# The Hakka Cookbook

# The Hakka Cookbook

# Chinese Soul Food from around the World

## Linda Lau Anusasananan

Art by Alan Lau

Foreword by Martin Yan

UNIVERSITY OF CALIFORNIA PRESS    Berkeley  Los Angeles  London

*The publisher gratefully acknowledges the generous support of the Sue Tsao Endowment Fund in Chinese Studies of the University of California Press Foundation.*

University of California Press, one of the most distinguished university presses in the United States, enriches lives around the world by advancing scholarship in the humanities, social sciences, and natural sciences. Its activities are supported by the UC Press Foundation and by philanthropic contributions from individuals and institutions. For more information, visit www.ucpress.edu.

University of California Press
Berkeley and Los Angeles, California

University of California Press, Ltd.
London, England

"the upside down basket" by Alan Chong Lau was previously published in *Songs for Jadina* (Greenfield Center, N.Y.: Greenfield Review Press, 1980) and is reprinted with permission.

Design and composition: Claudia Smelser
Text: Adobe Chaparral Pro
Display: PMN Caecilia
Index: Kevin Millham
Prepress and color: iocolor
Printing and binding: Imago

LIBRARY OF CONGRESS CATALOGING-IN-PUBLICATION DATA

Anusasananan, Linda Lau, 1947–
 The Hakka cookbook : Chinese soul food from around the world / Linda Lau Anusasananan ; art by Alan Lau ; foreword by Martin Yan.
  p. cm.
 Includes bibliographical references and index.
 ISBN 978-0-520-27328-3 (cloth : alk. paper)
 1. Cooking, Chinese—Hakka style.  2. Hakka (Chinese people).  3. Chinese diaspora.
I. Title.
 TX724.5.C5A64  2012
 641.5951—dc23                                                                    2012003052

Manufactured in China

21  20  19  18  17  16  15  14  13  12
10  9  8  7  6  5  4  3  2  1

The paper used in this publication meets the minimum requirements of ANSI/NISO z39.48–1992 (R 2002) *(Permanence of Paper)*.

*For Popo, who inspired me to discover what it means to be Hakka.*

*And for my daughters, Chalida and Lisa, and their children, who inspire me to pass on our history through word and food.*

*Most of all, this is for Hakkas throughout the world, so they can honor and preserve their roots with the foods of their ancestors.*

Popo

# the upside down basket

my grandmother
rakes up chicken shit
mixed with mud
to feed her roses

head protected
by an upside down basket
dares the sun to get closer

her shirt ablaze
with hawaiian pineapples
she imitates the cackle of hens
as they run merry off nests
wings flapping dust

an egg
still warm
cuddles the round
of my chin

a tickle unbearable
so i laugh
and she does too
so hard

the upside down
basket trembles
as though shaking
a fist
at the heat

we walk home
the musk of rotten apples everywhere
incense curling into skin
on the porch the upside down basket
sits rightside up

we drink gallons
of lemonade

*Alan Chong Lau*

# Contents

# Recipes

# Foreword  Martin Yan

My earliest memories of Hakka cooking date back to my childhood in Guangzhou. On several occasions, I sampled Hakka dishes at the homes of friends and neighbors. My mother, who was a formidable home cook, would graciously compliment our hosts on their delectable offerings. Afterward, on our way home, she would comment on some of the finer differences between Hakka and our day-to-day Cantonese cooking. Much of that went over my head. All I knew was that everything was delicious and that I wished that my stomach could hold twice as much food the next time we got invited.

Over the years, as my knowledge of Hakka food has deepened, so has my admiration for the Hakka culture. Chinese cuisine is largely divided into four geographical regions: Mandarin (north), Cantonese (south), Shanghai (east), and Sichuan (west). There are further subdivisions, but they are also mostly geographically based. The Hakka cuisine, on the other hand, is closely connected to its unique history rather than simple geography.

The Hakka people originated from Shanxi and Henan provinces in the Central Plains of China. Many centuries ago they migrated to the southeast, settling along the coastal regions of China, as well as westward, into Sichuan Province. As Linda points out in her introduction, the term *Hakka* literally means "guest" and "family." In other words, Hakkas were newer families settling alongside the natives who had been residing in those areas for centuries.

But the influence of the Hakka does not stop at national boundaries. There are many Hakkas who have immigrated abroad. Today one can find enclaves of Hakkas throughout Southeast Asia, Australia, Europe, and the Americas. The taping of the many seasons of the *Yan Can Cook* show allowed me to venture throughout mainland China, Hong Kong, and Indochina. Everywhere I went I would, sooner or later, meet Chinese immigrants who were Hakka in origin. In North America, I cannot think of a single Chinese community where Hakka Chinese are absent. Once, in the Caribbean, I actually ran into Chinese Jamaicans who claimed that their forbears were Hakkas.

Today an estimated 80 million people can trace their heritage to Hakka ancestors. Among them are famous politicians, artists, and literary luminaries—a group that includes Dr. Sun Yat-sen and Chinese Premier Deng Xiaoping.

I won't pretend that I am a scholar and expert on Hakka history. However, as an immigrant, I can appreciate the challenges in adapting and adjusting to a new cultural environment and the delicate balance we immigrants undertake in our effort to preserve our heritage. The fact that the Hakka culture is still recognized and honored by millions of its descendants all over the world is a testament to the strength and character of a proud people.

When Linda first approached me with her Hakka cookbook project, my reaction was "It's about time!" I have known Linda for many years, since her days at *Sunset* magazine, and she has always struck me as a truly dedicated professional. This book is the latest proof!

As much as I love cookbooks—and anyone who doubts that is welcome to tour my personal thousand-cookbook library—I must say that this book is more than a cookbook. It is also Linda's personal journey, her way to reconnect with her long-deceased grandmother and the roots of her Hakka culture.

And then there are the pages and pages of mouthwatering recipes, many of which I recognize and remember. Some even date back to the time when I was a child who wished he could have a bigger stomach.

Honoring our culture through delicious food: is there a better way?

# Acknowledgments

I first envisioned this book in 2001. Finally, with the help of a newfound global network of Chinese pioneers, I can share it. Hakka tenacity triumphs. I extend thanks to the many people who paved my journey of discovery with their good food, expertise, recipes, stories, experiences, time, support, and patience. This book wouldn't be possible without them.

Major contributions came from Alan Chong Lau and Fah Liong. Alan, my brother, created the art that personalizes this book. Fah, my Hakka mentor, cooked more than twenty Hakka dishes for me, answered my many questions, interpreted, and helped me understand the basics of the Hakka kitchen. Without the help of Alan and Fah, this book might not have seen print.

In China, Hong Kong, and Taiwan, many chefs cooked Hakka feasts for me. One of the most helpful was Yan Si Ming (now deceased) in Beijing. Scholars including Sidney Cheung, a professor at the Chinese University of Hong Kong, and May (Yu-Hsin) Chang at the Foundation of Chinese Dietary Culture shared their research with me. My Hakka Gourmet Group—which consisted of my husband, Terry; my daughter, Lisa; my brother Alan Lau and his wife, Kazuko Nakane; my brother Gene Lau; my cousins Sue Chee, Jeannie Chow, and Yau Lau; and my Hakka friend Rebekah Luke and her husband, Peter Krape—traveled with me and helped with my research by eating endless Hakka banquets.

In Kuala Lumpur, my friend Sally Painter Hussein introduced me to her coworker Loh Kwai Lai, who recruited her Hakka aunt Loh Sye Moi to cook for me. Amy Wong (Wong Choon Wei), owner of the Eiffel Restaurant and writer at *Famous Cuisine,* a food magazine in Kuala Lumpur, gave me Hakka recipes. She and the magazine staff shared their expertise over a delicious Hakka lunch.

Violet Oon introduced me to her Hakka friends in Singapore. Doreen Ho Fui Fah and her sister, Ho Huey Cheen, shared recipes and family history over lunch. Through Violet, I also met Wong Chee Leong at Moi Kong in Singapore.

From a brief meeting with Mee Lan Wong, I learned about the Hakka in Mauritius.

Liliana Com introduced me to the Hakka community in Lima, Peru. Her mother, Natalie Com Liu, prepared lunch and shared her recipes. Professor Jorge Salazar (now deceased) and Joseph Cruz described the history of the Chinese in Peru. Alfredo Valiente guided me through Lima's Chinatown.

In Hawaii, Kelley Oshiro and Paul Yuen told me about their shared family history. Another Hawaii resident, Margaret Lai, who originally came from Tahiti, described life growing up in French Polynesia.

Many friends in Toronto generously shared their contacts, recipes, and experiences. Filmmaker Cheuk Kwan introduced me to my key Hakka guides, Peter and Gladys Lee-Shanok, who in turn introduced me to an ever-growing circle of Hakkas in Toronto: Winston H. Chang Jr. and his family, P. K. Chen, Everard Hoo, Patrick Lee, Jennie Liao, Margarita Wong Liu, Liu Ying Hsien, Keith Lowe, Albert Lim Shue, and Carol Wong. At the Hakka Conference in 2008, Simone Tai introduced me to chefs Herbert Lee and Yong Soon, who both shared their Hakka specialties. At the conference I also met Ellen Oxfeld, a professor of anthropology at Middlebury College, who described her experience living in Meixian. Anthony Lin, of Danforth Dragon in Toronto, allowed me to watch him cook Hakka-Indian dishes in his kitchen.

In New York, Jacqueline Newman, editor of *Flavor and Fortune,* introduced me to the Lo family of Tangra Masala. I later interviewed Peter Lo, Lo Sim Fook, and Peter Tseng at their new restaurant, Tangra Asian Fusion Cuisine.

Back home in California, my uncle Hang Lau helped me with family history and shared his recipes. In San Francisco, chefs William Wong at Ton Kiang and Jin Hua Li at the Hakka Restaurant generously contributed their Hakka dishes.

Others also helped in many ways. Chih-Hui Burns translated English words into Chinese characters. Susan Stone proofread the pinyin and Chinese words. Grace Young showed me how to write a book proposal. Liv and Bill Blumer advised me on the book publishing business. Jerry Di Vecchio, my mentor at *Sunset* magazine, taught me how to write a recipe. Artist Chitfu Yu painted the beautiful calligraphy for the cover.

At the University of California Press, I appreciated Dore Brown's and Kate Marshall's thoughtful suggestions and Emily Park's sharp eyes. Claudia Smelser merged the text and art in a graceful design.

Many thanks to Martin Yan for graciously writing the foreword to this book.

Finally, thanks to my husband, Terry Anusasananan, who as the ever-present taster ate endless rounds of pork belly and other Hakka dishes with gusto.

# Notes to the Reader

The Chinese language is complex, with many different dialects that vary widely in their pronunciation. Throughout the text, the standard Mandarin (pinyin) is generally used. When pinyin is not used, the spelling of Chinese terms and names reflects the version given by the sources. The Hakka language is used with Hakka classic dishes and the names of some places in the Hakka heartland.

In the Hakka Pantry (page 247), standard Mandarin and several common dialects in phonetic spellings are included to provide the most help in finding ingredients. The phonetic spelling of Chinese words varies depending on the dialect used. The Chinese characters in that section are written in the traditional way.

Chinese people traditionally place their family name first, followed by their first name (usually two words, sometimes hyphenated or written together as one word). However, many Chinese, especially those who live in the West, reverse the order and state their given names followed by their surnames. Or they may adopt a Western first name. I have stated their names as they prefer or as commonly used.

If you're new to Chinese cooking, please read through the Hakka Kitchen (page 235) first to acquaint yourself with the cuisine's basic techniques and equipment. If you run across unfamiliar ingredients, check the Hakka Pantry. Before you begin a recipe, read through the instructions and prepare all ingredients for cooking; this is especially important for fast-paced stir-fries. Don't be put off by long recipes. The detailed steps will guide you through unfamiliar ingredients and techniques to successful and delicious results.

# Introduction

## Proud to Be Hakka

"You should be proud to be Hakka," my grandmother, or Popo, told my brother Alan and me over and over. But even with Chinese lessons after school, her efforts to instill ethnic pride in us were lost. As the only Chinese kids growing up in a small white community in Northern California, those sentiments meant little to us. Now that most of the relatives who could have filled in my family history have passed on, I wish I had paid closer attention. What does it mean to be Hakka?

Although I have been a food writer for over thirty-five years, my knowledge of Chinese food was superficial. After writing primarily about Western food for more than three decades at *Sunset* magazine, I found myself ready to delve more deeply into the cuisine of my youth. I had never lost interest in Chinese food, but my opportunities to explore it deeply and authentically were limited at a magazine that focused on living in the western United States. This book traces my exploration of Hakka culture through what I know best: food.

I grew up eating mostly Chinese food. I didn't know if the food we ate was Hakka; I simply thought of home cooking as a meal built around a bowl of steaming rice. Although my husband is Thai, not Chinese, we share a similar Asian food culture based around rice. When our children were young, I cooked mostly stir-fried meats and vegetables, noodles, soups, and stews. Of course, I also cooked favorite dishes from many other cultures. But my go-to home cooking was based on Chinese ingredients, techniques, and seasonings. Before Chinese markets opened nearby, we made a weekly shopping trip to San Francisco's Chinatown to buy Asian vegetables and ingredients, such as Chinese sausages, fresh Hong Kong–style noodles, and roast duck. Over the years, I added some Chinese regional seasonings to my pantry.

However, I never heard much about Hakka food. By the time I became curious about it, my parents and Popo were gone. So I asked one of the few Hakkas I knew, my *Sunset* colleague Fah Liong, to teach me about our cuisine. Fortunately, Fah is a very good cook and was happy to spend many afternoons with me, demonstrating her Hakka dishes. I began to recognize familiar flavors that reminded me of home. Fah became my Hakka mentor.

Many people are unfamiliar with Hakka food. The Hakkas' humble dishes have stayed largely sequestered in home kitchens, rarely appearing on restaurant menus. Even within Hakka families, much of the cuisine is not being passed on. With assimilation, mixed marriages, changing tastes, and busier lifestyles, Hakka food is disappearing. The new generation doesn't know how to cook its ancestors' dishes. I feel this Hakka identity slipping away in my own life. My brothers and I have lost the language, and none of us married someone Hakka, or even Chinese. We live in a multicultural society and cook and eat a wide variety of food.

With this book, I've discovered my family history and how it merges into the Hakka diaspora. I'm not alone, but one of millions who share a similar history and identity. I hope this book will preserve some Hakka classics, pass on recipes to the next generation, and encourage Hakka cooks to maintain and expand their culinary repertoires as they adapt to their ever-changing environment.

I finally understand what Popo was trying to tell me. Popo was proud to be Hakka. She had good reasons for her pride and loyalty. She grew up in the late 1800s, just as the Hakka were developing and solidifying their identity amid great turmoil in China. Her home was in Guangdong Province, where she lived with many others of her own kind. She married a Hakka. Then she left home and moved to America, a new frontier where again she was the uninvited guest. Her firsthand experiences developed her Hakka spirit and strength.

Two generations later in America, times have changed. I have grown through my own experiences, but my challenges seem minor compared to hers. I didn't grow up isolated in a Hakka incubator, but in a largely Western society. I'll never be as Hakka as Popo, but I inherited some of her Hakka virtues. She taught me to be independent, to work hard to attain my goals, and to adapt and grow. Now, I realize, I'm recapturing the flavor and spirit of my Hakka culture through her life and her food. Yes, Popo, I'm proud to be Hakka.

# The Hakka Story

A dandelion with a bright yellow flower defiantly emerges from a hairline crack in my driveway. When I see it, it reminds me that I am Hakka. The Chinese characters 客 家 (*Hakka* in Hakka dialect, or *Kejia* in Mandarin) literally mean

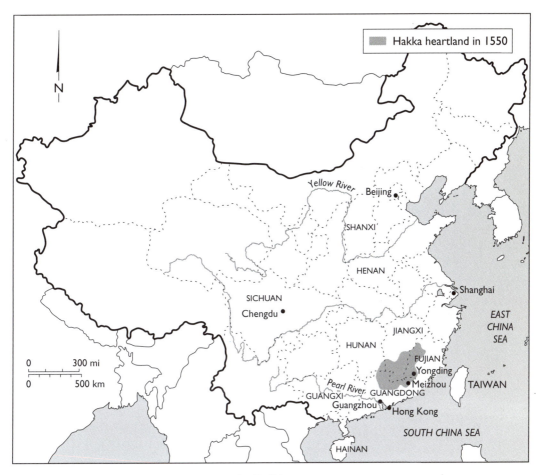

Areas where the Hakka have lived in China.

"guest family." Many other words have been used to describe us as well: *pioneers, nomads, migrants, gypsies.* But for me, *dandelion* hits the target. I find this popular metaphor, often used to symbolize the Chinese, on www.asiawind.com, an online community for Hakkas. Siu-Leung Lee, creator of the site, believes this symbol aptly describes the character and spirit of the Hakka. Like a dandelion, a Hakka can land anywhere, take root in the poorest soil, and flourish and flower.

Who are the Hakka? Almost seventeen hundred years ago, invaders forced the ancestors of the Hakka from their home in the plains of the Yellow River near Henan in north-central China, once the cradle of Han, or Chinese, culture. The Hakka, like many other peasant migrants, fled the miseries of war, famine, droughts, and floods. In a series of five mass migrations, they moved south. By the time they reached the southern provinces, most of the area was occupied. Unlike other Chinese groups who claim a connected homeland, Hakkas lived dispersed as minorities throughout southern China. Anthropologist G. William Skinner describes the Hakka as the only Chinese group who "had no drainage basin of their own."

Chinese society denied these homeless migrants social status and looked down on them with contempt. As a result of being landless and shunned, Hakka communities became expert at pulling up stakes, moving on, and starting over. They gained a reputation as pioneers, good at settling on land no one else wanted, usually in remote highlands or on hills. A Chinese saying states: "He is not a Hakka who is not on a hill; there is no hill but has Hakkas on it."

Several theories exist to explain the origin of the Hakka. The story most Hakkas and many scholars embrace follows historian Luo Xianglin's pioneering genealogical work in 1933. Luo claims that the Hakka are descendants of the Han dynasty (206 B.C. to 220 A.D.) and therefore members of the Chinese ethnic majority from central China. This is significant to the Hakka because it elevates their status; if the Hakka are Han, they are as Chinese as those who have long considered them lower class.

Critics suggest that Luo's theory is full of misconceptions. Asian studies scholar Sow-Theng Leong considers Luo's *Kejia yanjiu daolun* (Introduction to the study of the Hakkas) to be partly "ethnic rhetoric." He denies the Hakka what they prize the most, their pure Han heritage. Based on migration patterns, Leong concludes, the ancestors of the Hakka were likely local non-Han living in the southern mountain region now known as Meixian. Clyde Kiang, author of *The Hakka Search for a Homeland,* goes further, suggesting that the Hakka may be more closely related to Koreans and Japanese.

I am not a scholar, and to my mind, any of these origin theories may be valid. To me, the spirit and character that developed as the result of a challenge-filled history make up a large part of the Hakka identity. Let's look at their obstacles, how they overcame them, and the traits that emerged.

## The Migrations of the Hakka

The journey of China's unwanted migrants started in the fourth century, around 317 A.D., when invading barbarians from the north forced the Hakka ancestors from their home in Henan Province in central China. They fled south as far as central Jiangxi. This was the first of five mass migrations that continued into the nineteenth century.

The second migration began in the late Tang era (618 to 907), as Huang Chao rebels, in an attempt to overthrow the Tang dynasty, sought to destroy rich cities and fertile farms. Many people fled the north and pursued safety in remote regions of the more stable south. The Hakka found shelter in Jiangxi, southern Fujian, and neighboring Guangdong Province. The Huang Chao rebels left north-central Jiangxi Province undisturbed. From the end of the Tang dynasty through the Southern Song period, a concentration of Hakka speakers lived with non-Han neighbors in southwestern Fujian in relative isolation for almost four hundred years (907 to 1279). This period of seclusion allowed the Hakka to solidify their language, culture, and identity.

Around 1171, bandits grew more prevalent in Fujian. In the third migration, the Hakka sought safer terrain and moved from southern Jiangxi and southwestern Fujian across the border into northern and eastern Guangdong Province, where more land was available. A few lazy farmers owned the fields. The Hakka took advantage of the situation and as tenants farmed the neglected plots of poor hillside soil scattered between the fertile Cantonese-controlled lowlands. Locals labeled the unwelcome newcomers Hakka, meaning "guest family." It wasn't until the turn of the twentieth century that the name Hakka became familiar beyond the local area. By the end of the Yuan dynasty, northern and eastern Guangdong Province was solely Hakka. From the sixteenth century on, the Hakka started to identify the region centered near Meixian in Guangdong and the Jiaying Prefecture (now Meizhou City) as their homeland.

In the fourth migration, the Manchus of the Qing dynasty (1644 to 1911) sent the Hakka from northern and eastern Guangdong to the province's central and coastal regions, central and eastern Sichuan, eastern Guangxi, and Taiwan. Those from southern Jiangxi, southern Fujian, and Meixian moved into western Jiangxi and southern and central Hunan. Hakka speakers spread throughout Guangdong, especially in Guangzhou. They lived in small pockets scattered throughout the Cantonese villages. The Hakka grew more successful and began to compete for land, spurring violent conflict with the local Punti (mostly Cantonese). Although the Hakka were limited to the hillsides and least fertile lands, through their hard work, frugality, and entrepreneurship, they prospered and some became landlords. The Punti resented their success. Sparks flew. Fighting broke out, which led to wars in the West River region in the 1850s.

Out of this hostile environment and the poor economy, the Society of God Worshippers emerged. Hong Xiuquan, a Hakka convert, led this zealous religious group. He claimed he was Jesus's younger brother, delegated by God to restore China's great peace and equality. This new kind of Christianity promoted the people's welfare, endorsed equality for women, nationalized private property, and mandated monogamy. In 1851, Hong united many of China's oppressed—a great number of whom were Hakka—into the army of "Chosen People" to get rid of the Manchus and foreign rulers with God's benevolent rule. It grew into a revolutionary army that swept through China from 1851 to 1864 and nearly destroyed the Qing dynasty. Called the Taiping Rebellion, this civil war led to the loss of twenty million people. Although the Taiping Rebellion failed, its democratic and equalitarian ideals inspired Dr. Sun Yat-sen to overthrow the rule of powerful families and promote a nationalistic Republic of China. The world's bloodiest civil war ushered in the dawn of modern China.

The fifth migration began in 1867, when the fighting grew so violent in Guangdong that the governor established a subprefecture of Chiqi as a reservation for displaced Hakkas. Chiqi was too small to hold everyone, so others fled to the southwest tip of Guangdong, Hainan Island, and overseas. Danger followed the Taiping rebels in China. Survivors and others escaping the turmoil of China fled to Southeast Asia and Taiwan; others went farther, to North and South America, Mauritius, the Caribbean, and India. A majority worked as contract or "coolie" labor for colonists.

By the end of the nineteenth century, the Hakka proudly claimed their identity. Contact and conflict with other ethnic groups, especially during the Taiping Rebellion and the West River Hakka–Cantonese wars, fostered the development of an identifiable ethnic group with a shared identity, which developed further as the Hakka scattered throughout the world in a global diaspora. When Communist China opened its doors in 1979, some Hakkas returned to relatives who had never left the mainland.

In 1992, the International Association of Hakka estimated that the total Hakka population worldwide was about seventy-five million. Many Hakkas have quietly assimilated into the prevailing culture of their adopted homelands or a form of generic overseas Chinese. Others, such as those in Taiwan and Toronto, have stepped out to proudly reclaim their ethnic identity. About forty million Hakka live in mainland China, Hong Kong, and Taiwan. In China, they are concentrated primarily in northern Guangdong (the Hakka heartland), southwestern Fujian, southern Jiangxi, southeastern Hunan, and central Sichuan. Many settled in nearby Southeast Asia and India. Others migrated farther, to Australia, Canada, New Zealand, the Caribbean, and the United States. They now reside in over fifty countries, including Britain, Mauritius, Peru, South Africa, and Tahiti. Even in the past few decades, the Hakka population has shifted as political and economic situations force Hakkas to seek a better life. The Chinese pioneers are still on the move. Like the stubborn dandelion, they flourish wherever they land.

## The Hakka Spirit

Landlessness and frequent relocation have honed the Hakkas' ability to adapt and survive any situation. With a hardy fierceness, they cultivated lands no one else wanted. The dynasties regarded the Hakka as potential pioneers, good for establishing communities in unpopulated areas. This proved true in the mid-eighteenth to late nineteenth centuries, when the Hakka established settlements in Sarawak and along the uninhabited coasts of Sabah in the Federation of Malaysia, where other Chinese had failed.

The Hakkas' untraditional egalitarian gender roles strengthened their survival skills. The ever-practical Hakka women eschewed the prevailing practice of binding feet, which would cripple them. Enemies mocked them and called them "Big Feet." Hakka women did much of the farm work and tilled the fields. Men often worked outside jobs in mining, trade, handicrafts, teaching, and government to supplement the meager farm income. Others served as professional soldiers. Men and women became entrepreneurs, doing whatever they needed to survive.

Being shunned forced Hakkas to fight for everything. In their close-knit communities, they developed group identities and protected their own, as evidenced by the impenetrable round, multistory earth fortresses they built in Yongding in Fujian Province. Their distinct dialect bound them together, but it also distinguished them as outsiders.

With a shared history of hardship, many Hakkas have come to see themselves as highly independent, adaptable, and tenacious; hard working, frugal, and gutsy; and somewhat insular, contentious, and clannish. This Hakka spirit and collective identity helped them survive as they moved across the world.

## Chinese Soul Food

What is Hakka food? Hakkas I have asked reply that it is strong flavored, salty, fatty. It is country food, the "food of my people." Pork and soy sauce feature prominently. As I taste Hakka dishes all over the world, I find that many of these descriptions apply to the roots of this peasant food, but regional differences and creative cooks have stretched the definition, creating a diverse cuisine that could be described as fresh, natural, uncomplicated, satisfying, and direct. It's difficult to define a cuisine concisely, especially one like Hakka that has traveled the world and is a work in progress. The most insightful answer came from my youngest brother, Gene, who called it honest, earthy, and rustic—the simple, comforting soul food of the peasant. The clarity of his answer surprised me.

Gene was born sixteen years after I was, just two years before I left home for college. My parents separated when he was about seven. After the separation, Gene went with my mother and grandmother to Hong Kong for a year, then returned and lived in San Francisco. In the summers, he visited my father in Paradise, a small retirement community in the Sierra Nevada foothills. There he spent most of his time with our cousin Paul. Paul's mother and our aunt, whom we call Ah Sim, fed the boys wholesome soups, stuffed tofu, stir-fried vegetables, and glasses of cool, sweet soy milk. She had come to Paradise in 1963, when her husband, Hang (whom we call Uncle Henry or Ah Sook), went to work at my father's restaurant, The Pagoda. To this day, Ah Sim maintains many Hakka traditions, living like she did in her native village, Lop Muey. She raises chickens for eggs and meat, grows vegetables and fruits, and cooks from her garden, sometimes outside on a wok set over a fire contained in a large can. Gene told me that when he was young, he discovered his passion for food while eating a Hakka meal at our aunt's house.

During lunch there one day, Gene put the pieces together. Coming from sophisticated Hong Kong to my aunt's humble table, he realized what variety Chinese food could encompass. Both ends of the spectrum were good. It felt comforting to find home in Ah Sim's cooking. "It was a form of establishing an identity, a security in who I was," he said. "All the comfort, security, and warm feelings one could ask for were wrapped up in a simple bowl of soup." The soup came from homegrown vegetables and freshly slaughtered chickens—all cooked as if in a traditional Chinese village. "It was real, it was good, and some-how I belonged to it," he said.

Gene and I had learned when we were young that food feeds more than hungry stomachs. Growing up Chinese in a white town had made both of us sensitive. We always thought we were like the others until someone commented that we were different. For my brother and me, as for other Hakkas living an isolated and sometimes bleak life abroad, food offered familiarity and safety.

Hakka farmers lived off the land, eating vegetables they grew and raising pigs and chickens. Most lived on hills inland, so seafood was rare. Poverty forced them to be resourceful when finding food. Frogs and snakes found in the country were often eaten. And like most Chinese people, Hakkas ate every part of the animal, from head to tail. They filled their pantries with preserved, salted, and dried vegetables, cured meats, and seasonings to survive travel and time. Common Chinese seasonings such as soy sauce, rice wine and its by-products, red fermented bean curd, ginger, and garlic endowed some of the dishes with robust savory flavors. Other foods were served plain or lightly adorned to show off their natural goodness. Rice was the main starch. In southeast China's Guangdong Province—primarily around Meizhou, where most Hakkas eventually settled and the greatest concentration still live today—many of these plain, down-to-earth dishes still exist.

Some call Hakka food the country cousin of Cantonese cuisine. It's more straightforward and hearty than the urbane Cantonese. Flavors can be strong and dark, yet simple dishes balance the meal. Many dishes that Cantonese people eat at home, such as soy-braised meats, stews, stir-fried vegetables, and steamed meats, share similarities with Hakka dishes. For centuries, the two groups lived side by side in Guangdong Province as well as abroad, so there was much adaptation and borrowing from both sides.

## Traveling Cuisine

When the Hakka moved from one place to another, their cooking adapted to ingredients that were available in their new environments. Stuffed tofu, now a Hakka classic, was born from the desire to make dumplings similar to those they had consumed in northern China. With no flour in the south, inventive cooks substituted pieces of tofu for the flour-based dumpling wrappers. In China's mountainous Hakka heartland, tofu pieces were filled with seasoned ground pork and steamed, braised, or fried. When migrants went to Singapore or Hong Kong, they found seafood widely available and incorporated ground shrimp or fish into the stuffing.

The Hakka adopted local ingredients farther afield as well. In Jamaica, soup noodles are served with soy sauce laced with the local Scotch bonnet chile. In Peru, we will meet Natalie Com Liu, who substitutes local yuca for taro to steam with pork. My Hakka mentor, Fah Liong, originally from Indonesia, frequently adds fish sauce or sweet soy sauce, typical Southeast Asian seasonings, to her Hakka dishes in California. Chef Lin, originally from India, cooks Chinese ingredients with Indian spices, but adjusts the ingredients to the tastes of his Canadian customers. In Mauritius, Mee Lan Wong sometimes substitutes chayotes for Asian white radishes to make a more vibrant version of the steamed radish balls so typical in the Hakka heartland. When she cooks fried rice, she serves a fresh Indian-style tomato chutney alongside to cater to the island's Creole-fusion tastes.

The borrowing also worked the other way. The influence of Hakka cuisine can be found in Chinese restaurants run by Indians in New Delhi that serve dishes such as chow mein. In Peru, the popular dish *lomo saltado* mixes Chinese stir-fried beef with soy sauce and french fries. Hakka foods, even when adapted to new environments, retain a distinctly Hakka identity. In Singapore, stuffed tofu and vegetables can be found at street vendors everywhere. The rustic Hakka version uses a coarse mixture of ground pork and shrimp for the filling, whereas the subtler, more sophisticated Cantonese version would be likely to have a delicate, mousse-like seafood filling.

Sometimes tradition prevails, though the difference may be so slight that it's hard to discern the import from the original. Other times, dishes exhibit a change that reflects the prevailing flavor profile of the local cuisine. For instance, chow mein made in India may be spicier than the traditional Hakka version. Or a pork stew cooked in a city may be lighter and more refined than a version cooked at a country farm.

## Food for the New Generation

Hakka food has changed over time. Today, less active lifestyles mean that people don't need to eat as hearty foods as they did in the past. City dwellers and the younger generation tend to prefer lighter foods. Some restaurants invent new dishes or modify Hakka classics for the new generation. Health-conscious cooks may trim excess fat from meat, choose leaner cuts, use less salt, and try baking or broiling rather than deep-frying. They tend to cook lighter and fresher foods for everyday meals and save richer, more labor-intensive foods for special occasions.

In this book, I've streamlined some recipes with shortcuts to suit modern lifestyles. I've tried to preserve these dishes' Hakka soul but also make them accessible to today's home cook by offering supermarket alternatives for ethnic ingredients when the results are acceptable.

# HAKKA CLASSICS
## Dishes That Define

This book showcases the dishes I tasted around the world when I requested Hakka food. People presented easy everyday fare and banquet-worthy masterpieces. Some dishes were hard to distinguish from classic Chinese or Cantonese cuisine, while others bore the markings of a foreign home.

Yet some dishes seemed to define Hakka fare. I call them Hakka classics because they are the most characteristic of the cuisine. Many appear regularly on restaurant menus. The most famous Hakka dishes include salt-baked chicken *(yam kuk gai)*, stuffed tofu *(nyiong tiu fu)*, wine chicken *(jiu gai)*, and pork belly with preserved mustard greens *(kiu ngiuk moi choi)*. As the Hakka crisscrossed the globe, new regional classics appeared. In Singapore and Malaysia, I tasted taro abacus *(wu tiuh sun pan jue)*, a sort of Hakka gnocchi made with taro. I also found a rice bowl topped with healthy savory tea known as pounded tea rice *(lui cha fan)*. In a similar dish in Taiwan, the herbaceous tea took a sweeter form *(lui cha)*. Also in Taiwan, a popular stir-fry that used the elements of temple offerings acquired the name Hakka little stir-fry *(Hakka seow chow)*. Basin feast *(puhn choi)*, a banquet layered in a washbasin, gained popularity in Hong Kong for family festivals and Chinese New Year celebrations. Soup noodles *(sui men)*, brought to Jamaica by the Hakka, traveled to Toronto with the Hakka Jamaicans who migrated there. All over the world, Hakkas love their salted mustard greens *(hahm choi)* and pickled mustard greens *(soen choi)*. They are so common, they have become a classic in their own right. Back home in San Francisco, I tasted braised chicken with preserved mustard greens *(moi choi gai)*, a dish that captured the essence of Hakka flavor and could emerge as a new masterpiece.

Scattered throughout the book, you'll find these Hakka classics. Although many may not fit into your weeknight dinner schedule, they make grand choices for a festive dinner or party.

# My Hakka Journey

To research this book, I followed the footsteps of the Hakka diaspora, eating my way around the globe. I first planned to go to China, followed by a few trips to other Hakka hotspots. I knew that there were Hakka populations in Britain, Australia, and South Africa. But before I embarked on my travels, locations picked me. In 2004, I received a wedding invitation to Hawaii with a second ceremony in Kuala Lumpur. A chance meeting with an old friend from Singapore prompted me to add a stopover to my Malaysia trip. With a few extra days, I interviewed the local Hakkas in each city. On a business trip to New York City in 2005, a friend took me out for a Chinese-Indian dinner that was unlike any meal I had tasted before; the restaurant was run by a Hakka family from India.

Finally, in the fall of 2005, I embarked on a scouting trip to China. I had been to China once before, in 1987. At that time, I was on assignment for *Sunset* magazine to report on how people cooked and ate in this vast country that had recently opened its doors to the world. Now, eighteen years later, I had returned on a personal mission: to learn all I could about Hakka food. I planned to visit Guangdong Province—the Hakka heartland—in the south, but I also wanted to retrace the route of my previous trip, just to see the changes. I added Hong Kong and Taiwan to my itinerary, to meet Hakka scholars and taste the food.

With experience from my previous trip to China, I knew I would need tasters to help me get through the many multicourse banquets. I organized a group, mostly family, to share my eating adventure. We ate Hakka dishes in every city we visited, plus local regional cuisine to offer more variety. In Guangdong, we found my father's village.

The reportedly sizable Hakka population and the mystery of Machu Picchu beckoned me to Peru. Through Jacqueline Newman, editor of *Flavor and Fortune,* I met the perfect guide for my introduction to the Chinese face of South America. Liliana Com, a well-connected Hakka woman, introduced me to friends who told me how the Chinese influenced Peru. She showed me Lima's Chinatown, which I was surprised to find wasn't that different from other Chinese communities around the world, except for the Spanish accent. Most importantly, she invited me home to watch her mother cook a Hakka meal.

In 2006, I became fascinated by a DVD series about Chinese restaurants all around the world. Many of the restaurant owners were Hakkas. I contacted the producer, Cheuk Kwan. "Come to Toronto," he said. "I have a friend who can introduce you to many Hakkas." A few weeks later, I was eating dinner with over a dozen Hakkas from all over the world—Jamaica, Trinidad, India, Mauritius,

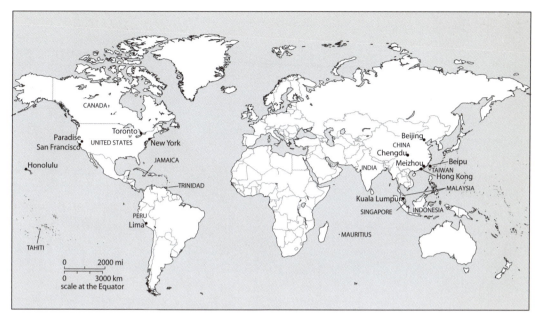

Hakka communities explored in this book.

Africa, Surinam, Malaysia—places often mentioned as Hakka settlements. Interviewing my dinner companions, I heard a common story: as the political and economic situations in their native countries had changed, many Hakkas had left. There seemed little reason to visit some countries on my list. I could meet many more Hakkas here, all in one place. In 2008, I returned to Toronto to attend the third Toronto Hakka Conference. An estimated twelve hundred people attended, more Hakkas than I've ever seen together sharing their culture.

I returned from my travels with a greater appreciation for Hakka food. Once I was back home in the San Francisco Bay Area, my friend and Hakka tutor, Fah Liong, introduced me to many dishes she had learned to cook from her Indonesian mother. With each bite of Fah's food, I appreciated the comfort of home cooking. Two San Francisco chefs expanded my collection of recipes with traditional dishes and newer creations.

For centuries, the Hakka were looked down upon as peasants. Their cuisine was often described negatively and remained relatively unknown, because it was rarely served outside the home. The Hakka diaspora infused new life and more variety into this once-isolated cuisine. Now it's time to discover the rustic, satisfying soul food of these Chinese pioneers.

Garlic

# ONE

# Popo's Kitchen
# on Gold Mountain California

## Pioneer in Paradise

On the deck of the *S.S. Nile,* the petite Chinese woman shivers with excitement as the ship pulls into view of San Francisco, the entry to Gold Mountain, the Chinese nickname for California. Fear tempers her joy as the ship anchors at the cove of Angel Island, where the immigration station for the Chinese is located. Her dream could end here.

Moist clouds of fog billow in as the immigration authorities lead the Chinese arrivals up the hill to the detention hall. The guards separate the men from the women. She is shunted into the women's barracks. Wind whistles through the cracks of the thin wood walls. Beds are stacked floor to ceiling, side by side. There are no walls, no privacy, no space to breathe. Some women have been here for years. They advise her to make sure she knows her facts. As the days pass, she replays in her mind every detail of her life in China. Finally, seven days later, she is called.

"What is your name?" barks a white man with a dark bushy mustache. She cringes at his rough, loud manner.

"Au Shee," she stammers.

As the interpreter translates, she feels herself floating outside of her body, viewing the surreal scene as a stranger. What is this tiny woman from a small village in southern China doing in this room with white ghosts screaming questions at her?

"When and where were you married?" cuts through her thoughts.

She shakes herself out of her fog. She must concentrate. She must remember every detail of her village. Her answers must match her husband's. If she falters, she could be forced to stay in this prison-like detention camp much longer, or even be deported. In this land with a law to ban Chinese, she knows she is not welcome.

"August 18, 1919, in Hong Kong," she answers.

She barely knew her betrothed before the wedding, more than a year ago. Koo Chong was fifty, twenty years her senior. He had gone to America in 1881, just one year before the Chinese Exclusion Act was signed. Thirty-eight years later, he had come back to find a wife. According to the matchmaker, he had all the important qualifications. He was from a nearby village, Suey Nom, located in the foothills of Guangdong Province. Like Au Shee, he was Hakka, and they spoke the same dialect. He was a merchant in Gold Mountain and known to be a hard worker. What more could she want?

"What is your mother's name?" comes the voice.

"Tai Shee," she murmurs. The hole in her heart grows larger.

At age thirty, Au Shee no longer cared about marriage. People had already labeled her a spinster. Her life as a teacher suited her. She was happy not to answer to a man. But her mother had begged her to consider his marriage offer. War and famine were sweeping through China. She knew her mother was right. There was no future in China for her, and Koo Chong offered her a way out. She agreed to the marriage. She would learn to live with him.

"Where was your home in the village?"

"It is the first house on the left side." Would she ever see her mother or home again, she wonders.

"Can you sign your name?" When will this end? She has already answered endless, insignificant questions.

"Yes," she tiredly replies.

"Admitted." Suddenly the interrogation ends.

On February 28, 1921, the bride and groom are allowed entry to Gold Mountain. Au Shee learns that her husband's careful planning in establishing merchant status before returning to China was crucial to her acceptance. Merchants composed one of the few exempt classes to the Chinese Exclusion Act of 1882. As the wife of a merchant, Au Shee was one of only about 150 Chinese women legally permitted to enter the United States during the period from 1906 to 1924.

After being admitted, Au Shee and Koo Chong went to Sacramento, where he had a job at the Lincoln Market as a bookkeeper. He later opened a barbershop. Although they were not rich, they belonged to the entrepreneur class, the petty bourgeois of Chinese American society. Au Shee acquired a new English name to fit her new American life: Jadina Ou. In 1922, about a year after the young couple left Angel Island, my mother, Lillian, was born; a sister and a brother soon followed. When my mother turned eight, her family moved to Stockton, where they ran a barbershop. Later they owned a cigar store and the American Restaurant on El Dorado Street.

I entered the world in 1947, becoming Au Shee's first granddaughter in Gold Mountain. She became my Popo. At that time, we lived in Oroville, about a three-hour drive from Stockton. My mother didn't drive and my father worked six days a week. When my father wasn't too tired or when he needed to buy ingredients for the restaurant in Sacramento, we sometimes visited my grandparents. Other times, my brother and I might ride the Greyhound bus that crawled from town to town. We usually found Popo working in their café, a gathering place for Filipinos looking for cheap, filling meals.

We delighted in the big metal basins filled with chunks of fried pork belly with crunchy, bubbly skin and golden layers of fat and lean. Grass jelly, a Jello-like dessert made from a special grass, was another treat for the sweltering Stockton summers. When sweat beaded on my nose, Popo scooped quivering spoonfuls of the dark jelly into bowls and poured sweet syrup over the top. The soft lumps coolly slithered down my throat. One of her jolly Filipina friends, Annie Bang Bang, always said, "Your grandma makes the best grass jelly." She was right.

Our visits were short and few. I didn't spend much time with Popo until the mid-1950s, when she came to live with us in Paradise, a small town about twenty miles north of Oroville. Popo epitomized a true Hakka woman. In the '50s and '60s, when divorce was taboo and men were king, she was a feminist living in a conservative small town. When her marriage fell apart, she left her husband and adult son in Stockton. She came to live with us and offered financial and moral support to my mom, who was having problems with her own marriage.

Popo soon became the matriarch in our family. At four feet ten, she was a small woman with a big presence. She chose commonsense comfort over vanity. While most women of her generation wore floral housedresses and permed their hair, Popo preferred aloha shirts and loose pants. She slicked back her barbershop clipper-cut hair with pomade, like a man. She ruled with a strict hand and a bamboo feather duster, ready to administer a sharp crack to the head if my brother or I showed disrespect. And she was smart with money. When it finally became legal for Asians to buy land in California in 1948, she eagerly bought investment property. Yet she generously rewarded us, especially when we received good grades. You didn't cross Popo. If she felt someone was not treating her loved ones fairly, she cut that person out of her life, even if they were another relative.

"You should be proud to be Hakka," Popo would say. Hakka identity was so important to her that she had insisted my mom marry my dad because he was Hakka. But her Hakka pride washed right over my brother and me. We were already oddities in our all-white community. None of our friends spoke Chinese, let alone Hakka. And at that age we didn't really want to be even more different; we just wanted to fit in.

Popo insisted she would teach us to speak Hakka. Every day, after American school, we climbed the back stairway to reach Popo's kitchen for our Chinese lessons. She had been a teacher in China and tried in vain to teach us how to speak our dialect. We could understand what was being said most of the time, but neither of us ever spoke the dialect fluently. Our vocabulary was limited to essential phrases: *food, bathroom,* and *thank you.* The lesson started with calligraphy, as we traced Chinese characters with ink-filled brushes on tissue paper, and was followed by reading from Chinese picture books.

After our Chinese lessons, Popo would clear the oilcloth-covered table and prepare dinner. She beat eggs with broth to make a delicate steamed custard, sometimes with bits of gelatinous black thousand-year-old eggs embedded inside. She directed us how to cook rice: "Wash the rice until the water runs clear. Add water until it reaches the first joint of your finger." Every time she ate tangerines, she would save the peels and dry them near the heater vent until they hardened. When she made soups, she might drop one or two pieces of dried tangerine peel into the broth to add a faint fruity aroma. She filled gallon jars with salt, water, and eggs to make salted eggs. We ate stir-fried garden vegetables, soups made from a chicken or pot of bones, sometimes steamed fish or braised meat. Popo's dishes were humble, savory, satisfying Chinese comfort food.

Popo loved to putter in the garden, coaxing green seedlings from the iron-rich red dirt. She raised chickens in the backyard and planted gourd seeds near their cage. As the chicken manure enriched the soil, the vines scrambled up the wire cages into the apple trees and soon pale green gourds hung heavy from above. Popo would slice the voluptuous gourds and stir-fry them with pork. She taught me to appreciate the crunch of stir-fried broccoli and the smooth, slippery texture of perfectly steeped chicken.

I learned to love food through Popo. Now I realize that I learned much more. She taught me to be Hakka; I just didn't know it at the time. She preached through example, by being self-reliant, hard working, frugal, practical, and painfully honest. Popo was a true Hakka pioneer. Indeed, she was someone to be proud of.

Like her thrifty Hakka ancestors, Popo was a master at foraging. One day, when we were driving through the flat farmlands near Oroville, Popo suddenly shouted for us to pull off the road. She had spied a stand of tall green plants growing in an irrigation ditch along the road and knew wild potatoes lay underneath. We plunged our hands into the cold water and dug into the muddy silt to search for bulbs attached to the green stems. We yanked them out and loaded them into the trunk. That night, Popo cooked the bulbs we had gathered, making a potato-like stew that filled the kitchen with a sweet, spicy perfume that both my brother and I remember to this day. We were amazed that she had created such a delicious meal with food we had literally found for free.

Arrowhead, bacon, and green onions

## FIVE-SPICE POTATOES AND CHINESE BACON

This dish is a Hakka version of meat and potatoes. Although Popo used arrowhead (*ci gu*) on the day when we found it by the irrigation ditch, she typically used readily available potatoes. Arrowhead, a bulb that resembles a tan-colored fresh water chestnut, has a crunchier texture than potatoes and a slightly bitter finish. You can sometimes find it in Asian markets, usually in the winter. In my attempts to recreate this dish, I found that I prefer potatoes. Maybe it's my American-bred taste buds, but I like the way the potatoes soften, thicken the juices slightly, and absorb the smoky-sweet spices of the dry Chinese bacon.

*Makes 2 to 3 servings as a main dish or 4 to 5 servings as part of a multicourse meal*

1 strip Chinese bacon (6 to 8 ounces)

1 tablespoon minced garlic

1 tablespoon minced fresh ginger

2 cups water, or as needed

2 tablespoons dark soy sauce

2 tablespoons Chinese rice wine (shaoxing) or dry sherry

1 tablespoon packed brown sugar

1 teaspoon five-spice powder

1 pound small red or white boiling potatoes, each about 1½ inches wide, or arrowhead (see note)

¼ cup thinly sliced green onions, including green tops

**1** Cut the bacon crosswise into ¼-inch-thick strips. Set a 14-inch wok or 12-inch frying pan over medium-high heat. When the pan is hot, after about 1 minute, add the bacon and stir occasionally until it is lightly browned, 3 to 5 minutes. Remove and discard all but 1 tablespoon of fat from the pan, leaving the bacon. Stir in the garlic and ginger; cook until the garlic begins to brown, about 30 seconds. Add the water, soy sauce, wine, sugar, and five-spice powder, and bring to a boil. Reduce the heat, cover, and simmer, stirring occasionally, until the bacon is almost tender when pierced, 20 to 30 minutes.

**2** Meanwhile, peel the potatoes or arrowhead. If using arrowhead, trim off and discard the ends and any spongy parts. Cut the potatoes or arrowhead crosswise into ¼-inch-thick slices.

**3** If the liquid in the pan is very thick and has reduced substantially, add enough additional water to bring the total volume to 1 cup. Add the potatoes to the bacon mixture and bring to a boil. Reduce the heat, cover, and simmer, stirring occasionally, until the potatoes are tender when pierced (arrowhead will have a firmer texture than potatoes), 20 to 30 minutes. Add more water if the potatoes begin to stick; if using a frying pan, watch closely, as the liquid will evaporate more quickly. You should have at least 1 cup liquid during cooking. When done, you want ¾ to 1 cup liquid in the pan; if needed, add more water or boil the juices, uncovered, to make this amount. Stir in the green onions, and spoon into a serving bowl.

**Note:** I found that the results for the arrowhead varied. Sometimes the arrowhead was just as mild and tender as potatoes; other times, it took much longer to cook and had a firmer, crunchier texture and slightly bitter taste. For best results, look for very fresh, large, firm arrowhead in Asian markets; avoid any that are spongy. ■

# STIR-FRIED LONG BEANS AND PORK

Popo loved to garden. One of my favorite vegetables that she grew were the Chinese long beans that dangled almost two feet from the vines. I was always puzzled as to why Popo cut those beautiful, slender beans into tiny pieces. Now, I realize that the small bits absorb more of the dark savory sauce she coated them in. Chinese long beans possess a heartier bean flavor than regular green beans, because they're related to cowpeas or black-eyed peas. If you can't find long beans, you can substitute common fresh green beans; the dish will have a crunchier texture and less intense flavor.

*Makes 2 servings as a main dish or 4 servings as part of a multicourse meal*

## SAUCE

¼ cup water

1 tablespoon Chinese rice wine (shaoxing) or dry sherry

1 tablespoon soy sauce

½ teaspoon sugar

½ teaspoon cornstarch

## STIR-FRY

8 ounces long beans or green beans

4 to 8 ounces boneless pork butt or pork shoulder, trimmed of fat

2 tablespoons vegetable oil

½ cup chopped onion

1 tablespoon minced garlic

1 tablespoon ground bean sauce or hoisin sauce (see notes)

⅓ cup water, or as needed

1 **FOR THE SAUCE:** In a small bowl, mix the water, wine, soy sauce, sugar, and cornstarch.

2 **FOR THE STIR-FRY:** Trim off the stem ends from the long beans, and cut the beans into ½-inch lengths. Cut the pork into ½-inch chunks.

3 Set a 14-inch wok or 12-inch frying pan over high heat. When the pan is hot, after about 1 minute, add the oil and rotate the pan to spread. Add the onion and garlic; stir-fry until the onion is lightly browned, about 1 minute. Add the pork and stir-fry until the meat is browned, 1 to 2 minutes. Stir in the bean sauce to coat the pork. Add the water and long beans. Cover and cook until the long beans are barely tender to the bite, 1 to 2 minutes. Stir the sauce mixture and add to the pan. Stir-fry until the sauce boils and thickens, about 30 seconds. With a frying pan, the sauce may be thicker. If the sauce is too thick, stir in 1 to 2 tablespoons more water. Transfer to a serving dish.

**Notes:** The bean sauce will produce a more intense, robust bean flavor than the hoisin sauce. Hoisin sauce contains bean paste with added sugar, vinegar, and spices.

For a shortcut, substitute ground pork for the pork butt and crumble into the pan. ▪

# STEEPED CHICKEN BREASTS

I've been told that most Hakkas like their meat well done. Well, Popo must have been a renegade or acquired her love of moist, tender chicken from her Cantonese neighbors. She was adamant that chicken not be overcooked and insisted that the flesh have a smooth, slippery texture. In fact, when Popo cooked a whole chicken, the bone marrow would still be bright red and a blush of pinkness would peek out at the joint. She would chew on the bone and suck the marrow.

I find that her technique, likely borrowed from the Cantonese, works well on lean chicken breasts, which turn dry and cottony when overcooked. Instead of boiling over direct heat, the chicken cooks in the residual warmth of the boiling water, gently steeping to a silky smoothness that Popo would approve of. Slice the breast to use in Ginger-Garlic Chicken (page 205), serve slathered with Fresh Ginger-Onion Sauce (page 66), or shred the meat for salads or sandwiches.

*Makes 4 to 6 servings as a main dish or 2 to 3⅓ cups shredded chicken*
*(each 8-ounce breast makes about 1¼ cups shredded chicken)*

6 thin slices fresh ginger, lightly crushed

2 or 3 boneless, skinless chicken breast halves (6 to 10 ounces each)

1 In a 5- to 6-quart pan, bring about 3 quarts water and the ginger to a boil over high heat. Add the chicken, stir to separate the pieces, and return to a boil. Cover and remove from the heat. Let stand until the chicken is no longer pink in the center of the thickest part (cut to test), 17 to 22 minutes. If still pink, cover and steep a few minutes longer.

2 Lift out the chicken using a slotted spoon. Immerse in ice or cold water briefly to cool down quickly, then drain and let rest for about 5 minutes. Slice the chicken across the grain. Or use your hands to tear the meat along the grain into coarse shreds to use as desired.

Note: To adapt this recipe for larger quantities, slightly bigger pieces, or skin-on, bone-in pieces, keep these factors in mind: It's important to have enough water to cover the chicken by at least 1 inch. Don't crowd the pan; water should be able to flow between the chicken pieces. If the chicken is quite underdone and the water is no longer steaming hot, return the pan to the heat and cook just until the water begins to simmer. Remove from the heat and let chicken stand, covered, for a few minutes longer.

**Steeped Whole Chicken**

Use a 10- to 12-quart pan and increase the water to about 5 quarts (so that it covers the chicken by at least 1 inch). After the water returns to a boil, lower the heat and simmer 1 whole chicken (3½ pounds), covered, for 30 minutes, then remove from the heat and let stand for about 30 minutes. Insert an instant-read thermometer through the center of the thickest part of the breast until it touches the bone; it should read about 170°F. Lift out the chicken. Immerse in ice or cold water briefly to cool down quickly, then drain and let rest for about 10 minutes. Cut the chicken (page 243) and arrange on a serving platter. ∎

# My Family's Frontier

When he was just ten, my father, Harry Chong Lau, left his village on the outskirts of Tong Sui Town, in Yah Young County, Guangdong, to work for an uncle in Hong Kong. He left behind his mother, a younger brother, and a merchant marine father he rarely saw and barely recognized. In his teens, he left to work in Singapore in the mines, then later on a Norwegian ship that sailed between Hong Kong, Malaysia, Australia, and the West Coast of the United States. Meeting foreigners and seeing new places stoked his desire to live in America. On one of these trips, he jumped ship at San Pedro, California. When he missed the train to San Francisco, he took a later bus and ended up in Sacramento. He worked as a farmhand in the Courtland/Walnut Grove area.

During World War II, Dad served as a cook and mess sergeant in the army. Like many illegal Chinese immigrants, he became a citizen through his military service. He gained citizenship in 1944, just one year after the passage of the Magnuson Act, which repealed the Chinese Exclusion Act, provided an annual quota of 105 Chinese immigrants, and allowed foreign-born Chinese the right to naturalization for the first time in sixty years.

My father met my mother in Stockton, perhaps at her family's restaurant. She was attending the University of the Pacific and studying home economics. Although Mom was dating other men at the time, Popo thought marriage to my father, a Hakka from a neighboring village to her own hometown in China, would be a good fit for her. Mom and Dad married in Reno on August 13, 1946. I was born in 1947, followed by my brother Alan in 1948; much later, in 1963, another brother, Eugene, was born.

After my parents married, my father became a partner at Pigg's Café in Oroville. When the property owner died, they lost the business. Customers coaxed him to open the first Chinese restaurant in Paradise, a town whose claim to fame was a fifty-four-pound gold nugget discovered there in 1859. We moved to Paradise in November 1949. We were the first and only Chinese family in town. My parents sold their Oroville house to Popo and used the proceeds to buy a building in Paradise that had once been a church.

We soon discovered that not everyone welcomed us. Paradise lies just ten miles east of Chico, where, in 1877, a group of white men broke into a cabin, shot five Chinese farm workers, and set them on fire. Although my father was ready to strike it rich in Paradise, this conservative all-white community needed convincing. It had been just seven years since the repeal of the sixty-one-year-old Chinese Exclusion Act. The Chamber of Commerce questioned the wisdom of my father's decision to move here. To persuade them, Dad brought white friends from out of town to supply character references for the "Chinaman." In spite of a bomb threat, my father opened The Pagoda in 1950. Racism and de-layed road construction from Chico nearly destroyed the business, but eventually bargain-priced platters heaped with mounds of chop suey, chow mein, and sweet-and-sour pork won over the town. Years later, when the Rotary decided to hold its weekly meetings at The Pagoda, perhaps my father felt a measure of victory.

## STUFFED BITTER MELON SOUP

Bitter melon is one of those vegetables people either love or hate. Though I've never acquired a taste for it, my father enjoyed these bumpy squash-like melons so much that he grew them in his garden. He sliced the green melons cross-wise into rounds, scooped out the seeds, and stuffed the rings with a pork and shrimp filling. To make the filling, he would use two cleavers, one in each hand, and tap dance over the pork and shrimp to turn them into a fine mince. He dropped the stuffed melon rings into bubbling broth and poached them gently until they became tender and their bitterness seeped into the broth.

My husband, another bitter melon fan, claims that if you cover the soup while cooking, it will be more bitter. If you leave the soup uncovered during cooking, the bitterness will escape. Frankly, I've tried it both ways and don't taste a discernable difference. I'll leave it to you to decide. If you simmer the soup uncovered, you may need to add a little extra water or broth to make up for the evaporation. You may want to try this dish once to see where your tastes lie.

*Makes 3 servings as a main dish or 6 servings as part of a multicourse meal*

## MELON RINGS

4 ounces peeled, deveined shrimp (about 8 shrimp, 31 to 35 per pound)

4 ounces boneless pork butt or ground pork

¼ cup minced green onions, including green tops

1 tablespoon Chinese rice wine (shaoxing) or dry sherry

2 teaspoons cornstarch

1 teaspoon minced garlic

½ teaspoon sugar

½ teaspoon salt

⅛ teaspoon ground white pepper

2 bitter melons, each about 2 inches wide (about 1 pound total)

## SOUP

6 cups chicken broth, homemade (page 267) or purchased

Salt and ground white pepper

¼ cup thinly sliced green onions, including green tops, for garnish

**1 FOR THE MELON RINGS:** Finely chop the shrimp and pork butt, if using (no need to mince ground pork), to make a coarse paste. In a bowl, mix the shrimp, pork, green onions, wine, cornstarch, garlic, sugar, salt, and white pepper until well blended. You will have about 1 cup of filling.

**2** Trim the ends off the bitter melons. Cut the bitter melons crosswise into ½-inch-thick rounds. With a small knife, cut out the spongy center with seeds from each round, push out, and discard. Pack the cavity of each bitter melon section with the pork mixture; the filling can mound slightly over the edges of the melon.

**3 FOR THE SOUP:** In a 4- to 5-quart pan over high heat, bring the broth to a boil. Add the bitter melon rings to the broth. Drop 1-inch chunks (about 1 tablespoon each) of any remaining filling into the broth. Bring to a simmer, cover, and cook over low heat until the filling is no longer pink in the thickest part and the bitter melon is tender when pierced, 12 to 15 minutes. Add salt and white pepper to taste. Ladle into bowls and sprinkle with the green onions. ■

Bitter melon

# MUSTARD GREEN AND PORK SOUP

Hakkas love mustard greens—fresh, salted, pickled, and preserved. This quick soup shows off the flavor power of fresh mustard greens. As the greens simmer, their pungency leaches into the broth to contrast with the rich pork. Use almost any type or maturity of mustard greens, from leafy to broad-stemmed varieties. I prefer the young stalks of Chinese mustard greens that I find at the farmers' market, but curly southern mustard greens from the supermarket also work well.

*Makes 6 to 8 servings as part of a multicourse meal*

6 cups chicken broth, homemade (page 267) or purchased

3 thin slices fresh ginger, lightly crushed

2 large cloves garlic, lightly crushed

8 ounces ground pork (see note)

2 teaspoons minced garlic

1 teaspoon cornstarch

½ teaspoon salt, or to taste

¼ teaspoon ground black pepper, or to taste

12 to 14 ounces mustard greens

1 In a 4-quart pan over high heat, bring the broth, ginger, and crushed garlic cloves to a boil.

2 Mix the pork, minced garlic, cornstarch, salt, and pepper. Drop ½-inch lumps (about 1 teaspoon each) of the pork mixture into the boiling broth. Return to a boil, cover, and simmer until pork is no longer pink in the center of the thickest part (cut to test), 3 to 5 minutes. Skim off the fat and discard.

3 Meanwhile, trim the tough stem ends off the mustard greens and discard. Cut the greens into pieces 2 to 3 inches long and ½ inch wide, to make about 8 cups. Rinse and drain. When the pork is done, add the mustard greens, return to a boil, and cook until bright green and crisp-tender, 3 to 5 minutes. Add salt and pepper. Ladle into individual bowls or a large serving bowl.

**Note:** For a richer soup, omit the ground pork and minced garlic and replace with 1½ pounds bite-sized chunks of bone-in pork neck or 12 ounces boneless pork butt, cut into ½-inch chunks. Simmer, covered, until the meat is tender when pierced, 45 minutes to 1¼ hours, before adding the greens. Add a little water or more broth, if some of the broth has evaporated. ∎

# STIR-FRIED ICEBERG LETTUCE AND GARLIC

My mother often stir-fried iceberg lettuce with garlic. It was sort of like eating a hot—but still crisp—salad. We thought it was a bit strange, because all our friends ate iceberg lettuce only raw in a sandwich or slathered with French dressing, and my brother suspected that Mom was just trying to use up old lettuce. As an adult, I've come to appreciate its fresh, clean flavor and quick preparation.

*Makes 4 to 6 servings as a side dish or as part of a multicourse meal*

1 small head iceberg lettuce
(about 12 ounces)

2 tablespoons vegetable oil

3 large cloves garlic, lightly crushed

½ teaspoon salt, or to taste

**1** Core the lettuce and discard the wilted outer leaves. Rinse and drain well. Tear the lettuce into 3- to 5-inch pieces to make 10 to 12 cups.

**2** Set a 14-inch wok or 12-inch frying pan over high heat. When the pan is hot, after about 1 minute, add the oil and rotate the pan to spread. Add the garlic and stir-fry until golden, about 30 seconds. Add the lettuce and salt and stir-fry just until the lettuce wilts slightly but still retains some crispness, about 2 minutes. Do not overcook. If all the lettuce doesn't fit in the frying pan, add half and stir-fry until slightly wilted, about 30 seconds, and then stir in the remainder. Transfer to a serving dish.

**Note:** If possible, use a wok. Its bowl shape contains the lettuce more effectively than a frying pan. ▪

# CAULIFLOWER AND BEEF IN BLACK BEAN SAUCE

Most people describe cauliflower as bland, but my mother's stir-fried version is packed with flavor. Her secret is fermented black beans. Soybeans go through a fermentation process that transforms them into soft capsules of earthy pungency. When combined with garlic, ginger, and soy sauce, the dark beans make a robust, appetizing sauce. When I went away to college, I asked her to send this recipe. It's simple, satisfying, and economical—Hakka virtues that a hungry student could appreciate. Broccoli can replace the cauliflower.

*Makes 2 to 3 servings as a main dish or 4 to 6 servings as part of a multicourse meal* ▶

## SAUCE

¾ cup water

2 tablespoons Chinese rice wine
(shaoxing) or dry sherry

1 tablespoon cornstarch

½ teaspoon sugar

¼ teaspoon salt

## STIR-FRY

1½ tablespoons fermented black
beans, rinsed and minced

1 tablespoon minced garlic

1 tablespoon minced fresh ginger

1 tablespoon soy sauce

2 tablespoons vegetable oil

8 ounces ground beef

1½ pounds cauliflower or broccoli, cut
into 1-inch chunks (about 6 cups)

¾ cup water, or as needed

½ cup thinly sliced green onions,
including green tops

**1** **FOR THE SAUCE:** In a small bowl, mix the water, wine, cornstarch, sugar, and salt.

**2** **FOR THE STIR-FRY:** In a bowl, combine the black beans, garlic, ginger, and soy sauce. (Or in a mortar and pestle, crush the black beans, garlic, and ginger into a coarse paste and then stir in the soy sauce.)

**3** Set a 14-inch wok or 12-inch frying pan over high heat. When the pan is hot, after about 1 minute, add the oil and rotate the pan to spread. Add the black bean mixture and stir-fry just until fragrant, about 10 seconds. Add the beef and stir-fry until the meat is crumbly and lightly browned, 2 to 3 minutes. Add the cauliflower and ¾ cup water, cover, and cook, stirring once, until the cauliflower is tender when pierced and most of the liquid has evaporated, 3 to 4 minutes.

**4** When the cauliflower is tender, stir the sauce mixture and add to the pan. Stir-fry until the sauce boils and thickens, about 30 seconds. If the sauce is thicker than desired, stir in 1 to 2 tablespoons water. Stir in the green onions, and transfer to a serving bowl.

Note: For a shortcut, use 1½ tablespoons purchased Chinese black bean–garlic sauce such as Lee Kum Kee, and eliminate the black beans, garlic, and soy sauce. In step 3, stir-fry the beef in oil with ginger, and then stir in the black bean sauce after the meat has browned. ■

# SOY-BRAISED OXTAIL AND RADISH STEW

I learned to love oxtails from my mother. She would braise a kettle of oxtails until they were so tender I could suck the meat off the craggy bones. My kids and husband used to turn them down, but after watching me strip the bones clean, they have become converts. Use a dark soy sauce for deep color and the all-purpose soy sauce for saltiness. Since oxtails take a few hours to cook, I make a pot big enough for a second meal; the stew tastes even better the second night. Serve with plenty of rice to soak up the aromatic juices.

*Makes 6 to 8 servings as a main dish or 12 to 14 servings as part of a multicourse meal*

2 quarts water

½ cup Chinese rice wine (shaoxing) or dry sherry

¼ cup dark soy sauce

3 tablespoons soy sauce

12 thin slices fresh ginger, lightly crushed

8 large cloves garlic, lightly crushed

3 tablespoons packed brown sugar

3 star anise

2 pieces dried tangerine peel, each about 1 inch wide, rinsed

2 oxtails (4½ to 5 pounds total)

1 pound Asian white radish, such as daikon

1 pound carrots (4 or 5 large)

¼ teaspoon salt, or additional soy sauce, to taste

¼ cup coarsely chopped cilantro, for garnish

2 tablespoons thinly sliced green onions, including green tops, for garnish

**1** In a 10- to 12-quart pan over high heat, combine the water, wine, dark soy sauce, soy sauce, ginger, garlic, sugar, star anise, and tangerine peel. Bring to a boil.

**2** If the oxtails are whole, cut between the joints to separate. Trim off the excess fat. Add the oxtails to the boiling water. Return to a boil, cover, and simmer, stirring occasionally, until the oxtails are just tender when pierced, 1½ to 2 hours.

**3** Meanwhile, peel the radish and carrots. Cut both vegetables into 1-inch chunks. Add the radish and carrots to the tender oxtails and return to a boil. Reduce the heat. Cover and simmer, stirring occasionally, until the oxtails and radish are very tender when pierced, about 30 minutes longer.

**4** With a slotted spoon, transfer the oxtails and vegetables to a serving dish. Skim off the fat and discard. Cover to keep warm or place in a warm oven. Taste the pan juices and, if watery, boil uncovered over high heat until the juices have reduced to about 2 cups and the flavor is concentrated to your taste. Add salt or more soy sauce to taste. Pour the sauce over the oxtails, and garnish with cilantro and green onions. ■

Star anise

# Tuesday's Family Banquet

In my first years of school, I always felt like an outsider. We were the only Chinese family in a conservative, all-white retirement town. My father had opened the first Chinese restaurant in town. He worked long hours. The only time we saw him was Tuesday, the day the restaurant closed.

Tuesday was the day of the family banquet. All through elementary school, I looked forward to this night of gluttony. My parents, brother, grandmother, two uncles, and I gathered together for an informal banquet that was like Chinese New Year and Thanksgiving rolled into one.

The meal often opened with bird's nest soup, an expensive and rare delicacy fit for an emperor. The soup was made from dried birds' nests—not the twiggy nests of North American birds, but nests made with the gelatinous saliva of a special breed of swifts in East Asia. When dried, the nests look a bit like coarse sea sponges. To Westerners, this oddity may sound unpalatable, but if you ate this soup not knowing what it was, you might find it delicious. Bird's nest has a neutral taste but a wonderful crunchy texture, like crisp seaweed. My grandmother or mother would simmer the soaked nest in a rich broth made with a whole chicken and bits of dried tangerine peel.

Our family banquets featured other delicacies as well. If we had recently visited San Francisco's Chinatown, we might have a roast duck with its crisp, burnished brown exterior. Sometimes Popo would cook our favorite dish, sliced potatoes and Chinese bacon braised in fragrant five-spice powder and soy. An uncle might bring braised pillows of tofu, stuffed with pork and shrimp, in a brown gravy. Mom would simmer dried dark mushrooms and chicken in soy and ginger until glossy and plump. We ate until we almost burst.

Those family banquets taught me to enjoy the pleasures of good food. Most important, I learned how food could satisfy the yearnings of not only a hungry stomach, but also of a lonely soul.

# HAKKA CLASSIC
# Stuffed Tofu

釀豆腐 Hakka: *nyiong tiu fu;* Mandarin: *niang dou fu*

Savory stuffed tofu morsels are a product of migration. When the Hakka moved south, there was little wheat to make wrappers for dumplings. To adapt, they replaced the wheat-based wrappers with tofu, or bean curd, made from ground soybeans. The neutral-flavored tofu encased a savory filling. These tofu pouches were amazingly versatile. Cooks browned, braised, poached, or steamed them to create many appetizing dishes.

In the basic Hakka version, the filling starts with ground pork. Some cooks add dried or fresh seafood to the mixture. Possible seasonings include garlic, ginger, green onions, cilantro, soy sauce, fish sauce, dried tangerine peel, salt, and pepper. You can interchange the fillings, using your favorite. The filling can also be used to stuff vegetables, such as mushrooms, bitter melon, mild chiles, and eggplant. You'll find delicious variations throughout the book, such as Braised Fried Tofu with Pork (76), Singapore Stuffed Vegetable and Tofu Soup (106), and Fah's Stuffed Tofu Triangles (215).

## UNCLE HENRY'S TOFU TRIANGLES

In my Uncle Henry's homestyle version of stuffed tofu, a slot-like pocket is carved into tofu triangles to cradle a filling of pork, fish, and shrimp. To preserve the natural flavor of the tofu, Uncle Henry browns just the narrow slits of exposed filling. Then he gently braises the filled triangles in broth and thickens the juices to make a light sauce.

*Makes 3 to 4 servings as a main dish or 6 to 8 servings as part of a multicourse meal*

### STUFFED TOFU

1 teaspoon dried shrimp,
 or ⅛ teaspoon salt

1½ ounces peeled, deveined shrimp
 (3 or 4 shrimp; see note)

1½ ounces skinless fillet from a white-
 fleshed fish, such as rockfish

**1 FOR THE STUFFED TOFU:** Rinse the dried shrimp and place in a small bowl. Cover with warm water and soak until soft, about 15 minutes. Drain and squeeze water out of the shrimp. Finely chop the dried shrimp. If not using dried shrimp, omit this step and add the additional salt to the filling in step 2.

**2** Rinse the fresh shrimp and fish. Cut both into ½-inch chunks. With a large knife, finely chop the shrimp ▸

4 ounces ground pork

2 tablespoons minced green onions

1 tablespoon beaten egg

1 teaspoon minced garlic

¼ teaspoon salt

¼ teaspoon sugar

⅛ teaspoon ground white pepper

1 pound firm tofu

## BRAISING

2 tablespoons vegetable oil

¾ cup chicken broth, homemade (page 267) or purchased

1 tablespoon Chinese rice wine (shaoxing) or dry sherry

2 teaspoons cornstarch

2 teaspoons soy sauce

1 tablespoon thinly sliced green onions, including green tops, for garnish

and fresh fish until they form a coarse, sticky paste. (Or place in a food processor and pulse just until a coarse, sticky paste forms.) In a small bowl, mix the dried shrimp, fresh shrimp and fish paste, ground pork, green onions, egg, garlic, salt, sugar, and white pepper until well blended.

3 Rinse the tofu, and then drain for about 5 minutes. Cut the tofu into 4 squares or rectangles, each about 1 inch thick and 2½ to 3 inches wide. Cut the pieces in half diagonally to make triangles. Lay the tofu in a single layer on a double thickness of towels. Set another double layer of towels on top and press gently to remove excess moisture. Cut a slit down the center of the widest side of each triangle so it comes within ½ inch of the ends. Cut around the slit to form a generous ¼-inch-wide opening and carefully dig out the tofu to form a pocket. Gently fill the pocket with about 1 tablespoon filling, using a chopstick to push the filling into the pocket; the filling can mound slightly on top. Repeat to fill all. Reserve the tofu scraps for another use.

4 FOR BRAISING: Set a 14-inch wok or 12-inch frying pan over medium-high heat. When the pan is hot, after about 1 minute, add the oil and rotate the pan to spread. Stand the triangles, filling side down, in the pan. If there's extra filling, break it into ½-inch chunks and add to the pan. Cook until the filling is browned, about 2 minutes.

5 Lay the tofu triangles flat. Add the broth, cover, and simmer over low heat, turning once halfway through, until the filling is no longer pink in the center (cut to test), 4 to 5 minutes total. With a slotted spatula, transfer the tofu to a serving dish, leaving behind the pan juices. In a small bowl, mix the wine, cornstarch, and soy sauce. Add to the pan juices and stir until the sauce reaches a boil, about 30 seconds. Pour over the tofu. Sprinkle with the green onions.

Note: Instead of using both fresh shrimp and fish, substitute 3 ounces of one kind of seafood, either all shrimp or all fish. ∎

# NATALIE COM LIU'S TOFU TOPPED WITH PORK

If filling a skinny pocket of delicate tofu proves too intimidating, try this easier open-faced method that Natalie Com Liu uses in Lima, Peru. She cuts the tofu into rectangles, scoops out a little cavity in the flat pieces, and mounds a simple pork mixture on top. She then steams the tofu rectangles and drains off the pan juices to create a brown sauce that cloaks the tofu with deep flavor.

*Makes 3 to 4 servings as a main dish or 6 to 8 servings as part of a multicourse meal*

## PORK-TOPPED TOFU

8 ounces ground pork

1 tablespoon soy sauce

2 teaspoons Chinese rice wine (shaoxing) or dry sherry

2 teaspoons cornstarch

¼ teaspoon salt

1 tablespoon grated fresh ginger (see note)

1 pound firm tofu

## SAUCE

2 tablespoons oyster sauce

⅞ cup chicken broth, homemade (page 267) or purchased, or as needed

2 teaspoons cornstarch

1 tablespoon vegetable oil

1 tablespoon minced garlic

3 tablespoons thinly sliced green onions, including green tops

**1  FOR THE PORK-TOPPED TOFU:** In a medium bowl, combine the pork, soy sauce, wine, cornstarch, and salt. Squeeze the ginger over the pork so the juice drips onto the pork; discard the ginger solids. Mix the pork well.

**2**  Rinse the tofu, and then drain for about 5 minutes. Cut the tofu into 12 pieces, each ½ to ¾ inch thick and about 2 inches square (or a similar-sized rectangle). Lay the pieces in a single layer on a double thickness of towels. Set another double layer of towels on top and press gently to remove excess moisture. With a small spoon, scoop out the tofu in the center of each piece to make a depression about ¼ inch deep, leaving a ¼-inch border around the sides. Reserve the tofu scraps for another use. Mound about 1 tablespoon of the pork filling in each depression, pressing gently so that it sticks to the tofu.

**3**  Place the tofu pieces in a single layer in a 9-inch shallow heatproof dish that will fit inside a steamer, such as a Pyrex pie pan. Set the dish on a rack over 2 to 4 inches boiling water in a steamer or wok (if the bottom is round, place on a wok ring to stabilize). If the steamer lid is flat metal, wrap the lid with a towel to reduce condensation dripping on the food. Cover and steam over high heat until the pork filling is no longer pink in the center (cut to test), 10 to 15 minutes. Watch the water level, adding more boiling water as needed. Carefully remove the dish from the steamer. ▸

**4 FOR THE SAUCE:** Tilt the dish slightly and spoon off the pan juices. Measure the liquid and add the oyster sauce and enough broth to make 1 cup. Stir in the cornstarch. Set a 10-inch frying pan over high heat. When the pan is hot, after about 1 minute, add the oil and garlic, and stir-fry just until the garlic is lightly browned, about 15 seconds. Add the oyster sauce mixture and stir until it boils, about 1 minute. Stir in the green onions and pour over the tofu.

**Note:** To grate the ginger, use a microplane or the rough round holes on a box grater. If you grate it over a plate, it is easier to collect the juices. ∎

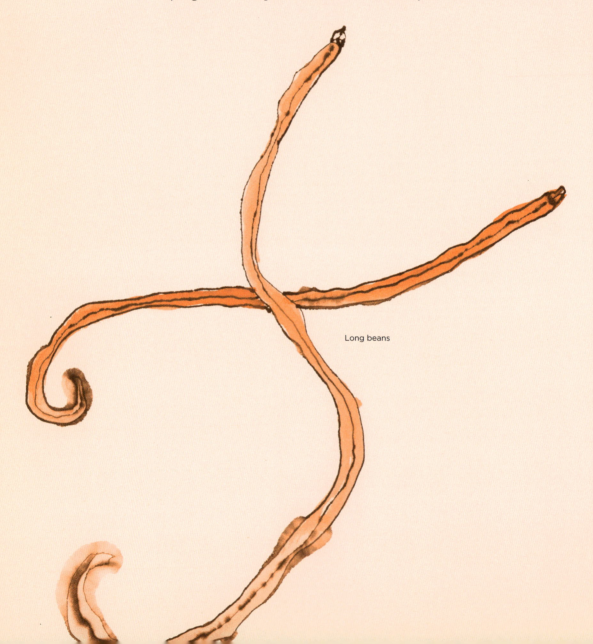

Long beans

# TWO

# Hakka Cooking in the Homeland China

After Popo passed away, reminders of my Hakka identity grew scarce. Although my parents were proud to be Chinese, they seldom spoke of their Hakka heritage. As I pursued a career and raised a family of my own, my Hakka identity slid into dormancy. Decades passed. As retirement approached, I decided I finally had time to research the food of my culture. The heart of my plan was a trip to China in the fall of 2005. My travel companions and I began in Guangdong Province, where I searched for my ancestral roots in Meixian and explored the home of Hakka cuisine and culture in Meizhou, the provincial capital. We then followed the Hakka food trail to Beijing, Luodai (a village in Sichuan Province), and Hong Kong. Eating in the country where my ancestors had come from taught me the taste of true Hakka food. As I continued my travels, I would have a baseline for comparison.

## Coming Home to Meixian

Meixian (Moiyen in Hakka) is the ancestral home to many Hakkas, including my family. I include it in our trip but am a bit nervous about tracking down family roots. Old quarrels, grudges, and hidden agendas haunt our family. My generation never understood the family politics. Going home might open a Pandora's box of secrets we were afraid to uncover.

Regardless, I feel we need to go. I press my father's younger brother, Uncle Henry, for details. Did he have the Chinese names for our family village? My grandparents' immigration papers are in English and the phonetic village names aren't precise enough. Also, the names of villages and cities have changed in China. Uncle Henry sends me the Chinese characters for his and my father's village, Lop Muey, but doesn't know the name of my mother's family's hometown. I show the characters to our guides, who locate the general area and feel that once we are there, locals will direct us.

For my travel companions, I recruit family members: my husband, Terry, my daughter, Lisa, my brothers, Gene and Alan, Alan's wife, Kazuko Nakane, and my cousins Sue Chee, Jeannie Chow, and Yau Lau. We need at least ten people to qualify for an additional national guide, so I ask my Hakka friend Rebekah Luke and her husband, Peter Krape, to join our eating adventure. After a few mammoth meals, our group names itself Linda's Hakka Gourmet Group.

We fly into Guangzhou, and then ride the bus to Huizhou. As we arrive, I'm surprised to see a large, bustling modern city with high-rise buildings, multi-story supermarkets, small factories, and even nuclear power stations. I had expected a country village. Tomorrow we'll look for our ancestral home, about a forty-five-minute bus ride away, say our guides.

The next day, as we drive through the countryside, with its reddish-orange dirt, fragrant pine trees, and hills, I am reminded of Paradise, the small town where my brothers and I grew up in Northern California. True, there are tropical plants at this latitude, but I feel that we might be at the same two-thousand-foot elevation as Paradise. Hakkas lived in the mountains of China, and our family had settled in the Sierra foothills—was that just a coincidence?

In Danshui, our guides stop locals and show them the Chinese characters for Lop Muey. We ask two or three people who don't recognize the name, but soon we're driving up a road to a small village. Our guides, both with the same surname as ours, Liu (in Hakka and Mandarin; Lau in Cantonese), point out the name on a plaque over a doorway. "This is a village of the family Liu," one says. We walk around and find the village mostly abandoned. Vines climb over deserted buildings and houses with no roofs and collapsed walls. We find two white-haired women chattering inside a dark shell of a building. They direct us to a neighborhood on the hill, where the houses are intact and more modern.

Yau, Uncle Henry's son, speaks Hakka but hasn't found anyone who can understand him so far. Finally, in our family's village, he can talk with the locals. He meets a woman in her seventies who claims to have known his mother and father. The woman introduces her son and grandson and invites us into her plain stucco house. She tells us that Yau has a relative who lives nearby and sends someone to fetch her. As we wait for the relative to arrive, we sip tea and eat bananas in the dark front room of the house.

Finally, another woman arrives and says that she is the wife of one of Yau's relatives. She leads us back through the village ruins to the family house, now deserted. She tells us that seventy years ago, three families shared the four-room house. My father and Uncle Henry lived here when they were young. Later, they both sent money to help renovate this place. Since then, the house has fallen into disrepair, like many of those around it. The woman tells us that bad karma drove our family away. The inhabitants feared they might die in the house after three of our grandfather's wives died there. We take several family photos and examine the broken pottery and weather-streaked furniture. My father was a quiet man and never spoke of his parents or his life in China. We knew nothing of his relatives in China. The discovery of the home of my great-grandparents and grandparents, people I never knew, seems almost unreal.

A couple of weeks after our trip, I get an email from Yau with a family photo of fifteen people. He writes:

Here's a photo you may find interesting. It is a picture taken in the house in Lop Muey. There is a very interesting story behind this picture. When your dad was only a child, his parents arranged to have a girl child be his future wife. That girl child lived with them from the time she was promised to your dad. When your dad was of age she became his wife. After your dad left for the U.S. he wanted to have a picture of his wife sent to him so that's why he sent money home and requested to have this picture taken. The Lau family in China did not treat his wife very well after your dad left, and she went back to live with her own family. Your dad was lied to. He was told that she was killed by the Japanese when they invaded China. He never found out the truth until my mom and dad came over to the U.S. My mom was the one who volunteered this information. My dad did not have much to say except that it is the past and that it doesn't matter now, since all have passed away. Those were different times.

Now back to the picture. "If you'll look closely, you will be able to see the stairs in the background on the right. It looks like they are standing just in front of the area where the rainwater is collected. They have draped some fabric to cover up the walls, so you can't see the rooms to the sides. I wonder if one of the chairs that great-grandfather and great-grandmother are sitting in is the same one that was left there."

I compare the two photos: the one we took a few weeks ago with the four of us, and the one taken almost sixty years ago. It does look like it was taken in the same place. We had found our roots in China.

# A Family Meal in Meixian County

We ate many meals in China, but we were never invited to a home-cooked meal in a village. A few years later, I learned more about country life from an anthropologist who had lived there.

"Food in rural Meixian is a total social experience. It is also a way to express ethnic identity. It is cultivated, wild, and a commodity," says Ellen Oxfeld, a professor at Middlebury College, at her presentation at the Roundhouse Reunion, a Hakka conference in Toronto in 2008. She has firsthand experience. She lived in a village in the county of Meixian that was settled in the seventeenth century. This county is one of seven—Meixian, Dapu, Wuhua, Pingyuan, Xingning, Fengshun, and Jiaoling—that are part of the greater Hakka area now known as Meizhou. Her presentation paints a picture of daily life there.

In Meixian, every rural family has land rights and is able to grow two crops of rice each year plus a wide variety of vegetables in a private garden. Women handle the farming, while men often cultivate fishponds and raise pigs. Some even recycle the methane fuel the animals produce. The Hakka forage wild greens, medicinal grasses, and twigs and catch highly prized snakes. For cash, they grow pomelos and make tofu.

A typical family meal might include rice, soup, a meat dish (usually with pork), and some stir-fried greens. Steamed fish is also common for lunch or dinner. For breakfast, congee, a rice porridge, is a staple, supplemented by salted dried vegetables and fried peanuts. Breakfast might also include a soup made from pork innards and *zao,* a red by-product of making sweet rice wine. In the city, *yang mian,* a boiled noodle dish garnished with stir-fried garlic and other ingredients, is very popular for breakfast.

# STEAMED FISH WITH GREEN ONIONS

Steamed fish is largely known as a Cantonese dish, but it often appears on the Hakka table. The Hakka use whole local fish—from a river or lake if they live inland, or from the ocean if they live on the coast. Seasonings vary by region. Sichuan chefs shower the fish with fresh green peppercorns and sliced hot chiles. In Beijing, one chef scatters dark mushrooms and strips of red pepper on the fish. Chef Li from San Francisco tops the fish with slivers of pickled mustard greens and fermented black beans. Finally, Winston and Marie Chang from Trinidad sometimes use canned pickled plums to add a tart, fruity accent. Start with this recipe for a basic steamed fish, and then add your own local accents.

*Makes 2 servings as a main dish or 4 servings as part of a multicourse meal*

1 small whole fish (1½ to 2 pounds), such as rock cod, tilapia, black bass, or striped bass, cleaned and scaled (see note)

2 tablespoons Chinese rice wine (shaoxing) or dry sherry

2 tablespoons soy sauce

⅛ teaspoon salt

2 tablespoons thinly slivered fresh ginger

⅓ cup thinly slivered green onions, including green tops

2 tablespoons vegetable oil

**1** Rinse the fish inside and out; pat dry. Place the fish in a 9- to 10-inch shallow heatproof dish that will fit inside a steamer, such as a Pyrex pie pan. If the fish is too long, remove the head and tail or cut it in half crosswise so it will fit inside the dish. Evenly drizzle wine and soy sauce over the inside and outside of the fish. Sprinkle salt lightly over the inside and outside of the fish. Distribute half of the ginger inside the fish, and sprinkle the remaining ginger over the top.

**2** Set the dish on a rack over 2 to 4 inches boiling water in a steamer or wok (if the bottom is round, place on a wok ring to stabilize). If the steamer lid is flat metal, wrap the lid with a towel to reduce condensation dripping on the food. Cover and steam over high heat until the fish is barely opaque in the center of the thickest part (cut to test), about 10 minutes per inch of thickness, measured at the thickest part. Watch the water level, adding more boiling water as needed. Carefully remove the dish from the steamer. Sprinkle the fish with green onions.

**3** In an 8- to 10-inch frying pan, warm the oil over high heat until it ripples, about 30 seconds. Drizzle the hot oil evenly over the green onions and fish.

**Note:** Asian markets sell small whole fish, sometimes alive and swimming. Chinese cooks leave the heads and tails on, but if you prefer, you may remove them. Or, instead of a whole fish, substitute 12 ounces to 1 pound fillet from a fish such as rockfish, halibut, or salmon. Reduce the wine, soy sauce, and salt by half. ∎

# Meizhou, Capital of the Hakka World

As we ride the bus to the city of Meizhou in northeast Guangdong Province, our local guide, Sister Liu, fills in the facts. Meizhou is the name of the district and a prefecture-level city. It is part of the mountainous area where Jiangxi, Guangdong, and Fujian provinces meet, often referred to the Hakka heartland. Almost everyone in the cities of Meizhou (in Guangdong) and Yongding (in Fujian) is Hakka.

After a long journey, we arrive at Wen Cho Low, a restaurant located in a picturesque eighty-year-old building owned by a Hakka woman from Taiwan. The sprawling compound also houses exhibits of Hakka history and rents four guest rooms. With one head chef and twenty-seven sous chefs, the restaurant offers a wide range of hearty soul food.

We taste fine examples of Hakka classics, such as steamed pork belly with preserved mustard greens, stuffed tofu, and salt-baked chicken. Chewy dried bamboo shoots simmer with pork in soy sauce. There's an herbal pork tonic with big chunks of fibrous root. Strands of chewy preserved radish lace a thin, browned omelet. In a riff on the Cantonese classic of steamed fish, the chefs embellish a local river fish with soy sauce and a generous tangle of green onion threads. Baseball-sized orbs of steamed pork, turnip, and taro surprise me with their somewhat sticky, dense texture; a dip in soy and red chile sauce sparks their otherwise bland flavor. For my vegetarian brother, there are browned bean curd triangles with strips of carrot, mushrooms, and green onions. It's a comforting meal to share with family in our ancestral homeland. After dinner, we head to the hotel downtown that serves as a base for our explorations around Meizhou.

Green onions

# FRIED EGGS AND PRESERVED RADISH

Beaten eggs bind a web of salty-sweet radish strips and sliced green onions to create a golden pancake, similar to a frittata. The chewy dried radish (also called Chinese turnip) lends an earthy substance to the eggs. Eat this dish with rice for a fast, homespun meal.

*Makes 1 serving as a main dish or 2 to 3 servings as part of a multicourse meal*

⅓ cup sweet or salted radish strips (see note)

2 large eggs

1 tablespoon water

3 tablespoons vegetable oil

⅓ cup thinly sliced green onions, including green tops

1 Rinse the radish strips. If they are too salty for your taste, cover them with water and soak for 5 to 15 minutes, then drain and squeeze out excess water.

2 In a small bowl, lightly beat the eggs and water to blend.

3 Set a 6-inch frying pan over medium-high heat. When the pan is hot, after about 1 minute, add 1 tablespoon of the oil and rotate the pan to spread. Add the radish strips and green onions. Stir-fry just until the radish strips are dried out and the green onions are bright green, 1 to 2 minutes. Stir the radish mixture into the beaten eggs.

4 Return the pan to medium-high heat. Add the remaining 2 tablespoons oil and rotate the pan to spread. Add the egg-radish mixture and spread it in an even layer. Shake the pan to level the egg. Cook the egg pancake until the top is almost set and the bottom is golden brown, 1 to 2 minutes. With a wide spatula, turn the egg pancake over and cook until browned on the other side, about 30 seconds longer. Slide out of the pan onto a serving dish.

Note: If the sweet or salted radish is not already in thin strips, cut into thin sticks about ¼ inch thick and 2 inches long. ∎

# HAKKA CLASSIC
# Pork Belly with Preserved Mustard Greens

扣 肉 梅 菜 Hakka: *kiu ngiuk moi choi;* Mandarin: *kou rou mei cai*

Pork belly with preserved mustard greens pairs two traditional humble Hakka ingredients. When pork belly is layered over dried mustard greens and steamed with soy sauce and wine, the parts meld into a soulful classic that melts in your mouth. What this dark dish lacks in looks, it makes up for with its enticing, salty-sweet flavors.

Pork belly, also called three-layer pork or five-flower pork, is highly valued by the Hakka. Basically, it is fresh side pork—the same cut used for bacon. When it is slowly cooked in moist heat, the fat, meat, and skin melt into soft succulence. The dried preserved mustard greens cut the pork's richness with their pungent bite.

Traditionally, the pork belly slices are arranged over the bottom of a dish, with the greens and sauce laid over them. After cooking, the dish is inverted so that the pork appears on top. This action may account for its name, *kiu ngiuk,* which loosely translates to "turn over meat."

For many Hakkas, this tribute to fat and salt is the ultimate comfort food: a dish to be enjoyed with great relish and a small measure of guilt. These days, most people don't burn off enough calories to justify eating this dish very often. When they indulge, it is savored almost as a stolen pleasure.

The first recipe is a simplified version for the home cook. The second recipe is a party-sized deluxe version with more complex flavors. Eat either one with hot cooked rice. Or, for a modern adaptation, serve as mini-sandwiches, with the pork and mustard greens tucked into folded buns. Look for the white steamed buns in the freezer, refrigerator, or deli section of Asian markets. Or use soft baked rolls instead.

Shop at an Asian market to gather the main ingredients. You may need to hunt for the preserved mustard greens since the label may be vague. Check the ingredients list and look for one that includes mustard greens or cabbage, sugar, and salt. If there's a choice, opt for the softer, lighter one, which will usually be less salty than the drier, darker version.

# STEAMED PORK BELLY WITH PRESERVED MUSTARD GREENS

In this classic, cherished pork belly and humble preserved mustard greens slowly steam together. The pork becomes juicy and tender, while the mustard greens provide a bed of savory pungency. In restaurants, the meat is usually parboiled and deep-fried before being steamed. To simplify the process for the home cook, I've substituted broiling for deep-frying. You can assemble the dish a day ahead, so that it is ready to steam the next day.

*Makes 6 to 8 servings as a main dish or 10 to 12 servings as part of a multicourse meal*

6 ounces preserved mustard greens

1 piece boneless pork belly with skin (1½ to 2 pounds), about 1½ inches thick

¼ cup dark soy sauce

1 tablespoon vegetable oil

1 tablespoon minced garlic

½ cup Chinese rice wine (shaoxing) or dry sherry

1½ tablespoons packed brown sugar

1 tablespoon oyster sauce

½ teaspoon five-spice powder

1  Chop the mustard greens into ½-inch pieces to make about 1½ cups, and place in a large bowl. Fill the bowl with hot water and rub the greens to remove the salt and sand; rinse and drain several times. Cover with more hot water and let stand, changing the water occasionally, until the thick stem pieces are soft, 30 minutes to 1 hour. Drain, rinse, and drain again. Press and squeeze the excess water out of the greens.

2  Cut the pork belly across the grain into 3-inch sections. In a 4-quart pan over high heat, bring about 6 cups water to a boil. Add the pork, return to a boil, and reduce the heat. Cover and simmer until the pork skin can be pierced with a fork, 30 to 40 minutes. Lift out the pork and pat dry.

3  Place the pork and 1 tablespoon of the dark soy sauce on a plate. Coat the meat in the soy sauce, and then set the pork pieces skin side down in the sauce. Let stand until the skin darkens slightly, 5 to 15 minutes. Preheat the broiler. Skim off and discard the fat from the cooking liquid. Reserve ⅔ cup liquid for the mustard greens; reserve the remainder for another use or discard. Blot the pork pieces dry with a towel. Set the pork pieces, skin side up, in a broiler pan. Broil, about 6 inches from the heat, until the skin is browned, about 15 minutes. (Fat may splatter the oven.) Let cool and chill until firm, about 1 hour.

4  Set a 14-inch wok or a 12-inch nonstick frying pan over medium-high heat. When the pan is hot, after about 1 minute, add the oil and rotate the pan to spread. Add the garlic and stir until it begins to brown, about 30 seconds. Stir in the mustard greens. Add the reserved ⅔ cup pork cooking liquid, remaining 3 tablespoons dark soy sauce, wine, sugar, oyster sauce, and five-spice powder. ▸

Bring to a boil, reduce the heat, and simmer, uncovered, stirring occasionally, until the greens absorb some of the sauce, about 10 minutes.

5   From the flesh side, cut each section of the pork along the grain into ½-inch-thick slices. Arrange the slices in 2 rows, skin side down, in the center of a shallow heatproof bowl that holds 5 to 6 cups and will fit inside a steamer. Distribute the chopped greens and sauce evenly over and around the pork slices.

6   Set the dish on a rack over 2 to 4 inches boiling water in a steamer or wok (if the bottom is round, place on a wok ring to stabilize). If the steamer lid is flat metal, wrap the lid with a towel to reduce condensation dripping on the food. Cover and steam over medium-high heat until the pork is very tender when pierced, 1½ to 2 hours. Check the water level often and add more boiling water as needed. With a bamboo steamer, keep the bottom rim covered with water to avoid burning. Carefully remove the dish from the steamer. Let rest about 5 minutes. Tilt the bowl to one side and spoon out most of the pan juices into a small bowl. Skim off and discard the fat from the pan juices.

7   Set a serving platter over the bowl. Holding both together tightly over the sink, carefully and quickly invert and remove the bowl. Serve the sauce alongside.

Note:   You can assemble the dish through step 5 up to 1 day ahead, cover, and chill. The next day, uncover the dish and steam. ▪

## CHEF SOON'S PORK BELLY WITH PRESERVED MUSTARD GREENS

Chef Yong Soon, originally from Malaysia, created this mouthwatering party-sized version of the Hakka classic. His professional training shows in the careful crafting of the dish. He blanches marinated pork belly skin with boiling water. When broiled, the skin blisters and produces an appealing texture. Long, slow baking crisps the skin and tenderizes the pork. Chef Soon then buries the pork in mustard greens and an aromatic spiced sauce, which contains fresh grated orange zest instead of dried tangerine peel for a modern fusion flavor. It's likely to be one of the best versions of this dish you'll ever taste.

This classic takes time to make, but Chef Soon's technique is easy to manage and the parts can be made ahead. Prepare the parts to fit your schedule over two or three days, then assemble and steam.

*Makes 8 to 10 servings as a main dish or 16 to 18 servings*
*as part of a multicourse meal*

## PORK

1 piece boneless pork belly with skin (2 to 2½ pounds), about 1½ inches thick

1 tablespoon salt

2 teaspoons packed brown sugar

1 teaspoon five-spice powder

7 cups water

2 tablespoons cider vinegar

1 to 2 tablespoons vegetable oil, or as needed

## PRESERVED MUSTARD GREENS

1 package (1 pound) preserved mustard greens

2 tablespoons vegetable oil

1 tablespoon minced shallots

1 tablespoon minced garlic

1 tablespoon minced fresh ginger

## SAUCE

3 cups chicken broth, homemade (page 267) or purchased

½ cup Chinese rice wine (shaoxing) or dry sherry

¼ cup hoisin sauce

2 ounces brown slab sugar (a 2½-by-1-inch piece), or 2 tablespoons packed brown sugar

1 tablespoon soy sauce

1 tablespoon oyster sauce

1 teaspoon dark soy sauce or additional all-purpose soy sauce

1 teaspoon fennel seeds

**1 FOR THE PORK:** With a sharp knife, score the skin of the pork belly, making cuts about ⅛ inch deep and ½ inch apart, vertically and diagonally across the whole surface. In a small bowl, mix the salt, sugar, and five-spice powder. Rub the mixture all over the pork and place the pork, skin side up, in a 9-by-13-inch roasting or baking pan. Do not use glass, which may crack. Chill for about 1 hour.

**2** In a 3- to 4-quart pan over high heat, bring the water and vinegar to a boil. Remove the meat from the refrigerator. Pour the boiling water and vinegar over the pork to cover completely. Let stand about 1 minute, and then pour off the water. (This blanching encourages the skin to blister and crackle when broiled and adds texture to the finished product.) Preheat the broiler. Remove the meat from the pan and pat dry. Rinse the pan and dry. Line the pan with foil and coat lightly with oil. Return the meat to the pan, skin side up.

**3** Broil the meat 6 to 7 inches from the heat until the skin is browned and crisp, 25 to 30 minutes. Reduce the heat to 250°F and bake for 1 hour. Let cool. Lift out the meat and discard excess fat. Cut the pork along the grain into ½-inch-thick slices. Then cut the slices into 2- to 3-inch lengths.

**4 FOR THE MUSTARD GREENS:** Chop the mustard greens into ½-inch pieces to make about 4 cups, and place in a large bowl. Fill the bowl with hot water and rub the greens to remove salt and sand; rinse and drain several times. Cover with more hot water and let stand, changing water occasionally, until the thick stem pieces are soft, 30 minutes to 1 hour. Drain, rinse, and drain again. Squeeze the excess water out of the greens.

**5** Set a 14-inch wok or 5- to 6-quart pan over medium-high heat. When the pan is hot, after about 1 minute, add the oil and rotate the pan to spread. Add the shallots, garlic, and ginger, and stir-fry until the shallots ▸

½ teaspoon Sichuan peppercorns or white peppercorns

3 thin slices fresh ginger, lightly crushed

1 cinnamon stick (3 inches long)

1 cardamom pod, crushed (optional)

1 whole clove

1 star anise

¾ teaspoon grated orange peel, orange part only, or to taste

Thin orange slices for garnish

are limp, about 1 minute. Add the preserved greens and stir-fry until the greens are dry and well mixed with the seasonings, about 2 minutes. Remove from the heat.

6 **FOR THE SAUCE:** In a 2- to 3-quart pan over high heat, combine the broth, wine, hoisin sauce, sugar, soy sauce, oyster sauce, dark soy sauce, fennel seeds, Sichuan peppercorns, ginger, cinnamon stick, seeds from the crushed cardamom pod, clove, and star anise. Bring to a boil, reduce the heat to medium to medium-high, and gently boil 20 to 30 minutes until the sauce has reduced by one-half, to about 2 cups. Pour the sauce through a fine strainer set over a bowl; discard the solids. Stir the orange peel into the sauce.

7 To assemble, arrange the pork, skin side down, in 1 or 2 rows in the center of an 8- to 10-cup shallow heatproof dish that will fit inside a steamer, such as a 9- to 10-inch cake pan with 2-inch sides. (Or place half of the ingredients in each of 2 shallow heatproof dishes, each holding 4 to 5 cups.) Spread the mustard greens over and around the pork. Pour the sauce evenly over the top.

8 Set the dish on a rack over 2 to 4 inches boiling water in a steamer or wok (if the bottom is round, place on a wok ring to stabilize). If the steamer lid is flat metal, or if steaming in 2 layers and the upper layer is a flat metal rack, wrap the lid or metal rack with a towel to reduce condensation dripping on the food. Cover and steam over medium-high heat until the pork is very tender when pierced, about 2 hours. With this long steaming time, check the water level often so that the pan does not boil dry, and add more boiling water as needed. With a bamboo steamer, keep the bottom rim covered with water to avoid burning. Carefully remove the dish from the steamer. Let rest 5 minutes. Set a large, rimmed serving dish over the bowl. Holding both tightly together over the sink, carefully and quickly invert and remove the bowl. If desired, garnish the platter with orange slices.

Note: If making up to 3 days ahead, prepare the pork, mustard greens, and sauce; cool, cover, and chill separately. Up to a day ahead, assemble the dish through step 7, cover, and chill. ∎

# BRAISED TOFU AND VEGETABLE CLAY POT

My vegetarian brother welcomed this satisfying mélange of pan-browned tofu, dark mushrooms, and fresh bok choy and carrots. The clay pot makes for a handsome presentation. Use a wok or frying pan if you don't have a clay pot.

*Makes 3 to 4 servings as a main dish or 6 to 8 servings as part of a multicourse meal*

6 dried shiitake mushrooms, each about 2 inches wide (see note)

2 cups hot water

1 pound firm tofu (see note)

2 small heads baby bok choy or *choy sum* (about 4 ounces total)

1 large carrot (about 5 ounces total)

2 green onions, including green tops

2 tablespoons vegetable oil

1 tablespoon minced garlic

2 tablespoons soy sauce

2 tablespoons Chinese rice wine (shaoxing) or dry sherry

1 tablespoon oyster sauce or hoisin sauce

½ teaspoon sugar

2 tablespoons cold water

1 tablespoon cornstarch

¼ teaspoon salt, or to taste

1 Rinse the mushrooms. In a medium bowl, soak the mushrooms in the hot water until soft, 20 minutes for thin caps to 2 hours for thick caps. Lift out the mushrooms and squeeze dry. Carefully pour the soaking liquid into a measuring cup and reserve 1½ cups, leaving the sediment behind. Remove and discard the stems of the mushrooms. Cut the caps into ¼-inch-wide strips.

2 Meanwhile, rinse and drain the tofu. Cut the tofu into triangles about ½ inch thick and 3 inches long across the widest side. Pat dry and drain on towels. Gently press the top surface with towels to remove excess moisture.

3 Cut each head of bok choy lengthwise into sections about ½ inch thick and 3 to 4 inches long; rinse well. Peel the carrot and cut diagonally into ¼-inch-thick slices. Cut the green onions into 2-inch lengths; slice the thick ends in half lengthwise.

4 Set a 14-inch wok or 12-inch nonstick frying pan over medium-high heat. When the pan is hot, after about 1 minute, add the oil and rotate the pan to spread. Lay the tofu in a single layer and cook, turning once, until golden-brown on both sides, 5 to 7 minutes total. Stir the garlic into the oil and cook until soft, about 30 seconds. Transfer the tofu and garlic to a 1½- to 3-quart Chinese clay pot, if using. Use a heat diffuser if cooking on an electric burner.

5 Add the reserved 1½ cups mushroom-soaking liquid, carrot, mushrooms, soy sauce, wine, oyster sauce, and sugar to the tofu. Bring to a boil over high heat. Reduce the heat, cover, and simmer for 5 minutes, stirring occasionally. Add the bok choy and green onions; cover and simmer until the carrot and mushrooms are tender when pierced, about 5 minutes. ▸

6 In a small bowl, mix the cold water, cornstarch, and salt. Add to the pan and stir gently until the sauce boils and thickens, about 30 seconds. Transfer to a serving dish or serve directly from the clay pot.

Note: For a faster version, use purchased fried tofu and skip the browning in step 4. Substitute fresh shiitake mushrooms for the dried and skip the soaking in step 1. Replace the mushroom-soaking water with 1½ cups chicken or vegetable broth. ■

## STIR-FRIED SNOW PEAS AND TOFU

I love the mix of textures in this uncomplicated vegetarian stir-fry—crisp edible-pod peas, lightly fried tofu, and crunchy black fungus. A light sauce ties the elements together.

*Makes 2 servings as a main dish or 4 to 6 servings as part of a multicourse meal*

### SAUCE

⅔ cup chicken broth, homemade (page 267) or purchased, or vegetable broth

2 tablespoons Chinese rice wine (shaoxing) or dry sherry

2 teaspoons cornstarch

½ teaspoon salt

⅛ teaspoon ground white pepper

### STIR-FRY

⅓ cup dried black fungus, such as cloud ears

8 ounces fried tofu or pressed tofu

1 tablespoon vegetable oil

1 teaspoon minced fresh ginger

6 ounces snow peas or sugar snap peas, strings removed

⅓ cup chicken broth, homemade (page 267) or purchased, or vegetable broth

1 **FOR THE SAUCE:** In a small bowl, mix the broth, wine, cornstarch, salt, and white pepper.

2 **FOR THE STIR-FRY:** Rinse the fungus and place in a medium bowl. Cover with hot water and soak until soft, 15 to 20 minutes. Rinse well and squeeze excess moisture out of the fungus. Pinch out and discard the hard knobby centers. Cut the fungus into 1-inch pieces.

3 Meanwhile, cut the tofu into thin strips, about 3 inches long.

4 Set a 14-inch wok or 12-inch frying pan over high heat. When the pan is hot, after about 1 minute, add the oil and rotate the pan to spread. Add the ginger and peas; stir-fry until the peas are bright green, about 1 minute. Add the broth, tofu, and fungus; stir-fry until the tofu is hot, about 1 minute. Stir the sauce mixture and add to the pan. Stir until the sauce boils, about 30 seconds. Transfer to a serving dish. ■

# STEAMED SHRIMP AND GARLIC

This dish, part of a Hakka lunch with Cantonese overtones, impressed me with its no-fuss simplicity and good looks. Shrimp in their shells are slit down the back and tucked with minced garlic. As the shrimp steam, the garlic mellows slightly. The dish is finished with a drizzle of soy sauce and aromatic sesame oil and a shower of green onions.

*Makes 2 to 3 servings as a main dish or 6 to 8 servings as part of a multicourse meal*

1 pound shrimp (16 to 20 per pound), in their shells

2 tablespoons Chinese rice wine (shaoxing) or dry sherry

½ teaspoon salt

⅛ teaspoon ground white pepper

2 tablespoons minced garlic

2 teaspoons soy sauce

2 teaspoons Asian sesame oil

2 tablespoons thinly sliced green onions, including green tops, for garnish

1 With scissors or a small sharp knife, cut the shrimp lengthwise along the center of the back through the shell and about halfway through the flesh of the shrimp. Lift out and discard the dark back vein, if present. Rinse the shrimp and drain well. In a 9- to 10-inch shallow heatproof dish that will fit inside a steamer, such as a Pyrex pie pan, mix the shrimp with the wine, salt, and white pepper. Arrange the shrimp, cut side up, in a single layer. Sprinkle the shrimp evenly with the garlic, pushing the garlic into the slits in the shrimp.

2 Set the dish on a rack over 2 to 4 inches boiling water in a steamer or wok (if the bottom is round, place on a wok ring to stabilize). If the steamer lid is flat metal, wrap the lid with a towel to reduce condensation dripping on the food. Cover and steam over high heat until the shrimp are barely opaque in the center of the thickest part (cut to test), 4 to 5 minutes. Watch the water level, adding more boiling water as needed. Carefully remove the dish from the steamer. Drizzle the shrimp evenly with the soy sauce and sesame oil. Sprinkle with the green onions and serve. ▪

Garlic

# STIR-FRIED CHINESE LETTUCE AND WINE RICE

In the mountains of Meizhou, we ate lunch at the Hakka-owned Yearning Tea Plantation. Hills surrounded us with rows of tea bushes undulating in rhythmic waves of green. We sipped *dancong* tea, a high-quality local oolong noted for its ability to soothe the throat. Yearning's logo features a flying wild goose that represents the Hakka fleeing from the north to the south.

One dish announced its arrival with the fragrant scent of rice wine. A reddish mound of soft rice and big cloves of garlic crowned stir-fried celtuce, often called Chinese lettuce. In this modified version, the wine rice is loosely distributed throughout the greens. The rice used in the dish was the by-product of making sweet glutinous rice wine. Hakkas often add the soft fermented rice, sometimes mixed with red yeast rice for color, to give a sweet, heady accent to savory stir-fries and desserts. You can buy fermented sweet wine rice in Asian markets, refrigerated or in a jar on the shelf.

*Makes 4 to 6 servings as part of a multicourse meal*

1 teaspoon red yeast rice (optional)

1 tablespoon boiling water

¼ cup fermented sweet wine rice, including liquid

2 tablespoons Chinese rice wine (shaoxing) or dry sherry

12 to 16 ounces celtuce tops or romaine lettuce

2 tablespoons vegetable oil

6 cloves garlic, each about ½ inch thick

½ teaspoon salt

2 tablespoons cold water

1 In a fine strainer, rinse and drain the red yeast rice. Place the red rice in a small bowl and cover with the boiling water. Let stand until the rice is soft, 5 to 15 minutes. Add the fermented sweet wine rice and wine to the soaked red yeast rice in water (if not using red yeast rice, just add 1 tablespoon water).

2 Meanwhile, trim and discard the stem ends of the celtuce and separate into leaves. If the leaves are wider than 3 inches, cut them in half lengthwise. Cut the leaves crosswise into 3- to 4-inch lengths to make 8 to 12 cups. Rinse the greens and drain well.

3 Set a 14-inch wok or 12-inch frying pan over high heat. When the pan is hot, after about 1 minute, add the oil and rotate the pan to spread. Add the garlic and salt; stir-fry just until the garlic begins to brown, about 15 seconds. Add the greens and the cold water. (If they don't all fit at one time, stir-fry about half the greens just until they begin to wilt, then add the remainder.) Stir-fry just until the greens barely wilt, 1 to 2 minutes. Add the sweet wine rice mixture and stir until hot, about 30 seconds. Transfer to a serving bowl. ∎

# RED-BRAISED PORK AND GARLIC ON STIR-FRIED CHINESE LETTUCE

For our final meal in Meizhou, the chef of the Fortune Grand Hotel prepared a Hakka meal, Cantonese-style. He describes Hakka food as a branch of Cantonese cuisine. Since both Hakkas and Cantonese live in Guangdong Province, it's easy to see where some dishes—especially homestyle fare—overlap. One of my favorite results of this culinary cross-pollination is this red-braised pork served on a bed of greens. Dried red yeast rice, ground into a powder, imbues the luscious slow-cooked pork belly with a rich mahogany hue. If you omit the red yeast rice, you still have a delicious stew, but the color will be less vibrant. Whole cloves of garlic add lumps of soft, mellow sweetness.

*Makes 6 servings as a main dish or 10 to 12 servings as part of a multicourse meal*

2 teaspoons red yeast rice (optional)

1½ to 2 pounds boneless pork belly, with skin, or boneless pork butt, trimmed of fat

2 to 3 tablespoons vegetable oil

18 cloves garlic, each about ½ inch thick

2 cups water, or as needed

¼ cup Chinese rice wine (shaoxing) or dry sherry

2 tablespoons dark soy sauce

1 tablespoon sugar

12 to 16 ounces celtuce tops or romaine lettuce

¼ teaspoon salt, or to taste

1 In a blender or with a mortar and pestle, whirl or crush the red yeast rice until finely ground. Cut the pork into 1-inch chunks.

2 Set a 14-inch wok or 5- to 6-quart pan over medium-high heat. When the pan is hot, after about 1 minute, add 1 tablespoon of the oil (2 tablespoons if using pork butt) and rotate the pan to spread. Add the garlic and stir-fry until lightly browned, 1 to 2 minutes. With a slotted spoon, lift out the garlic and set aside.

3 Return the pan to high heat. Add the pork and stir occasionally until the pork is lightly browned, 4 to 5 minutes. Add the water, wine, dark soy sauce, sugar, ground red yeast rice, and 6 cloves of the garlic. Bring to a boil over high heat. Reduce the heat, cover, and simmer, stirring occasionally, for 45 minutes. (If most of the liquid has evaporated, add an additional 1 to 1¼ cups water.) Add the remaining garlic and return to a boil over high heat. Reduce the heat, cover, and continue simmering, stirring occasionally, until the pork is very tender when pierced, 20 to 30 minutes longer.

4 Meanwhile, trim and discard the stem ends of the celtuce and separate into leaves. If the leaves are wider than 3 inches, cut them in half lengthwise. Cut the leaves crosswise into 3- to 4-inch lengths to make 8 to 12 cups. Rinse the greens and drain well. ▸

**5** When the meat is tender, set a 14-inch wok or 12-inch frying pan over high heat. When the pan is hot, after about 1 minute, add the remaining 1 tablespoon of oil and rotate the pan to spread. Add the salt, celtuce, and 2 tablespoons water. (If the greens don't all fit at one time, stir-fry about half the greens just until they begin to wilt, then add the remainder.) Stir-fry just until the greens barely wilt, 1 to 2 minutes. Drain off any excess liquid and transfer to a rimmed serving dish.

**6** With a slotted spoon, lift out the meat and garlic and place on the bed of greens. Skim off and discard the fat from the pan juices. Measure the juices. If more than ½ to ¾ cup, boil, uncovered, over high heat until reduced to that amount. If less than ½ to ¾ cup, add water to make that amount and bring to a boil. Pour over the pork. ■

## GINGER-SCENTED SQUASH, PEAS, AND LILY BULBS

In Meizhou, we ate this colorful combination of ginger-scented orange squash, green pea pods, and white lily bulbs. The lily bulbs were new to me. They looked much like small onions or large garlic cloves and tasted mildly sweet, with a slightly starchy texture and a bit of crunch. Back home, I found vacuum-packed fresh lily bulbs in an Asian supermarket. Use shallots as an alternative. Serve as a vegetable side dish in a Chinese or Western meal; it's a lovely companion to chicken or pork.

*Makes 4 to 6 servings as part of a multicourse meal*

8 ounces winter squash, such as kabocha or butternut (see note)

2 fresh lily bulbs or shallots, each about 1½ inches wide

¾ cup water, or as needed

2 tablespoons Chinese rice wine (shaoxing) or dry sherry

½ teaspoon sugar

½ teaspoon salt, or to taste

1 tablespoon vegetable oil

**1** Peel the squash, cut in half, and remove the seeds. Cut the squash into strips about ¼ inch thick, ½ inch wide, and 2 inches long to make 1½ to 2 cups. If needed, use a flat mallet or hammer to help force the knife through the squash.

**2** Trim off the base and any soft or discolored parts from the lily bulbs. Separate the bulbs into layers to make about 1 cup. (If using shallots, trim the ends and cut in quarters lengthwise. Peel and separate into layers.)

**3** In a small bowl, mix the water, wine, sugar, and salt.

1 tablespoon minced fresh ginger

4 ounces snow peas or sugar snap peas, strings removed

**4** Set a 14-inch wok or 10-inch frying pan over medium-high heat. When the pan is hot, after about 1 minute, add the oil and tilt the pan to spread. Add the ginger and squash; stir-fry to coat with oil. Add the water mixture. Cover and cook over medium-high heat until the squash is almost tender when pierced, 3 to 5 minutes. Stir in the lily bulbs and peas. If almost all the liquid has evaporated, add 2 to 3 more tablespoons water. Cover and cook just until the peas are crisp-tender, 2 to 3 minutes longer. Transfer to a serving dish.

**Note:** Although you may sometimes find small kabocha or squash pieces at farmers' markets, it's likely you may have to buy a larger squash. Cover and chill the leftover squash and reserve for another use. ■

Snow peas and squash

# BRAISED PORK AND WATER SPINACH

The chef at the Fortune Grand Hotel wilted leafy greens in a soupy stew of pork, whole garlic cloves, mushrooms, and ginger slices. He used water spinach, a hollow-stemmed green with long pointed leaves. Spinach works as an alternative. For a casual one-bowl supper, spoon the green-streaked stew over rice.

*Makes 3 to 4 servings as a main dish or 6 to 8 servings as part of a multicourse meal*

8 to 12 ounces boneless pork butt, trimmed of fat

2 tablespoons vegetable oil

1⅓ cups chicken broth, homemade (page 267) or purchased

⅓ cup Chinese rice wine (shaoxing) or dry sherry

2 tablespoons soy sauce

½ teaspoon sugar

8 thin slices fresh ginger

10 to 12 ounces water spinach or spinach

1 medium carrot (about 3 ounces), peeled and sliced ¼ inch thick

8 garlic cloves, each about ½ inch thick

1 can (15 ounces) straw mushrooms, rinsed and drained, or 8 ounces fresh button mushrooms, each about 1½ inches wide, cut lengthwise in halves

¼ teaspoon salt, or to taste

1 Cut the pork into ½-inch chunks. Set a 14-inch wok or 5- to 6-quart pan over high heat. When the pan is hot, after about 1 minute, add the oil and rotate the pan to spread. Add the pork and stir occasionally until lightly browned, 4 to 5 minutes. Add the broth, wine, soy sauce, sugar, and ginger, and bring to a boil. Reduce the heat, cover, and simmer for 30 minutes.

2 Meanwhile, remove and discard any yellow or wilted leaves from the greens. Trim off and discard the woody ends from the water spinach, usually the bottom 3 to 4 inches. Cut the tender stems with leaves into 3- to 4-inch lengths. If the stems are woody and tough, discard them and use only the leaves. (For spinach, trim off the root ends and tough stems and cut into 4-inch lengths.) Wash well and drain. You should have 8 to 10 cups of greens.

3 After the pork has simmered for 30 minutes, stir in the carrot, garlic, and mushrooms, and bring to a boil. Reduce the heat, cover, and simmer until the pork and carrot are tender when pierced, 10 to 15 minutes.

4 Increase the heat to high. Add the water spinach. Stir until the greens wilt, 1 to 2 minutes, and add the salt. Transfer to a serving bowl. ∎

# Peasant Food for City Slickers in Beijing

Our van slowly crawls its way through the bumper-to-bumper traffic of the capital. The perpetually smoggy gray sky testifies to the high density of cars. In 1987, when I first visited Beijing, the traffic was mostly a sea of bicycles; now cars and trucks replace them. Restaurants that were once dowdy and run-down now look trendy or overdone, gaudy with Las Vegas excess.

We arrive at our destination: the Hakka restaurant Han Kejia. Appropriately rustic and understated, the restaurant is located in a rambling old house where many families once lived, and faces the tranquil Back Lakes. The character and old age of the building show through in the coarse stone walls, now artistically decorated with faded black calligraphy and rough-hewn wood doors and posts. We're directed upstairs and past countless rooms to our own private space, which once housed a family. The owners are not Hakka, but they sent chefs south to Hakka country to learn. In this artful restaurant, peasant home cooking is adapted to city tastes. The restaurant hums with life and feels much like a trendy restaurant in the West.

The similarity to America ends when the food starts to arrive. It comes with the speed of McDonald's, but with a seemingly never-ending procession of delicious variety. I'm floored by the choices; the menu runs twelve pages. Within minutes, our heavy wood table is buried under an avalanche of dishes. I try to taste everything and take photos and notes, but I can't keep up. Over twenty dishes blanket the table. Even with eleven people eating, we barely make a dent in the meal. We feel guilty leaving so much food, but Leon, our guide who has ordered the meal, assures us that the food will go to the pigs and eventually those pigs will end up on the table.

The next night, we eat at Lao Hanzi, an older restaurant that Han Kejia was modeled after. The building is smaller, but the atmosphere and food are similar. With such a vast menu, there are few repeats. The characteristic Hakka simplicity comes through in the food, although some dishes taste and look a bit more refined than their country counterparts. We sip the sweet yellow rice wine that Hakkas are noted for. To me, it tastes like a mellow cream sherry with a plum finish. Our guide has learned to gauge the size of our appetites, and there isn't much left for the pigs this night.

# STIR-FRIED SPINACH AND PEANUTS

At Lao Hanzi in Beijing, we ate a platter of stir-fried spinach laced with peanuts. The nuts lend substance, texture, and a hearty flavor to the greens.

*Makes 4 servings as part of a multicourse meal*

10 to 12 ounces spinach

2 tablespoons vegetable oil

⅓ cup roasted, salted peanuts

1 tablespoon minced garlic

¼ teaspoon salt, or to taste

1 tablespoon black vinegar or balsamic vinegar

1 Trim and discard any yellow leaves or tough stems and roots from the spinach. Wash the spinach thoroughly and drain well to make 8 to 10 cups.

2 Set a 14-inch wok or 12-inch frying pan over medium-high heat. When the pan is hot, after about 1 minute, add the oil and rotate the pan to spread. Add the peanuts, garlic, and salt. Stir-fry until the peanuts are lightly browned, 30 seconds to 1 minute. Increase the heat to high and add the spinach. (If all the spinach doesn't fit in the frying pan, add about half and turn just until it slightly wilts and shrinks, and then add the remainder.) Stir-fry until the spinach is barely wilted, 1 to 2 minutes, and then stir in the vinegar. Transfer to a serving dish. ■

# GARLIC-CHILE EGGPLANT STICKS

In Beijing, these spiced eggplant sticks were served as one of many room-temperature starters. They are also delicious served hot as a side dish. With quick braising, the eggplant softens to a creamy texture that absorbs the spicy heat of the chiles and garlic.

*Makes 4 servings as part of a multicourse meal or 6 to 8 servings as an appetizer*

1 pound Asian eggplant or globe eggplant (see note)

2 tablespoons vegetable oil

2 tablespoons minced garlic

1 teaspoon minced fresh ginger

½ teaspoon dried hot chile flakes

¾ cup water, or as needed

2 tablespoons soy sauce

1 Trim and discard the stem ends of the eggplant. Cut the eggplant into 2- to 3-inch lengths, then vertically into about ¾-inch-thick wedges or sticks.

2 Set a 14-inch wok or 12-inch frying pan over high heat. When the pan is hot, after about 1 minute, add the oil and rotate the pan to spread. Add the garlic, ginger, chile flakes, and eggplant. Stir-fry until the eggplant is lightly browned, 1 to 2 minutes. Add the water, soy sauce, vinegar, sugar, and salt. Reduce the heat, cover,

1 teaspoon rice vinegar or black vinegar

½ teaspoon sugar

¼ teaspoon salt, or to taste

2 tablespoons chopped cilantro

and simmer, stirring occasionally, until the eggplant is tender, 6 to 8 minutes. (If all the water evaporates before the eggplant is done, add 2 to 3 tablespoons more water.)

3 Transfer the eggplant to a serving dish, and sprinkle with the cilantro. Serve hot or at room temperature.

**Note:** Slender Asian eggplant works best because each piece is likely to have some skin attached, so the sticks hold together better. You can also use globe-shaped eggplant; the pieces without skin attached may fall apart and the result may have more seeds, but it will still be delicious. ∎

# STIR-FRIED CHINESE LETTUCE, GARLIC, AND BLACK BEANS

The Chinese love a vegetable not often seen in the United States. They call it lettuce; in America it might be labeled celtuce, stem lettuce, *woh sun,* or Chinese lettuce. In my local Asian market, it is labeled A-choy. With leafy greens sprouting from a long, thick stem, it looks like a little tree. The tops resemble romaine lettuce, which makes a fine substitute. The thick, tender stems have the texture of broccoli stems or kohlrabi, with a lettuce-like flavor. In America, the tops and stems are generally sold separately. Fermented black beans, whole cloves of garlic, and soy sauce add a pungent kick to the stir-fried lettuce tops.

*Makes 3 to 4 servings as part of a multicourse meal*

12 ounces celtuce tops or romaine lettuce

1 tablespoon vegetable oil

8 cloves garlic, each about ½ inch thick

1 tablespoon fermented black beans, rinsed and coarsely chopped

1 teaspoon minced fresh ginger

1 tablespoon water

1 teaspoon soy sauce, or to taste

1 Trim off and discard the stem ends from the celtuce and separate into leaves. If the leaves are wider than 3 inches, cut them in half lengthwise. Cut the leaves crosswise into 3- to 4-inch lengths to make about 8 cups. Rinse the greens and drain well.

2 Set a 14-inch wok or 12-inch frying pan over high heat. When the pan is hot, after about 1 minute, add the oil and rotate the pan to spread. Add the garlic; stir-fry just until the garlic begins to brown, 15 to 30 seconds. Stir in the black beans and ginger. Add the greens and water. Stir-fry just until the greens slightly wilt, about 1 minute, and then stir in the soy sauce. Transfer to a serving bowl. ∎

# Mama's Soul Food Comes to Beijing

With his wispy goatee, shaved head, and dark-rimmed glasses, Yan Si Ming, or Simon Yan, looks and speaks more like a Chinese scholar than the owner of a casual hip café. Simon used to be an engineer. But in 2004, fueled by a desire to own a business and share his Hakka food, he opened Paddy Field Hakka Restaurant (Shui Tian Kejia Cai), a cozy art-filled café that has become a gathering place for the Hakka in China's capital. "Hakka food is quite different and not too well known here," says Simon. "The restaurant reminds Hakkas living in Beijing of their childhood. There aren't many restaurants here that do that."

"My mama taught me to cook," he continues. "Every day we ate this kind of food." Now his chef has taught him how to cook for a restaurant, and Simon admits it's a little different from home cooking. But as we savor the dishes, tastes from our childhood greet us. My brother Gene sums it up: "This food tastes like Mom's." As we leave, I ask Simon to write down the name of his village. His hometown, Huizhou, is not far from our family's village. No wonder his cooking tastes like home.

Chinese lettuce

# FRAGRANT RICE

"Hakka food has a heavier flavor than Cantonese," says Simon as he introduces his Fragrant Rice. Most Hakkas live in rural areas and like to eat meat. Preserved pork products, such as *lop chong* (Chinese sausage) and *lop ngiuk* (Chinese bacon), are typical Hakka food, popular because they keep for a long time.

This rice pot contains staples of the Hakka diet—rice, sausage, and pork. Sweet cured Chinese sausage and marinated Chinese bacon infuse fragrance into white rice as they steam together. A final dressing of soy sauce and oyster sauce and a sprinkling of fried shallots tie the elements together. Simon prefers to cook the rice in a clay pot for a pure, sweet flavor with a toasty crust on the bottom. Serve the rice directly from the rustic clay pot or spoon into small bowls.

*Makes 6 servings as part of a multicourse meal*

2 cups jasmine rice

2¾ cups water

1 Chinese sausage (about 2 ounces)

2 ounces Chinese bacon, or
   1 additional Chinese sausage

3 tablespoons vegetable oil

½ cup thinly sliced shallots
   (see notes)

2 tablespoons soy sauce

1 tablespoon oyster sauce

½ teaspoon sugar

¼ teaspoon salt

**1** Place the rice in a 1½- to 2-quart clay pot or a 2- to 2½-quart heavy metal saucepan. Cover the rice generously with water and swish with your hands until the water is very cloudy. Carefully pour off most of the water and repeat until the water is just slightly cloudy, 2 or 3 times more. Holding the rice back with your hand, drain off all the water (or pour the rice and water into a wire strainer to drain and return the rice to the pot). Level the rice and add the water. Cook over high heat, uncovered, until most of the water has evaporated and the surface of the rice is exposed, 7 to 10 minutes.

**2** Meanwhile, thinly cut the sausage crosswise into ⅛-inch-thick slices. Cut the bacon crosswise as thinly as possible to make about ⅓ cup. Sprinkle the sausage and bacon evenly over the partially cooked rice. Cover the pot and cook over very low heat until the rice is tender and the meat is hot, 15 to 20 minutes. Uncover and continue cooking until the bottom is toasted and slightly crisp, 3 to 5 minutes. Remove from the heat.

**3** Meanwhile, set an 8- to 10-inch frying pan over medium-high heat. When the pan is hot, after about 1 minute, add the oil and heat until it ripples when the pan is tilted. Add the shallots and cook, stirring often, until golden, 2 or 3 minutes. Remove from the heat. With a slotted spoon, lift out the shallots and drain on a plate lined with paper towels. ▸

**4** In a small bowl, mix the soy sauce, oyster sauce, sugar, and salt. Just before serving, drizzle the sauce evenly over the rice. Sprinkle the rice with the fried shallots. Stir lightly and scrape the pan bottom to get chunks of crisp crust. Spoon the rice into individual bowls.

**Notes:** Cooking is slower and gentler in a clay pot; avoid extreme changes in temperature to reduce the chance of breakage. Use a heat diffuser with electric burners.

In step 3, instead of frying the shallots, you can use ⅓ cup fried shallots found in Asian markets. Or if you're in a hurry, use ¼ cup thinly sliced green onions. ■

## PICKLED CARROTS AND RADISHES

These easy refrigerator pickles, spiked with ginger and chiles, are often served as a refreshing cold dish to open a meal. Keep them in the refrigerator for an instant snack or appetizer, or serve as an accompaniment to spicy foods.

*Makes 3 cups*

8 ounces carrots (about 2 large)

8 ounces Asian white radish, such as daikon (see note)

3 teaspoons sea salt or table salt

1 cup water

½ cup distilled white vinegar or rice vinegar

¼ cup sugar

6 thin slices fresh ginger, lightly crushed

2 dried small hot red chiles, broken in half, or 8 to 10 thin rings fresh red chile, such as Fresno

**1** Peel the carrots and radish. Cut the vegetables crosswise into strips 2 inches long, ¼ inch thick, and ½ inch wide. You should have about 3 cups vegetable pieces total. In a medium bowl, mix the vegetables with 2 teaspoons of the salt. Let stand until the vegetables are slightly limp, about 20 minutes. Rinse and drain.

**2** Pack the vegetables in a clean wide-mouth quart jar.

**3** In a 1- to 2-quart pan over high heat, bring the water, vinegar, sugar, remaining 1 teaspoon of salt, ginger, and chiles to a boil. Let cool about 20 minutes. Pour over vegetables and cover. Chill until the vegetables are pleasantly piquant, at least 2 days. Keep up to 2 weeks in the refrigerator.

**Note:** For the best texture, choose an Asian white radish, such as daikon, with a green top, firm flesh, and smooth skin. Farmers' markets often offer the freshest options. ■

# BRAISED PORK-STUFFED MUSHROOMS

Meaty shiitake mushroom caps hold seasoned ground pork. Braise the mushrooms in broth, and then thicken the pan juices for a light sauce to gild them.

*Makes 2 to 3 servings as a main dish or 4 to 6 servings as part of a multicourse meal*

## MUSHROOMS

2 teaspoons dried shrimp, or
¼ teaspoon salt

12 fresh shiitake mushrooms, each
about 2 inches wide

8 ounces ground pork

2 tablespoons minced green onions

1 tablespoon cornstarch

1 tablespoon Chinese rice wine
(shaoxing) or dry sherry

1 tablespoon soy sauce

1 teaspoon minced fresh ginger

## BRAISING

1 cup chicken broth, homemade
(page 267) or purchased

1 tablespoon oyster sauce

¼ teaspoon sugar

2 tablespoons vegetable oil

2 tablespoons Chinese rice wine
(shaoxing) or dry sherry

1 tablespoon water

2 teaspoons cornstarch

2 tablespoons thinly sliced green
onions, including green tops, for
garnish

**1** **FOR THE MUSHROOMS:** Rinse the shrimp. In a small bowl, soak the shrimp in warm water until soft, about 15 minutes. Squeeze out excess water from the shrimp and mince to make about 1 tablespoon. (Omit this step if using salt.)

**2** Meanwhile, remove and discard the stems from the mushrooms. Rinse the mushrooms quickly (to avoid waterlogging them) and drain well.

**3** In a medium bowl, mix the shrimp or salt, pork, green onions, cornstarch, wine, soy sauce, and ginger. Mound a rounded tablespoon of the pork mixture on the stem side of each mushroom, pressing slightly so it sticks to the mushroom.

**4** **FOR BRAISING:** In a small bowl, mix the broth, oyster sauce, and sugar.

**5** Set a 12-inch frying pan over medium-high heat. When the pan is hot, after about 1 minute, add the oil and rotate the pan to spread. Place the mushrooms in the pan, filling side down. Cook until lightly browned, 1 to 2 minutes. Add the broth mixture and bring to a simmer. Reduce the heat to low, cover, and cook for 4 minutes. Carefully turn the mushrooms over and cover. Simmer until the mushrooms are tender and the filling is no longer pink in the center of the thickest part (cut to test), 3 to 4 minutes longer.

**6** With a slotted spatula, transfer the mushrooms to a serving dish. Skim off and discard the fat from the pan juices. Measure the juices. If more than ¾ cup, boil, uncovered, over high heat until reduced to that amount. ▸

If less than ¾ cup, add water to make that amount and bring to a boil. In a small bowl, mix the wine, water, and cornstarch and stir into the pan juices. Stir the liquid over high heat until it boils, about 30 seconds. Pour the sauce over the mushrooms and sprinkle with the green onions. ∎

## SALT-BAKED SHRIMP

Chef Simon Yan tells us that many years ago, some Hakkas who lived by the sea developed the technique of baking food in a pit with salt to promote the sale of this valuable mineral. This method sold a lot of salt. It also imparts subtle flavor into the food being baked. Rather than baking in a pit, Simon cooks his shrimp on skewers in a large pan over high heat. Translating this technique to a Western oven makes this dramatic and unique way to cook shrimp quite easy. Use jumbo shrimp in the shell. The shell keeps the juices in and prevents the shrimp from getting too salty. Slit the back shell to remove the vein and provide an opening for the shrimp to pick up flavors from the marinade and a few crunchy crystals of salt.

*Makes 2 to 3 servings as a main dish or 6 to 8 servings as an appetizer or part of a multicourse meal*

1 pound shrimp (16 to 20 per pound), in their shells

2 tablespoons minced green onions, including green tops

2 tablespoons Chinese rice wine (shaoxing) or dry sherry

1 tablespoon minced garlic

1 tablespoon minced fresh ginger

1 tablespoon minced red or green jalapeño chiles

6 pounds rock salt, or as needed

1 With scissors or a small sharp knife, cut through the shells of the shrimp along the center of the back and make a slit about ¼ inch deep into the flesh. Lift out and discard the dark back vein, if present. Rinse the shrimp and drain well. In a medium bowl, mix the shrimp, green onions, wine, garlic, ginger, and chiles. Cover and chill at least 30 minutes or up to 1 hour.

2 About 1 hour before serving, preheat the oven to 400°F. Choose a deep ovenproof container about 10 to 12 inches wide and 4 to 6 inches deep (at least as tall as the length of the shrimp), such as a 5- to 8-quart kettle, metal bowl, or 3- to 4½-quart clay pot. Place a layer of rock salt, about ½ inch deep, in the bottom of the container. Place the remaining rock salt in a 9-by-13-inch baking pan. As the oven heats, set the shallow pan of salt on the top rack and the deep pan of salt on the bottom rack. Bake until the salt is very hot in the center (insert a knife

tip and leave for a few seconds, then withdraw and briefly touch the blade to see if hot), 30 to 45 minutes.

3 Meanwhile, run a thin wooden skewer (6 to 8 inches long) from the tail to the head of each shrimp, pushing the shrimp to the tip of the skewer. Rub some of the marinade seasonings into the slits of the shrimp. Place 1 shrimp on each skewer.

4 When the salt is hot, remove the deep pan from the oven. Stick the shrimp, head first, vertically, and slightly apart, into the salt layer. Pour the remaining pan of hot salt over the shrimp and spread to bury completely. Remove the top rack from the oven, if needed, to fit. Place the pan with the shrimp on the bottom rack. Bake until the shrimp are barely opaque in the thickest part (cut to test), 8 to 10 minutes. If not done, rebury the shrimp and return to the oven for a few minutes longer. Serve immediately from the pan, or transfer the shrimp to a serving platter. If not ready to eat, pull the shrimp from the hot salt and invert, placing the stick end into the salt. Peel the shrimp to eat. ■

Salt-baked shrimp

# HAKKA CLASSIC
## Salt-Baked Chicken

鹽 焗 雞 Hakka: *yam kuk gai;* Mandarin: *yan ju ji*

The Chinese nomads had no ovens. To roast a chicken, the resourceful cooks buried the bird in a pit of hot salt and rocks. The salt absorbed the heat and transferred it to the chicken. The result was an aromatic, lightly browned bird with juicy flesh.

This signature dish, salt-baked chicken, frequently appears on Cantonese and Hakka restaurant menus. We ate it many times in China, where restaurants have a large kitchen staff to cook the chicken traditionally, which demands time and some attention. Outside of China, it is rarely prepared in the traditional way. Most restaurants and home cooks take shortcuts and poach the bird in brine or steam a salt-rubbed chicken. These techniques result in a bird with juicy, smooth flesh and white skin that somewhat resembles the Steeped Whole Chicken (page 23) that cooks in residual heat.

This recipe follows the traditional technique of baking in salt but uses a Western oven to simplify the process. Turn to page 226 for a version that uses a faster poaching technique.

## SALT-BAKED CHICKEN

Chef Simon Yan in Beijing buried a marinated, paper-wrapped chicken in a big, wide pan of hot salt. He cooked it over high heat, turning the bird occasionally. In Western kitchens, using an oven results in less work and greater control. The chicken emerges juicy and moist. Once you find the right pan for baking, this is an easy preparation. Allow a couple of hours to heat the salt and bake the chicken. After cooking, the dry salt can be recycled for another use. Because the chicken in this dish is undisguised, the flavor and quality of the meat show through. If you are going to make the effort to prepare this dish, choose a quality bird—preferably organic or free-range.

Chef Yan served his chicken with a pungent sauce made with ground dried galangal, a peppery rhizome related to ginger. In China, it is called sand ginger or *sha jiang.* Look for dried galangal in Asian markets. If unavailable, make the zesty fresh ginger sauce that follows. Or make both sauces. The leftover chicken and sauces can be served with warm noodles or salad greens.

*Makes 5 to 6 servings as a main dish or 10 to 12 servings as part of a multicourse meal*

## CHICKEN

1 chicken (about 4 pounds), preferably free-range or organic

2 tablespoons dark soy sauce

1 tablespoon Chinese rice wine (shaoxing) or dry sherry

2 teaspoons kosher salt

1 teaspoon ground ginger

¼ teaspoon ground white pepper

About 10 pounds rock salt, for baking

## GARLIC-GALANGAL SAUCE

1½ tablespoons minced garlic

½ teaspoon kosher salt

3½ tablespoons vegetable oil

1 tablespoon ground galangal

1 teaspoon onion powder

**1 FOR THE CHICKEN:** If the head, neck, and feet of the chicken are attached, remove for another use or leave attached. If the neck and giblets are in the body cavity, remove for another use. Remove and discard the large pads of fat near the entrance of the body cavity. Rinse the bird inside and out; pat dry with towels. In a large bowl, mix the dark soy sauce, wine, kosher salt, ginger, and pepper. Set the chicken in the bowl and turn to coat completely, spooning the excess marinade into the cavity. Chill, uncovered, in the refrigerator, 2 to 4 hours, turning chicken over halfway through.

**2** About 2½ hours before serving, preheat the oven to 425°F. Remove the chicken from the refrigerator. Choose a deep ovenproof container, 11 to 14 inches wide and 4½ to 8 inches deep, such as a metal mixing bowl or pan, Dutch oven, or 12- to 14-inch wok. If the container has handles, make sure they are ovenproof. The container should be at least 2 inches deeper than the height of the chicken and 1 to 2 inches wider than the bird. If the container is on the shallow side, or to help contain salt, line the container with heavy-duty foil to extend over the sides by 4 to 6 inches. Pour rock salt into the deep container to a depth of ¾ to 1 inch. Place the remaining salt in a shallow 12-by-17-inch roasting or baking pan. Place the deep pan on the bottom rack of the oven and the shallow pan on the top rack or in another oven. Bake, stirring the salt in the roasting pan after about 20 minutes, until the salt is very hot in the center (insert a knife blade and leave for a few seconds, then withdraw and briefly touch the blade to test), 30 to 40 minutes total.

**3** Meanwhile, drain the chicken and pat dry. Set the chicken, breast side up, in the center of a 15-by-30-inch piece of cooking parchment. If the head and feet are attached, fold the head under the body and tuck the feet into the body cavity. Bring the ends of the parchment together and fold the edges over several times to enclose the chicken. Fold the remaining parchment ends over together several times to seal the chicken completely in a packet. Starting on the breast side, wrap a cotton string around the width and length of the chicken, and tie a knot on top of the chicken like a package. Let the chicken stand at room temperature while the salt heats. ▸

**4** When the salt is hot, lay the wrapped chicken, breast side up, on top of the hot salt in the deep container. Spoon the hot salt from the other pan over the chicken, shaking the pan slightly so that the salt settles around the chicken, and cover the chicken completely with a ½- to 1-inch-thick layer of salt. Cup the foil, if used, around the salt to help contain it. Set the chicken on the bottom rack of the hot oven, removing the top rack if necessary. Roast the chicken for 1 hour and 15 minutes.

**5** Remove the pan from the oven and push away or scoop off enough salt to reveal the top of the chicken. Insert an instant-read thermometer (see note) through the parchment and into the center of the thickest part of the breast until it reaches the bone; it should read about 170°F. If the temperature is lower, leave the thermometer in the chicken and push the salt back over the breast. Let the chicken rest in the salt, out of the oven, 5 to 10 minutes longer. When the internal temperature reads about 170°F, push aside the salt on top. With the strings and a potholder, lift out the chicken and place on a rimmed plate. Unwrap the chicken carefully, trying to keep the rock salt from tumbling into the juices, and let rest on the parchment about 15 minutes.

**6** **FOR THE GARLIC-GALANGAL SAUCE:** In a small heatproof bowl, mix the garlic and salt. In a 1-quart or smaller pan, over high heat, warm the oil until it ripples when the pan is tilted, about 30 seconds. Pour the hot oil over the garlic mixture. Stir to blend. Stir in the ground galangal and onion powder.

**7** Transfer the chicken from the parchment to a cutting board. Pour any juices from the chicken cavity and any accumulated juices in the parchment packet into a small bowl. Skim off and discard the fat. Cut the chicken into pieces for serving (page 243). Arrange the pieces attractively on a platter. Serve the chicken with the garlic-galangal sauce and the reserved juices.

**Note:** If you don't have an instant-read thermometer, remove the chicken from the oven and salt after 1 hour and 15 minutes. It is likely done or very close to it if you used a 4-pound chicken.

**Fresh Ginger-Onion Sauce**

In a 1½- to 2-cup heatproof bowl, mix ⅓ cup minced fresh ginger, 3 tablespoons minced green onions, including green tops, and 1 tablespoon minced garlic. In a 6- to 8-inch frying pan over high heat, warm ⅓ cup vegetable oil until it ripples when the pan is tilted, 1 to 2 minutes. Pour the hot oil over the ginger mixture (it will bubble vigorously) and mix well. Add ½ teaspoon kosher salt, or to taste. ∎

# Luodai: Hakka Village Food in the Land of Chiles

A broad stone-paved pedestrian boulevard leads to a five-tier pagoda. Shop-keepers beckon with bubbling soup tonics, leaf-wrapped sticky rice on sticks, and tiny cups of sweet yellow rice wine. People gather in courtyards under leafy trees to drink tea and shuffle mahjong tiles in a noisy click-and-clack. Some sit back to have their ears cleaned by a slender man equipped with long-handled scoops and brushes to dig wax and debris from the ear canal. Customers line up to buy bowls of hand-cut rice noodles with a choice of spicy toppings. Shiny black rickshaws with red seats attended by gray-uniformed drivers stand ready to serve riders. People leisurely stroll by.

We're in Luodai, a suburb of Chengdu, the capital of Sichuan Province. Luodai is the largest Hakka town in Sichuan, and about 90 percent of the twenty-three thousand residents are Hakka. Did it look like this when the Manchus forced the Hakka from Guangdong here during the Qing dynasty, I wonder? I feel almost like we are in a Chinese version of Disneyland's Main Street. Everything is pleasant and enjoyable, but seems sanitized and a bit too picture perfect.

Our guide, Monica, tells us that last year the township was renovated into a picturesque Qing dynasty–style village with tiled roofs, upward-curving eaves, and cobbled walkways to attract tourists, Chinese as well as foreign. The Twentieth World Hakka Convention is in town, so there is pressure to put on a good face. Sichuan Province is home to three million Hakkas.

When we stray off the main street, we discover the old Luodai, with its ramshackle rutted dirt pathways. Along the lanes, small stores sell dry goods, cakes, and pans. A grandmother carries her grandson on her back. A young woman delivers disks of coal for cooking from her scooter-powered minitruck. A covered open-air market sells fresh mushrooms, greens, and crushed dried red chiles. This must be where the residents shop.

Being a tourist town isn't a bad thing. It attracts people and money and exposes a wider audience to Hakka culture. Unlike most Hakka villages, Luodai lies a short bus ride away from a major tourist city. The town houses several large guild complexes representing different provinces in China. They function as social halls, with teahouses, restaurants, and meeting rooms. We visit the Jiangxi and Guangdong provincial guilds, which were both built using donations given by Hakkas from those provinces.

At the Jiangxi Guild, we sit down to a lunch prepared by a young chef who learned to cook Hakka food from his teacher in a commune. The chef marries local ingredients with Sichuan flavors for his own personal take on Hakka food. Chiles are used liberally in the meal, and some dishes taste Sichuan, rather than

Hakka. Other dishes feature the plainer, more natural flavors typical of Hakka food.

A few hours later, we dine at the Guangdong Guild, built in 1747 by the Hakka. Our host's ancestors came from Meizhou. His grandparents moved here. He donates his money to this guild to preserve the Hakka tradition. "The Hakka people always work hard, no matter where they go," he says. "They always make a fortune. There's a strong spirit in their mind. I spend my money here because of that spirit." He hopes to pass the Hakka culture down to the next generation. "Young people are interested in preserving the culture."

In the almost three-hundred-year-old dining room, lined with Chinese brush paintings, dishes come out in rapid procession. Some are similar to ones that we ate at lunch. Some show characteristic Sichuan spice. A steamed fish buried in fresh green peppercorns and sliced green chiles singes my tongue with its fiery bite. Sliced fresh green chiles and crushed dried red chiles top braised black fungus. Pickled long red chiles refresh the palate. Our host explains that although the traditional Hakka flavor profile is not spicy, after the Hakka came to Sichuan they integrated the dry pepper into their cooking to match the climate. There are some plainer foods on the table, too, such as boiled corn on the cob (which is simply called American corn), steamed chunks of pumpkin, and steeped white chicken, which comes with a saucer of vivid red chile sauce. Other dishes taste very Hakka, often with the addition of Sichuan peppercorns or chiles in various forms.

Before we departed for China, Uncle Henry told me that our family may have passed through Sichuan Province. As we end our day in this Hakka wonderland, I wonder if my attraction to spice comes from ancestors in this chile-obsessed region.

## DEEP-FRIED MUSHROOMS WITH SICHUAN PEPPER SALT

The chef at Jiangxi Guild House fried local mushrooms in a light coating of egg and flour to make fritters. He offered a roasted salt with numbing Sichuan peppercorns and a touch of aromatic five-spice powder as a dip. Choose a selection of mushrooms for an interesting variety, from crisp, craggy enoki fritters to meaty, succulent king oyster slices. The fried mushrooms can be held in a warm oven for about 30 minutes.

*Makes about 3 dozen pieces, enough for 6 to 8 servings as part of a multicourse meal or 8 to 10 servings as an appetizer*

## SICHUAN PEPPER SALT

2 tablespoons kosher salt

1 tablespoon Sichuan peppercorns
(see notes)

¼ teaspoon five-spice powder,
or to taste

## MUSHROOMS

8 ounces fresh mushrooms, such as
oyster, king oyster, shiitake, button,
beech, or enoki (choose one or
several kinds; see notes)

2 large eggs

⅛ teaspoon salt

¾ cup all-purpose flour, or as needed

**1 FOR THE SICHUAN PEPPER SALT:** Set a 6- to 10-inch frying pan over medium-high heat. When the pan is hot, after about 1 minute, add the salt and peppercorns. Stir often, until the mixture is fragrant and the salt begins to brown, about 2 minutes. Add the five-spice powder. Finely grind the mixture in a mortar and pestle, or whirl in a blender. Transfer to a small bowl.

**2 FOR THE MUSHROOMS:** Trim off the ends and any soft or discolored portions from the mushrooms. If the mushrooms are fairly clean, gently brush off any debris. Otherwise, lightly rinse the mushrooms, drain well, and pat dry. Remove and discard the stems of the shiitake mushrooms. If the oyster and shiitake mushrooms are wider than 3 inches, cut in half through the caps. Slice the king oyster and button mushrooms lengthwise about ½ inch thick. If desired, cut the long king oyster mushrooms in half crosswise. Separate clumps of beech and enoki mushrooms into clusters about ½ inch wide and leave whole.

**3** In a medium bowl, lightly beat the eggs and salt. Spread the flour on a plate. With chopsticks or fingers, lightly coat a few mushroom pieces or clusters with the egg, and let the excess egg drain off. Then coat with flour and shake off the excess. Place the pieces slightly apart on a baking sheet. Repeat to coat all.

**4** Set a 14-inch wok (if the bottom is round, place on a wok ring to stabilize) or 5- to 6-quart pan over medium-high heat. Fill the pan with oil to a depth of about 1½ inches. Heat the oil until it reaches 375°F on a thermometer. Adjust the heat to maintain the temperature.

**5** Gently drop 6 to 8 mushroom pieces into the hot oil, pushing them slightly apart with chopsticks. Fry until they are crisp and golden, turning as needed to brown evenly, about 1 minute total. With a slotted spoon or wire strainer, lift out and drain the fried mushrooms on baking sheets lined with paper towels. Repeat to fry the remainder. Serve at once or keep warm in a 200°F oven up to about 30 minutes. Serve hot with the Sichuan pepper salt to dip into.

**Notes:** If Sichuan peppercorns are not available, use 1 tablespoon white peppercorns and ½ teaspoon dried hot chile flakes.

If the varieties of mushrooms specified are not available, choose local mushrooms or more common varieties. ■

# BRAISED MOUNTAIN MUSHROOMS

Hakka chefs in Luodai often braise the mushrooms that grow in the nearby mountains in a rich meat broth to emphasize their natural goodness. For a vegetarian version, use mushroom or vegetable broth.

*Makes 4 to 6 servings as part of a multicourse meal*

12 ounces fresh mushrooms, such as oyster, king oyster, shiitake, button, beech, or enoki (choose 2 to 5 kinds; limit enoki to 2 to 3 ounces; see note)

1 small leek (about 6 ounces untrimmed)

2 tablespoons vegetable oil

2 tablespoons thinly sliced garlic

8 thin slices fresh ginger, lightly crushed

1 cup chicken broth, homemade (page 267) or purchased, or vegetable broth

2 tablespoons Chinese rice wine (shaoxing) or dry sherry

1 tablespoon soy sauce

¼ teaspoon salt, or to taste

⅛ teaspoon ground white pepper

2 tablespoons water

1 tablespoon cornstarch

1   Trim off and discard the ends and any soft or discolored portions from the mushrooms. If the mushrooms are fairly clean, gently brush off any debris. Otherwise, lightly rinse the mushrooms, drain well, and pat dry. Remove and discard the stems of the shiitake mushrooms. If the oyster and shiitake mushrooms are wider than 3 inches, cut in half through the caps. Slice the king oyster and button mushrooms lengthwise about ½ inch thick. If desired, cut the long king oyster mushrooms in half crosswise. Separate clumps of beech and enoki mushrooms into clusters about ½ inch wide and leave whole.

2   Trim off and discard the root end and tough dark-green top from the leek. Cut the leek in half lengthwise and rinse well under running water, separating the layers to remove the grit. Thinly slice the leek crosswise.

3   Place a 14-inch wok or 12-inch frying pan over medium-high heat. When the pan is hot, after about 1 minute, add the oil and rotate the pan to spread. Add the garlic, ginger, and leek; stir-fry until the leek is limp, about 30 seconds. Add the mushrooms (except for the enoki), and stir-fry until they are lightly browned, 2 to 3 minutes. Add the broth, wine, soy sauce, salt, and white pepper. Bring to a boil, reduce the heat, and simmer, stirring often, until the mushrooms are limp, 2 to 3 minutes.

4   Meanwhile, in a small bowl, mix the water and cornstarch. Add the cornstarch mixture to the pan and stir until the sauce boils, about 30 seconds. Stir in the enoki mushrooms (if using). Transfer to a serving bowl.

Note:   If the varieties of mushrooms specified are not available, choose local mushrooms or more common varieties. ∎

# STIR-FRIED WATER SPINACH AND CHARRED RED CHILES

In Sichuan Province, chiles sneak their way into many dishes. At the Jiangxi Guild, the chef threw a handful of dried red chiles that resembled jalapeños into a simple dish of stir-fried greens. The chiles look deadly, but their effect is surprisingly mild; if the chile remains whole, much of the heat is contained inside. In this recipe, I've used widely available small hot dried chiles, and their effect is minor as long as you don't break open the pods or eat them. Charring the chiles in hot oil seasons the oil with a very subtle spicy smokiness. Want more heat? Just break a few chiles in half to unleash their fire.

*Makes 2 to 4 servings as part of a multicourse meal*

10 to 12 ounces water spinach or spinach

2 tablespoons vegetable oil

1 tablespoon minced garlic

½ teaspoon salt

6 to 8 dried small hot red chiles

1   Remove and discard any yellow or wilted leaves from the greens. Trim off and discard the woody stem ends from the water spinach, usually the bottom 3 to 4 inches. Cut the tender stems with leaves into 3- to 4-inch lengths. If the stems are woody and tough, discard them and use only the leaves. (For spinach, trim off and discard the root ends and tough stem ends and cut the tender portion into 4-inch lengths.) Wash well and drain. You should have 8 to 10 cups.

2   Set a 14-inch wok or 12-inch frying pan over high heat. When the pan is hot, after about 1 minute, add the oil and rotate the pan to spread. Add the garlic, salt, and chiles (break 2 or 3 chiles in half, if you want it spicy). Stir-fry just until the chiles are lightly browned, about 10 seconds. Add the water spinach and a tablespoon of water (if the spinach is very dry); stir-fry just until the greens wilt, about 1 minute. Transfer to a serving dish. ∎

Mushrooms

# PICKLED RED CHILES

We welcomed these pickled red chiles in a twenty-plus-dish banquet in Luodai. The chiles' vivid red color and tart-sweet heat cleansed our palate in the midst of excess. In the fall, you can often find fresh red chiles at the farmers' market, and Asian markets carry them year round. Long, slim cayenne chiles are hot, but pickling tames much of their heat. If you can't find them, use another mild to hot red chile.

*Makes 7 to 8 servings*

7 or 8 fresh red chiles, such as cayenne, jalapeño, or Fresno (4 to 6 ounces total)

1 cup rice vinegar

⅓ cup water

2 tablespoons packed brown sugar

1 tablespoon sea salt or table salt, or 1½ tablespoons kosher salt

Half of a star anise (4 sections)

¼ teaspoon Sichuan peppercorns (optional)

2 tablespoons Chinese rice spirits or vodka

1  Wash the chiles and trim their stems to about ¼ inch. Cut a 1-inch slit down 2 sides of each chile. Pack the chiles into a sterilized heatproof wide-mouth pint jar.

2  In a 1- to 2-quart pan over high heat, bring the vinegar, water, sugar, salt, star anise, and peppercorns to a boil. Add the rice spirits. Pour the hot mixture over the chiles to within ¼ inch of the top of the jar. Screw on the lid. Let stand at room temperature for 2 to 3 days, then refrigerate for at least 2 days or up to 3 months. ■

Chiles

# Hong Kong: Low to High Cuisine, Rustic and Nouvelle

My maternal grandparents married in Hong Kong more than nine decades ago. The certificate of marriage reads: "On the 18th August, 1919, Koo Chong, Age 50, Bachelor and Accountant married Au Na Sheung, Age 30, Spinster and Teacher in To Tsai Church at Victoria in Hong Kong."

Now I'm in the city where their life together began. I'm here to learn about their food. Sidney Cheung, a professor of anthropology at the Chinese University of Hong Kong, tells me, "Low cuisine depends on basic ingredients; it's country-style cooking. High cuisine builds up from daily life. It's everyday food made into cuisine." Two to three hundred years ago, the Hakka came to villages in Hong Kong. Now most Hakkas live in the northern part of the New Territories, where there's farming and river and ocean fishing.

In his essay "Food and Cuisine in a Changing Society," Cheung states that Hakka food developed along the East River in Guangdong Province in mainland China. During the Liberation in 1949, many Hakkas fled for Hong Kong. They lived in the Shek Kip Mei squatter settlements and worked in light industry and cottage factories. Hakkas from Xingning in Guangdong Province ran many of the area's restaurants. They fed tired workers with satisfying, country-style Hakka dishes that used salt, preserved vegetables, and the residue from red rice wine to season meat. The food was filling and provided energy.

When fire roared through the settlements in 1953, the displaced residents of Shek Kip Mei moved to public housing projects. As they moved throughout the region, so did their Hakka food. It grew popular with Hong Kong residents. It was eaten with rice, like their Cantonese diet. Yet it was different than the typical fish and vegetables that most Cantonese ate at home. Common Hakka food began to change to high cuisine as it began to incorporate more exotic seasonings, such as wine, preserved vegetables, and sand ginger (ground dried galangal, a rhizome related to ginger). Large quantities of meat satisfied the cravings of hungry factory workers. Many dishes still popular in Hong Kong today—beef balls, pork with preserved vegetables, bean curd with fish, and fried large intestine—originated with the Hakka during this time.

In the 1970s, hearty peasant-based Hakka food lost favor as the economy and lifestyles soared upward. Expensive, exotic, and delicate foods were in vogue as nouvelle Cantonese cuisine became the new darling. But since the late 1990s, Hakka food has won new fans. After the economic downturn following the British handover to the Chinese in 1997, upscale dining lost its appeal. People began to appreciate the simple and inexpensive food that Hakka cuisine embodies. Many Hong Kong residents travel to the mainland to find traditional foods and local culture. Hong Kong is similar to the Hakka homeland.

Tonight, we're dining at the stylish Hakka 3 Generations, a contemporary restaurant with a spare, rustic ambience. The menu boasts both traditional and modern dishes. "Modern Hakka means new combinations," Sidney says. The salt-baked chicken tastes traditional, but steamed pork belly with preserved mustard greens takes on a new form here: the dark, savory pork and vegetables are chopped and used as a filling for steamed buns. The ingredients and flavors are Hakka, but they're combined in a new way.

The next night, we dine at Cho Choy Go (roughly translated to "Rustic Dishes"), a small, noisy café. The buzz of satisfied diners and a busy kitchen forecasts that we'll eat well. Although the Cantonese embrace the tasty meat dishes of the Hakka, we dine mostly on minimalist seafood and vegetable dishes here. Dishes tend to focus on one main ingredient with just a few key seasonings to spice it up. The combination offers a fresh interpretation.

A mere few hours from our ancestral village, the cuisine begins to expand with more seafood, new combinations, and more spices. As we eat our last meal in Hong Kong, I wonder what Popo would think of the low and high cuisine of the Hakka.

# BITTER MELON STUFFED WITH STICKY RICE

At the Hakka 3 Generations restaurant in Hong Kong, we sampled a modern version of stuffed bitter melon. Usually pork fills the green rings, but these are plump with sticky rice laced with bits of cured pork and preserved vegetables. A savory sauce flows over the filled rings.

*Makes 4 to 6 servings as part of a multicourse meal*

## MELON RINGS

⅔ cup long-grain glutinous rice

1 tablespoon Tianjin (Tientsin) preserved vegetable

2 tablespoons minced Chinese sausage or Chinese bacon

⅔ cup water

1 **FOR THE MELON RINGS:** Place the rice in a wire strainer and rinse well, stirring the rice occasionally. Spread an even layer of rice in a 9- to 10-inch shallow heatproof dish that will fit inside a steamer, such as a Pyrex pie pan. Rinse the preserved vegetable, squeeze dry, and finely chop. Sprinkle the preserved vegetable and sausage over the rice. In a small bowl, mix the water and soy sauce and pour over the rice.

1 teaspoon soy sauce

2 bitter melons, each about 2 inches wide (about 1 pound total)

## SAUCE

¾ cup chicken broth, homemade (page 267) or purchased

2 tablespoons oyster sauce

2 tablespoons Chinese rice wine (shaoxing) or dry sherry

2 teaspoons cornstarch

¼ teaspoon sugar

1 tablespoon vegetable oil

¼ cup thinly sliced green onions, including green tops

1 tablespoon minced fresh ginger

1 teaspoon minced garlic

2 Set the dish on a rack over 2 to 4 inches boiling water in a steamer or wok (if the bottom is round, place on a wok ring to stabilize). If the steamer lid is flat metal, wrap the lid with a towel to reduce condensation dripping on the food. Cover and steam over high heat until the rice is soft when pressed, 25 to 35 minutes. Watch the water level, adding more boiling water as needed. Carefully remove the dish from the steamer. Transfer the rice to a medium bowl and mix gently to blend. Wash the steaming dish, dry, and lightly oil the bottom.

3 Trim off the ends from the bitter melon. Cut the bitter melon crosswise into 1-inch rounds. With a small knife, cut around the inside edges of the bitter melons from both ends, push out the spongy centers with seeds, and discard. Scrape out the white pith from the inside edges. Fill each of the bitter melon rings with the rice mixture, mounding the filling on top. Arrange the filled bitter melon rings slightly apart on the oiled dish.

4 Return the dish to the steamer. Cover and steam over high heat until the bitter melon is tender when pierced, about 15 minutes. Watch the water level, adding more boiling water as needed. Carefully remove the dish from the steamer. If desired, transfer the bitter melon rings to a serving dish.

5 FOR THE SAUCE: In a small bowl, mix the broth, oyster sauce, wine, cornstarch, and sugar. When the bitter melon is done cooking, set a 10-inch frying pan over high heat. When the pan is hot, after about 1 minute, add the oil and rotate the pan to spread. Add the green onions, ginger, and garlic; stir-fry just until the green onions are limp, about 30 seconds. Stir the broth mixture and add to the pan. Stir until the sauce boils, about 30 seconds. Pour the sauce over the bitter melon rings and serve. ∎

# BRAISED FRIED TOFU WITH PORK

At Hong Kong's Hakka 3 Generations restaurant, we ate braised deep-fried tofu topped with pork. Restaurants often fry tofu to deepen the flavor and enrich the color. When braised, the fried tofu soaks up the juices like a sponge and swells with flavorful succulence. The braising liquid turns into a warm brown sauce.

*Makes 3 to 4 servings as a main dish or 5 to 6 servings as part of a multicourse meal*

## FRIED TOFU

8 ounces ground pork

1 tablespoon soy sauce

1 tablespoon minced fresh ginger

2 teaspoons Chinese rice wine (shaoxing) or dry sherry

2 teaspoons cornstarch

¼ teaspoon salt

1 pound firm tofu

Vegetable oil, for frying

## BRAISING

1 tablespoon vegetable oil

1 tablespoon minced garlic

1 tablespoon minced fresh ginger

1 cup chicken broth, homemade (page 267) or purchased

2 tablespoons oyster sauce

2 tablespoons Chinese rice wine (shaoxing) or dry sherry

2 tablespoons water

2 teaspoons cornstarch

2 tablespoons thinly sliced green onions, including green tops, for garnish

**1  FOR THE FRIED TOFU:** In a medium bowl, combine the pork, soy sauce, ginger, wine, cornstarch, and salt. Mix pork well.

**2** Rinse the tofu, and then drain for about 5 minutes. Cut the tofu into 12 pieces, each about ½ to ¾ inch thick and 2 inches square (or a similar-sized rectangle). Lay the pieces in a single layer on a double thickness of towels. Set another double layer of towels on top and press gently to remove moisture. With a small spoon, scoop out the tofu in the center of each piece to make a depression about ¼ inch deep, leaving a ¼-inch border around the sides. Reserve the tofu scraps for another use. Mound about 1 tablespoon of the pork filling in each depression, pressing gently so it sticks to the tofu.

**3** Set a 14-inch wok (if the bottom is round, set on a wok ring to stabilize) or 5- to 6-quart pan over medium-high heat and add oil to a depth of about 2 inches. Heat the oil until it reaches 350°F on a thermometer. Adjust the heat to maintain the temperature. Fry 4 pieces of tofu at a time, placing the pieces filling side down. Fry until golden, turning once, 1½ to 2 minutes total. With a slotted spoon, lift out and drain on a plate lined with paper towels. Repeat to fry the remaining pieces.

**4  FOR BRAISING:** Set a 10-inch frying pan over high heat. When the pan is hot, after about 1 minute, add the oil and rotate the pan to spread. Add the garlic and ginger and stir-fry until golden, about 15 seconds. Add the broth, oyster sauce, and wine; stir until smoothly blended. Add the fried tofu, filling side down. Reduce the heat, cover, and simmer for 2 minutes. Turn the tofu over, cover, and continue simmering until the filling is hot in the center of the thickest part (cut to test), about 2 minutes.

5 With a slotted spoon or spatula, transfer the tofu to a serving platter. In a small bowl, mix the water and cornstarch. Add to the pan juices and stir until the sauce boils. Pour the sauce over the tofu and sprinkle the green onions on top.

Note: If making up to 1 day ahead, prepare the tofu through step 3, cool, cover, and chill. The next day, continue at step 4. ■

## PAN-FRIED FISH, GREEN ONIONS, AND CHILES

At Cho Choy Go in Hong Kong, fish are coated with five-spice powder, deep-fried, and then briefly stir-fried with a few bold seasonings—thin coins of pungent ginger and spicy fresh chile slices. I've simplified the process for home cooks and pan-fry the fish in a little oil, skipping the messy deep-frying. Popo cooked a plainer version of this dish. Perhaps she learned the recipe while living in Hong Kong.

*Makes 2 to 3 servings as a main dish or 4 to 6 servings as part of a multicourse meal*

### FISH

1 pound skinless fillet from a firm, white-fleshed fish, such as halibut

½ teaspoon salt

⅛ teaspoon five-spice powder

⅛ teaspoon ground white pepper

2 tablespoons cornstarch, or as needed

2 tablespoons vegetable oil

### STIR-FRY

1 tablespoon vegetable oil

3 green onions, cut into 3-inch lengths, including green tops

1 **FOR THE FISH:** Rinse the fish and pat dry. Cut the fish into sticks ½ inch thick and 2 to 3 inches long. On a large plate, mix the salt, five-spice powder, and white pepper. Coat the fish with the salt mixture. Shortly before frying, sprinkle the cornstarch over the fish to lightly coat; shake off the excess.

2 Set a 12-inch nonstick frying pan over medium-high heat. When the pan is hot, after about 1 minute, add the oil and rotate the pan to spread. Place the fish in a single layer in the pan and cook, turning once, until the fish is browned on the outside and barely opaque in the center of the thickest part (cut to test), 4 to 5 minutes total. With a slotted spatula, transfer the fish to a serving dish. ▸

12 thin slices fresh ginger

5 to 8 thin rings fresh chile (preferably red), such as Fresno or jalapeño, or to taste

⅛ teaspoon salt, or to taste

⅛ teaspoon five-spice powder

**3 FOR THE STIR-FRY:** Return the pan to medium-high heat. When the pan is hot, add the oil and rotate to spread. Add the green onions, ginger, chile, salt, and five-spice powder. Stir-fry until the green onions begin to wilt, about 30 seconds. Return the fish to the pan and stir-fry gently until the seasonings coat the fish, about 30 seconds. Transfer to a serving dish. ∎

## SHRIMP WITH FRIED GARLIC AND CHILES

Sprinkle toasty fried garlic spiked with chiles over stir-fried shrimp in their shells. At the Rustic Dishes Café in Hong Kong, the shrimp were deep-fried, but I find stir-frying a neater and equally delicious alternative for home cooks.

*Makes 3 to 4 servings as a main dish to 6 to 8 servings as part of a multicourse meal*

1 pound shrimp (31 to 35 per pound), in their shells (see note)

1 tablespoon Chinese rice wine (shaoxing) or dry sherry

½ teaspoon salt

2 cups thinly sliced iceberg or romaine lettuce

¼ cup minced garlic

3 tablespoons vegetable oil

1 to 2 tablespoons minced fresh chile (preferably red), such as Fresno or jalapeño

**1** With scissors or a small sharp knife, cut through the shell of the shrimp along the center of the back and make a slit about ½ inch deep into the flesh. Lift out and discard the dark back vein, if present. Rinse the shrimp and drain well. In a small bowl, mix the shrimp with the wine and salt. Line the serving dish with the lettuce.

**2** In a 14-inch wok or 12-inch nonstick frying pan over medium heat, stir the garlic with the oil just until it begins to turn gold, about 2 minutes. Stir in the chile and remove from the heat. Pour the mixture into a fine strainer set over a bowl.

**3** Return the pan to high heat. When the pan is hot, return the strained oil to the pan. Add the shrimp and stir-fry until pink, 2 to 3 minutes. Transfer the shrimp to the lettuce-lined dish. Sprinkle evenly with the garlic-chile mixture.

**Note:** For a shortcut or easier eating, you can use peeled, deveined shrimp. ∎

# STIR-FRIED LOTUS ROOT AND PORK

On the outside, lotus root looks like a string of fat, ivory-colored sausages. When cut crosswise into thin slices, it blossoms into lacy snowflakes. Lotus root has a crisp texture and mild sweetness. In Hong Kong, we ate it stir-fried with pork, lots of green onions, and rings of hot chile. If you can't find lotus root in an Asian market, substitute an Asian white radish such as daikon, which is available in many supermarkets.

*Makes 2 servings as a main dish or 4 to 6 servings as part of a multicourse meal*

## SAUCE

⅓ cup water

1 tablespoon Chinese rice wine (shaoxing) or dry sherry

2 teaspoons soy sauce

2 teaspoons ground bean sauce or hoisin sauce

1 teaspoon cornstarch

½ teaspoon sugar (omit if using hoisin sauce)

## STIR-FRY

8 ounces lotus root (a 4- to 5-inch section) or Asian white radish, such as daikon

8 ounces boneless pork shoulder, trimmed of fat

2 teaspoons soy sauce

5 green onions, including green tops

2 tablespoons vegetable oil

1 tablespoon minced garlic

5 to 8 thin slices fresh chile (preferably red), such as Fresno or jalapeño

**1** **FOR THE SAUCE:** In a small bowl, mix the water, wine, soy sauce, bean sauce, cornstarch, and sugar.

**2** **FOR THE STIR-FRY:** In a 3- to 4-quart pan over high heat, bring about 6 cups water to a boil. Meanwhile, peel the lotus root or radish and trim off and discard the ends. If the root is more than 2 inches wide, slice it in half lengthwise. Thinly slice crosswise ⅛ inch thick to make 1½ to 2 cups. Drop the slices into the boiling water, and stir to separate. Return to a boil and cook until the slices are crisp-tender, 1 to 2 minutes. Drain, rinse, and drain again.

**3** Cut the pork into slices ⅛ inch thick, 2 inches long, and 1 inch wide. In a small bowl, mix the pork with the soy sauce. Trim off and discard the ends of the green onions. Cut the green onions, including the green tops, into 2-inch lengths.

**4** Set a 14-inch wok or 12-inch frying pan over high heat. When the pan is hot, after about 1 minute, add the oil and rotate the pan to spread. Add the garlic, chile, and pork and stir-fry until the pork is lightly browned, about 2 minutes. Add the lotus root. Stir-fry until the slices are hot, about 1 minute. Add the green onions. Stir the sauce mixture and add to the pan. Stir-fry until the sauce boils, about 30 seconds. Transfer to a serving dish. ▪

# FRIED EGGS AND CHIVES

We tasted thin, browned, frittata-like fried eggs throughout Asia and America. This straightforward version is heavily laced with bits of garlic chives. It's my fallback choice for a quick emergency meal.

*Makes 1 serving as a main dish or 2 to 4 servings as part of a multicourse meal*

2 large eggs

1 tablespoon water

⅛ teaspoon salt

3 tablespoons vegetable oil

¾ cup thinly sliced garlic chives, or ¾ cup thinly sliced green onions plus 1 tablespoon minced garlic

Chile sauce, homemade (page 268) or purchased

**1** In a small bowl, lightly beat the eggs, water, and salt to blend.

**2** Set a 6-inch frying pan over high heat. When the pan is hot, after about 1 minute, add 1 tablespoon of the oil and rotate the pan to spread. Add the chives and stir-fry just until slightly wilted and bright green, about 30 seconds. Scoop out the chives and stir into the eggs.

**3** Return the pan to high heat. Add the remaining 2 tablespoons of oil and rotate the pan to spread. Pour the egg mixture into the pan and shake to spread egg evenly.

As the egg sets, lift the cooked portion up slightly around its edges so the raw egg can flow underneath. When the bottom is golden brown and the top is almost set, about 2 minutes, use a wide spatula to turn the eggs over and cook until browned on the other side, about 30 seconds longer. Slide out of the pan onto a serving dish. Serve with chile sauce, if desired.

## Fried Eggs and Bitter Melon

Replace the chives with 1 small bitter melon (4 to 6 ounces). Trim off and discard the ends. Cut the melon in half lengthwise, then use a spoon to scoop out and discard the seeds. Thinly slice the bitter melon crosswise to make about ½ cup. You may have leftover melon. Reduce heat to medium-high in steps 2 and 3. After cooking the melon in step 2, leave the slices in the pan and spread in a single layer. Drizzle the remaining oil over the slices. Pour the egg mixture over the melon and cook as directed in step 3. ∎

# STEAMED LOOFAH SQUASH WITH TOASTED GARLIC CROWNS

Bits of crisp fried garlic adorn rounds of silky white-fleshed squash. Look for the long, slender angled loofah (also known as sponge squash) at farmers' markets and Asian grocery stores. You can identify the long squash by its dull, rough green skin and protruding vertical ridges. The clean, cool, refreshing quality of the fresh loofah squash is a perfect base for the crunchy topping of toasty garlic.

*Makes 3 to 4 servings as part of a multicourse meal*

3 tablespoons evenly minced garlic (see note)

1½ tablespoons vegetable oil

1 large angled loofah squash, or 3 or 4 medium zucchini (12 to 16 ounces total)

Salt

2 tablespoons thinly sliced green onions, including green tops, for garnish

1  In a 6- to 8-inch frying pan over medium heat, stir the garlic with the oil until the garlic turns light gold, 2 to 3 minutes. Remove from the heat; garlic may continue to brown slightly.

2  Peel the skin and ridges from the loofah (zucchini needs no peeling); discard the ends. Cut the squash crosswise into ¾-inch-thick rounds. Place the squash in a single layer, flat side down, on a 9- to 10-inch shallow heatproof plate that will fit inside a steamer. Lightly sprinkle the squash with salt.

3  Set the dish on a rack over 2 to 4 inches boiling water in a steamer or wok (if the bottom is round, place on a wok ring to stabilize). If the steamer lid is flat metal, wrap the lid with a towel to reduce condensation dripping on the food. Cover and steam over high heat until the squash is tender when pierced, about 5 minutes for the loofah or 10 minutes for the zucchini. Watch the water level, adding more boiling water as needed. Carefully remove the dish from the steamer and drain off any accumulated water. Transfer to a serving dish, if desired.

4  Place a spoonful of garlic on each round and add salt to taste. Sprinkle with the green onions.

Note:  Finely chop the garlic so the pieces are close to the same size. When fried in oil, the pieces will cook more evenly. If there's a great variation in size, some pieces of garlic will burn while others remain raw. The goal is golden toasted garlic. ■

# ADOPTED HAKKA CLASSIC
## Basin Feast

盆 菜  Hakka: *puhn choi;* Mandarin: *pen cai*

The waitress set a huge metal basin, mounded high with food, in front of us on a portable burner. Our eyes popped. We were at Chung Shing Restaurant in Tai Po, New Territories. The dish was called basin feast for the container that it was served in. Cooks layer many ingredients, from humble white radish to stately shrimp, in a large washbasin or wide bowl to serve a crowd. Guests gather around the basin and eat from the top down. This is a specialty in the New Territories, where many Hakkas live. We also saw this dish served in a Hakka restaurant in Beijing. Some claim it to be a Hakka classic.

Baby bok choy and mushrooms

Stories of the origin of this dish vary. One popular story suggests that when Emperor Bing of Song and his entourage moved south during the Mongolian invasion in the late Song period, there weren't enough dishes to hold food for everyone. Inventive villagers filled their washbasins with the army's banquet. Another version claims that the dish started as leftovers given to royalty. When the Qianlong Emperor visited Guangdong, he enjoyed eating the village banquet leftovers.

*Puhn choi* (also called *sihk puhn* by locals) represents the cultural traditions of the Punti lineage-oriented social structure in the New Territories of Hong Kong. Residents of local single-surname villages ate this one-bowl feast together to signify their connection, while excluding Hakkas from their circle. *Sihk puhn* has been considered the real food of the New Territories since the earliest days. Hakka villages that moved to the New Territories in the mid-Qing dynasty may have adopted this *puhn choi* tradition in the last few decades, says Hong Kong anthropology professor Sidney Cheung.

Since the late 1990s, this New Territory specialty has been reinvented as a symbol of Hong Kong heritage and serves as a popular feast dish for wedding banquets, Chinese New Year dinners, ancestral worship rites, and large family gatherings at ancestral halls. It's popular with local tourists and even sold as takeaway food in Hong Kong. Five years after visiting Hong Kong, I see local cafés and delis in California selling it as a take-out Chinese New Year feast. Most restaurant versions have gone upscale, as humble leftovers have been replaced with more expensive ingredients. For many in Hong Kong, eating *puhn choi* reinforces their cultural identity and returns them to their family roots.

This feast in one big bowl is a perfect party dish. Although it takes time to assemble, it can be made completely ahead. Parts can be prepared over a period of a few days to spread out the work and then layered in a bowl on the day of the party. When guests arrive, turn on the heat and set the hot bowl in the center of the table on a portable burner or trivet. Guests gather around the big bowl and serve themselves, starting with the top layer and working their way to the bottom. Offer hot cooked rice to soak up the savory juices.

For your big bowl, choose a wide heatproof container. A 12- to 14-inch wok, Chinese clay pot, or metal mixing bowl are possibilities. If you use a carbon-steel wok, make sure it is well seasoned first. A brand-new unseasoned wok may react with the sauce if it stands in the pan for a long time. The ideal pan size for the following recipe is around 4 quarts; however, a container that holds anywhere from 3½ to 6 quarts will work. For easier serving and presentation, it works best when the bowl is filled almost to the top.

# BASIN FEAST

Layer the elements of a banquet—pork, chicken, shrimp, mushrooms, and vegetables—into a big bowl, and then heat it up for a generous meal to feed a crowd. Layer the components with a pungent sauce made from red fermented bean curd, or, for a milder flavor, use soy sauce. Although the ingredients list is long, remember that this is a seven-course banquet in a bowl. Since most of it can be prepared in advance, there is very little last-minute cooking. Just turn on the heat and let the dish slowly warm up. Then, right before eating, add the bok choy and shrimp. Serve with hot cooked rice.

*Makes 8 to 10 servings as a main dish*

## SAUCE

2½ cups water

⅓ cup Chinese rice wine (shaoxing) or dry sherry

¼ cup oyster sauce

3 tablespoons mashed red fermented bean curd (3 to 5 pieces) or soy sauce (see notes)

1 tablespoon dark soy sauce

1 tablespoon sugar

1 teaspoon five-spice powder

½ teaspoon salt

## PORK

2 tablespoons vegetable oil

3 tablespoons minced garlic

3 tablespoons minced fresh ginger

1½ to 2 pounds boneless pork butt, trimmed of fat and cut into 1-inch chunks

**1 FOR THE SAUCE:** In a medium bowl, combine the water, wine, oyster sauce, fermented bean curd, dark soy sauce, sugar, five-spice powder, and salt. Whisk or stir until smoothly blended.

**2 FOR THE PORK:** Set a wok or 5- to 6-quart pan over high heat. When the pan is hot, after about 1 minute, add the oil and rotate the pan to spread. Add the garlic and ginger; stir-fry until the garlic begins to brown, about 15 seconds. Add the pork and stir occasionally until the meat is lightly browned, 5 to 7 minutes. Add the sauce mixture, cover, and simmer, stirring occasionally, until the pork is tender when pierced, 45 minutes to 1 hour. With a slotted spoon, transfer the pork to a medium bowl. Skim off and discard the fat from the pan juices. Measure the juices. If more than 2 cups, boil, uncovered, over high heat, until reduced to that amount. If less than 2 cups, add water to make that amount and bring to a boil.

**3 FOR THE CHICKEN:** Set a 14-inch wok or 12-inch frying pan over high heat. When the pan is hot, after about 1 minute, add the oil and rotate the pan to spread. Add the chicken and stir occasionally until it begins to brown, about 5 minutes. Add the wine and dark soy sauce. Reduce the heat, cover, and simmer, stirring occasionally, until the chicken is no longer pink in the cen-

## CHICKEN

2 tablespoons vegetable oil

1½ to 2 pounds boneless, skinless chicken thighs, cut into 1-inch chunks

¼ cup Chinese rice wine (shaoxing) or dry sherry

1 tablespoon dark soy sauce

## MUSHROOMS

12 dried shiitake mushrooms, each about 2 inches wide

3 cups hot water

1 tablespoon dark soy sauce

## VEGETABLES

1 pound Asian white radish, such as daikon

12 ounces napa cabbage

1 tablespoon vegetable oil

3 tablespoons water

4 or 5 small heads baby bok choy, each 2 inches wide at the base (6 to 8 ounces total)

## SHRIMP

1 pound peeled, deveined shrimp (16 to 20 per pound)

2 tablespoons Chinese rice wine (shaoxing) or dry sherry

2 tablespoons thinly sliced green onions, including green tops

1 tablespoon minced fresh ginger

½ teaspoon salt

¼ teaspoon ground white pepper

ter of the thickest part (cut to test), about 5 minutes. Transfer the chicken and juices to a medium bowl.

4 **FOR THE MUSHROOMS:** Rinse the mushrooms and place in a medium bowl. Cover with the hot water and soak until soft, 20 minutes for thin caps to 2 hours for thick caps. Squeeze the water out of the mushrooms, and reserve the soaking water. Cut off and discard the stems. Cut the mushrooms in half. Carefully pour 2½ cups of the reserved mushroom-soaking water into a 2-quart pan, leaving the sediment behind. Add the dark soy sauce and mushrooms to the pan, and bring to a boil over high heat. Reduce the heat, cover, and simmer, stirring occasionally, until the mushrooms are tender when pierced, 10 to 20 minutes. Transfer the mushrooms, including their juices, to a small bowl.

5 **FOR THE VEGETABLES:** Peel the radish and cut it into ¾-inch cubes to make about 2 cups. Place the radish cubes in a 2- to 3-quart pan, over high heat, with enough water to cover; bring to a boil. Reduce the heat, cover, and simmer until the radish is tender when pierced, 20 to 30 minutes. Drain and transfer to a medium bowl.

6 Cut the cabbage into 1-inch-by-3-inch strips to make about 4 cups. Set a 14-inch wok or 12-inch frying pan over high heat. When the pan is hot, after about 1 minute, add the oil and rotate the pan to spread. Stir in the cabbage. Add the water. Stir-fry until the cabbage wilts, about 2 minutes. Transfer the cabbage to a medium bowl.

7 Cut each head of bok choy in half lengthwise, rinse well, and drain.

8 To assemble: Up to 8 hours ahead, in a wide 3½- to 6-quart metal basin, metal bowl, pan, clay pot, or 12- to 14-inch well-seasoned steel, nonstick, or stainless steel wok, starting at the bottom, layer in the following ▸

order: the radish, pork, cabbage, chicken with juices, and mushrooms with juices; evenly drizzle each layer with ⅓ cup sauce from the pork. Pour any remaining sauce evenly over the top. If not cooking within 1 hour, cover and chill.

**9** **FOR THE SHRIMP:** Up to 1 hour before serving, in a medium bowl, mix the shrimp with the wine, green onions, ginger, salt, and pepper.

**10** Cook the layered container, covered, over medium heat until the juices simmer around the edges, 10 to 15 minutes. Attractively arrange the bok choy over the top. Simmer, covered, until the juices bubble in the center and the bok choy begins to wilt, 5 to 10 minutes. Arrange the shrimp in a single layer over the top. Cover and simmer until the shrimp are barely opaque in the thickest part (cut to test), 3 to 6 minutes. To serve, set the pan on a on a portable burner over low heat or a large trivet. If not using a portable burner, return the pan to the stove and reheat as needed. Guests help themselves from the pan with large serving spoons or chopsticks, working from the top layer to the bottom.

**Notes:** Fermented red bean curd has a strong funky flavor and aroma that Hakkas enjoy. Look for it in Asian markets. If you prefer a milder flavor, use the soy sauce alternative.

Up to 2 days ahead, you can make the sauce, cook the meats, and prepare the vegetables through step 7; cool, cover, and chill the parts separately. Up to 8 hours ahead, you can completely assemble the bowl through step 8, cool, cover, and chill. Take the bowl out of the refrigerator about 1 hour before heating. ∎

# THREE

# Leaving the Mainland
# Taiwan, Singapore, Malaysia, and Mauritius

Once we leave the Hakka heartland in mainland China, the food loses the narrowness of a singular society. On Taiwan, just over one hundred miles from the mainland, the Hakka food scene expanded as the result of a movement to preserve Hakka culture and reinvigorate and reinvent the cuisine. In Singapore and Malaysia, some dishes tasted livelier, with a more varied palette of fresh ingredients. Farther south, on the island of Mauritius in the Indian Ocean, the multicultural society brought fusion elements to the Hakka table.

The Chinese influence on the countries of Southeast Asia is felt in all areas of life, from business to food. Migrants from China started coming to this region as early as the fourteenth century and spread to every country. Great numbers of Chinese, many of whom were Hakkas, migrated to Southeast Asia during the late 1800s to feed the colonists' hunger for cheap labor. Southeast Asia now holds the largest Chinese population outside of mainland China and Taiwan— about 27 million people, according to 2005 figures. The biggest concentrations are in Thailand and Indonesia (each about 7.5 million), Malaysia (about 6 million), and Singapore (about 2.5 million).

In 2004, I visit Singapore and Malaysia to taste their contributions to the multicultural food scene. I meet Hakka home cooks and restaurant chefs; some cook traditional dishes, while others adapt to the tastes of the new generation with lighter variations.

# Proud to Be Hakka in Taiwan

We fly across the Taiwan Strait to the island of Taiwan (also known as the Republic of China). Taiwan shows a growing Hakka activism. Instead of assimilating and fading into the background, the Hakka now step out to claim their identity. As the second-largest group in Taiwan, composing 15 to 18 percent of the total population, the Hakka hold some power. It wasn't always this way.

The Hakka came to Taiwan in the seventeenth century, over three hundred years ago, claiming to be descendants of Chinese nobility. In their new island home, however, they were treated not as nobles, but as unwanted intruders. Their new enemies were the Hokkien from Fujian, who had arrived earlier. As descendants of Chinese nobles, the Hakka were viewed as having a strong connection with mainland China rather than Taiwan. The strong Taiwanese nationalist movement threatened the Hakka identity and suppressed its culture for decades. The Hakka became Taiwan's invisible minority.

In 1987, political activists created a new identity and term, "the new Hakka." This group of Hakkas no longer focused on its past mainland connection but on its new island home, Taiwan. A year later, a demonstration with the slogan "Returning My Mother Language to Me" united Taiwanese Hakkas in a cause they all could support. As the government began to recognize the power of the Hakka and other minorities, it created "Multicultural Taiwan," a government-supported public policy that promoted the culture, language, and community of minorities. This culture was almost lost. Now people are proud to be Hakka.

I see the results of these programs when I visit May (Yu-Hsin) Chang, director of the Foundation of Chinese Dietary Culture in Taipei. This private corporate body dedicates itself to the research of Chinese dietary culture. May interviews elderly Hakkas to record their food culture. She shares their stories and recipes.

"Hakka food reflects the spirit of the Hakka people," she says. "They work hard, always saving money. They're poor people and must use every resource at their disposal. Pork is the most important ingredient, and Hakkas use every part of the pig. In Hsinchu and Miaoli Counties, where the Hakka make up about half of the population, the food is very traditional."

In Taipei, the capital of Taiwan, Hakka food is very different. Many city people, with their urbane tastes, don't like the rustic qualities of traditional food. Taipei restaurants reduce salt and oil in Hakka dishes and add Taiwanese food to the menus of Hakka-owned restaurants. Hakka food in Taiwan is different than that in mainland China. Chefs here follow tradition, but change the taste a little to adapt to local ingredients.

In Beipu, a Hakka village in the foothills of eastern Hsinchu County, in the northern part of the island, we see evidence of this Hakka pride. The majority of the residents here are Hakka. Well-maintained temples and historic buildings, such as the grand baroque-style mansion of the prosperous Jiang family, show the success of the Hakka. Small shops, teahouses, and restaurants line the cobblestone streets of the old town, tempting tourists to experience the local culture.

We stop for dinner at Kwang Fu Cha Fung, a teahouse known for its fine Hakka food and tea. A dish of wilted greens, drizzled with a squiggle of fruity dressing and encircled with passion fruit halves, doesn't look Hakka—or, for that matter, like any Chinese dish I have ever seen. When I ask if the dish is Hakka, the chef says, "Hakka cooks adapt." He created the dish using wild mountain greens and local ingredients from the neighborhood. This self-taught chef is an inventive Hakka cook who takes advantage of what he has. A parade of other dishes follows. Some display the effect of local ingredients, while others show the more traditional salty, savory Hakka flavor profile.

# NEW HAKKA CLASSIC
## Hakka Little Stir-Fry

客家 小 炒 Hakka: *Hakka seow chow;* Mandarin: *ke jia xiao chao*

No one knows exactly how Hakka little stir-fry was invented. One story claims that a Hakka hostess had many leftovers after a party. With frugality in her genes, she didn't want to waste the food, so she created this new dish, adding some Chinese celery and stir-frying it to add fragrance.

Another tale has roots in Taoist culture. On the first and fifteenth of the month, worshippers gave an offering of pork belly, dried squid, green onions, and sometimes tofu at the temple or at home. Afterward, the offering was stir-fried with soy sauce and eaten.

Regardless of its origin, this popular dish has become a new classic.

## HAKKA LITTLE STIR-FRY

This stir-fry of pork belly, dried squid, tofu, and celery produces an appetizing mix of crisp and chewy textures that has found favor with Taiwanese customers.

A couple of the ingredients in this dish need some advance preparation. Boil the pork belly and soak the dried squid before stir-frying. These steps take only an hour, but for a head start, prepare them a day ahead and refrigerate overnight.

*Makes 4 servings as a main dish or 6 to 8 servings as part of a multicourse meal*

6 to 8 ounces boneless pork belly, skin on

1 teaspoon baking soda (if using squid)

1 piece dried squid, 3 to 4 inches square (optional)

2 tablespoons Chinese rice wine (shaoxing) or dry sherry

2 to 3 tablespoons soy sauce

¼ teaspoon sugar

5 ounces five-spice pressed tofu (about 2 squares)

1 In a 3- to 4-quart pan, combine about 4 cups water and the pork belly. Bring to a boil over high heat. Reduce the heat, cover, and simmer until the skin of the pork is easily pierced, 45 minutes to 1 hour. Lift out the pork and let cool briefly. Reserve the cooking water for another use or discard.

2 Meanwhile, in a small bowl, mix about 1 cup warm water and the baking soda. Rinse the squid and soak in the soda water until soft, 15 to 30 minutes. Lift out the squid. If present, remove and discard the long, transparent, sword-shaped shell and ink sac from the body. With scissors, cut the squid into thin slivers, about ¼ inch

6 ounces Chinese celery or common thick-stalked celery

4 green onions, including green tops

2 tablespoons vegetable oil

1 tablespoon minced garlic

5 to 8 thin rings fresh chile (preferably red), such as jalapeño or Fresno

½ cup flat-leaf parsley leaves (optional)

1 tablespoon water

Chinese celery

wide and 2 to 3 inches long, to make about 3 table-spoons. Return the squid slivers to the soda water and let stand until they plump slightly, 15 to 30 minutes. (Baking soda tenderizes squid.) Rinse well and soak in plain water to remove the soda, at least 10 minutes or up to the next day, changing water occasionally. Drain and squeeze the water out of the squid. In a small bowl, mix the squid with the wine.

3 Slice the pork belly through all layers to make match-sticks about ¼ inch thick and 2 to 3 inches long. In a small bowl, mix the pork with 1 tablespoon of the soy sauce and the sugar.

4 Cut the tofu into matchsticks ¼ inch thick and 2 to 3 inches long to make about 1 cup. Trim off and discard the stems ends from the celery. Cut the stalks into matchsticks ¼ inch thick and 3 inches long to make 1½ to 2 cups. Reserve about ½ cup of the celery leaves. Trim off and discard the ends from the onions. Cut the green onions, including green tops, into 3-inch lengths; split the thick stem ends in half lengthwise to make about 1 cup total.

5 Set a 14-inch wok or 12-inch frying pan over high heat. When the pan is hot, after about 1 minute, add the oil and rotate the pan to spread. Add the garlic and pork; stir-fry until the pork is lightly browned, 1 to 2 minutes. Add the celery sticks and leaves, chile, parsley, tofu, and water. Stir-fry until the celery is crisp-tender, 1 to 2 minutes. Add the green onions, squid mixture (or wine, if not using squid), and remaining 1 to 2 tablespoons of soy sauce to taste. Stir-fry until the green onions begin to brown, about 1 minute. Transfer to a serving dish. ■

# STIR-FRIED PORK AND PINEAPPLE

In Taiwan, people tend to be health conscious, so Hakka chefs sometimes reduce the amount of salt and fat in their dishes. This popular stir-fry is a good example. Chunks of locally grown fresh pineapple, bits of crunchy black fungus, and rings of hot chile bring a lively character to the pork. Traditionally, frugal Hakkas use pork lung in this colorful dish, but pork shoulder is a suitable alternative. This dish reminds me of sweet-and-sour pork without the rich heaviness and syrupy sauce.

*Makes 2 servings as a main dish or 4 servings as part of a multicourse meal*

## PORK

8 ounces boneless pork shoulder, trimmed of fat

2 teaspoons soy sauce

1 teaspoon vegetable oil

1 teaspoon cornstarch

## SAUCE

2 tablespoons rice vinegar

1 tablespoon sugar

1 tablespoon soy sauce

½ teaspoon salt

## STIR-FRY

8 pieces dried black fungus, such as cloud ears, each about 1 inch wide

3 green onions, including green tops

2 tablespoons vegetable oil

2 tablespoons thinly slivered fresh ginger

8 ounces fresh pineapple, cut into ¾-inch chunks (about 1 cup)

5 to 8 thin rings fresh chile (preferably red), such as jalapeño or Fresno

**1 FOR THE PORK:** Cut the pork into slices ⅛ inch thick, 2 inches long, and 1 inch wide. In a small bowl, mix the pork with the soy sauce, oil, and cornstarch.

**2 FOR THE SAUCE:** In a small bowl, mix the vinegar, sugar, soy sauce, and salt.

**3 FOR THE STIR-FRY:** Rinse the fungus. In a medium bowl, soak the fungus in hot water until soft and pliable, 5 to 15 minutes, and then drain. Pinch out and discard any hard knobby centers. Cut the fungus into 1-inch pieces. Trim the ends off the green onions. Cut the green onions, including green tops, into 2-inch lengths.

**4** Set a 14-inch wok or 12-inch frying pan over high heat. When the pan is hot, after about 1 minute, add the oil and rotate the pan to spread. Add the ginger and pork; stir-fry until the meat is lightly browned, about 2 minutes. Add the pineapple, black fungus, sauce mixture, green onions, and chile. Stir-fry until the pineapple is hot, 1 to 2 minutes. Transfer to a serving dish. ■

# BRAISED EGGPLANT, PORK, AND MUSHROOMS

The chef at Kwang Fu Cha Fung braises eggplant with pork, chiles, garlic, and soy sauce until the spongy vegetable softens into creamy morsels packed with robust flavors. He finishes the dish with long, slender enoki mushrooms to add a slightly crisp texture.

*Makes 2 to 3 servings as a main dish or 4 to 6 servings as part of a multicourse meal*

12 ounces Asian eggplant or globe eggplant (see note)

¾ cup water

3 tablespoons Chinese rice wine (shaoxing) or dry sherry

2 tablespoons soy sauce

1 tablespoon sugar

1 tablespoon black vinegar or balsamic vinegar

¼ teaspoon ground black pepper

2 tablespoons vegetable oil

6 to 8 ounces ground pork

2 tablespoons minced garlic

2 dried small hot red chiles

3 ounces enoki mushrooms, trimmed of ends, rinsed, and separated (optional)

⅓ cup chopped cilantro

1 Trim off the stem ends from the eggplant. If using Asian eggplant, slice into 2-inch lengths, and then cut lengthwise into ½-inch-thick wedges. If using globe eggplant, cut into ½-inch cubes. In a small bowl, mix the water, wine, soy sauce, sugar, vinegar, and pepper.

2 Place a 14-inch wok or 12-inch frying pan over high heat. When the pan is hot, after about 1 minute, add 1 tablespoon of the oil and rotate the pan to spread. Add the pork and garlic, and stir-fry until the pork has broken into small chunks and is lightly browned, 3 to 5 minutes. Reduce the heat to medium-high. Add the remaining 1 tablespoon of oil, chiles, and eggplant; stir-fry until the eggplant begins to brown, 2 to 3 minutes.

3 Add the water mixture. Bring to a boil. Reduce the heat, cover, and simmer, stirring occasionally, until the eggplant is soft when pressed, 7 to 9 minutes. Stir in the mushrooms and remove from the heat. Transfer to a serving bowl and sprinkle with cilantro.

**Note:** Slender Chinese or Japanese eggplants hold their shape better and are less seedy than larger, more common globe eggplants. ∎

Asian eggplant

# PORK DRUMSTICKS

Chicken symbolizes wealth to the Chinese. It's more highly prized than pork and is often served for festive events or to special guests. May (Yu-Hsin) Chang tells a story to illustrate this point. An eighty-year-old grandmother invented this dish using common pork to resemble coveted chicken. She molded a typical Hakka mixture of ground pork and fish paste around pork spareribs, and then steamed and deep-fried them so that they resembled fried chicken drumsticks.

Dip the crisp faux chicken legs in chile sauce to eat. I like the Mae Ploy sweet chile sauce from Thailand with the fried drumsticks. Fresh fish paste is readily available in Asian supermarkets; if you can't find it, make your own.

*Makes 6 servings as a main dish or 10 to 12 servings as part of a multicourse meal*

8 ounces ground pork

8 ounces fresh fish paste, homemade (page 225) or purchased

2 tablespoons minced peeled fresh or canned water chestnuts

2 tablespoons minced carrots

2 tablespoons minced green onions, including green tops

¾ teaspoon salt

¼ teaspoon sugar

¼ teaspoon ground white pepper

6 baby back pork ribs (about 1¼ pounds total)

½ cup cornstarch, or as needed

Vegetable oil, for frying

Chile sauce, homemade (page 268) or purchased

1 In a medium bowl, mix the ground pork, fish paste, water chestnuts, carrots, green onions, salt, sugar, and white pepper. Divide into 6 equal portions.

2 Cut the ribs apart between the bones. For each piece, with wet hands, mold 1 portion of the pork mixture completely around the thicker end of the rib bone and gradually taper down the sides so it resembles a chicken drumstick. Place the ribs slightly apart on 1 or 2 oiled rimmed heatproof dishes that will fit inside a steamer.

3 To steam: Set the dishes on a rack over 2 to 4 inches boiling water in a steamer or wok (if the bottom is round, place on a wok ring to stabilize). If the steamer lid is flat metal, wrap the lid with a towel to reduce condensation dripping on the food. Cover and steam over high heat until a thermometer inserted in the center of the thickest part of the meat reads 165°F to 170°F, or until the meat is no longer pink in the center of the thickest part (cut to test), 20 to 30 minutes. Watch the water level, adding more boiling water as needed. Carefully remove the dish from the steamer. If desired, reserve the juices for another use.

4 To deep-fry: Set a 14-inch wok (if the bottom is round, place on a wok ring to stabilize) or 5- to 6-quart pan over medium-high heat. Fill the pan with the oil

to a depth of about 2 inches. Heat the oil until the temperature reaches 350°F on a thermometer. Adjust the heat to maintain the temperature.

5  Meanwhile, place the cornstarch on a plate and coat each drumstick with the starch. Shake off the excess. Carefully place 2 or 3 pieces in the hot oil. Fry, turning once, until crisp and golden, 3 to 4 minutes total. With a slotted spoon or tongs, lift out and drain the drumsticks on plates lined with paper towels. Repeat to fry the remainder. Place on a serving dish and serve at once, or keep warm in a 200°F oven for up to 30 minutes. Offer chile sauce to add to taste.

Note:  These drumsticks taste best freshly made, but you can make them in advance and reheat them in the oven. Up to 1 day ahead, make them completely ahead. Cool, cover, and chill. To serve, place the pieces slightly apart on a shallow rimmed baking pan and bake in a 350°F oven until crisp on the outside and hot inside or until a thermometer reads 140°F when inserted in the center of the thickest part, 20 to 30 minutes. ▪

## PEPPERY ROAST PORK BELLY WITH GARLIC-VINEGAR SAUCE

At Taiwan's Hungry Ghost Festival, a celebration to honor ancestors, it is said that ghosts travel back to earth to visit the living and eat their food offerings. The Hakka offer a pig—not any pig, but the fattest specimen available. Families compete to raise the "divine pig." One year the winning swine weighed in at fifteen hundred pounds.

One winner created this recipe to preserve the prized pork belly. He coated strips of pork belly with salt and aromatic spices, then stashed some in the refrigerator (the rest went in the freezer) for five or six days to allow the seasonings to permeate and cure the meat. He steamed the pork until tender, roasted it until brown, then sliced the strip into succulent bite-sized pieces and laid them on a bed of green onion shreds. To cut the richness, he served the fat-streaked pork with garlic paste tempered with vinegar. In my version, you'll still need to plan in advance to cure the pork for several days, but the cooking process is simplified: the pork is steamed in the oven and then roasted in the same pan.

For a modern variation, serve the pork as an appetizer, tucked with green onions and garlic paste into small steamed buns or baked rolls to make mini-sandwiches. Asian supermarkets sell the steamed folded buns in the refrigerator or freezer section.

*Makes 3 to 4 servings as a main dish or 6 to 8 servings as part of a multicourse meal* ▸

1½ tablespoons kosher salt

2 teaspoons black peppercorns

½ teaspoon five-spice powder

¼ teaspoon ground white pepper

1 pound boneless pork belly with skin, in a single piece (see note)

½ cup water

2 tablespoons minced garlic

¼ cup rice vinegar

4 green onions, including green tops

**1** In an 8- to 10-inch frying pan over medium heat, stir the salt and black peppercorns until the peppercorns begin to pop, 5 to 6 minutes. Remove from the heat. Stir in the five-spice powder and white pepper. With a large spoon, coarsely crush the peppercorns in the pan. Let cool.

**2** Set the pork on a sheet of plastic wrap. Rub the salt mixture all over the pork, wrap tightly, and place in a plastic bag. (For longer storage, freeze up to 4 weeks.) Place in the refrigerator and let cure 5 to 6 days. (If the pork is frozen, add an extra 24 hours to allow meat to thaw in refrigerator first).

**3** Preheat the oven to 250°F. Rinse the pork well and rub lightly to remove the salt; pat dry. Place the strip, skin side up, in a 9-by-13-inch rimmed baking pan. Add the water. Cover the pan tightly with foil and bake until the pork is tender when pierced, about 1¼ hours. Pour off any juices and reserve for another use, or discard. Increase the oven temperature to 400°F. Bake, uncovered, until the pork strip is browned, 25 to 30 minutes. Remove the pork from the oven and let rest about 5 minutes.

**4** Meanwhile, crush the garlic in a mortar and pestle or press with the flat side of a knife to make a coarse paste. In a small pan, bring the vinegar to a boil; stir in the garlic and remove from the heat. Pour into a small serving bowl. Trim off the ends from the green onions. Cut the green onions, including tops, into 3-inch lengths, then cut lengthwise into thin slivers to make about ¾ cup. Spread the green onions in a thin layer on a serving plate. Cut the pork strip crosswise into ½-inch-thick slices. Arrange the pork on the green onions. Offer the garlic vinegar to add to taste.

**Note:** Look for an evenly thick piece of boneless pork belly with skin, preferably with a high portion of lean meat, about 1½ inches thick. If you buy a larger, 3- to 4-pound, slab of pork belly, slice the belly along the grain into 3 or 4 strips, about 1 pound each. Increase the salt mixture proportionately and rub each strip with the salt mixture; wrap and freeze. Six to seven days before serving, take out the amount you plan to serve, thaw, let cure, and then bake. ∎

# CHEWY RICE MORSELS IN SWEET PEANUT POWDER

These soft, chewy rice morsels have a texture similar to Japanese mochi and are made in a similar manner: by pounding cooked glutinous rice into a smooth dough-like paste. The process can become messy and sticky. To make it easier and neater, place the cooked rice into a heavy-duty plastic freezer bag and pound until it has reduced to a paste. With the bag, you avoid touching the gluey rice. Then, use the bag like a pastry bag to squeeze out the rice paste, either in one big log or in small balls, onto a bed of ground peanuts and sugar. In this rustic version, some of the texture of the rice still remains.

Make these rice balls shortly before serving, or ask your guests to help pound the rice as part of the experience. You can make the peanut powder a day ahead and store it in an airtight container. Serve with Pounded Tea with Sweets (page 100) or with plain hot green or oolong tea.

*Makes 8 to 10 servings*

¾ cup roasted, salted peanuts

⅓ cup sugar, or to taste

¾ cup short- or long-grain glutinous rice

1 cup water

**1** In a food processor, pulse the peanuts and sugar just until peanuts are finely ground and almost powdery; do not overprocess. Pour into a shallow rimmed dish.

**2** Rinse the rice in a fine strainer until the water runs almost clear. Place the rice and water in an 8- to 9-inch shallow heatproof dish that will fit inside a steamer, such as a Pyrex pie pan. Set the dish on a rack over 2 to 4 inches boiling water in a steamer or wok (if the bottom is round, place on a wok ring to stabilize). If the steamer lid is flat metal, wrap the lid with a towel to reduce condensation dripping on the food. Cover and steam over high heat until the rice is soft when pressed, 20 to 25 minutes. Watch the water level, adding more boiling water as needed. Carefully remove the dish from the steamer.

**3** Let the rice cool about 5 minutes, stirring occasionally. Place the rice in a 1-gallon heavy-duty plastic ziplock bag. Press the air out of the bag and seal. With a rolling pin or flat mallet, roll or pound the rice until a smooth paste forms, turning the bag over occasionally.

**4** To let guests serve themselves at the table: Press or roll the rice paste into the shape of a log toward the bag opening. Open the bag and squeeze the rice log onto the peanut mixture. Spoon the peanut mixture over the log to coat. Have guests place a chopstick on each side of the rice log and cross in the center in ▸

the shape of an *X,* and then cut through the rice paste by bringing chopsticks together to make a small bite-sized piece. Or cut with a knife into bite-sized pieces. Roll in the peanut mixture to coat.

To form into small morsels in the kitchen: Press or roll the rice paste into the bottom of the bag. Cut about 1 inch off a corner of the bag. Twist the top of the bag down tightly until the rice paste is compacted in the corner of the bag with the hole. Using the bag like a pastry bag, press from the top to squeeze out 1-inch portions of rice paste onto the peanut mixture. Coat the rice pieces in the peanut mixture. Using chopsticks, lift the rice pieces out of the peanut coating and arrange on a serving plate. Serve warm. ∎

# A Singapore Chef Lightens Up

In Singapore, Chinese faces seem to outnumber Indians, Malays, and all others. I ask our taxi driver about the country's Chinese residents. Our talkative driver opens up. "I'm Cantonese," he says. "The Chinese make up about 75 percent of the population here, with Hokkiens being the biggest group." "What about Hakka?" I ask. "The fourth largest," he responds. "The government wants everyone to speak Mandarin rather than dialects. Our first president, Lee Kwan Kee, a Hakka, started that."

He drops us off at Moi Kong Hakka Restaurant. This family restaurant goes back to the 1950s, with the last twenty-plus years at this Maxwell Street location (which has since closed). Rick Wong (Wong Chee Leong), the chef and owner, tells us that his father originally came from Meixian in China. He went to Ipoh in Malaysia, and then settled in Singapore, where Rick was born.

Chef Wong offers authentic Hakka food, but admits that "this old traditional restaurant has changed for the new generation. Hakka food uses lots of salt, oil, preserved vegetables, and pork belly, but stewed pork belly is too fatty for the new generation. I serve just a few slices with steamed buns to make a sandwich. I make up some dishes to appease the younger tastes." He emphasizes fundamental flavors but takes into consideration nutritional value. As we eat our way through the menu, I taste traditional Hakka flavors but often in a lighter form. I like his approach.

# NEW HAKKA CLASSIC
## Pounded Tea with Sweets

擂茶 Hakka: *lui cha;* Mandarin: *lei cha*

In Taiwan we visit Kwang Fu Cha Fung, a teahouse in the Hakka village of Beipu in Hsinchu County. After a big Hakka dinner, we learn that we'll be making the specialty of the house, pounded tea with sweet side dishes. The chef claims that this tradition originated almost two thousand years ago during China's Three Kingdoms era. As General Zhang Fei prepared to capture Chengdu, the capital at the time, a plague struck down his troops. An old doctor prescribed a tea made from pounded tea leaves, sesame seeds, and peanuts. Miraculously, the brew cured the soldiers and they fought their way to victory. The recipe was passed through the generations. This modern adaptation was developed as a teahouse Hakka specialty to draw visitors and keep the town alive.

The chef divides us into groups of four. Each group gets a deep, rough bowl, a thick wooden stick, and small bowls of green tea leaves, seeds, and nuts. He directs us to put the tea, seeds, and nuts into the big bowl and grind the mixture with the stick to make a paste. We all take turns trying to beat it into a pulp. Finally, his skinny assistant rescues us and demonstrates how a professional does it. He tucks his necktie into his shirt, and then whirls the stick around the bowl like a human food processor. In seconds, the coarse mound collapses into a smooth paste. He stirs steaming water into the green paste to make a thick, creamy tea. Into small bowls, we spoon dry puffed rice (sort of like a white version of Rice Krispies cereal) and a sweet mix of chewy tapioca pearls, dates, ginger, and beans. Then he ladles the hot, slightly creamy, greenish-gray tea over the sweet condiments in our bowls.

The chef also presents a big lump of pounded glutinous rice resting in a bowl of ground peanuts and sugar. He brings together two chopsticks to cut off a small piece, and then rolls the mochi-like lump in the sweet peanut mixture and offers it to us. The Hakka brought this delicacy from the North. They pounded leftover rice to make this sweet treat so that guests always had more than enough to eat. Sometimes thrifty hosts served it before the main courses to fill up empty stomachs so guests wouldn't eat too much. I find I can't stop eating this sweet, chewy confection.

The next day, May (Yu-Hsin) Chang at the Foundation of Chinese Dietary Culture tells me the story of the Taiwanese version of this unique tea. Centuries ago on the mainland, when the Hakka moved south to Fujian, Jiangxi, and

Guangdong provinces, they couldn't carry many ingredients, but tea was easy to pack. The tea quenched their thirst, and when they added ingredients from the local region, such as rice puffs, it sated their hunger. They brought this tea tradition with them to Taiwan.

Originally, this special tea was served as part of a savory rice bowl (page 119). In 1998, the Beipu Agricultural Department searched for a local specialty to generate tourism and keep their Hakka village alive. They interviewed Yei Pong Shell, an eighty-four-year-old grandmother who came from China's Guangdong Province to Taiwan when she was twenty-eight. Her family drank the tea to promote health. Its original ingredients were green tea, sesame seeds, and peanuts. Yei added extra nuts and seeds to provide more nutrition. When she went to Beipu to demonstrate how to make the tea, she was asked if it could be sweetened. She said that adding sweets would not hurt. Since then, this savory tea from mainland China has developed into a distinctive tea ceremony dish with sweet condiments served in Hakka villages in Taiwan.

## POUNDED TEA WITH SWEETS

In essence, the basic tea is a nutritious health drink. It's not a clear beverage, but a creamy, slightly thick, greenish-gray drink that has a pronounced tea taste, made smooth and rich by the addition of nuts and seeds. For a simplified home version, an electric blender makes the pounding step effortless. Spoon a sweet mixture of dates, goji berries, sweet beans, crystallized ginger, and chewy tapioca pearls into the tea; it balances the tea tannins.

For an everyday version, make just the tea portion of this recipe. Store it in the refrigerator and reheat small portions in the microwave. For a quick breakfast on the go, stir in some chopped candied ginger, a few goji berries or raisins, bits of dried fruit, raw or brown sugar, and rice cereal. I have seen a powdered form manufactured in Taiwan in my local Asian supermarket to which you just stir in boiling water for an instant healthy snack.

To enjoy the special teahouse experience, make both the sweet condiments and tea and serve the dish with Chewy Rice Morsels in Sweet Peanut Powder (page 97). Both the condiments and tea can be made up to three days ahead. Reheat to serve. Reheat them separately, covered, over low heat, stirring occasionally. Add a little water to the condiments. If the tea is too thick, thin with a little water.

*Makes 8 to 10 servings*

## CONDIMENTS

12 dried red dates, rinsed

1 cup dried tapioca pearls (see notes)

⅓ cup dried goji berries, rinsed

1 cup water

½ cup chopped brown slab sugar (two 5-by-1-inch slabs) or packed brown sugar, or to taste

⅓ cup chopped crystallized ginger

1 cup cooked red beans or adzuki beans, rinsed (see notes)

1½ to 2 cups dried puffed rice cereal

## POUNDED TEA

⅓ cup pumpkin seeds

3 tablespoons raw or roasted peanuts

2 tablespoons pine nuts

1 tablespoon chopped walnuts

¼ cup white sesame seeds

1 tablespoon black sesame seeds or more white sesame seeds

2 tablespoons dried green tea leaves

3 cups boiling water

**1 FOR THE CONDIMENTS:** In a small bowl, soak the dates in hot water until soft enough to remove pits, 5 to 10 minutes.

**2** In a 3-quart pan, over high heat, bring about 1½ quarts water to a boil. Add the dates, reduce heat to low, cover, and simmer until soft, about 10 minutes. Increase the heat to high, add the tapioca pearls, and boil until the pearls float. Reduce the heat, cover, and simmer until the pearls are soft but still chewy, about 5 minutes or according to the package directions. Stir in the goji berries. Drain and rinse well. Rinse the pan.

**3** In the rinsed pan over high heat, combine the water, sugar, and ginger. Bring to a simmer, stirring until the sugar dissolves. Stir in the tapioca mixture and beans. (If not serving soon, let stand at room temperature up to 2 hours or cover and chill up to 3 days.) Shortly before serving, stir the mixture over low heat until most of the syrup is absorbed, 5 to 7 minutes. Transfer the mixture to a serving bowl; keep warm. Pour the puffed rice into a serving bowl.

**4 FOR THE POUNDED TEA:** In a 10-inch frying pan over low heat, stir the pumpkin seeds, peanuts, pine nuts, and walnuts until the nuts begin to lightly brown, 2 to 4 minutes. Add the white and black sesame seeds and stir until the white sesame seeds begin to pop and turn golden, 1 to 2 minutes longer. Cool about 5 minutes.

**5** In a blender, combine the tea and nut mixture. Whirl until finely ground. Add 1 cup of the boiling water. With a potholder firmly holding down the blender lid, blend on low speed, then increase to high and whirl until smooth. Pour the mixture into a 2- to 3-quart pan. Pour another 1 cup boiling water into the blender container, whirl to remove any remaining residue, and add to the pan. Pour the remaining 1 cup water into the pan. Stir the tea over low heat until hot and thick, 2 to 4 minutes.

**6** Pour the tea into small bowls. Offer the sweet condiments and puffed rice to add to taste. ▸

**Notes:** Dried tapioca pearls, found in Asian markets to make *boba* or pearl or bubble tea, vary in their cooking times. I used pearls that cooked in 5 minutes. If you buy tapioca with a longer cooking time, cook it separately, and then combine with the dates. I prefer the black or green tea tapioca pearls.

To cook red beans: In a 2-quart pan, bring about 1 quart water and ½ cup rinsed dried Chinese red beans or adzuki beans to a boil. Cover and let stand for about 1 hour. Drain and add 1 quart water. Bring to a boil, cover, and simmer until beans are tender, 25 to 45 minutes.

Some Japanese markets sell sweetened cooked red beans vacuum packed; however, most red beans are sold in Asian markets as a sweet paste. For a shortcut, used rinsed canned pinto beans.

The sweet condiments and pounded tea can be made up to 3 days ahead, cooled, covered, and chilled. Reheat them separately, covered, over low heat, stirring occasionally. Add a little water to the condiments if they stick to the bottom of the pan. Add a little water to the tea if it is thicker than desired. ▪

# POACHED SHRIMP IN GINGER BROTH

Pour a ginger-spiked broth over lightly poached shrimp and bean sprouts for a refreshing and colorful dish that comes together in minutes. This recipe was inspired by a dish served by Chef Wong at Moi Kong Hakka Restaurant in Singapore to please his younger customers.

*Makes 2 to 3 servings as a main dish or 4 to 6 servings as part of a multicourse meal*

1 pound shrimp (21 to 25 per pound), in their shells

2 cups bean sprouts (about 4 ounces)

⅓ cup cilantro leaves

⅓ cup flat-leaf parsley leaves

2 tablespoons thinly sliced garlic chives, or 2 tablespoons thinly sliced green onions, including green tops, plus ½ teaspoon minced garlic

1 to 2 tablespoons thinly slivered fresh chile (preferably red), such as jalapeño or Fresno

¾ cup chicken broth, homemade (page 267) or purchased

1 tablespoon thinly slivered fresh ginger

2 teaspoons fish sauce, or to taste

2 teaspoons Asian sesame oil

1 In a 3- to 4-quart pan over high heat, bring about 2 quarts of water to a boil. Meanwhile, peel the shrimp. Cut a lengthwise slit along the center of the back about ¾ inch deep and remove the dark vein. Rinse the shrimp. Add the shrimp to the boiling water and stir to separate. Cover and cook over low heat just until the shrimp are barely opaque in the center of the thickest part (cut to test), 1 to 2 minutes.

2 Meanwhile, place the bean sprouts in a large colander. Pour the shrimp and their cooking liquid over the sprouts. Drain and put the shrimp and sprouts into a wide serving bowl. Sprinkle with the cilantro, parsley, chives, and slivered chile to taste.

3 In the same pan (no need to wash) over high heat, bring the broth and ginger to a boil. Add the fish sauce and sesame oil and pour over the shrimp. Mix lightly and serve. ∎

# NOODLES WITH MUSHROOM PORK SAUCE

This comforting noodle dish from Moi Kong Hakka Restaurant in Singapore pleases all generations. Think of it as a Hakka version of pasta with Bolognese sauce. Stir-fry ground pork, mushrooms, and garlicky Chinese chives with soy sauce. Toss with noodles, crisp bean sprouts, and a little broth for a speedy meal in a bowl.

*Makes 3 to 4 servings as a main dish or 6 to 8 servings as part of a multicourse meal*

8 ounces fresh mushrooms, such as shiitake, king oyster, cremini, or button

2 tablespoons vegetable oil

8 ounces ground pork

1 cup thinly sliced garlic chives, or 1 cup thinly sliced green onions, including green tops, plus 1 tablespoon minced garlic

2 tablespoons dark soy sauce

¼ teaspoon salt, or to taste

¼ teaspoon ground black pepper, or to taste

1 pound fresh Chinese wheat or egg noodles, or 12 ounces dried

4 cups bean sprouts (about 8 ounces)

¼ cup thinly sliced green onions, including green tops

1¼ cups chicken broth, homemade (page 267) or purchased

**1** Lightly rinse and drain the mushrooms. If using shiitake mushrooms, trim off and discard the tough stems. Chop the mushrooms into ½-inch pieces to make 2½ to 3½ cups.

**2** In a 6- to 8-quart pan over high heat, bring about 3 quarts water to a boil.

**3** Meanwhile, set a 14-inch wok or 12-inch frying pan over high heat. When the pan is hot, after about 1 minute, add 1 tablespoon of the oil and rotate the pan to spread. Add the pork and stir-fry until the meat is loose and crumbly, 2 to 3 minutes. Add the remaining 1 tablespoon oil, mushrooms, and chives; stir until the liquid evaporates and the mixture browns, 3 to 5 minutes. Stir in the dark soy sauce, salt, and pepper. Cover to keep warm.

**4** If the noodles are fresh, pull them apart to separate. Add the noodles to the boiling water and stir to separate; cook just until barely tender, 2 to 3 minutes for fresh, 5 to 6 minutes for dried. Meanwhile, rinse the bean sprouts in a large colander and drain; leave in the colander. When the noodles are done, pour the noodles and their cooking liquid over the sprouts in the colander. Drain well and transfer to a large, wide serving bowl. Sprinkle with green onions.

**5** Reheat the pork, stirring over high heat, and pour over the noodles. Add the broth and bring to a boil, scraping free the browned bits and brown film clinging to the pan. Pour the broth over the noodles. Mix lightly and serve. ■

# Three Sisters in Singapore

My foodie friend Violet Oon, who seems to know everyone in Singapore, introduces me to Doreen Ho Fui Fah. Doreen's eldest sister, Ho Huey Cheen, is an excellent cook. She agrees to show me a few Hakka dishes at Doreen's high-rise apartment. Huey Cheen is already at work in the kitchen when we arrive. Trim and energetic, she doesn't look like a seventy-year-old grandmother with six children and thirteen grandchildren. As she squats by the thick chopping block on the kitchen floor, cutting up chicken and vegetables, she shares tips on how to make the sweet Hakka rice wine that she will cook with the chicken. Soon Doreen and Huey Cheen's middle sister, Ah Kum, arrives and the three women reminisce about their family.

Their father came from Meixian in China to Singapore in 1920 to work as an apprentice in a relative's medical practice. He married a Hakka woman and started a family that grew to twelve children. In the 1950s, he left Singapore to set up his own medical practice in the small town of Kluang, in the Malaysian state of Johor. "He was well liked because he rode an old bicycle to make house calls. Patients fondly called him *fat sinseh* [Chinese physician]," says Fui Fah. Their mother joined him in the business in the 1960s. While their parents worked, the girls, starting when they were twelve, cooked and took care of the household.

Soon we sit down to a lunch of traditional home-cooked wine chicken and mashed eggplant, supplemented by purchased favorite dishes that their mother used to cook for festivals, such as abacus taro and stuffed tofu and vegetables.

Noodles and mushrooms

# SINGAPORE STUFFED VEGETABLE AND TOFU SOUP

In Singapore's street markets, customers can choose from a wide selection of tofu and vegetables filled with fish paste and poached in a light broth. In the Cantonese style, the fish paste is light, smooth, and delicate. The Hakka version mixes pork into the filling for a deeper flavor and coarser texture. The stuffed vegetables and tofu flavor the broth as they poach in it. Cook this soup gently over low heat and without vigorous stirring so the filling remains inside the vegetables. If you don't like bitter melon, omit it and replace with more chiles, eggplant, or tofu. If desired, offer hot rice to spoon into the broth or to eat alongside.

*Makes 4 to 6 servings as a main dish or 8 to 10 servings as part of a multicourse meal*

## FILLING

8 ounces skinless fillet from a firm, white-fleshed fish, such as rockfish or tilapia

12 ounces ground pork

¼ cup minced green onions, including green tops

1 large egg white

2 tablespoons fish sauce

1 tablespoon cornstarch

1 teaspoon minced garlic

1 teaspoon minced fresh ginger

¼ teaspoon salt

¼ teaspoon ground white pepper

## SOUP

1 pound firm tofu

4 slender, straight, mild to medium-hot red chiles, such as Anaheim, New Me xican, or sweet Italian (6 to 8 ounces total), or 1 red bell pepper (about 8 ounces)

**1 FOR THE FILLING:** Rinse the fish and cut into ½-inch chunks. Whirl in a food processor until you have a paste or finely chop with a knife. Transfer the fish to a medium bowl and mix in the pork, green onions, egg white, fish sauce, cornstarch, garlic, ginger, salt, and white pepper until well blended. At this point, you can cover and chill the mixture for up to 1 day.

**2 FOR THE SOUP:** Rinse the tofu, and then drain for about 5 minutes. Cut the tofu into 6 equal slabs, ¾ to 1 inch thick. Place on a double layer of towels and pat dry. Using a spoon, scoop out a cavity about ½ inch deep from the center of each tofu slab, leaving a ¼-inch border around the edges. Reserve the tofu scraps. Mound about 1 rounded tablespoon of pork filling in each cavity, smearing the filling around the edges so that it sticks to the tofu.

**3** Cut the chiles in half lengthwise through the stems or cut the bell pepper lengthwise through the stem into 8 equal wedge-like strips. Scrape out the seeds and leave the stems attached. Trim stems to about ¼ inch long. Fill the chile or pepper cavities with the pork mixture, mounding slightly and smearing the filling around the cut edges of the chile, using about 1 rounded table-spoon for each.

1 bitter melon, about 2 inches wide (about 8 ounces)

1 Asian eggplant, about 1½ inches wide (about 8 ounces)

4 tablespoons vegetable oil, or as needed

8 cups chicken broth, homemade (page 267) or purchased

3 thin slices fresh ginger, lightly crushed

Salt

Cilantro leaves, for garnish

Chile sauce, homemade (page 268) or purchased

**4** Trim off and discard the ends from the bitter melon. Cut the melon crosswise into 1-inch rounds. With a small knife, cut around the inside edges of the melon from both ends, push out the spongy centers with seeds, and discard. Scrape out the white pith from the inside edges. Fill the cavities with about 1 rounded tablespoon of filling, mounding the filling slightly over the top and smearing it around the cut edges of the melon.

**5** Slice the eggplant on the diagonal into ¾-inch sections; discard the ends. Cut through the center of each section almost to the skin, but not completely through to the other side. Fill the center of each piece with about 1 rounded tablespoon of filling and gently press the eggplant together against the filling.

**6** Set a 12-inch nonstick frying pan over medium-high heat. When the pan is hot, after about 1 minute, add 2 tablespoons of the oil and rotate the pan to spread. In several batches, place the bitter melon, tofu, chile, and eggplant pieces slightly apart in a single layer in the pan, filling side down (or flesh side down for the eggplant). Cook, turning over halfway, until lightly browned on both sides, 3 to 5 minutes. Add 1 to 2 tablespoons oil to the pan for each batch, as needed. With a slotted spatula, transfer the pieces as done to a large platter.

**7** In a 6- to 8-quart pan over high heat, bring the broth and ginger to a boil. Add the bitter melon rings to the broth, reduce the heat, cover, and simmer for 10 minutes. Add the eggplant, tofu, chiles (filling side up), and any accumulated juices to the broth. If desired, add the tofu scraps and bite-sized lumps of leftover filling or reserve for another use. Return to a simmer, reduce the heat, cover, and cook over low heat until the vegetables are tender when pierced, 10 to 12 minutes. Carefully transfer the bitter melon, tofu, chiles, and eggplant into 4 to 6 large, wide soup bowls or a large serving bowl. Skim off and discard the fat from the broth. Add salt to taste. Ladle the broth into the bowls. Sprinkle with the cilantro. Offer the chile sauce to add to taste. ■

# MASHED EGGPLANT WITH WATER SPINACH

After Ho Huey Cheen boils eggplant and mixes in blanched water spinach, Ah Kum beats it with a spoon. "Mash them so they taste good," Huey Cheen directs. Mashing releases the eggplant's earthy essence and creamy texture. The soft pulp readily soaks up the robust spiciness of the garlic and chile. Bits of water spinach streak through with trails of green. The Ho sisters call this dish "Beaten Eggplant Mud." With such a name, it's not likely to win a beauty contest, but eggplant lovers will appreciate the pure taste of the vegetable in this dish.

*Makes 6 servings as part of a multicourse meal*

8 ounces water spinach or spinach

1 pound Asian eggplant or globe eggplant

3 tablespoons vegetable oil

1½ teaspoons salt

2 tablespoons minced garlic

6 to 9 thin rings fresh chile (preferably red), such as jalapeño or Fresno

1 tablespoon fish sauce or soy sauce, or to taste

**1** Trim off and discard the woody stem ends from the water spinach, usually the bottom 3 to 4 inches. If the stems are woody and tough, discard them and use only the leaves. (For spinach, trim off the root ends and tough stem ends.) Wash well and drain. Coarsely chop the tender leaves and stems to make about 3 cups.

**2** Trim off the stem ends from the eggplant. If using Asian eggplant, cut in half lengthwise. Cut long pieces crosswise into ½-inch-thick slices. (If using globe eggplant, cut lengthwise into 1½-inch wedges.)

**3** In a 14-inch wok or 5- to 6-quart pan over high heat, bring about 2 quarts water, 1 tablespoon of the oil, and 1 teaspoon of the salt to a boil. Add the eggplant and cook until soft when pressed, 5 to 7 minutes. Stir in the spinach and cook just until it turns bright green, about 30 seconds; drain well.

**4** Rinse and dry the pan and set it over high heat. When the pan is hot, after about 1 minute, add the remaining 2 tablespoons oil and rotate the pan to spread. Add the garlic, remaining ½ teaspoon salt, and chile, and stir-fry until the garlic is lightly browned, about 30 seconds. Stir in the eggplant, spinach, and fish sauce. Stir-fry to blend the eggplant with the seasonings, about 1 minute. The eggplant will likely fall apart. If needed, with a large spoon, lightly mash the eggplant until it is creamy and has absorbed the flavors. Scoop into a serving dish. ■

# HAKKA CLASSIC
# Wine Chicken

酒 雞 Hakka: *jiu gai;* Mandarin: *jiu ji*

In Singapore and Malaysia, when I ask for Hakka recipes, Loh Sye Moy, Amy Wong, and Ho Huey Cheen all suggest wine chicken. This version is my adaptation of their recipes for braised chicken in sweet rice wine and ginger. This stew might be considered a tonic and is most traditionally served to a new mother after childbirth. The wine increases the mother's supply of breast milk; the ginger builds her *chi,* or energy; and dried black fungus improves her blood circulation. Even if you're not a new mother, you will welcome this soupy stew, with its generous portion of warming wine and ginger, on a cold winter's night.

The Hakka use a special wine in this dish that is made by fermenting cooked glutinous rice with wine yeast. As the sweet wine ages, it becomes dark, mellow, and nutty—much like a cream sherry or tawny port, which make fine substitutes. Some of my Hakka tutors made their own wine. However, my attempts rendered inconsistent results. The wine can sometimes be found in Asian markets and may be called Tung Kiang glutinous rice wine. The only brand I found was made by Pearl River. If you cannot find it, use one of the readily available substitutes.

## WINE CHICKEN

Serve this warming stew with hot cooked rice to sop up the gingery wine-infused juices. Some cooks believe that the chicken tastes sweeter when braised in a Chinese clay pot. If you have one, after browning the chicken, transfer the pan contents to the clay pot and continue braising. Serve directly from the clay pot.

*Makes 4 to 6 servings as a main dish or 8 to 10 servings as part of a multicourse meal*

5 pieces dried black fungus, such as cloud ears, each about 1 inch wide (optional)

2 tablespoons vegetable oil

½ teaspoon Asian sesame oil

1  Rinse the black fungus and place in a small bowl. Soak in hot water until the fungus is soft, 15 to 20 minutes. Rinse the fungus well, and squeeze out excess water. Pinch out and discard the hard knobby center of the fungus. Cut the remaining fungus into thin strips. ▸

¾ cup minced fresh ginger (about 4 ounces)

1 chicken (about 4 pounds), rinsed and cut into 3-inch pieces with bone (see note)

2 cups glutinous rice wine, cream sherry, or tawny port

1½ cups water

1 teaspoon sugar

1 teaspoon salt

**2** In a 14-inch wok or 5- to 6-quart pan over medium-high heat, stir the vegetable oil, sesame oil, and ginger until the ginger begins to brown, 4 to 5 minutes. Add the chicken, except the breast pieces, and stir often until the chicken begins to lightly brown, about 8 minutes. (If desired, transfer the contents to a 3- to 5-quart Chinese clay pot.)

**3** Add 1 cup of the wine and the water, sugar, and fungus to the chicken. Bring to a boil over high heat. Reduce the heat, cover, and simmer, stirring occasionally, for 15 minutes. Add the remaining 1 cup wine and the breast pieces. Cover and simmer, stirring occasionally, until the chicken is tender when pierced, about 10 minutes longer. Skim off and discard the fat. Add salt to taste. Spoon the chicken and juices into a serving dish. (If using a Chinese clay pot, serve directly from the pot.)

**Note:** Chinese cooks often chop chicken through the bone into bite-sized pieces so they can handle them with chopsticks. See page 243 for directions for cutting a whole chicken. If you prefer not to chop the chicken this way, you can cut it into larger pieces or substitute 3 to 4 pounds small whole bone-in chicken thighs. You may need to increase the cooking time for the larger chicken pieces by 10 to 15 minutes. ∎

Fresh ginger

# Passing Recipes Down to the Next Generation in Malaysia

Laden with bags of food and pots and pans, Loh Sye Moi arrives at our hotel apartment in Kuala Lumpur with her niece, Loh Kwai Lai, known also as Lee. Loh Sye Moi has come to demonstrate some Hakka dishes. The Hakka are the second-largest Chinese dialect group in Malaysia, where they are known as *Khek.*

Lee is as excited as I am to learn about Hakka food. Although her grandmother and father (Loh's brother) are Hakka, she doesn't know how to cook many Hakka dishes. Her mother is half Cantonese and half Babba (Chinese-Malay) and cooks most of the meals at home.

In just minutes, Loh starts the first dish. She cooks with quiet efficiency and confidence. Today she prepares typical Hakka dishes for us, but I sense that she is an intuitive cook who puts her own signature on every dish she creates. As I try to keep up with her rapid pace, I learn that her great-grandparents came from China, from a province next to Guangdong. Her grandparents were born here and worked in the tin mines in Ipoh. Her mother taught her how to cook Hakka food. Hopefully, the tradition will continue and this seventy-two-year-old mother of five and grandmother of ten will pass on her recipes to future generations. As the aromas of her steamed pork and taro fill the kitchen, they remind me of my own grandmother's cooking.

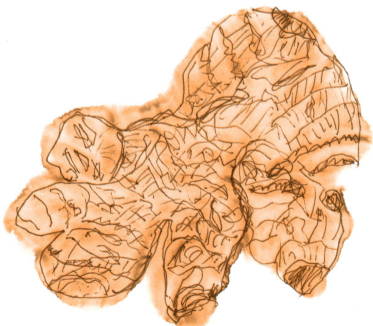

# STEAMED PORK AND TARO

Fermented bean curd enriches potato-like taro and succulent pork with a deep umami flavor akin to Japanese miso. Loh uses both pork belly and pork butt in this steamed dish, but many use only the belly. Russet potatoes make a good substitute for the taro in this dish, if taro is unavailable.

*Makes 4 servings as a main dish or 6 to 8 servings as part of a multicourse meal*

## PORK AND TARO

8 ounces boneless pork belly with skin

8 ounces boneless pork butt, trimmed of fat, or additional boneless pork belly with skin

1 pound large taro or russet potatoes

2 tablespoons vegetable oil

## SAUCE

2 or 3 squares red fermented bean curd (about 2 ounces total)

1 cup water

2 tablespoons minced onion

2 tablespoons oyster sauce

2 tablespoons Chinese rice wine (shaoxing) or dry sherry

1 tablespoon minced garlic

1 teaspoon raw sugar or packed brown sugar

½ teaspoon five-spice powder

2 or 3 large iceberg lettuce leaves, for garnish

1  **FOR THE PORK AND TARO:** Cut the pork belly across the grain into 2-inch-long strips, then lengthwise into ¼-inch-thick slices. Cut the pork butt into ¾-inch cubes. Wearing rubber gloves or under running water, peel the taro and cut into slices ½ inch thick, 2 inches long, and 2 inches wide.

2  Set a 14-inch wok or 10- to 12-inch frying pan over medium-high heat. When the pan is hot, after about 1 minute, add 1 tablespoon of the oil and rotate the pan to spread. Add the pork belly and cook, turning as needed, until browned on all sides, 8 to 10 minutes. With a slotted spatula, remove the slices from the pan. Add the pork cubes to the pan and stir often until browned, about 5 minutes. With a slotted spatula, remove the pork from the pan. Add the remaining 1 tablespoon oil and the taro slices to the pan and cook, turning once, until lightly browned on both sides, 5 to 7 minutes total. With a slotted spatula, remove the taro from the pan. Remove and discard all the fat from the pan.

3  **FOR THE SAUCE:** With a fork, mash enough fermented bean curd to make 2 tablespoons. In a small bowl, whisk together the mashed fermented bean curd, water, onion, oyster sauce, wine, garlic, sugar, and five-spice powder.

4  Return the pork belly and pork cubes to the pan over low heat. Add ¾ cup sauce, cover, and simmer, turning meat once, until the meat absorbs most of the sauce, 10 to 12 minutes.

5 In a wide, heatproof 4- to 5-cup bowl that will fit inside a steamer, arrange the pork belly slices, skin down, and taro, alternating the slices in 2 or 3 rows. Mound the pork cubes around and over the slices. Pour the remaining sauce over the meat.

6 Set the dish on a rack over 2 to 4 inches boiling water in a steamer or wok (if the bottom is round, place on a wok ring to stabilize). If the steamer lid is flat metal, wrap the lid with a towel to reduce condensation dripping on the food. Cover and steam over high heat until the meat and taro are very tender when pierced, 50 to 60 minutes. Watch the water level, adding more boiling water as needed. Carefully remove the dish from the steamer.

7 Let rest about 5 minutes. Tip the dish to one side and spoon off the sauce into a small bowl. Skim off and discard the fat from the sauce. Place the lettuce leaves over the steaming dish so the leaves extend over the sides. Set a rimmed serving platter over the pork-filled dish. Holding both dishes tightly together, quickly invert and carefully lift off the bowl. Serve the sauce alongside. ∎

## VEGETABLE TEA

Loh Sye Moi makes this healthy light soup for special occasions, such as the birth of a son, or during the first ten days of Chinese New Year. She arranges eight different vegetables in a bowl to create a pretty kaleidoscope of greens. Each vegetable contributes a different texture and flavor—from mild to bitter, sweet to pungent. A clear broth is poured over the arrangement, and a spoonful of coarse ground peanuts and sesame seeds tops it off.

Much of the prep can be done a day in advance. Slice the vegetables into thin strips, about ¼ inch wide and 2 to 3 inches long. For most greens, simply slice the leaves crosswise and cut in half if too wide. Include the tender stems, unless the recipe specifies only leaves. To find descriptions of unfamiliar vegetables, check the Hakka Pantry (page 247). If you can't find all the vegetables, let the bounty of your farmers' market guide you in choosing alternatives. Basically, you want an assortment of vegetables that will contribute different flavors and textures. Keep in mind that leafy vegetables shrink greatly, while dense, drier vegetables may not. You should end up with about the same amount of each vegetable. Serve any leftover vegetables in broth for second helpings, or reserve for another use.

*Makes 8 to 10 servings as part of a multicourse meal* ▸

## FISH BROTH (SEE NOTE)

10 cups water, or as needed

2 cups dried anchovies (about
    2 ounces), rinsed

6 ounces Asian white radish, such as
    daikon, peeled and chopped (about
    1 cup)

6 thin slices fresh ginger, lightly
    crushed

1 teaspoon Asian sesame oil

½ teaspoon salt, or to taste

## VEGETABLES

2 medium leeks (1 to 1½ pounds total,
    untrimmed weight)

⅓ cup vegetable oil, or as needed

4 teaspoons minced garlic

6 to 8 ounces spinach leaves, thinly
    sliced (about 5 cups)

Salt

6 to 8 ounces amaranth or red chard
    leaves, thinly sliced (about 5 cups)

4 ounces green cabbage, thinly sliced
    (about 1½ cups)

7 ounces napa cabbage, thinly sliced
    (about 1½ cups)

6 ounces baby bok choy or white-
    stemmed bok choy, thinly sliced
    (about 2 cups)

5 ounces *yao choy* or mustard greens,
    thinly sliced (about 2 cups)

7 ounces Chinese celery or common
    celery, thinly sliced (about 1½ cups)

**1** **FOR THE FISH BROTH:** Up to a day ahead, in a 5- to
6-quart pan over high heat, combine the water, dried
anchovies, radish, and ginger; bring to a boil. Reduce
the heat and simmer, covered, until the broth is well
flavored, about 1 hour. Pour through a fine strainer into
a bowl; discard solids. If needed, add water to make
2 quarts. Shortly before serving, return the broth to a
boil over high heat. Add the sesame oil and salt to taste.

**2** **FOR THE VEGETABLES:** Trim off and discard the root
ends and dark green tops from the leeks. Cut the white
parts in half lengthwise, rinse well between the layers,
and drain. Thinly slice the leeks crosswise to make about
1½ cups.

**3** Up to a day ahead, cook the vegetables. Set a 14-inch
wok or 12-inch nonstick frying pan over medium-high
heat. When the pan is hot, after about 1 minute, add
2 teaspoons of the oil and rotate the pan to spread.
Add ½ teaspoon of the garlic and stir until it softens,
about 30 seconds. Add the spinach and stir-fry until it
wilts slightly, 1 to 2 minutes. Add salt to taste. Mound
the cooked spinach on a large plate or in a small bowl.
Repeat, using the same pan (no need to wash unless
you're using red chard), with the amaranth, green cabbage, napa cabbage, bok choy, *yao choy,* celery, and leeks;
cook in separate batches until the leafy greens wilt or
the denser vegetables are crisp-tender, 1 to 2 minutes,
adding a little water if the vegetables are dense or begin
to burn. Place in separate mounds on the plate or in
individual small bowls. Each vegetable should measure
about 1 cup cooked.

**4** **FOR THE GARNISH:** In a mortar and pestle or food
processor, coarsely grind the peanuts and sesame seeds.

**5** To serve: In eight to ten 1½- to 2-cup bowls, attractively
arrange equal portions of all the cooked vegetables in
separate mounds. If made up to 1 day ahead, cover and
chill. Arrange the bowls on a shallow baking pan and

## GARNISH

¼ cup roasted, salted peanuts

¼ cup toasted sesame seeds

lightly cover. If refrigerated, let the bowls warm to room temperature for at least 2 hours. Shortly before serving, place the pan of covered bowls in a 250°F oven until the vegetables are hot to the touch, about 10 minutes.

Slowly ladle the boiling broth over the vegetables without disturbing the arrangement. Place a spoonful of the peanut-sesame mixture in the center of each bowl and serve.

**Note:** Instead of making the fish broth, you can substitute 2 quarts chicken or vegetable broth. Season the broth with the ginger, sesame oil, and salt to taste. ▪

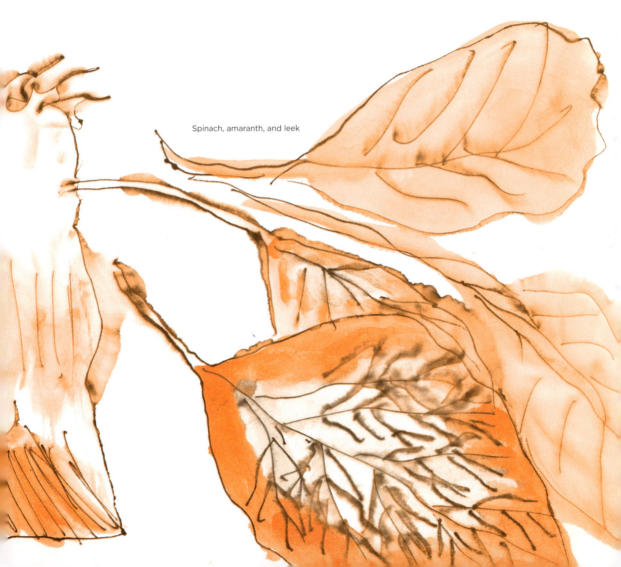

Spinach, amaranth, and leek

# GINGER SOUP WITH SWEET RICE BALLS

In December, Chinese people around the world celebrate the Winter Festival. This festival marks the turning point between winter and spring, when days start to grow longer. It coincides with the winter solstice, which usually falls on December 21 or 22 on the Gregorian calendar. Families worship their ancestors and gods and enjoy a traditional feast. People celebrate by eating rice balls in soup. The round balls symbolize unity and completion. These days, most people use purchased glutinous rice flour to make the chewy rice balls rather than soaking and grinding the rice by hand, as their ancestors did.

The rice balls can be white or colored, plain or filled, sweet or savory. Popo filled her rice balls with chunks of Chinese brown slab sugar so that we would end the cycle with a sweet taste in our mouths. In Malaysia, Loh Sye Moi uses ground peanuts and sesame seeds for her festive filling and serves the dumplings in a sweet soup, redolent with the warmth and fragrance of fresh ginger. I add a Chinese sesame paste to make the filling more cohesive and easier to handle.

If you like, make the filled dumplings ahead of time and store them in the freezer. The soup may also be made up to three days ahead and chilled. Fresh pandan leaf, common in Southeast Asia, adds a toasty aroma, but can be omitted if unavailable.

*Makes 6 to 8 servings as a dessert or snack*

## GINGER SOUP

5 cups water, or as needed

½ cup raw sugar or packed brown sugar

½ cup thinly sliced fresh ginger

1 fresh pandan leaf, about 8 to 12 inches long, rinsed and twisted (optional)

## FILLING

⅓ cup minced roasted, salted peanuts

¼ cup Chinese sesame paste

2 tablespoons raw sugar or packed brown sugar

**1 FOR THE GINGER SOUP:** In a 2- to 3-quart pan over high heat, combine the water, sugar, ginger, and pandan leaf. Bring to a boil, reduce the heat, cover, and simmer until the water is infused with ginger flavor, 15 to 20 minutes. With a slotted spoon, remove and discard the ginger and pandan. If the liquid is too sweet or gingery, dilute with a little water to taste. Cover the ginger soup and set aside.

**2 FOR THE FILLING:** In a small bowl, mix the peanuts, sesame paste, and sugar.

**3 FOR THE DOUGH:** In a medium bowl, stir together the flour and ¾ cup boiling water. Then gradually stir in more boiling water, 1 tablespoon at a time, to form a soft, moist dough. Stir vigorously until smooth. Cover

## DOUGH

2 cups glutinous rice flour (9¼ ounces), or as needed

¾ cup boiling water, plus 1 to 2 additional tablespoons, and more as needed

the bowl and let stand until the dough is cool, 10 to 15 minutes. Transfer the dough to a lightly floured board. With lightly floured hands, knead the dough until smooth and pliable, about 1 minute. If the dough is sticky, knead in a little more rice flour as needed.

4 Roll the dough into a 1-inch-thick rope and cut crosswise into 20 equal pieces. Roll each piece of dough into a ball. Set the pieces slightly apart on the floured board and cover with plastic wrap.

5 To fill: On a lightly floured board, roll or lightly press each ball into a disk about 2½ inches in diameter and ¼ inch thick (if too thin, filling will poke through). Use your fingers to gently flatten the outer edge of each disk. Place 1 teaspoon peanut filling in the center of each disk. Gather opposite edges and bring them together, and then gather remaining edges and bring them together; press to seal. If the edges do not stick, moisten lightly with a little water. Gently roll between flour-dusted palms to make smooth balls. Place slightly apart on a plate dusted with flour. Repeat to fill the remainder. Cover with plastic wrap.

6 In a 4- to 5-quart pan over high heat, bring 2 to 3 quarts water to a boil. Add all of the rice balls, stir once so they don't stick to the pan bottom, and return to a boil. Reduce the heat to medium and cook until the balls float, about 3 minutes, then cook 2 to 3 minutes longer. Lift out the balls with a slotted spoon and place in a bowl of hot water.

7 To serve: Reheat the ginger soup to boiling. For each serving, with a slotted spoon, lift out 2 or 3 rice balls and place into a small bowl. Ladle the hot ginger soup over the rice balls.

Note: To make ahead: In step 1, make the ginger soup up to 3 days ahead, cool, cover, and chill. After step 5, freeze the filled dough until hard. If desired, transfer to a plastic bag and seal airtight. In step 6, cook the frozen rice balls until they float, 6 to 8 minutes, then cook 3 to 5 minutes longer.

## Sweet Rice Brown Sugar Balls

Omit the peanut-sesame filling and replace with twenty ½-inch-square chunks of brown slab sugar. In step 5, instead of flattening the dough into a thin disk, simply push one sugar chunk into the center of each dough piece and roll between your palms to make a smooth ball. When cooking, after the balls float, cook about 5 minutes longer. ■

# A Cantonese Preserves Hakka Tradition in Kuala Lumpur

While in Kuala Lumpur, I hear of a talented female chef at a Hakka restaurant and seek her out. Since 1999, Amy Wong (Wong Choon Mui) has run the Eiffel Restaurant and Dessert House, a restaurant known for its Hakka specialties. With thirty years' cooking experience, she has also taught Asian cooking, written the book *Malaysian Gourmet,* and contributed recipes to *Famous Cuisine,* a Chinese/English food magazine for home cooks. (In 2011, she sold the restaurant, and she no longer writes for *Famous Cuisine.* She continues to teach cooking classes, consult for commercial kitchens, and write recipes for another publisher.)

I meet this energetic woman at her restaurant with members of the *Famous Cuisine* editorial staff. Wong learned to cook from old women in the Hakka village of Perak, long ago. Many of her teachers have since passed away. Luckily, Wong carries on their food traditions even though she is not Hakka—her parents are Cantonese and Malaysian. Other members of the magazine staff have Hakka roots. Kevin Chai, the pastry expert, learned how to cook a few Hakka specialties from his mother, also from Perak. James Wan, the magazine's executive editor, has a Hakka mother and Cantonese father.

At lunch the group, who all love to eat, tell me about Hakka food in Malaysia. Here there are many types of Chinese food—Hokkien, Cantonese, Teochiu, and Hainanese. Hakka food used to be eaten only at home, but now it is available in restaurants. People choose Hakka dishes for their strong flavors and cheap prices. As the food flows out of the Eiffel's kitchen, I savor the robust flavors but don't find the food overly salty or oily. It's just right for my Hakka tastes.

# HAKKA CLASSIC
## Savory Pounded Tea Rice

擂 茶 飯 Hakka: *lui cha fan;* Mandarin; *lei cha fan*

The Hakka specialty pounded tea rice may have acquired its name from the sound made when the herb and nut mixture is ground in a special bowl to make the tea. It is also known as thunder tea. The dish comes from the Ho Po clan, a Hakka subgroup who serve it during Chinese New Year.

I first taste this dish in a little café in Singapore. It promises miracles—to reinvigorate me, lower my cholesterol, boost my immune system, and provide fiber and antioxidants. I order it and receive a small bowl of thick, green, soup-like tea and a larger bowl of rice topped with vegetables, nuts, and tofu. I pour the green tea over the rice and mix it up. The tea is made from a secret combination of green tea leaves, fresh herbs, nuts, and seeds. The tea rice tastes refreshingly healthy.

A few days later, in Kuala Lumpur, I learn the secret from Amy Wong, who graciously shares her recipe for this popular rice dish, which she published in *Famous Cuisine Home Recipes*. I've adapted and simplified it for Western kitchens. Amy shows me the sturdy branch of a guava tree and the big, rough-textured bowl that she uses to crush green tea leaves, peanuts, sesame seeds, and fresh herbs to make the nutritious pounded tea. When the aromatic green tea is mixed with rice and a medley of vegetables, it makes a wholesome and surprisingly delicious meal.

When I serve this dish to my family, both vegetarians and omnivores love it. Each element of the topping contributes a different flavor and texture. The unique tea, made with an abundance of fresh green herbs, dried green tea leaves, nuts, and seeds, is smooth, creamy, and herbaceous. When combined with the garlic-scented rice, the dish satisfies and energizes.

## SAVORY POUNDED TEA RICE

There are three main elements to this healthy rice bowl: the toppings, the garlic rice, and the herbaceous tea. Although traditionally the tea is pounded with a mortar and pestle, an electric blender makes the process easier.

This unique dish uses a variety of different vegetables and fresh herbs (see the Hakka Pantry for descriptions). If you can't find all of them, adjust your ▸

choices to your local market. You can also reduce the variety of vegetables and cook larger amounts of fewer kinds. If the ingredients list looks too daunting, ask a few friends to help cook or bring the vegetable toppings. This dish is well worth trying for a special occasion. Follow the note at the bottom for make-ahead directions.

You can assemble the rice bowls in the kitchen or present the elements as a party buffet and let guests serve themselves.

*Makes 6 to 8 servings as a main dish*

## TOPPINGS

5 ounces salted radish, cut into ½-inch pieces (about 1 cup)

⅓ cup vegetable oil, or as needed

2 tablespoons minced garlic

4 cups sliced garlic chives (about 9 ounces), or 4 cups sliced green onions plus 2 tablespoons minced garlic

Kosher salt, to taste

8 ounces amaranth leaves or spinach leaves, cut into ½-inch pieces (about 3 cups)

8 ounces Chinese broccoli or common broccoli, cut into ½-inch pieces (about 2 cups)

7 ounces cabbage, cut into ½-inch pieces (about 2 cups)

5 ounces green beans, thinly sliced crosswise (about 1 cup)

4 tablespoons dried shrimp, rinsed and chopped (optional)

3 medium leeks (1½ to 2 pounds total, untrimmed weight)

8 ounces plain or five-spice pressed tofu, cut into ½-inch cubes

1 cup roasted, salted peanuts

1 **FOR THE TOPPINGS:** Up to 3 hours before serving, cook the toppings. In a small bowl, soak the salted radish in water for 10 to 20 minutes, draining and changing the water occasionally. Drain the radish and squeeze out excess water.

2 Meanwhile, set a 12-inch nonstick frying pan over medium-high heat. When the pan is hot, after about 1 minute, add 2 teaspoons of the oil and rotate the pan to spread. Add about 1 teaspoon of the garlic and stir until it softens, about 30 seconds. Add the chives and stir-fry until they wilt slightly, 1 to 2 minutes; add a spoonful of water if the vegetables begin to burn. Add salt to taste. Pour the vegetables into a small bowl. Repeat, using the same pan (no need to wash), with the amaranth, broccoli, cabbage, and green beans; cook in separate batches until leafy greens wilt or denser vegetables are crisp-tender, 1 to 2 minutes, adding a little water if the vegetables begin to burn. Place each cooked vegetable in a separate bowl. Each vegetable should measure about 1 cup cooked.

3 Return the unwashed pan to medium-high heat and add 2 teaspoons oil, 2 tablespoons of the dried shrimp, and all the radish. Stir-fry until fragrant, about 1 minute. Place in a small bowl.

4 Trim and discard the root ends and dark green tops of the leeks. Cut the white parts in half lengthwise, rinse well between the layers, and drain. Thinly slice the leeks

## TEA

1 ounce Thai basil or Italian basil
  leaves (about 2 cups)

1 ounce fresh mint leaves (about
  2 cups)

2 teaspoons vegetable oil

1 teaspoon chopped garlic

¼ cup chopped cilantro

2 tablespoons dried green tea leaves

6 black peppercorns

⅔ cup roasted, salted peanuts

3 tablespoons toasted sesame seeds

1 cup cold water

4 cups boiling water

1 teaspoon kosher salt, or to taste

## GARLIC RICE

3 cups jasmine rice

¼ cup vegetable oil

3 tablespoons minced garlic

4 cups water

1 teaspoon kosher salt

crosswise to make about 2 cups. Return the unwashed pan to medium-high heat and add 2 teaspoons oil and the remaining garlic. Stir until the garlic softens, about 30 seconds. Add the leeks, the remaining 2 tablespoons dried shrimp, and tofu; stir-fry until the leeks wilt and the tofu is hot, 2 to 3 minutes. Add salt to taste and place in a small bowl. Pour peanuts into a small bowl.

5 **FOR THE TEA:** Up to 2 hours before serving, coarsely chop the basil and mint. Set a 10- or 12-inch frying pan over medium-high heat. When the pan is hot, after about 1 minute, add the oil and rotate the pan to spread. Add the garlic and stir until it softens, about 30 seconds. Add the basil, mint, and cilantro; stir-fry just until the herbs wilt and turn bright green, about 30 seconds. Remove the herbs from the pan.

6 In a blender, finely grind the tea leaves and pepper-corns. Add the peanuts and sesame seeds; blend until finely ground. Add the basil mixture and cold water, and blend until smooth. Let stand, covered, until shortly before serving.

7 Just before serving, add 1 cup of the boiling water to the herbs in the blender and whirl until smooth, holding the blender lid down with a towel. Pour into a 2-quart pan. Add the remaining 3 cups boiling water and salt; whisk until blended. Cover to keep hot.

8 **FOR THE GARLIC RICE:** About 30 minutes before serving, place the rice in a fine wire strainer; rinse with water, stirring rice occasionally, until the water runs almost clear. Drain well. Set a 3- to 4-quart pan over medium-high heat. When the pan is hot, after about 1 minute, add the oil and garlic, stirring until the garlic softens, about 30 seconds. Add the rice; stir until all the grains are thoroughly coated with oil. Add the water and salt; bring to a boil. Reduce the heat to low. Cover and cook until the rice is tender to the bite, about 20 minutes.

9 To assemble, scoop the hot rice into six to eight large (2½- to 3-cup) bowls and spread the rice to level. Mound equal portions of the toppings over the rice. Reheat the tea, if cool, and pour the hot tea into small bowls to serve with ▶

the rice. Or pour ½ to ¾ cup hot tea over each bowl of rice. To eat, mix the tea and rice together to moisten.

Or, to serve buffet style, arrange the rice, toppings, and tea on the table. Provide large bowls. Guests fill bowls with rice, cover with toppings, and ladle enough hot tea over the rice to moisten.

Note: To make this recipe more manageable, wash and prep the vegetables up to 1 day ahead, wrap each separately in a towel, and place in a plastic bag. Measure out the other ingredients. Up to 3 hours before serving, cook the vegetable toppings and let stand at room temperature. Up to 2 hours ahead, start the tea mixture. Shortly before serving, cook the rice. Just before serving, blend the ground tea mixture with boiling water. ▪

# STIR-FRIED TOFU AND PORK HASH

Amy Wong converts the elements and flavors of complicated stuffed tofu into an everyday stir-fry. She strips away the time-consuming filling process of the classic and simply crumbles tofu and ground pork into a pan, and then stir-fries the ingredients to make a loose savory hash. Serve with rice and stir-fried greens for a satisfying supper.

*Makes 4 servings as a main dish or 6 to 8 servings as part of a multicourse meal*

12 to 16 ounces firm tofu

8 ounces ground pork

1 tablespoon Chinese rice wine (shaoxing) or dry sherry

¼ teaspoon five-spice powder

¼ teaspoon salt

¼ teaspoon ground black pepper

2 tablespoons vegetable oil

1 tablespoon minced garlic

2 tablespoons soy sauce

¼ teaspoon sugar

½ cup thinly sliced green onions, including green tops

1 Rinse the tofu and drain. With your hands, crumble the tofu into ½-inch chunks in a colander; let drain thoroughly, at least 5 minutes.

2 In a small bowl, mix the pork, wine, five-spice powder, salt, and pepper.

3 Set a 14-inch wok or 12-inch frying pan over high heat. When the pan is hot, after about 1 minute, add the oil and rotate the pan to spread. Add the garlic and pork mixture. Stir-fry until the pork is crumbly and begins to brown, 2 to 3 minutes. Add the tofu, soy sauce, and sugar. Stir-fry until the tofu begins to brown, 2 to 3 minutes. Stir in the green onions, and transfer the mixture to a serving dish. ∎

# BRAISED PIG'S FEET IN SWEET VINEGAR

Pig's feet, also known as trotters, turn dark and glossy when braised in sweetened black vinegar and ginger. This lush transformation of a humble cut of pork is commonly served to new mothers to replenish their bodies after childbirth. But its fans extend far beyond new mothers. It's pure comfort to suck the tangy-sweet meat off the bones of these soft and velvety braised feet. Amy Wong's version uses palm sugar, common in her home in Malaysia, but brown sugar works as well.

Slowly braise the pork in a Chinese clay pot or other nonreactive pan for a pure, natural flavor. Make it a day ahead for deeper flavor, and then reheat to serve. ▸

*Makes 5 to 6 servings as a main dish or 8 to 9 servings as part of a multicourse meal*

2 tablespoons vegetable oil

1 or 2 pig's feet (3 to 4 pounds total), sawed crosswise into 1- to 1½-inch-wide sections (see notes)

2 tablespoons Asian sesame oil

2 cups thinly sliced fresh ginger (about 12 ounces), lightly crushed

3 cups water

1 bottle (20 ounces, or 2¾ cups) sweetened black vinegar

1 cup black vinegar

½ cup chopped packed palm sugar or packed brown sugar

1 teaspoon salt, or to taste

**1** Set a nonreactive 14-inch wok or 5- to 6-quart pan over medium-high heat. When the pan is hot, after about 1 minute, add the vegetable oil and rotate the pan to spread. Add a single layer of pig's feet and cook, turning occasionally, until lightly browned on all sides, 10 to 12 minutes; you may need to brown the meat in 2 batches. Remove the pork from the pan and set aside. Remove and discard the fat from the pan.

**2** Reduce the heat to medium and add the sesame oil and ginger to the pan. Stir to loosen the browned bits and cook until the ginger begins to brown, 1 to 2 minutes. Transfer the pork and ginger to a 3½- to 5-quart clay pot or return to the pan. Add the water, sweetened black vinegar, black vinegar, and sugar. Cover and bring to a boil over high heat. Reduce the heat, cover, and simmer, turning meat over halfway if it sits above the liquid, until the skin is very tender when pierced and the meat almost falls from the bone, 2 to 2¼ hours. Skim off and discard the fat. Add the salt. Serve from the clay pot or transfer to a serving dish.

**Notes:** You can buy pig's feet in most Chinese markets. Sometimes they are labeled "front" or "back." Front feet tend to be meatier; back feet are more flavorful. Ask the butcher to saw the feet across the bone into 1- to 1½-inch sections.

Since the pork cooks in vinegar for a long time, it's best not to use a new carbon steel wok. A nonstick or stainless steel wok or other pan will work fine.

If made ahead, cool, cover, and chill up to 3 days. Lift off and remove the solidified fat from the pan juices. Reheat, covered, over medium heat. ■

# HAKKA CLASSIC
# Taro Abacus Beads

芋頭算盤子 Hakka: *wu tiuh sun pan jue;* Mandarin: *yu tou suan pan zi*

The curious name of these chewy pasta rounds, taro abacus beads, comes from their shape, which resembles the pierced disks on a Chinese abacus, a sort of ancient, low-tech adding machine. Hakkas often make this special dish for Chinese New Year to bring wealth and good luck in business. Taro, commonly called yam in Asia, is a starchy tuber that is used much like a potato.

Singapore cooking expert Violet Oon, who is part Hakka, describes taro abacus beads as "Hakka gnocchi." Both mix a starchy tuber with flour; in the Hakka version, potato is replaced with taro and wheat flour with tapioca starch. The result has a nuttier flavor from the taro and a chewier texture from the tapioca starch.

## TARO ABACUS BEADS

Small disks of taro abacus resemble a springy, sticky version of Italian gnocchi. Asians like the chewy texture, but others may find it too gummy for their tastes. The tapioca starch produces a texture similar to Japanese mochi. The soft disks of fresh pasta readily absorb the seasonings and sauces they cook with.

You can make and boil the fresh pasta disks up to two days ahead, and then cover and refrigerate them. They will be a bit firmer and chewier than fresh-cooked pasta.

*Makes 6 to 7 dozen taro abacus beads, enough for 3 to 4 servings as a main dish or 6 to 8 servings as part of a multicourse meal*

1 teaspoon salt

1 pound small or large taro (see note)

1¼ cups tapioca starch or flour (5¾ ounces), or as needed

1 tablespoon vegetable oil

1 In a 6- to 8-quart pan, bring about 2 quarts water and the salt to a boil over high heat. Meanwhile, wearing rubber gloves or under running water, peel and rinse the taro. Cut the taro into ½-inch chunks to make 3 to 3½ cups. Add the taro to the boiling water and return to a boil. Reduce the heat and simmer, partially covered, until the taro is soft when pressed, 8 to 15 minutes. Set aside about ½ cup of the cooking water, and then drain the taro. ▸

**2** Pour the taro into a medium bowl or return to the pan. With an electric mixer on medium to high speed, beat the hot taro until smooth. Gradually add the tapioca starch and beat on low speed until the mixture is blended and forms a soft dough. If the mixture doesn't hold together, beat in just enough of the reserved hot water to form a soft dough. Beat on medium to high speed until the dough is smooth, supple, and not sticky to the touch. If the dough is too heavy for the mixer, scrape the dough with a spatula or dough scraper onto a board lightly dusted with tapioca starch. With starch-dusted hands, knead the dough until smooth, supple, and not sticky. If the dough is still sticky, knead in more tapioca starch as needed.

**3** On a board lightly dusted with tapioca starch, divide the dough into 4 equal portions. Keep the dough covered with plastic wrap to keep moist while working with each portion. Roll out 1 portion of the dough into a ¾-inch-thick rope. Cut the rope crosswise into ½-inch-wide pieces. Roll the pieces into ¾-inch balls. Gently press the end of a chopstick into the center of each ball on both sides to make a slight indentation. Place the taro abacus beads, as formed, in a single layer, slightly apart, on starch-dusted baking sheets or plates, and cover with plastic wrap to prevent drying. Repeat until all are formed.

**4** In a 6- to 8-quart pan over high heat, bring 3 to 4 quarts water to a boil. Fill a large bowl or pan with about 3 quarts water and the oil. Add the taro abacus beads to the boiling water and stir to separate; simmer until the abacus beads are cooked through, 2 to 3 minutes; they will be sticky. Drain in a colander and immediately immerse in the water with oil, separating the pieces. If using within a few minutes, leave in the water and drain just before using. If allowed to stand together out of the water, they will stick.

If preparing up to 2 days ahead, when the abacus beads are cool, drain them well in a colander, and then pour onto oiled plates or pans and spread the pieces slightly apart in a single layer. Cover and chill. When ready to use, immerse the abacus beads in a bowl of very hot water and let stand about 5 minutes. Drain just before stir-frying.

**Note:** I've had consistent results with both small and large varieties of taro with a dark, shaggy exterior. With other larger, drier varieties, you may need to add extra hot water to make a moist, supple dough. ∎

# STIR-FRIED TARO ABACUS BEADS AND VEGETABLES

I love the intriguing contrast of textures and flavors in this stir-fried pasta dish: chewy taro abacus beads, crisp carrot shreds, bits of salty radish, dried shrimp, and meaty mushrooms. Eat this vegetarian main-dish pasta with a light simple soup and a platter of stir-fried greens. To simplify last-minute cooking, shape and boil the taro abacus beads a day or two ahead. This recipe is adapted from *Malaysian Gourmet*.

*Makes 3 servings as a main dish or 6 to 8 servings as part of a multicourse meal*

## SAUCE

1 tablespoon oyster sauce

4 teaspoons soy sauce

2 teaspoons sugar

1 teaspoon Asian sesame oil

½ teaspoon five-spice powder

½ teaspoon salt

½ teaspoon ground black pepper

## STIR-FRY

6 dried or fresh shiitake mushrooms, each about 2 to 3 inches wide

3 tablespoons chopped salted radish

2 tablespoons dried shrimp (optional)

3 ounces pressed tofu

2 medium carrots (about 4 ounces total)

8 sprigs flat-leaf parsley or cilantro

2 green onions, including green tops, ends trimmed

Taro abacus beads (page 125)

3 tablespoons vegetable oil

2 tablespoons chopped shallots

2 teaspoons minced garlic

**1 FOR THE SAUCE:** In a small bowl, mix the oyster sauce, soy sauce, sugar, sesame oil, five-spice powder, salt, and pepper.

**2 FOR THE STIR-FRY:** Rinse the mushrooms. If using dried mushrooms, place in a small bowl and cover with hot water. Soak until soft, 20 minutes for thin caps to 2 hours for thick caps. Drain and squeeze excess water out of the soaked mushrooms. Remove and discard the stems from the dried or fresh mushrooms. Cut the caps into thin strips. Rinse the salted radish. In a small bowl, soak the radish in water 5 to 15 minutes. Drain and squeeze the water out of the radish. Rinse the shrimp. In a small bowl, soak the shrimp in water until softened, 5 to 15 minutes. Drain and squeeze excess water out of the shrimp, and then chop the shrimp.

**3** Cut the tofu into matchsticks, ¼ inch thick and 2 to 3 inches long, to make about ¾ cup. Slice the carrots diagonally into ¼-inch-thick ovals, stack a few slices, and cut lengthwise into ¼-inch-wide slivers, to make about 1 cup. Cut the parsley and green onions, including the green tops, into 3-inch lengths. Cut the thick white portions of the green onions in half lengthwise.

**4** Boil the taro abacus beads or place made-ahead cooked abacus beads in very hot water as directed in step 4 on page 126. ▸

5 Set a well-seasoned or nonstick 14-inch wok or 12-inch nonstick frying pan over medium-high heat. When the pan is hot, after about 1 minute, add the oil and rotate the pan to spread. Add the tofu and stir occasionally until golden, 2 to 3 minutes. With a slotted spoon, lift out the tofu and drain on a plate lined with paper towels.

6 Set the pan on high heat. Add the carrots, shallots, and garlic, and stir-fry until the shallots turn limp, about 1 minute. Add the mushrooms, salted radish, dried shrimp, and fried tofu strips, and stir-fry until the mushrooms are lightly browned, 1 to 2 minutes. Drain the abacus beads and add to the pan along with the sauce mixture. Cook and turn the abacus beads over gently until lightly browned on both sides, 1 to 2 minutes. Stir in the parsley and green onions. Spoon the abacus beads onto plates or a serving dish. ■

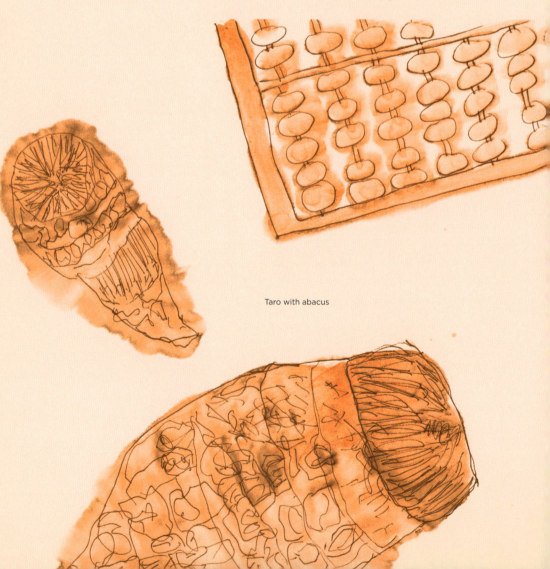

Taro with abacus

# TARO ABACUS BEADS WITH MUSHROOM PORK SAUCE

A glossy brown sauce freckled with bits of ground pork, mushrooms, and green onions cloaks chewy taro abacus beads. We ate this fresh pasta dish as a part of a multicourse Chinese meal at Doreen Ho's home in Singapore. It can also be served as a satisfying main dish with a side of stir-fried greens.

*Makes 4 servings as a main dish or 8 servings as part of a multicourse meal*

## SAUCE

1½ cups chicken broth, homemade (page 267) or purchased

2 tablespoons soy sauce

1 tablespoon dark soy sauce

4 teaspoons cornstarch

1½ teaspoons sugar

¼ teaspoon salt

## STIR-FRY

16 fresh or dried shiitake mushrooms, each about 2 to 3 inches wide

6 green onions, including green tops, ends trimmed

Taro abacus beads (page 125)

2 tablespoons vegetable oil

1 tablespoon minced garlic

8 ounces ground pork

**1** **FOR THE SAUCE:** In a small bowl, mix the broth, soy sauce, dark soy sauce, cornstarch, sugar, and salt.

**2** **FOR THE STIR-FRY:** Rinse the mushrooms. If using dried mushrooms, place in a small bowl and cover with hot water. Soak until soft, 20 minutes for thin caps to 2 hours for thick caps. Drain and squeeze excess water out of the soaked mushrooms. Remove and discard the stems from the dried or fresh mushrooms. Cut the mushroom caps into ¼-inch-wide strips. Cut the green onions, including green tops, into 3-inch lengths, and then cut lengthwise into ¼-inch-thick slivers.

**3** Boil the taro abacus beads or place made-ahead cooked abacus beads in very hot water as directed in step 4 on page 126.

**4** Set a well-seasoned or nonstick 14-inch wok or 12-inch nonstick frying pan over high heat. When the pan is hot, after about 1 minute, add the oil and rotate the pan to spread. Add the garlic and pork; stir-fry until the pork is browned and crumbly, about 2 minutes. Stir in the mushrooms and stir-fry until lightly browned, 1 to 2 minutes.

**5** Drain the taro abacus beads. Add the abacus beads and green onions to the pan. Cook and turn the abacus beads gently until lightly browned on both sides, 1 to 2 minutes. Stir the sauce mixture and add it to the pan. Stir gently until the sauce thickens and boils, about 1 minute. Spoon the abacus beads onto plates or a serving dish. ■

# Mauritius: A Melting Pot

On our bus ride from Meizhou to Hong Kong, we share the vehicle with a large group of Hakkas from Mauritius. They are on their way home from the Twentieth World Hakka Conference in Luodai. A very outgoing woman, Patricia, tells us about her country.

Mauritius, an independent island state, lies in the Indian Ocean off the southeastern shores of the African state of Mozambique. The Dutch first colonized the island in 1638, followed by the French in 1715 and the British in 1810. In 1860, the first Hakka immigrants entered Mauritius. Soon, many more followed, especially after the colonial government eased immigration restrictions in 1877. Patricia's father came from China to work on the island in 1926. Originally he thought it was a temporary move, but as her family grew and prospered, he stayed on. Although the thirty to forty thousand Chinese make up only about 3 percent of the population, the Hakka constitute about 90 percent of the Chinese population. "The Hakka have a very close-knit community there," Patricia says.

When I ask about Hakka food in Mauritius, Patricia introduces me to her friend Mee Lan Wong. Mee Lan's father came to Mauritius in 1930 to work for a shop. Eventually he started his own business and married a Chinese woman born in Mauritius. Mee Lan, a gentle-mannered woman, explains, "Mauritius is a multiethnic island, which allows us to get Chinese, Indian, Muslim, European, and local food. On top of that, we can eat American, Spanish, Italian, and Japanese cuisine in restaurants. Since many of us have roots in Meixian, the Chinese food in Mauritius is similar. Many of the cooking methods are the same, but the ingredients may be different." Mee Lan's statement sums up the Hakka food trail. On this isolated island, Hakka food, like the people, survive, adapting to their new environment.

## CHICKEN FRIED RICE WITH FRESH TOMATO CHUTNEY

Mee Lan makes basic fried rice. However, in multiethnic Mauritius, she serves the rice with an Indian fresh tomato chutney. Add the tart-hot chutney to spice the rice to your taste.

The secret to fried rice is to use leftover cold cooked rice. When you collect enough rice, try this infinitely versatile basic recipe. Vary the meats and vegetables based on what you have on hand.

*Makes 2 to 3 servings as a main dish or 4 to 6 servings as part of a multicourse meal*

## TOMATO CHUTNEY

1 cup chopped firm ripe tomatoes

¼ cup chopped onion, rinsed and drained

2 tablespoons chopped fresh mint or cilantro

2 tablespoons white wine vinegar

2 teaspoons minced fresh ginger

2 to 4 teaspoons minced jalapeño chiles

¼ teaspoon salt, or to taste

## FRIED RICE

4 cups cold cooked long-grain rice

3 tablespoons vegetable oil

2 large eggs, lightly beaten

1 cup chopped shallots or red onion

1 cup thinly sliced green beans, snow peas, or sugar snap peas

½ cup finely chopped carrots

1 tablespoon minced garlic

8 ounces boneless, skinless chicken breasts or thighs, cut into ½-inch chunks (about 1 cup)

2 tablespoons soy sauce

½ teaspoon salt, or to taste

¼ teaspoon ground black pepper

2 to 3 tablespoons thinly sliced green onions, including green tops, for garnish

**1 FOR THE TOMATO CHUTNEY:** In a small bowl, mix the tomatoes, onion, mint, vinegar, ginger, chiles, and salt.

**2 FOR THE FRIED RICE:** With your hands, break up the rice so that the grains are loose and separate.

**3** Set a 14-inch wok over high heat. When the pan is hot, after about 1 minute, add 2 tablespoons of the oil and rotate the pan to spread. Add the eggs and rotate the pan again to spread. As they set, lift up the sides so the raw egg flows underneath. When the eggs are almost completely set, after about 1 minute, transfer with a slotted spatula to a plate, leaving the oil in the pan.

**4** Add the shallots, beans, carrots, and garlic to the pan; stir-fry until the shallots are limp, 1 to 2 minutes. Add the chicken and stir-fry until it is lightly browned, 2 to 3 minutes.

**5** Reduce the heat to medium-high. Add the remaining 1 tablespoon oil to the pan. Add the rice and stir-fry until it is hot, 2 to 3 minutes. Stir in the soy sauce, salt, and pepper. Add the fried eggs, and with the spatula, break the eggs into small pieces and stir into the rice. Scoop the rice into bowls or plates and sprinkle with green onions. Offer the tomato chutney to add to taste. ∎

Cilantro

# STEAMED PORK AND VEGETABLE BALLS

When Mee Lan first describes these meatballs, I'm skeptical as to whether the recipe will work. She cooks all the elements separately, including the pork, and then mixes them together with cornstarch and steams. Doubtful that the components will hold together, I follow her directions. Success! The cornstarch literally glues the ingredients together. Mushrooms, dried shrimp, rice noodles, and fish sauce lace the steamed pork meatballs with flavor and lighten the texture. I prefer her version to the heavy, dense meatballs I ate in China.

Mee Lan uses the local island vegetable chayote or the traditional long Asian white radish. Chayote (also known as vegetable pear, *mirliton, chocho,* or *chouchou*) is a pale-green, pear-shaped gourd that can be found in Asian and Latino markets. In North America I've seen it only with smooth skin; however, it may also have prickly (though not sharp) spines. The texture of the smooth white flesh is like a cross between zucchini and cucumber, and the flavor is mild and neutral. The seed is soft and edible.

*Makes 3 to 4 servings as a main dish or 6 to 8 servings as part of a multicourse meal*

5 dried or fresh shiitake mushrooms, each about 2 inches wide

1 tablespoon dried shrimp, or ¼ teaspoon salt

12 ounces chayote or Asian white radish, such as daikon

2 ounces dried thin rice noodles

3 tablespoons vegetable oil

8 ounces ground pork

1½ tablespoons fish sauce, or 2 tablespoons soy sauce

½ cup cornstarch (2¼ ounces)

Soy sauce, to taste

Chile sauce, homemade (page 268) or purchased

1 Rinse the mushrooms and shrimp (use salt later). Place the dried mushrooms and shrimp in separate small bowls and cover with hot water. Soak the mushrooms until soft, 20 minutes for thin caps to 2 hours for thick caps. Soak the shrimp until soft, about 10 minutes. Squeeze the water out of the soaked mushrooms. Cut off and discard the tough stems from the dried or fresh mushrooms. Squeeze the water out of the shrimp. Finely chop the mushrooms and shrimp.

2 Peel the chayote. Using a food processor or the large smooth holes of a box grater, coarsely shred the chayote, including the soft edible seed. Squeeze the excess liquid out of the raw chayote. (If using radish, in a 10- to 12-inch frying pan over high heat, bring 3 to 4 cups water to a boil. Stir in the radish and return to a boil, then drain. Rinse the pan and dry. When the radish is cool, after about 10 minutes, press and squeeze the liquid out.)

**3** Inside a large bag to contain the noodles, use scissors to cut the noodles into 1-inch lengths to make about ½ cup.

**4** Set a 10- to 12-inch frying pan over medium-high heat. When the pan is hot, after about 1 minute, add 2 tablespoons of the oil and rotate the pan to spread. Add the noodles, stirring and turning until they are golden and slightly puffy, 1 to 2 minutes. With a slotted spoon, transfer the noodles to a medium bowl. Return the pan to medium-high heat and add the mushrooms and shrimp; stir-fry until they begin to brown, about 1 minute. Add the mushrooms and shrimp to the noodles. Return the pan to medium-high heat and add the remaining 1 tablespoon oil. Add the pork and stir-fry until the meat is crumbly and has lost its pinkness, about 2 minutes. Remove from the heat. Add the mushroom-noodle mixture, 1 cup of the raw chayote or blanched radish, ¼ teaspoon salt (if not using dried shrimp), and fish sauce. Stir the mixture until blended. Let stand until cool, 5 to 10 minutes.

**5** Add the cornstarch to the pork mixture and stir until well blended. Scoop out ⅓-cup portions of the mixture and, with your hands, squeeze firmly to form balls. Place the balls slightly apart on an oiled heatproof plate that will fit inside a steamer.

**6** Set the dish on a rack over 2 to 4 inches boiling water in a steamer or wok (if the bottom is round, place on a wok ring to stabilize). If the steamer lid is flat metal, wrap the lid with a towel to reduce condensation dripping on the food. Cover and steam over high heat until the meatballs hold together and no sign of powdery cornstarch remains in the center (cut to test), about 15 minutes. Watch the water level, adding more boiling water as needed. Carefully remove the dish from the steamer. Serve the pork and vegetable balls with soy sauce and chile sauce mixed together to add to taste. ∎

Sweet rice balls

# FOUR

# Across the Pacific
# Peru, Hawaii, and Tahiti

During the latter half of the nineteenth century, Hakkas crossed the Pacific to Peru, Hawaii, and Tahiti. They came as contract or indentured workers. In Peru and Hawaii, the need for laborers at sugar plantations brought the first wave of immigrants. Most came from the Pearl River Delta.

In Tahiti, the first Hakkas arrived in 1865 to work for a cotton plantation. When the plantation went bankrupt, some workers stayed on to develop businesses while many others returned to China. The unrest in China brought a new wave of Hakka immigrants in 1907. Women were included and a family society took root, establishing a sizeable Hakka community on this Pacific island.

I meet descendants of these early Hakka in Peru and Hawaii. In both these regions, signs of the Chinese legacy linger in the facial features of the people. Some have assimilated, but even those who are no longer 100 percent Chinese boast of Hakka relatives in their family trees. Although they adapt to the ingredients of their new home, some hold tight to their culture by maintaining the foods and flavors of their ancestral culinary kitchens.

A chance interview with a Honolulu resident raised in Tahiti gives me a glimpse into her life growing up in her French Polynesian home, where she ate Hakka village food. Now she adapts to her adopted home in Hawaii.

# Hakka Lunch in Lima

A lively Hakka woman, Liliana Com, leads me on a whirlwind tour of Lima's Chinatown, the largest in South America. She tells me that the Chinese make up 10 percent of the city's population. Many Hakkas used to live here, but now the largest Chinese community is Cantonese. At first glance, this neighborhood looks like any other Chinatown. Restaurants, gift shops, temples, and markets line the streets. Cabbages the size of bowling balls, long beans, bok choy, and silvery bean sprouts are mounded high on store shelves. Roast ducks the color of polished mahogany and glistening red barbecued pork hang in restaurant windows. Steamed pork buns, sweet dumplings, and cakes tempt from their glass cases. Yet a Latin vibe pulsates through this Chinatown: Spanish phrases are interspersed with Chinese, signs are written in Spanish, and hungry Peruvians rove the streets, searching for a good Chinese meal.

We stop for a midmorning snack of noodles with plump pork and chive dumplings at a branch of Wa Lok, the restaurant at which Liliana works as a hostess. There, we meet her Hakka friends, who also work in Chinatown. With their busy lives, the friends confess that they rarely cook. Liliana doesn't need to cook. Her mother, Natalie Com Liu, a former restaurant owner and chef, often prepares lunch for the family. Today, I'm invited.

When we arrive, Liliana's seventy-six-year-old mother is cooking in the kitchen. Liliana has brought some small whole fish from Chinatown. Her mother quickly browns the fish and braises it. She drains off the juices from steamed stuffed tofu to make a sauce. A pot of watercress soup bubbles on the range; she tells me it is a tonic to help clear the throat. She rapidly stir-fries blanched greens with golden lumps of fried tofu and assembles fried chicken and ham rolls. A few minutes later, we sit down to a home-cooked lunch of Hakka and Cantonese dishes.

Natalie was born in Peru in 1934 but returned to China when she was two. She lived in Guangdong Province with her family, who farmed and sold produce in the city. When she was twenty, she married Com Tack On, then forty, and they returned to Peru. In the 1950s, she worked for her husband's import firm. There, she learned to cook Cantonese dishes and mastered banquet dishes from one of her husband's business partners. In 1975, Natalie shocked the community when she became one of the first Chinese women in Lima to open her own restaurant, Chifa Siu Lan. She wooed doubters with her charm and fine cooking and ran the business successfully for four years, and then sold it. Now she cooks her Hakka and Cantonese dishes mostly for family and friends. I'm glad to be included.

# BRAISED FISH IN BLACK BEAN SAUCE

Liliana Com takes me to a small Chinese market where she selects small whole fish called *pejasapo*. Their scrunched-up faces make them look somewhat like frogs. "Peruvians don't appreciate these ugly fish, but the Chinese love their smooth flesh," says Liliana.

Adapt this recipe to your local fish. If you can't find whole fish, substitute boneless fish fillets.

*Makes 2 to 3 servings as a main dish or 4 to 6 servings as part of a multicourse meal*

## SAUCE

1 tablespoon grated fresh ginger (see notes)

¾ cup water

2 tablespoons Chinese rice wine (shaoxing) or dry sherry

1 tablespoon black bean sauce, or 1 tablespoon fermented black beans, rinsed and minced, plus 1 teaspoon soy sauce

1 teaspoon soy sauce

½ teaspoon sugar

1 teaspoon cornstarch

## FISH

2 small whole fish (12 to 16 ounces each), such as tilapia or white bass, cleaned and scaled (see notes)

Salt and freshly ground black pepper

⅓ cup all-purpose flour, or as needed

3 tablespoons vegetable oil

3 tablespoons thinly sliced green onions, including green tops

2 tablespoons thinly slivered fresh ginger

1 tablespoon minced garlic

**1 FOR THE SAUCE:** Over a small bowl, squeeze the grated ginger with your hands to extract the juice; discard the pulp. Add the water, wine, black bean sauce, soy sauce, sugar, and cornstarch to the ginger juice. Mix and set aside.

**2 FOR THE FISH:** Rinse the fish and pat dry. Lightly sprinkle salt and pepper over the inside and outside of the fish. Lightly coat the fish in flour; shake off excess.

**3** Set a 12-inch nonstick frying pan over medium-high heat. When the pan is hot, after about 1 minute, add the oil and rotate the pan to spread. Lay the fish in a single layer in the pan. Cover and cook until browned, 3 to 4 minutes. With a wide spatula, carefully turn the fish over. Scatter half the green onions and all the ginger and garlic around the fish. Cook just until the fish is browned, 2 to 3 minutes. Stir the sauce mixture and add to the pan. Cover and simmer over low heat just until the fish is barely opaque in the center of the thickest part (cut to test), 3 to 5 minutes.

**4** With a slotted spatula, transfer the fish to a serving platter. Stir the sauce in the pan until blended and pour over the fish. Sprinkle the fish with the remaining green onions.

**Notes:** To grate the ginger, use a microplane or the rough round holes on a box grater. If you grate over a plate, it is easier to collect the juices. ▶

Small whole fish are readily available at Asian makets. Choose fish that will fit in your pan. Chinese cooks prefer to leave the head and tail on; remove if desired. If you can't find whole fish, substitute 1 pound white-fleshed fish fillets (1 inch thick), use a 10-inch frying pan, and reduce the oil to 2 tablespoons. ■

## STEAMED EGGS AND PICKLED GINGER

This dish is comfort food for Liliana Com. Eggs steam atop of a bed of thinly sliced ginger bathed in sugar and vinegar. The sweet-sour ginger cuts through the richness of the soft egg yolk.

*Makes 2 servings as a main dish or 4 servings as part of a multicourse meal*

2 tablespoons sugar

2 tablespoons rice vinegar

10 to 12 very thin slices fresh ginger (see notes)

4 large eggs

⅛ teaspoon salt, or to taste

1 tablespoon thinly sliced green onions, including green tops, for garnish

1 In a 6- to 7-inch shallow rimmed dish that will fit inside a steamer, mix the sugar and vinegar. Lay the ginger slices evenly over the bottom of the dish. Crack the eggs and gently place over the ginger, taking care not to break the yolks. Sprinkle the salt lightly over the eggs.

2 Set the dish on a rack over 2 to 4 inches boiling water in a steamer or wok (if the bottom is round, place on a wok ring to stabilize). If the steamer lid is flat metal, wrap the lid with a towel to reduce condensation dripping on the food. Cover and steam over medium-high heat until the eggs are set to desired doneness, 4 to 5 minutes for soft yolks. Watch the water level, adding more boiling water as needed. Carefully remove the dish from the steamer. Sprinkle with the green onions.

Notes: Peel the ginger and slice crosswise as thinly as possible.

If you use a wider dish, increase the recipe as needed so the eggs cover the bottom of the dish completely. ■

Asian white radish

# STEAMED RADISH CAKE

This Hakka version of a savory steamed radish cake, also known as turnip cake or pudding, is packed with shreds of Asian white radish such as daikon or *lo bok*. Natalie Com Liu studs the thick rice-flour batter with bits of sweet Chinese sausage, five-spice–scented Chinese bacon, and tiny dried shrimp. When steamed, the mixture firms into a dense pudding-like cake that the Chinese enjoy. Serve the savory slabs steamed or pan-fried as a dim sum dish or appetizer.

*Makes about 12 servings as an appetizer*

¼ cup dried shrimp

1½ to 2 pounds Asian white radish, such as daikon

2¼ cups water, or as needed

1 teaspoon salt

1 strip Chinese bacon (about 4 ounces)

1 Chinese sausage (about 2 ounces)

2 cups rice flour (9¼ ounces)

½ teaspoon five-spice powder

¼ teaspoon ground white pepper

¼ cup thinly sliced green onions, including green tops

Soy sauce, to taste

Chile sauce, homemade (page 268) or purchased, to taste

**1** Place the shrimp in a small bowl and soak in warm water until soft, 10 to 20 minutes. Drain and squeeze out excess liquid.

**2** Peel the radish and trim the ends. With a food processor or the large smooth holes of a box grater, coarsely shred the radish to make about 4 cups. In a 5- to 6-quart pan over high heat, combine the radish shreds, 1¼ cups of the water, and ¼ teaspoon of the salt. Bring to a boil. Reduce the heat, cover, and simmer, stirring occasionally, until the radish shreds are very tender, 15 to 20 minutes. Pour the radish shreds into a colander set over a large bowl to collect the juices. Let the radish shreds cool, stirring occasionally, 10 to 15 minutes. Press firmly to remove excess liquid. Measure the liquid and add water, if necessary, to make 1 cup. Rinse and dry the pan.

**3** Meanwhile, dice the bacon and sausage into ¼-inch cubes; you should have about 1 cup bacon cubes and ¼ cup sausage cubes. In the same 5- to 6-quart pan over medium heat, stir the sausage until lightly browned, 1 to 2 minutes. Add the drained shrimp and stir until lightly browned, about 30 seconds. With a slotted spoon, lift out the sausage and shrimp and place in a small bowl. Add the bacon and remaining 1 cup water to the pan (no need to wash) and bring to a boil over high heat. Reduce the heat, cover, and simmer until the bacon is tender when pierced, 20 to 25 minutes. If liquid remains, cook, uncovered, over medium-high heat until it evaporates. Stir often until the bacon is lightly browned, about 1 minute. With a slotted spoon, lift out the bacon and add it to the sausage. ▸

4. In a medium bowl, mix the flour, five-spice powder, remaining ¾ teaspoon salt, and white pepper. Gradually stir in the radish water to make a smooth, thick batter. Stir in the radish shreds, sausage, shrimp, and bacon. Scrape the mixture into an oiled 9-inch cake pan that will fit inside a steamer and spread to level.

5. Set the pan on a rack over 2 to 4 inches boiling water in a steamer or wok (if the bottom is round, place on a wok ring to stabilize). If the steamer lid is flat metal, wrap the lid with a towel to reduce condensation dripping on the food. Cover and steam over high heat for 10 minutes. Sprinkle the cake evenly with the green onions and continue steaming until a toothpick inserted in the center comes out clean, or the center of the cake is firm to the touch, 5 to 10 minutes longer. Watch the water level, adding more boiling water as needed. Carefully remove the pan from the steamer.

6. Let the cake cool about 5 minutes. Run a knife around the edges of the pan, and then cut the cake into about 12 diamonds or rectangles. With a spatula, lift out pieces of the cake and place on a platter. Serve hot with soy sauce and chile sauce to add to taste.

Note: The cake pieces may also be pan-fried. Let cool at least 15 minutes or cover and chill up to 3 days. To pan-fry, set a nonstick frying pan over medium heat. When the pan is hot, after about 1 minute, add 1 to 2 tablespoons vegetable oil and rotate the pan to spread. Place pieces of the radish cake slightly apart in the pan and cook, turning once, until lightly browned on both sides, 4 to 6 minutes total. Repeat to cook the remainder, adding more oil as needed. ∎

## Chinese Change the Peruvian Diet

That evening we dine at another branch of Wa Lok in the upscale Milaflores District. Liliana has invited friends who can tell me more about the Chinese in Peru. Apparently, many Peruvians have Chinese connections.

Professor Jorge Salazar has a Chinese grandmother and is an expert on the history of the Chinese in Peru. He suggests that Chinese servants of a Spaniard delegation may have introduced Chinese food to Peru as early as the sixteenth century. Their greatest contribution came in the quarter century that followed 1849, when over one hundred thousand Chinese migrants, mostly from Canton (now Guangdong) replaced black workers after Peru abolished slave labor. The Chinese migrants worked as contract laborers in sugar plantations, on the Andean railroad, and in guano mines. Some moved into domestic service. Although they worked under exploitative contracts, the Chinese laborers demanded rice, essential to their diet, as part of their payment. This forced landowners to grow and import rice, a new food for this South American country.

"Westerners viewed these people from the East with fear. They all looked the same to them. Peruvians saw no difference between Hakkas and Cantonese," says Jorge. After surviving their contracts, the Chinese gained their freedom and set up their own trades and business. Some started restaurants. In 1921, the first Chinese restaurant, Kuong Tong, opened on Capon Street in the center of Lima's Chinese neighborhood. The restaurant stayed in business for over fifty years. Other restaurants opened nearby, and Peruvians embraced Chinese cuisine. Now there are Chinese restaurants all over Lima.

Other guests at the table—including Alfredo Valiente, who also has a Chinese grandmother; Joseph Cruz, a Chinese expert and teacher; and Joseph's Chinese girlfriend, a recent immigrant from Fukien—cite other Chinese contributions to Peruvian cuisine. The Chinese introduced the wok. Peruvians borrow the stir-fry technique in popular dishes like *steak à la chorrillana* (stir-fried beef strips with tomato, onion, garlic, and pepper) and *lomo saltado* (stir-fried beef strips with french fries, tomatoes, and onions). The Chinese adopted local fish that the Peruvians didn't know how to eat. They grew their Chinese vegetables here year round.

Peruvians love Chinese food. *Chifa,* which sounds somewhat like the words for "eat rice" in Mandarin, is the name for a place that serves Chinese food. *Chifas* can be found all over the city, packed with Peruvians. Most serve cheap, colorful fast food. Jorge says, "Fifty years ago, Chinese food here was closer to the original. Now, there is greater Peruvian influence. The majority of the food is sweet-sour pork, fried rice, and fried noodles." Liliana says some of the Chinese food in Peru tastes sweeter, and cooks often use Peruvian peppers, red onion, and tamarind.

Tonight's dinner shows that the purer, more traditional cuisine still exists. Wa Lok identifies itself as an "Oriental" restaurant to distinguish itself from the less expensive *chifas*. Its food mirrors a fine Chinese banquet that you might eat at a high-class Cantonese restaurant in San Francisco or Vancouver, Canada. As I bite into the fresh langoustines steamed with garlic, silky shreds of white-cut chicken, and fried baby pigeon with tangy lime sauce, I can taste the fresh, subtle sophistication of Cantonese cuisine.

We end the meal with Liliana's own version of fortune cookies. When the restaurant first opened, she couldn't find cookies with fortunes written in Spanish.

Her parents always talked in aphorisms. So she wrote her own Spanish fortunes based on her parents' phrases, wrapped them in plastic, encased them in sweet dough so they resembled toothpicks, and baked them. Her favorite phrase is: "The one who is always right can die of hunger."

The evening ends with a musical fusion of cultures as Joseph plays panpipes called *sampoño,* Alfredo plays an African drum known as *bombo,* and they sing, with Joseph's girlfriend, a Chinese song about the poet Li Po talking about the moon. This performance reflects the new Peruvian style that Jorge has described to us; as he says, it is "open to everyone, and everyone mixes."

The next day I meet Alfredo for a tour of Chinatown. We start at Calle Capón, the main street of Chinatown. At many small cafés, signs advertise something called *rachi con yuca.* We order one to eat. A large bowl of white Chinese rice soup arrives. The consistency looks like loose oatmeal. The rice grains are plump and recognizable, but the ends are just beginning to split open. A mound of crunchy bean sprouts, strips of tripe, big Peruvian corn kernels, slivers of green onion and ginger, and a sprinkle of white pepper sit on top. "Where's the yuca?" I ask. Alfredo points to the fried doughnut that is served alongside. It looks much like the typical fried doughnut that accompanies Chinese congee, but it is short and stubby, rather than long and slender. The Peruvians call it *yuca* because it resembles the popular fried starchy, potato-like tuber. When the Chinese invented this dish in the 1940s, the Peruvians fell in love with it. It shows how the Chinese have adapted their food to Peruvian tastes.

Later I meet Joseph for lunch. Although Joseph looks Spanish, his soul is Chinese. He teaches Chinese language, writing, and traditions and knows more about Asian culture and history than I do. He explains that the Hakka influence was strong in Lima, especially in martial arts. The Hakka brought kung fu here. Tomas Kam, a banished monk from China, came to Peru in the 1950s and introduced the lion dance to Lima. The Hakka societies have performed it at the carnival to celebrate Chinese New Year since 1956.

We eat dishes that remind me of my childhood: anise-flavored beef stew, steamed chicken and sweet sausage, and stir-fried greens. Our chef today is Hakka, but Joseph says that as the Hakka have grown successful, many have left Lima and moved north along the coast. The new Chinese immigrants come from Fukien.

# STEAMED CHICKEN AND CHINESE SAUSAGE

Hakka chef Andy Wong, known as "A-Man," runs Chun Koc Sen, a restaurant in Lima's Chinatown that is popular with both Peruvians and Chinese. This home-style dish doesn't stray far from A-Man's roots in China. It reminds me of a dish my grandmother used to cook in California. Sliced chicken, sweet cured Chinese sausage, dark meaty mushrooms, and crunchy black fungus steam together with pungent ginger, soy sauce, and wine. As all these elements cook together in a bath of steam, their natural juices merge in delicious harmony. Simple and comforting, its appeal spans the globe.

*Makes 3 to 4 servings as a main dish or 6 to 8 servings as part of a multicourse meal*

5 dried shiitake mushrooms, each about 1½ inches wide

5 dried black fungus, such as cloud ears, each about 1 inch wide, or 2 additional dried shiitake mushrooms

2 cups hot water

1 green onion, including green tops, ends trimmed

12 ounces boneless, skinless chicken thighs or breasts

1 Chinese sausage (about 2 ounces)

2 tablespoons soy sauce

2 tablespoons Chinese rice wine (shaoxing) or dry sherry

1 tablespoon cornstarch

1 teaspoon vegetable oil

½ teaspoon sugar

2 tablespoons thinly slivered fresh ginger

1 Rinse the mushrooms and fungus. Place both in a medium bowl and cover with the hot water. Soak until soft, 20 minutes for thin caps to 2 hours for thick caps. Lift out the mushrooms and fungus, rinse well, and squeeze out excess water. Reserve the soaking water. Remove and discard the tough stems from the mushrooms. Pinch out and discard the hard knobby centers from the fungus. Cut the mushrooms and fungus into 1-inch pieces. Cut the green onion, including green tops, into 2-inch lengths, and then cut lengthwise into ¼-inch slivers.

2 Meanwhile, trim off and discard the excess fat from the chicken. Cut the chicken across the grain into strips about ½ inch thick, 2 inches long, and ¾ inch wide. Cut the sausage diagonally into ¼-inch-thick slices. In a 9-inch shallow heatproof dish that will fit inside a steamer, such as a Pyrex pie pan, mix ¼ cup of the reserved mushroom-soaking water, soy sauce, wine, cornstarch, oil, and sugar. Add the chicken, sausage, mushrooms, fungus, and ginger; mix to coat. Spread the mixture to level.

3 Set the dish on a rack over 2 to 4 inches boiling water in a steamer or wok (if the bottom is round, place on a wok ring to stabilize). If the steamer lid is flat metal, wrap the lid with a towel to reduce condensation dripping on the food. Cover and steam over high heat ▸

until the chicken is no longer pink in the center (cut to test), 20 to 25 minutes. Watch the water level, adding more boiling water as needed. Carefully remove the dish from the steamer. Sprinkle with green onions and serve. ■

# A Hakka Matriarch in Hawaii

In the melting pot culture of Hawaii, it hasn't taken long for the Hakka to assimilate. You can see it in Kelley Oshiro's face—a melding of Swedish, English, and Asian features. You might not even know she has Chinese roots until she talks about her Hakka grandmother, Yun Tsin.

"Yun Tsin was the matriarch in the family," says Kelley in Honolulu. "She was such a strong woman. Everyone gathered around her." She was such a force, in fact, that she served as the inspiration for the character of Wu Chow's Auntie, Nyuk Tsin, in James A. Michener's best seller *Hawaii*.

"Food was always around," Kelley continues. "Yun Tsin always made great Chinese food. Her husband was Cantonese, but she cooked mostly Hakka dishes that she learned from her family. Everything was made from scratch. She made wontons filled with pork hash and water chestnuts, fried crisp and served with soy and mustard."

As Kelley tells me about her grandmother, her cousin Paul Yuen cooks *jai* (*zhai*, in Mandarin). He learned to cook this Buddhist vegetarian dish, which is traditionally eaten as part of the first meal of the Chinese New Year, from his paternal grandmother. While the *jai* gently simmers, Paul brings out the family history book. He tells me about Yun Tsin's father, Chong How Kong, who sailed from eastern Guangdong Province to Hawaii to work in the sugar plantations, and about his great-grandfather Yap See Young, who became a ward of the Anglican bishop and helped lay the foundation for many of the historical Chinese Episcopal churches in Hawaii.

Paul, a fourth-generation Hawaiian Hakka who is now an attorney but once taught ethnic studies, theorizes on the Hakka journey: "Chinese is Chinese. We don't make a distinction between groups. We are all Pakes [a Hawaiian term used to refer to all Chinese]. If we had been rich, we wouldn't have left China; only the homeless poor left. Now we're pretty much acculturated here in Hawaii. In our society you take part in the dominant culture. We're here doing what we do because our ancestors took a risk."

# HAKKA CLASSIC
# Salted and Pickled Mustard Greens

鹹菜 Salted greens—Hakka: *hahm choi;* Mandarin: *xian cai*

酸菜 Pickled greens—Hakka: *soen choi;* Mandarin: *suan cai*

Hakka women gained a reputation as master pickle makers. They would immerse vegetables in a brine or sauce or pack them dry in salt. Doreen Yuen from Hawaii writes that her maternal grandmother, En Fah Kong Yap, rubbed Hawaiian salt into mustard cabbage and then hung the heads of cabbage on a clothesline until dry. The pickles could be easily transported and kept for months. For the practical and thrifty Hakka family, pickles and preserved vegetables were like rainy-day savings. In the Hakkas' remote mountain homes, food could be scarce and difficult to come by. With preserved food in their pantry, they always had something to eat and food to serve to guests. A bowl of rice with a few pickles could fill a farmer's stomach in the field. Preserved vegetables cooked with fresh foods could deepen and boost the flavor.

One indispensable Hakka pickle is salted mustard greens. Pickled mustard greens are similar but have a sweet-sour tang. Both contribute a salty pungency or piquant lift to stir-fried dishes, stews, and soups. They can also be served as a condiment to add to rice, soup, or noodles.

Salted and pickled mustard greens are easy to make. Today, most modern cooks rely on the refrigerator to store pickles for more control and to use less salt. Start with large, fresh heart-shaped heads of jade-colored mustard greens (also called mustard cabbage or *dai gai choy*) and use the thick, wide stems to make the pickles. Most Asian markets sell mustard greens with the leaves trimmed off.

# SALTED MUSTARD GREENS

Many Hakka dishes call for this common preserved vegetable. Although it's readily available in Asian markets, it's easy to make if you can find fresh broad-stemmed mustard greens. Although the pickle is customarily made from mustard green stems, Natalie Com Liu from Peru includes some of the leaves as well. Her homemade salted mustard greens maintain more crunch and texture than purchased greens and are less salty.

*Makes 3 to 4 cups*

¾ to 1¼ pounds broad-stemmed Chinese mustard greens (see note)

4 cups water

2 tablespoons sea salt or table salt

1 Pull apart the mustard greens and separate the stems. Cut the stems and thicker part of the leaves into 1-inch pieces to make 4 to 5 cups. Wash and drain the greens. Place the greens into a 3-quart heatproof nonreactive bowl (preferably made of ceramic or glass).

2 In a 2- to 3-quart pan over high heat, bring the water and salt to a boil. Stir until the salt dissolves. Pour over the greens. Let stand until the water is cool, about 20 minutes. Cover and let stand at room temperature for 2 to 3 days.

3 If desired, transfer the greens and their liquid to smaller nonreactive containers. Cover and chill. The salted mustard greens are best used within 2 to 3 weeks but will keep up to 2 to 3 months.

**Note:** If most of the leaves are not trimmed off, buy the larger quantity. Extra leaves can be used in soups. ■

Mustard greens

# PICKLED MUSTARD GREENS

When I tried Margaret Lai's easy no-cook recipe for pickled mustard greens, I realized they taste almost like my father's—crunchy, sweet, and tart, with an underlying mustard pungency. Margaret says that years of eating Japanese pickled cucumbers and sweeter versions of pickled mustard greens at Chinese restaurants gave her a preference for a stronger sweet-and-sour punch. I like to serve a bowl of these crunchy pickles for a cool starter or as a cleansing condiment with a meal. They add a refreshing contrast to fried or rich appetizers. Or eat them like a pickle with sausages. They can be used in recipes calling for pickled mustard greens; however, this homemade version possesses more tang and crunch than most purchased versions.

*Makes 3 to 4 cups*

¾ to 1¼ pounds broad-leaf Chinese mustard greens

⅔ cup rice vinegar or distilled white vinegar

⅔ cup sugar

½ teaspoon sea salt or table salt

1 Pull apart the mustard greens and separate the stems. Cut the stems and thicker part of the leaves into 1-inch pieces to make 4 to 5 cups. Wash and drain the greens.

2 In a 3- to 4-quart pan over high heat, bring about 1½ quarts water to a boil. Add the mustard greens to the boiling water. Stir to separate. Drain and rinse with cold water to cool.

3 In a large bowl, mix the vinegar, sugar, and salt until the sugar dissolves. Stir in the mustard greens. Cover the bowl and let stand at room temperature overnight or about 12 hours. Transfer the mixture to a smaller container. Cover and chill in the refrigerator until the pickles are yellowish-green and sweet and tangy, 2 to 3 days. Store in the refrigerator up to 2 to 3 months.

**Pickled Cucumbers**

Substitute 8 ounces Persian or Japanese cucumbers for the mustard greens. Slice the cucumbers ¼ inch thick to make about 2 cups. Do not cook. Add the cucumbers to the vinegar mixture. Cover and let stand 8 to 12 hours at room temperature, and then refrigerate overnight. Store in the refrigerator up to 1 to 2 weeks. ∎

# STEAMED PORK HASH

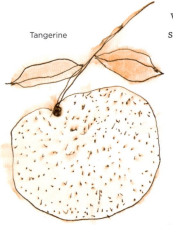

Tangerine

This moist steamed pork dish is pure comfort food. It's like a Chinese version of meatloaf and just as satisfying. Many Hakkas refer to this savory ground pork mixture as hash or pork cake. This version contains aromatic dried tangerine peel and Tianjin (Tientsin) preserved vegetable. The dry, chewy shreds of fermented vegetable add a savory, garlicky saltiness. Water chestnuts add crunch. Look for fresh water chestnuts in Asian markets. They resemble flower bulbs with dark brown skin. Peel off the skin to reveal the sweet crisp flesh. If unavailable, use canned water chestnuts. Some cooks might add a salted duck egg or salted fish. Because the hash is steamed in a thin layer, it cooks in about twenty minutes. Kelley's grandmother Yun Tsin also used this mixture to fill wontons.

*Makes 3 to 4 servings as a main dish or 6 to 8 servings as part of a multi-course meal*

1 piece dried tangerine peel, about 1 inch wide, or ¼ teaspoon grated fresh orange peel

2 tablespoons Tianjin (Tientsin) preserved vegetable, or 1 tablespoon soy sauce

12 ounces ground pork

1 large egg

½ cup finely chopped peeled fresh or canned water chestnuts

⅓ cup minced green onions, including green tops

1 teaspoon cornstarch

½ teaspoon salt

¼ teaspoon ground black pepper

3 tablespoons thinly sliced green onions, including green tops, for garnish

1  If using dried tangerine peel, rinse and soak in hot water until soft, about 20 minutes. Squeeze out excess water and finely chop the peel to make about ½ teaspoon. Rinse the preserved vegetable, squeeze dry, and finely chop.

2  In a medium bowl, mix the ground pork, egg, water chestnuts, minced green onions, tangerine peel, preserved vegetable, cornstarch, salt, and pepper until well blended. Lightly pat the mixture into an even layer in an 8- to 9-inch shallow heatproof dish that will fit in a steamer, such as a Pyrex pie pan.

3  Set the dish on a rack over 2 to 4 inches boiling water in a steamer or wok (if the bottom is round, place on a wok ring to stabilize). If the steamer lid is flat metal, wrap the lid with a towel to reduce condensation dripping on the food. Cover and steam over high heat until the meat is no longer pink in the center (cut to test), about 20 minutes. Watch the water level, adding more boiling water as needed. Carefully remove the dish from the steamer. Sprinkle with the sliced green onions and serve. ∎

# FRIED PORK HASH WONTONS

Yun Tsin used the raw pork hash as a filling for crisp fried wontons. Fill, fry, and even freeze the wontons in advance. To serve, crisp them in the oven. You can also use them in Fried Wontons with Vegetable Egg Flower Sauce (page 189).

*Makes 5 to 6 dozen wontons*

Steamed Pork Hash (page 148), uncooked

1 teaspoon water

5 to 6 dozen wonton skins (12 to 16 ounces)

Vegetable oil, for frying

Soy sauce, for serving

Chile sauce, homemade (page 268) or purchased, or hot mustard

1 For the filling, make Steamed Pork Hash (page 148) as directed, except lightly beat the egg first and reserve 1 teaspoon. In a small bowl, mix the 1 teaspoon egg with the water to use to seal the wontons. Mix the remaining egg into the pork hash.

2 To fill the wontons: Place a wonton skin on a flat surface with a corner facing you. Cover the remaining skins with a lightly damp towel or plastic wrap to keep moist. Mound 1 level teaspoon of the pork filling in the center of the wonton skin. Fold the bottom half of the skin over the filling to make a triangle. Moisten one side corner of the base of the triangle with the egg-water mixture. Pull the side corners down below the filling and overlap; press to seal. They should resemble tortellini with a triangular flap. Place the filled wontons in a single layer slightly apart on baking sheets dusted with flour. Cover with plastic wrap while filling the remaining skins.

3 To fry the wontons: Set a 14-inch wok (if the bottom is round, place on a wok ring to stabilize) or a 5- to 6-quart pan over medium-high heat. Fill the pan with oil to a depth of about 1½ inches. Heat the oil until the temperature reaches 350°F on a thermometer. Adjust the heat to maintain the temperature. Add 6 to 8 wontons and fry, turning occasionally, until the outsides are golden and the filling is no longer pink in the center (cut to test), 1½ to 2 minutes. With a slotted spoon or wire strainer, lift out the wontons and drain in a single layer on pans lined with paper towels. Repeat to fry the remainder. Serve at once or keep warm in a 200°F oven up to 30 minutes. Serve with soy sauce to mix with chile sauce or hot mustard.

Note: If made ahead, after the wontons are fried and drained, let cool and pack in a rigid container. Chill up to 1 day or freeze up to 1 month. To reheat, arrange the wontons in a single layer, slightly apart, on shallow baking pans. Bake the wontons in a preheated 350°F oven until crisp and hot, 10 to 12 minutes. ▪

# STEAMED SAVORY EGG CUSTARD

While in college, Kelley Oshiro would make her grandmother's steamed egg custard plain with just water. I enrich it with broth and bits of meat or seafood to make a plush savory custard. Another common addition would be thousand-year-old eggs. My Popo embedded chunks of the preserved eggs in the tender custard. The eggs aren't really as old as their name suggests. Duck eggs are coated with ash, lime, salt, and tea leaves and go through a hundred-day preservation process that firms their texture and changes the egg white to a translucent blackish brown and the yolk to grayish green. With their slight fermented flavor and startling appearance, they are an acquired taste. This recipe is adapted from *Everyone, Eat Slowly: The Chong Family Food Book*.

*Makes 2 servings as a main dish or 4 servings as part of a multicourse meal*

4 large eggs

1¼ cups chicken broth, homemade (page 267) or purchased

¼ teaspoon salt

1 teaspoon vegetable oil or Asian sesame oil

½ cup chopped cooked ham, Chinese barbecued pork, or peeled cooked whole tiny shrimp

2 tablespoons thinly sliced green onions, including green tops, for garnish

1  In a medium bowl, beat the eggs. Add the broth, salt, and oil; beat until well blended.

2  Pour the egg mixture into an 8- to 9-inch shallow heatproof dish that will fit inside a steamer, such as a Pyrex pie plate. Or use four ¾- to 1-cup bowls. Distribute the ham evenly in the dish and cover tightly with foil. Set the dish on a rack over 2 to 4 inches boiling water in a steamer or wok (if the bottom is round, place on a wok ring to stabilize). Cover and steam over medium-high heat until the center of the custard feels set when gently touched or barely jiggles when gently shaken, about 10 minutes for the large dish or 7 to 9 minutes for smaller bowls. Watch the water level, adding more boiling water as needed. Carefully remove the dish from the steamer. Garnish with green onions. ■

# From Tahiti to Hawaii

Margaret Lai came to Hawaii via Tahiti, but her roots stretch to Longgang, a small village near Shenzhen, China. In the early 1900s, a number of Chinese migrants from Longgang were working in French Indochina (now Vietnam). They were sent to Tahiti, along with the Vietnamese, as laborers. These early workers sent word to their fellow villagers and encouraged them to come to Tahiti. Lai's father arrived around 1910 to work in a store. Later, he brought his wife and child to Tahiti. They had ten children; Margaret was the youngest.

Says Margaret: "When I was growing up in Tahiti, Hakka was the language for the Chinese except for a few Punti (Cantonese) families. We were part of a close-knit Chinese community. Multiple generations lived together in a big house. We socialized with mostly Chinese friends. In school, we had Tahitian friends and a few French classmates." Most stores were run by Chinese shopkeepers, and Hakka was the language of business. Now big companies from France and its former colonies have opened stores in Tahiti, and the language of commerce is primarily French.

Margaret continues: "We ate mostly Chinese food growing up. At home, we ate village food. Steamed or fried fish, white-cooked chicken, pork, and stir-fries. On weekends, we ate tofu, bitter melon, and eggplant stuffed with a mixture of fish cake, ground pork, and saltfish. Tahiti has really good saltfish." Once a year, on Chinese Memorial Day, the entire Lai family would gather together for a feast of special dishes cooked by the men, such as pork braised in soy sauce with dried oysters, garlic, shallots, crunchy wood fungus, and arrowhead.

In 1948, after Margaret finished middle school, her parents sent her to study in Hong Kong, where she learned English. After high school, she went to America to continue her education and pursue a career in medicine. "I was tired of dorm food," she says. "I hungered for home-cooked food. When my parents came to visit while I was doing my internship in San Francisco, I watched my mother cook. I learned from her and started to improvise. I enjoy cooking. I like my own cooking."

Margaret married William Won, also an American-trained Hakka medical doctor, in New York. When they both completed all their medical training, they returned to Honolulu, where William was raised. They frequently entertained, showcasing Margaret's inventive cooking. Now Margaret cooks mostly uncomplicated dishes for her son's family.

# TANGY-SWEET RAW FISH SALAD

In Tahiti, the Chinese encountered *poisson cru,* raw fish marinated in coconut milk and lime juice. The Hakka created their own raw fish preparation, a mouthwatering salad bursting with crisp texture and vibrant tastes. Margaret Lai arranges slices of raw fish on a platform of crunchy slivers of fresh and pickled vegetables. Zesty fresh ginger and tart lemon juice, tempered with a bit of sugar and oil, dress the salad.

In Hawaii, Margaret initially used a local white fish known as jack to make this raw fish salad. Now she buys readily available sashimi-grade tuna. Shop at a Japanese market or seafood market that sells fresh tuna for sashimi. You can also buy the sweet pickled shallots and pickled ginger at the Japanese store. Look for the sweet preserved cucumber at a Chinese supermarket.

*Makes 2 servings as a main dish or 4 to 6 servings as an appetizer or part of a multi-course meal*

## DRESSING

¼ cup fresh lemon juice

4 teaspoons sugar

1 tablespoon Asian sesame oil

1 tablespoon minced fresh ginger

2 teaspoons honey mustard or Dijon mustard

¾ teaspoon salt or 1½ teaspoons soy sauce, or to taste

## SALAD

1 cup thinly slivered red bell pepper

½ cup thinly slivered carrots

½ cup thinly slivered Asian white radish, such as daikon

½ cup thinly slivered sweet pickled shallots

¼ cup thinly slivered preserved white cucumber in syrup (see note)

1 **FOR THE DRESSING:** In a small bowl, whisk together the lemon juice, sugar, sesame oil, ginger, mustard, and salt.

2 **FOR THE SALAD:** In a large bowl, mix half of the dressing with the red pepper, carrots, radish, shallots, cucumber, and pickled ginger. Mix lightly to blend. Arrange the lettuce in an even layer on a serving platter or individual plates, and mound the vegetable mixture over the bed of lettuce. Slice the fish about ¼ inch thick across the grain, and arrange the fish slices on top. Drizzle the remaining dressing over the fish. Sprinkle with peanuts, if desired.

Note: Margaret Lai uses small whole cucumbers packed in syrup from Hong Kong. They are sweet and crunchy and can be found in Asian markets. If you can't find them, omit them and use more pickled shallots. ∎

¼ cup thinly slivered pickled ginger

2 to 3 cups shredded iceberg lettuce

6 to 8 ounces very fresh sashimi-grade
tuna

¼ cup chopped salted, roasted peanuts,
for garnish

Red bell pepper

# STEAMED SALMON WITH SWEETENED PRESERVED LEMON

The Hakka often preserve citrus in salt to use as a seasoning, in sauces, or mixed with hot water and honey to make a soothing elixir for sore throats. Long ago, Margaret Lai's husband used to make salted lemons. Now her supply of home-made salted lemons comes from friends or the local Chinese market. She minces and mashes the lemons with garlic and sugar to make a paste that captures the key elements of Chinese flavor: sweet, sour, salty, and bitter. She spreads the paste over the fish and steams it. In Tahiti, mullet is commonly used, but she finds that salmon works well. I like to squeeze a wedge of lemon or lime over the moist fish to brighten the citrus presence.

*Makes 2 servings as a main dish or 4 servings as part of a multicourse meal*

1½ tablespoons seeded minced preserved lemon or lime, including peel (see note)

1½ tablespoons sugar, or to taste

1 tablespoon minced garlic

1 pound salmon fillet

2 tablespoons thinly sliced green onions, including green tops

Fresh lemon or lime wedges (optional)

Salt

**1** In a small bowl, mash and mix the lemon, sugar, and garlic.

**2** Rinse the salmon and pat dry. Set the salmon, skin side down, in an 8- to 9-inch shallow heatproof dish that will fit inside a steamer, such as a Pyrex pie pan. Spread the lemon mixture evenly over the fish.

**3** Set the dish on a rack over 2 to 4 inches boiling water in a steamer or wok (if the bottom is round, place on a wok ring to stabilize). If the steamer lid is flat metal, wrap the lid with a towel to reduce condensation dripping on the food. Cover and steam over high heat until the salmon is barely opaque in the center of the thickest part (cut to test), about 10 minutes per inch of thickness. Watch the water level, adding more boiling water as needed. Carefully remove the dish from the steamer. Sprinkle with the green onions and serve. If desired, offer lemon wedges to squeeze over the salmon and add salt to taste.

**Note:** To make salted lemons: Wash and dry small lemons or *calamansi* (also known as *calamondin* or Philippine lime). Layer the lemons with coarse salt in a large clean, dry glass jar. Close the jar and store at room temperature until the lemons turn brown and soft, 1 to 2 months. Liquid will gradually appear as the salts draws out the juice. If you can't wait, buy preserved or pickled lemons or limes from Asian markets. ∎

# BRAISED DUCK WITH PLUM SAUCE

Margaret Lai cooks her signature dish for her son and his family once a year. She fills the cavity of a duck with homemade plum sauce and steams it until tender. The sauce, made from purchased pickled plums, permeates the duck as it steams. After steaming, she empties the sauce into the pan juices and boils the mixture down to make a fruity sweet and sour sauce that complements the rich, moist duck. If you like roast duck, try the variation that follows.

*Makes 3 to 4 servings as a main dish or 6 to 8 servings as part of a multicourse meal*

1 Pekin duckling (4 to 5 pounds), thawed if frozen (see note)

2 tablespoons dark soy sauce

12 Chinese pickled plums, pitted

¾ cup sugar, or to taste

2 tablespoons minced garlic

2 tablespoons fresh lime juice, or to taste

1 teaspoon cornstarch

1 tablespoon water

Cilantro sprigs, for garnish

**1** Preheat the broiler. If the head, neck, and feet are present on the duck, remove them, leaving a few inches of neck skin attached. If the neck and giblets are in the body cavity, remove and reserve for another use. Remove and discard the lumps of fat near the entrance of the body cavity. Rinse the bird inside and out; pat dry. With a fork, prick skin all over the duck. Rub the dark soy sauce all over the surface of the duck. Place the duck in a 12-by-15-inch broiler pan lined with foil and broil 4 to 5 inches from the heat until well browned, 6 to 9 minutes. Turn the duck over and brush with any remaining soy sauce and broil until browned, 6 to 9 minutes.

**2** In a bowl, mash the plums with a potato masher or fork. Add the sugar, garlic, and lime juice. Tuck the neck skin under the body to cover the cavity; weave a toothpick through the skin to secure. Place the browned duck, breast side up, in a large, heavy, nonreactive pan just wide and deep enough to hold it, such as a 14-inch wok (if the bottom is round, place on a wok ring to stabilize) or 6- to 8-quart pan. Lift the rear of the duck up slightly and pour the plum sauce into the cavity, then set the duck down. Add water to the pan to a depth of about 1 inch (3 to 4 cups) and bring to a boil. Reduce the heat, cover, and simmer until the duck is tender when pierced, about 1½ hours.

**3** With tongs or a large spoon inserted into the body cavity, lift the duck out, draining the plum sauce out of the duck cavity into the pan, and set the duck on a platter. Scrape any remaining plum sauce from the duck cavity and add to the pan juices. Let the duck rest on a platter for 5 to 10 minutes. ▸

**4** Meanwhile, skim off and discard the fat from the pan juices. Boil the pan juices over high heat, uncovered, until slightly thickened and reduced to about 1½ cups. Chop the duck into pieces for serving (see page 243) and arrange on a platter. Taste the reduced pan juices and add more sugar or lime juice to taste, if needed. In a small bowl, mix the cornstarch with the water and add to the reduced pan juices. Stir over high heat until the sauce boils and thickens, about 30 seconds. Pour a little sauce over the duck and serve the remainder in a bowl to add to taste. Garnish the duck with cilantro.

**Note:** In Asian markets, ducks are often sold frozen and sometimes labeled young duckling (also called roaster, broiler, or fryer duckling). Lai uses a tender young duckling with head and feet removed. Pekin duck, also known as Long Island duck, is the most common type sold. If frozen, thaw the duck in the refrigerator for 1 to 2 days.

### Roast Duck with Plum Sauce

Remove any fat from the broiler pan. After braising, return the duck to the broiler pan, breast side up. Brush the duck all over with a few tablespoons of the reduced plum sauce. Roast in preheated 400°F oven until browned and glazed, 15 to 20 minutes. Serve the duck with the remaining plum sauce. ∎

# FIVE

# Multiple Migrations
# Toronto and New York

I knew I couldn't visit every Hakka enclave in the world. As I wrestled with the choice of my next destination, a fortuitous meeting with a Canadian filmmaker, Cheuk Kwan, sent me to Toronto. There, I met more than a dozen Hakkas. They weren't from just one country but, rather, they represented the worldwide Hakka migration in one place. Some had started in China, migrated once, and then moved again, settling in Canada. Others were descendants of Hakka nomads who had settled elsewhere. This was a new wave of migration, largely created when former British colonies gained independence in the twentieth century. Most Hakkas in this new Canadian wave are now professionals and businesspeople living in the metropolitan area around Toronto.

A few of the newcomers are chefs from India, who merge Chinese techniques and Indian spices to create a fusion cuisine popular with their restaurant customers. They remind me of another Hakka family from India in the restaurant business near New York City, whom I met early in my journey, just as I was formulating my book proposal. A friend brought me to their restaurant. There I tasted Hakka-Indian cuisine for the first time and loved it. That memorable meal showed me the global scope my book could take. This family, like the chefs in Toronto, left India when life became difficult for the Chinese and have successfully adapted to their new home. These transplants all share a common appreciation for their Hakka roots and culinary traditions.

# The Hakka Melting Pot in Toronto

As the economic and political climate turned against the Hakkas in their former homes, many sought a better life in Canada. Ironically, until the 1950s and even the 1960s, Canada discriminated against and rejected the Chinese through restrictive immigration practices and denied opportunities. Now Canada welcomes the Chinese as strong players in the country's economic growth. In 2001, Canada counted over one million Chinese residents, the largest non-European ethnic group. In 1999, about 10 percent of the Chinese were Hakkas. 72 percent of Canadians of Chinese origin were born outside of the country. Of these, more than 77 percent arrived since 1981. Chinese is Canada's third most spoken language, after English and French. Canada has become the new land of opportunity for the Hakka.

Keith Lowe, former director of the Chinese Cultural Centre of Greater Toronto, explains the increase in numbers. Beginning in the 1950s, many former British colonies and territories, including those now known as South Africa, Jamaica, Malaysia, Mauritius, Hong Kong, and India, gained independence. Nationalism flourished in these countries, and new people came into power. Political and economic turmoil forced minorities out. Many of the Chinese residents of these countries fled to Canada, once also part of the British Empire, and settled in the Toronto area, a business center.

I meet this new generation of Hakka nomads when I visit Toronto in 2006. My self-appointed guides, Peter and Gladys Lee-Shanok, set out to introduce me to the Hakka community, which is concentrated in the suburbs north of Toronto. As one of the organizers of the Toronto Hakka Conference in 2000 and past president of the Mauritius Chinese Association of Ontario, Peter has many contacts, and his easy charm brings people together effortlessly.

Both Peter and Gladys were born in Mauritius and grew up in large families, each with twelve children. Their fathers came from Meixian, China, and both were shopkeepers in Mauritius, a common occupation for Hakkas on the island. In 1968, Peter moved to Canada to work for a Canadian bank and attend McGill University in Montreal. There, he met his wife, Gladys. In 1982, when Peter was recruited by an international bank, the couple moved to Toronto with their young family.

My first night in Toronto, Peter and Gladys introduce me to a melting pot of the local Hakka community. We meet at Royal Chinese Seafood Restaurant in Scarborough, a northern suburb of Toronto noted for its concentration of Chinese restaurants and markets. Owner Margarita Wong Liu greets us. Liu's grandparents originally came from Meixian, and her parents were born in India.

In 1992, she and her husband, Danny, migrated to Canada to seek a better life for their children. Tonight, her husband prepares a typical Hakka feast.

Gathered around the table are about a dozen Hakkas from all over the world. As we eat our way through the menu, I feel like I'm back in Meizhou. This is not flashy restaurant food, but the honest, straightforward cooking of a home meal. We start with soup. Pork liver slices and pickled mustard green strips thread the broth, colored a warm rusty hue from dried red yeast rice. The red yeast rice, often used as a colorant, tints the stew of streaky pork belly, taro, black fungus, dried shrimp, and dark soy sauce. Steamed mounds of shredded white radish, ground pork, dried shrimp, and rice noodles taste more flavorful than those I ate in China. Tofu triangles filled with ground pork and braised in a golden sauce are a Hakka classic. A braise of fresh bamboo shoots with a tumble of mushrooms shows off the inherent flavors of the ingredients. I'm surprised that in Canada, the food tastes so true to what I ate in the Hakka homeland.

At this table sits a microcosm of the worldwide Hakka community. The guests were born in India, Jamaica, Trinidad, Mauritius, and Surinam. Now they all live here. Tonight we share a meal of a cuisine that ties us together. They tell their stories, which are similar in many ways.

## FRESH BAMBOO SHOOTS AND MUSHROOMS

If you've eaten only bland, fibrous bamboo shoots from a can, you're in for a surprise when you taste them fresh. Fresh bamboo shoots possess a natural sweetness and a smooth, crisp texture. When paired with tender mushrooms and lightly sauced, they make a satisfying vegetable dish. Look for the tan cone-shaped shoots in the produce section of your local Asian supermarket. Do not eat fresh bamboo shoots raw. They need to be cooked before eating. If they are not available, use canned or vacuum-packed whole winter bamboo shoots, which have a smooth, tender texture.

*Makes 4 to 6 servings as part of a multicourse meal*

1 large fresh cone-shaped bamboo shoot, about 1 pound (see note)

4 ounces fresh shiitake mushrooms, each about 2 inches wide

4 ounces oyster mushrooms

1 Cut about ½ inch off the tip and base of the bamboo shoot. Peel off and discard the tough outer layers until you reach the pale, tender edible core. Cut off the tough tip of the core. Cut the tender core into ½-inch-thick slices, then into strips about ½ inch wide and 3 inches long. You should have about 1½ cups. ▸

1 teaspoon salt

2 tablespoons vegetable oil

1 tablespoon minced fresh ginger

1 cup chicken broth, homemade (page 267) or purchased, or vegetable broth

2 tablespoons oyster sauce

2 tablespoons Chinese rice wine (shaoxing) wine or dry sherry

2 tablespoons water

1 tablespoon cornstarch

**2** Lightly rinse the mushrooms; drain well. Trim off and discard the stems from the shiitake mushrooms and cut their caps in half. Separate the oyster mushrooms into individual pieces, if they are in clumps. Cut the oyster mushrooms in half if wider than 3 inches.

**3** In a 14-inch wok or 12-inch frying pan over high heat, bring about 1 quart of water to a boil. Add the bamboo shoot strips and salt. Cook until the bamboo shoot strips are crisp-tender and not bitter, 5 to 7 minutes. If bitter, cook a few minutes longer and taste again. Drain well. Rinse the pan and dry.

**4** Set the pan over medium-high heat. When the pan is hot, after about 1 minute, add the oil and rotate the pan to spread. Add the ginger and mushrooms. Stir-fry until the oyster mushrooms begin to brown, 2 to 3 minutes. Add the bamboo shoot strips, broth, oyster sauce, and wine. Cook, stirring often, until the bamboo shoot strips are hot and the mushrooms are tender, about 2 minutes. In a small bowl, mix the water and cornstarch. Add the cornstarch mixture to the pan and stir until the sauce boils. Transfer to a serving dish.

**Note:** If fresh bamboo shoots are not available, use 1 can (about 1 pound) whole winter bamboo shoots (not the canned strips) or refrigerated vacuum-packed trimmed bamboo shoots. Skip the trimming directions, and just cut into strips to make 1½ to 2 cups. Skip step 3 and eliminate the salt. Rinse the shoots with hot water and drain. Then cook as directed in step 4. ∎

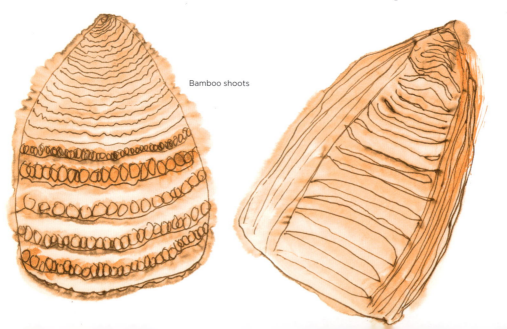

Bamboo shoots

# The Hakkaologist from Trinidad

Winston H. Chang Jr. calls himself a "Hakkaologist"—a name he coined to describe an expert on Hakka culture. He claims that the Chang surname is the third most common in the world. His family can trace back two hundred generations to one man, Chang Kim Yit, who founded the Chang village of Hoc Foo Do. Winston started research on his father's experiences as a Hakka shopkeeper and ended up writing two books, *The Legacy of the Hakka Shopkeepers of the West Indies* and *Foods of the Hakka Shops*.

Winston's father, a former schoolteacher, came from Guangdong Province to Trinidad in 1938. He first worked for a cocoa trader, where he danced on cocoa beans with his bare feet to polish them, and later became a manager and entrepreneur. He married a local Cantonese woman, and the family business grew to include more relatives and eventually a supermarket complex. Many Hakka families, including that of Winston's wife, Marie, have similar backgrounds. The shop dictated the lifestyle, diet, and living conditions of the family, and everyone ate what the shop provided—often leftovers or slow-selling items.

"Our generation didn't want to run shops," says Winston. Many left Trinidad when the island gained independence from Britain in 1962. Winston and Marie went to school in Canada. Others went to England, the United States, or Hong Kong. The year 2006 marked the two-hundredth anniversary of the Chinese presence in Trinidad. Once there were twenty thousand people of Chinese descent on the island. Now the population has greatly diminished. "There's brain drain in Trinidad. Social and political unrest makes life dangerous there, and everyone I know left," he continues. "The opportunities are all in Canada," adds Marie. In Canada, the Changs' hard work has been rewarded with education, good careers, and a home for their family.

I see this success two years later, when I meet Winston and Marie's daughters. I ask twenty-eight-year-old Melanie, "What does it mean to you to be Hakka?" This bright young woman, who knows more about being Hakka than I did at her age, responds:

I finally understand how I'm different from other Chinese people. Most Hakkas come from all over. Some people think all Chinese are alike, but Hakkas are not. We have a different culture, food, and music. Our Hakka habits and traits are quite different than those of my Cantonese and Mandarin friends. We believe in family. We even go to parties with our family. I've learned that the Hakka are enterprising and hardworking, especially the women. They are strong willed and ambitious, and they put their foot down. We have a strong sense of community, and we come together for a common cause: to keep Hakka culture alive.

# STIR-FRIED CHICKEN AND SALTED MUSTARD GREENS

Salted mustard greens, a beloved Hakka ingredient, find their way into many stir-fries. Winston Chang adds red bell pepper slivers to bring a jolt of bright color and fresh sweetness to contrast the salty mustard greens in this chicken stir-fry.

*Makes 2 to 3 servings as a main dish or 4 to 6 servings as part of a multicourse meal*

## CHICKEN

12 ounces boneless, skinless chicken thighs

2 teaspoons soy sauce

½ teaspoon five-spice powder

## STIR-FRY

¾ cup thinly slivered salted or pickled mustard greens, homemade (pages 146 and 147) or purchased

3 tablespoons water

1 tablespoon Chinese rice wine (shaoxing) or dry sherry

1 tablespoon rice vinegar

1 tablespoon soy sauce

1½ teaspoons sugar

1 teaspoon cornstarch

2 tablespoons vegetable oil

1 tablespoon minced fresh ginger

1 tablespoon minced garlic

1 small red bell pepper (about 6 ounces), cut into sticks ¼ inch wide by 2 inches long

**1 FOR THE CHICKEN:** Trim and discard the excess fat from the chicken and cut into 1-inch chunks. In a small bowl, mix the chicken, soy sauce, and five-spice powder.

**2 FOR THE STIR-FRY:** Rinse the mustard greens and place in a small bowl. Cover with water and soak for about 5 minutes. Drain the greens and squeeze out excess water.

**3** In a small bowl, mix the water, wine, vinegar, soy sauce, sugar, and cornstarch.

**4** Set a 14-inch wok or 12-inch frying pan over high heat. When the pan is hot, after about 1 minute, add the oil and rotate the pan to spread. Add the ginger, garlic, and chicken. Stir-fry until the chicken is browned, about 3 minutes. Add the mustard greens and red pepper. Stir-fry until the red pepper is crisp-tender, 1 to 2 minutes. Stir the cornstarch mixture and add to the pan; stir-fry until the sauce boils, about 30 seconds. Transfer to a serving dish. ∎

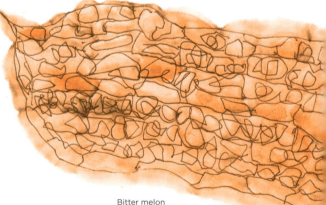

Bitter melon

# STUFFED BITTER MELON IN TOMATO SAUCE

Marie Chang adds a secret ingredient to bitter melon to defuse its quinine pungency: tomato sauce. In her recipe, the bitterness doesn't completely disappear, but the natural sweetness of the tomato gently mellows and blunts the bitter melon's bite. This recipe is adapted from her contribution to her husband's book *Foods of the Hakka Shops.*

*Makes 2 to 3 servings as a main dish or 4 to 6 servings as part of a multicourse meal*

2 bitter melons, each about 2 inches wide (about 1 pound total)

12 ounces ground pork

¼ cup minced green onions, including green tops

1 tablespoon minced fresh ginger

1 teaspoon minced garlic

½ teaspoon salt

¼ teaspoon ground black pepper

2 tablespoons vegetable oil

¾ cup chopped ripe tomatoes

¾ cup plus 1 tablespoon water, or as needed

2 tablespoons oyster sauce

½ teaspoon sugar

1 teaspoon cornstarch

1. Trim off and discard the ends from the bitter melons. Cut the melons crosswise into 1-inch-thick rounds. With a small knife, cut out the spongy center with seeds, push out, and discard. Scrape out the remaining white pith.

2. In a medium bowl, mix the pork, green onions, ginger, garlic, salt, and pepper. Pack the cavity of each melon section with the pork mixture, smearing the filling onto the cut edges; filling can mound slightly.

3. Set a 12-inch frying pan over medium heat. When the pan is hot, after about 1 minute, add the oil and rotate the pan to spread. Set the melon sections, pork side down, in the pan. Cook until browned on both sides, turning over halfway through, 4 to 5 minutes total.

4. Push the melon pieces to one side of the pan. Add the tomatoes to the empty part of the pan. Stir the tomatoes often until they begin to soften, 1 to 2 minutes. Add the ¾ cup water, oyster sauce, and sugar. Cover and simmer over medium-low heat, turning the pieces halfway, until the melon is soft when pierced, 12 to 15 minutes total. (If the pan juices evaporate before the melon is done, add a few tablespoons water as needed, and continue cooking.)

5. With a slotted spatula or spoon, transfer the melon pieces to a serving platter. Skim off and discard the fat from the pan juices. Measure the juices. If more than ¾ cup, boil, uncovered, over high heat, until reduced to that amount. If less than ¾ cup, add water to make that amount and bring to a boil. In a small bowl, mix the 1 tablespoon water with the cornstarch and add to the pan juices. Stir until the sauce boils. Spoon the sauce over the melon pieces. ∎

# Jamaican-Hakka Groupies

At the Tsung Tsin Association of Ontario, I meet Keith Lowe, a multicultural activist and professor of literature. With black-rimmed glasses and a thick mane of white-streaked hair, he looks a bit like the "absent-minded professor," an affectionate term his friends call him. Lowe's family originally came from Longgang in Shenzhen, China. His father went to Jamaica as a shopkeeper and later brought his Hakka wife over. After graduating with honors from Harvard, Keith received a PhD from Stanford in the 1960s. He returned to Jamaica for ten years, and then settled in Canada in 1979.

Keith explains that this branch of the Tsung Tsin Association was started in 1985 and has three to four hundred members, most of whom are Hakkas from Jamaica. (There are other Chinese associations that represent other countries, such as Trinidad, Mauritius, Malaysia, and India.) The organization's name, Tsung Tsin, means "upholding Hakka values," and the organization's main purpose is to pass on the Hakka principles of respecting elders, helping others, and taking care of the young. Concerned that when the older generation dies, Hakka culture would also die, members made it their mission to recruit young people. Keith suggested that they start by educating the new generation about its culture. He cofounded the first Hakka conference in Toronto in 2000, and other conferences followed in 2004 and 2008. Since then, organizers have created a festival atmosphere to bring Hakka culture to a larger and younger audience.

Keith and I sit down with Patrick Lee, an author and historian, who fills me in on the history of the Hakka in Jamaica. Starting in 1854, Hakkas were brought to Jamaica to work in sugar plantations, and some eventually settled there. Hakkas once made up about 95 percent of the Chinese population in Jamaica. Now it is estimated that about 80 percent are of Hakka descent, and the rest are Mandarin and Cantonese speakers from mainland China.

Everard Hoo, editor and writer of a website for Hakka Chinese Jamaicans (www.chinesejamaican.com), comments on the rapid Hakka population decline in Jamaica. In the mid-1970s, 90 percent of the Jamaican population was black. When Democratic Socialist Michael Manley became Jamaica's prime minister in 1972 and was reelected in 1976, the black population felt entitled to more economic power. The Hakka population—businesspeople mainly in retail trades—felt their future economic opportunities would be limited. Many migrated to Canada, the United States, and other countries.

In their new homes, these Hakkas have prospered through hard work in their businesses and careers. They've been assimilated into the multicultural society of their adopted home. And with their Hakka associations, they've kept their culture and traditions alive. As I feel the enveloping warmth and comfort radiating from the people I met here, I realize this peer reinforcement has been missing in my life. I have friends, but I've never felt like I had a group to call my own. Now I do. "You're one of us," says Keith.

## STEAMED BLACK BEAN PORK

Everard Hoo suggests that I check the website www.chinesejamaican.com for recipes. "Look for Uncle Boogsie," he says. "He is a frequent contributor." Born in Jamaica and now living in Toronto, William Lue-Tenn (also known as "Uncle Boogsie" or "Chef Boog") learned to cook by watching his father. One of his father's favorite recipes has become one of mine. Steam a chunk of fat-marbled pork butt, generously coated with fermented black beans, until the meat is so tender you can tear it apart with chopsticks. Serve with plenty of rice to absorb the plentiful juices. Chef Boog says this dish tastes even better the next day. His version of this recipe was published on the website in April 2007.

*Makes 6 to 8 servings as a main dish or 10 to 12 servings as part of a multicourse meal*

1 piece dried tangerine peel, about 2 inches wide (optional)

¼ cup fermented black beans, rinsed and chopped

3 tablespoons soy sauce

2 tablespoons minced fresh ginger

2 tablespoons minced garlic

2 tablespoons Chinese rice wine (shaoxing) or dry sherry

1 tablespoon packed brown sugar

2 to 2½ pounds boneless pork butt, in a single piece

2 tablespoons vegetable oil

3 tablespoons thinly sliced green onions, including green tops, for garnish

1  In a small bowl, soak the tangerine peel in hot water until soft, 10 to 15 minutes. Squeeze out excess water and mince the tangerine peel.

2  In a small bowl, mix the black beans, soy sauce, ginger, garlic, wine, sugar, and tangerine peel.

3  If the pork is too tall to fit under the steamer lid, cut the meat in half lengthwise. Set a 14-inch wok or 12-inch frying pan over medium-high heat. When the pan is hot, after about 1 minute, add the oil and rotate the pan to spread. Add the pork and cook, turning as needed to brown all sides, 5 to 8 minutes total. Lift out the meat and place in a 9- or 10-inch heatproof bowl that will fit in a steamer and hold the meat plus about 2 cups juice. Add the black bean mixture to the pan and bring to a boil, stirring to free any browned bits. Pour the sauce evenly over the pork.

4  Set the dish on a rack over 2 to 4 inches boiling water in a steamer or wok (if the bottom is round, place on a ▶

wok ring to stabilize). If the steamer lid is flat metal, wrap the lid with a towel to reduce condensation dripping on the food. Cover and steam over high heat until the meat is very tender in the center of the thickest part when pierced, or until you can pierce the center or thickest part with a chopstick, 2 to 2½ hours. Watch the water level, adding more boiling water as needed. If using a bamboo steamer, remember to keep the bottom rim of the steamer rack immersed in water so it doesn't burn. Carefully remove the dish from the steamer. Skim off and discard the fat from the pan juices. If desired, with a spoon, break the pork into smaller chunks and spoon the juices over it. Sprinkle with the green onions and serve. ▪

## SPICED GOAT STEW WITH PRESERVED LIME SAUCE

Albert Lim Shue, a second-generation Hakka-Jamaican who now lives in Toronto, loves to cook. This businessman injects Jamaican accents—handfuls of spice, fresh citrus leaves plucked from trees in his garden, and goat—into a typical Hakka soy-braised stew. He serves the aromatic, inky stew with a tart preserved-lime sauce that magically brightens the flavor. Albert calls his stew "Smile Hakka Jamaica," or Tai Sui Fee. If you can't find goat, use lamb instead.

*Makes 4 to 6 servings as a main dish or 8 to 12 servings as part of a multicourse meal*

### STEW

2½ to 3 pounds bone-in or boneless goat shoulder or leg (see note) or bone-in or boneless lamb stew meat from the shoulder, leg, or neck

⅓ cup thinly sliced fresh ginger

4 large cloves garlic

4 tablespoons dark soy sauce

5 pesticide-free fresh lime or lemon leaves, lightly crushed (optional)

2 tablespoons vegetable oil

5 cups water, or as needed

¼ cup coriander seeds

**1  FOR THE STEW:** Trim off and discard the excess fat from the meat. Cut the meat into 1½-inch chunks. With the flat side of a knife blade, lightly crush the ginger and garlic to release flavor. In a large bowl, mix the meat, 2 tablespoons of the dark soy sauce, garlic, ginger, and lime leaves. Cover and chill, stirring occasionally, 45 minutes to 1 hour.

**2**  Place a 14-inch wok or 5- to 6-quart pan over medium-high heat. When the pan is hot, after about 1 minute, add the oil and rotate the pan to spread. Add the marinated meat and cook, turning occasionally, until the meat is browned, 10 to 15 minutes. (If it begins to burn, reduce the heat slightly.) Add the water, remaining 2 tablespoons dark soy sauce, coriander seeds, and star anise, and bring to a boil. Reduce the heat, cover,

6 star anise

Cilantro leaves, for garnish

### SAUCE

⅓ cup distilled white vinegar

3 tablespoons seeded minced preserved lime or lemon, including peel

1½ teaspoons sugar

and simmer until the meat is tender when pierced, 1½ to 2 hours. (If the liquid reduces by more than half, add more water as needed.)

**3** With a slotted spoon, transfer the meat to a serving bowl and cover to keep warm. Skim off and discard the fat from the pan juices. Measure the juices. If more than 2 cups, boil, uncovered, over high heat, until reduced to that amount. If less than 2 cups, add water to make that amount and bring to a boil. Pour the juices over the meat and sprinkle with cilantro.

**4** **FOR THE SAUCE:** In a small bowl, mix the vinegar, minced lime, and sugar to taste. Offer the lime sauce to spoon over the stew.

**Note:** Look for goat in Asian, Hispanic, and halal meat markets. It may be frozen. If the meat is not boned, ask the butcher to saw the goat into 1½-inch chunks. Goat is quite lean, so it may seem a bit chewier and drier than other fat-marbled meats. It may absorb more liquid than the lamb so you may need to add more water as the liquid evaporates. ∎

## Computer Programmer to Chef

"I like to make good food," says Yong Soon. A noble ambition, since Yong is a chef, one with an impressive background. I met Yong at the Toronto Hakka Conference in 2008 as he was giving a cooking demonstration. He came from Malaysia when his brother offered him and his parents a chance to immigrate to Canada. As a computer programmer, he yearned for a career change. When he arrived in Toronto, he enrolled at the George Brown College Chef School. He was lucky to work under Susur Lee, a rising Hong Kong chef who cooked innovative French food. Yong worked in Singapore and Hong Kong, then traveled through China exploring regional cuisine.

I didn't get to sample Yong's cooking on my brief trip, but he promised to send me some Hakka recipes. His skill revealed itself in my kitchen as I tested and tasted his food. Both dishes were humble Hakka favorites that used pork belly. He enhances his versions with extra seasonings and techniques that elevate peasant food to gourmet status. Although he wishes to go into the corporate side of the food business, I secretly hope he opens a Hakka restaurant, preferably in my neighborhood.

# TRANSPLANTED HAKKA CLASSIC
## Hakka Soup Noodles with Egg Roll

水 麵 Hakka: *sui men;* Mandarin: *shui mian*

Carol Wong, the 2009 president of the Tsung Tsin Association of Ontario, says that when she grew up in Jamaica, soup noodles were considered a Jamaican-Hakka specialty. Although the literal translation for the words means "water noodles," they referred to noodles in soup. Typical toppings included Chinese barbecued pork, roast duck, shrimp, mushrooms, and bok choy or other green vegetables. The signature Jamaican-Hakka element—slices of egg roll (an egg crêpe filled with seasoned ground pork)—topped it off. A dish of soy sauce with minced local Scotch bonnet chiles was served alongside to add to taste.

Now it's hard to find these Jamaican-Hakka dishes. Says Wong:

When I was in Jamaica recently, I could not find this item in the Chinese restaurants anywhere on the island, because the Hakka people have emigrated and the restaurant trade has been taken over by Cantonese and new immigrants from mainland China. When I was growing up in Jamaica, this dish was also popular among black Jamaicans, who enjoyed it as a complete lunch despite the tropical heat.

In the Caribbean, Hakka soup noodles are a specialty among the Jamaican Chinese only. And while in Ontario, they and other Caribbean Hakkas eagerly await our "Shui Mein Nite" at our Tsung Tsin Association branch in Toronto. Undoubtedly, this event is usually oversold because this specialty is not obtainable elsewhere . . . not even in the Hakka Chinese restaurants around town.

Napa cabbage

# HAKKA SOUP NOODLES

"There is no hard and fast recipe for *sui men*," says Carol. "Each home has its own variation." Feel free to vary the recipe given here. You can buy barbecued pork, roast duck, and soy-sauce chicken at most Chinese delis or restaurants. Or substitute other toppings of your choice, such as roast chicken, roast pork, or ham.

This recipe makes enough noodles for a family of four. You can easily expand it for a festive party buffet. Just double the ingredients and the pan sizes for eight servings. If you like, add a few more topping options, such as blanched snow or sugar snap peas, Chinese broccoli, or bean sprouts. Arrange the cooked vegetables, meats, egg rolls, cilantro, green onions, and soy sauce with chiles in separate dishes. Cook the noodles and heat the broth shortly before serving; keep the broth hot over low heat. Place the hot noodles in large bowls, then invite guests to select toppings and ladle broth over the top.

*Makes 3 to 4 servings as a main dish or 6 to 8 servings as part of a multicourse meal*

6 to 7 cups chicken broth, homemade (page 267) or purchased

½ cup thinly sliced carrots

3 or 4 fresh shiitake mushrooms, each about 2 inches wide, stems removed

Salt

6 to 8 peeled, deveined shrimp (31 to 35 per pound; see note)

6 ounces napa cabbage, cut into thin strips (about 3 cups), or baby bok choy (2 to 3 small heads), cut lengthwise in quarters

1 pound fresh or dried Chinese wheat or egg noodles

9 to 12 slices Chinese barbecued pork (about 8 ounces total), warm or at room temperature

6 to 8 pieces Chinese roast duck or chicken (about 8 ounces total), warm or at room temperature

1  In a 6- to 8-quart pan over high heat, bring 3 to 4 quarts water to a boil for the noodles.

2  Meanwhile, in a 3- to 4-quart pan over high heat, bring the broth, carrots, and mushrooms to a boil. Add salt to taste. Reduce heat, cover, and simmer until the carrots are tender when pierced, about 5 minutes. With a slotted spoon or shallow wire strainer, lift out the vegetables and place on a plate or in a bowl.

3  Add the shrimp to the broth and cook until pink and barely opaque in the center of the thickest part (cut to test), 30 seconds to 1 minute. With a slotted spoon, lift out the shrimp and place in a small bowl. Add the cabbage to the broth and stir until it barely wilts, 30 seconds to 1 minute. With a slotted spoon or shallow wire strainer, lift out the cabbage, drain briefly, and place in a bowl. Reduce the heat to low and cover the broth to keep hot.

4  When the water for the noodles boils, pull the fresh noodles apart. Add the noodles to the water, stirring to separate. Cook until the noodles are barely tender, 2 to 3 minutes for fresh, 5 to 6 minutes for dried. Drain ▸

1 egg roll (recipe follows), without sauce, sliced ¼ inch thick diagonally, warm or at room temperature

¼ cup chopped cilantro, for garnish

¼ cup thinly sliced green onions, including green tops, for garnish

⅓ cup soy sauce

2 to 4 teaspoons minced or thinly sliced Scotch bonnet or other hot chile

and equally distribute the noodles among three or four large (2- to 3-cup) bowls. (If the noodles stick together and are difficult to separate, rinse with very hot water and drain.)

5 Attractively arrange equal portions of the carrots, mushrooms, shrimp, cabbage, pork, duck, and egg roll slices on top of each bowl of noodles. Ladle the hot broth over the noodles. Sprinkle with the cilantro and green onions. In a small bowl, combine the soy sauce and chiles; offer the soy mixture to add to taste.

**Note:** If desired, use whole unshelled shrimp with heads, which are often sold in Asian supermarkets. ■

## EGG ROLL

The Caribbean slang flies fast and funny between the audience and the cooking demonstrator, Chef Herbert A. Lee, an eighty-four-year-old living legend of Toronto's Caribbean Chinese community. The rapid-fire exchange of questions sounds hilarious, but I have no idea what they are saying. Winston Chang later informs me this friendly banter is typical between shopkeepers and their customers in the West Indies. It is called "fatigue" (derived from English) or "pecong" (derived from Creole French.)

As the crowd quiets, the self-taught cook demonstrates how to make a Hakka egg roll. It starts with a thin egg crêpe, which is filled with ground pork and rolled up like a jelly roll. After baking, the roll is sliced and served with gravy or used plain as a topping for noodles (page 169).

*Makes 4 rolls, enough for 4 servings as a main dish or 8 servings as part of a multi-course meal*

### FILLING

1 pound ground pork

2 tablespoons thinly sliced green onions, including green tops

1 tablespoon soy sauce

1 large egg

1 **FOR THE FILLING:** In a medium bowl, mix the pork, green onions, soy sauce, egg, salt, ginger, five-spice powder, and white pepper until well blended.

2 **FOR THE EGG WRAPPERS:** In a small bowl, beat the eggs until well blended. Place a nonstick frying or crêpe pan that measures 7 to 8 inches across the bottom over

½ teaspoon salt

¼ teaspoon ground ginger

¼ teaspoon five-spice powder (optional)

⅛ teaspoon ground white pepper

## EGG WRAPPERS

4 large eggs

Vegetable oil, as needed

## SAUCE

1 cup chicken broth, homemade (page 267) or purchased

2 tablespoons oyster sauce

2 tablespoons Chinese rice wine (shaoxing) or dry sherry

1 tablespoon cornstarch

¼ cup thinly sliced green onions, including green tops

1 teaspoon Asian sesame oil

medium heat. When the pan is hot, after about 1 minute, very lightly brush oil over the pan bottom and sides. Fill a ¼-cup measuring cup about three-fourths full with beaten egg. Pour the beaten egg into the pan all at once and quickly rotate the pan so that the egg coats the bottom in a thin, even layer. If there are large holes, drizzle with a little beaten egg to fill in. Cook until the egg feels dry on top and the bottom is lightly browned, about 1 minute. Loosen around the pan edges, if needed, and with a wide spatula, place the wrapper, browned side down, on a plate. Repeat to make remaining wrappers, stacking them as made. You will have 4 wrappers.

3 Preheat the oven to 350°F. Place a quarter of the pork filling (about ½ cup) on the pale side of each wrapper. With the back of a spoon or using wet hands, press the pork filling into a ¼-inch-thick layer to within ¼ inch of the edges. Roll each wrapper up like a jelly roll. Place the egg rolls, seam side down, slightly apart on an oiled shallow 9-by-13-inch baking pan.

4 Bake the rolls until the filling is firm to the touch and no longer pink in the center of the thickest part (cut to test), 15 to 20 minutes. Let rest about 5 minutes. Cut the egg rolls diagonally into ½-inch-thick slices and arrange on a platter.

5 FOR THE SAUCE: In the frying pan used for the wrappers or a 1- to 2-quart pan, stir together the broth, oyster sauce, wine, and cornstarch. Stir over high heat until the sauce boils and thickens, about 1 minute. Stir in the green onions and the sesame oil. Pour the sauce over and around the egg rolls. Omit the sauce if using the egg rolls as a topping for noodles.

Notes: When cooking the wrappers, don't use too much oil in the pan. Coat the pan very lightly; otherwise, the egg cannot grip the sides of the pan and will slide to one side and make a thick wrapper.

Prepare the rolls through step 3 (except for preheating the oven) up to 1 day ahead. Cover and chill, and then bake shortly before serving. ■

# BRAISED PORK BELLY AND BLACK FUNGUS

Like many Hakka stews, Yong Soon's pork belly version emanates a dark, umami-rich intensity. Known as *zha zhu rou,* it's a favorite of his parents, who love the smooth, yielding texture of the meat. The chef soaks chunks of pork belly in a soy sauce and spice marinade, and then fries them. He braises the seasoned meat in a broth enriched with oyster sauce and robustly flavored *sa cha* sauce, sometimes labeled Chinese barbecue sauce. As the chunks of pork slowly braise, they soften into meltingly tender morsels. Dried black fungus cooks with the pork to provide crunch and perhaps a cholesterol antidote; the Chinese believe that this black mushroom improves blood circulation and makes the blood more fluid, so in this pairing the fungus may also help neutralize the effects of the pork fat. Traditionally, the pork is deep-fried, but I find baking a far easier and neater (not to mention less caloric) option. The stew can be made ahead and reheated.

*Makes 6 to 8 servings as a main dish or 10 to 12 servings as part of a multicourse meal*

## PORK

2½ to 3 pounds boneless pork belly with skin or pork butt

¼ cup dark soy sauce

3 tablespoons Chinese rice spirits or vodka

3 tablespoons cornstarch

1 large egg

1 tablespoon five-spice powder

1 teaspoon ground star anise

1 teaspoon salt

½ teaspoon ground ginger

½ teaspoon ground white pepper

## STEW

2 cups dried thick black fungus, such as wood ears (about 2 ounces; see notes)

3 to 4 tablespoons vegetable oil

**1** **FOR THE PORK:** Cut the pork into 1½-inch chunks. In a large bowl, mix the dark soy sauce, rice spirits, cornstarch, egg, five-spice powder, star anise, salt, ginger, and pepper. Add the pork and mix to coat. Cover and chill for at least 30 minutes, and up to 2 hours, stirring occasionally.

**2** **FOR THE STEW:** Rinse the black fungus and place in a large bowl. Cover with hot water and let soak until soft and pliable, 15 to 30 minutes. Pinch out the hard knobby centers of the fungus. Tear the fungus into 1-inch pieces, rinse well, and drain.

**3** Preheat the oven to 425°F. Line two 10-by-15-inch baking pans with foil and coat each pan with about 1 tablespoon oil. Drain the excess marinade from the meat and discard. Arrange the pork pieces in a single layer slightly apart on the pans. Bake, switching the pan positions halfway, until the pieces are lightly browned, 18 to 20 minutes.

**4** Set a 14-inch wok or 5- to 6-quart pan over medium-high heat. When the pan is hot, after about 1 minute,

2 tablespoons minced shallots

1 tablespoon minced garlic

1 tablespoon minced fresh ginger

2 tablespoons Chinese rice wine
(shaoxing) or dry sherry

1 tablespoon *sa cha* sauce (see notes)

4 cups chicken broth, homemade
(page 267) or purchased

2 tablespoons oyster sauce

½ teaspoon sugar

¼ teaspoon salt, or to taste

add 1 tablespoon oil and rotate the pan to spread. Add the shallots, garlic, and ginger; stir-fry until the shallots begin to brown, about 30 seconds. Stir in the wine and *sa cha* sauce. Add the broth, pork, wood ears (if using cloud ears, add about 1 hour later), oyster sauce, sugar, and salt.

**5** Bring to a boil, reduce the heat, cover, and simmer, stirring occasionally, until the pork and skin are very tender when pierced, 1½ to 2 hours. Add more water if the liquid evaporates before the meat is done; you want at least 1⅓ cups water in the pan. With a slotted spoon, transfer the pork to a serving dish. Skim off and discard the fat from the pan juices. Measure the juices. If more than 1⅓ cups, boil, uncovered, over high heat, until reduced to that amount. If less than 1⅓ cups, add water to make that amount and bring to a boil. Add salt to taste and pour the juices over the meat.

**Notes:** If you can, select the thicker wood ear fungus, which will hold its texture during the long cooking of the pork. If you use the thinner cloud ear fungus, add it halfway through cooking to preserve its texture.

If you can't find *sa cha* sauce, omit and increase the oyster sauce to 3 tablespoons.

If making the stew up to 2 days ahead, cool, cover, and chill. Reheat, covered, over low heat, adding a little water if it is too dry or begins to stick; stir occasionally, until hot. ■

## The Royal Route from Calcutta to Canada

When Jenny Liao (Chi-Ying Liao) tells me that she used to work at a hotel in Copenhagen, I wonder if it is the same one that I worked at from 1969 to 1970. "Is it the Royal?" I ask. Her eyes open wide. "How did you know?" When I worked at the Royal Hotel in Copenhagen, it was a mini–United Nations. The hotel hired people from all over the world—Indians, Thais, Filipinos, Poles, Norwegians, Japanese, Swiss, Dutch, Danes, and Nigerians. Jenny and I discover that we were both chambermaids there. We also both met our husbands there: I married a Thai coworker, and she married a Chinese man from India. Both men had traveled overland from their homes in Asia to Denmark. If I had continued working at the Royal just a few months longer, I would have met Jenny thirty-six years ago.

Jenny and I share another connection: we're both Hakka. Jenny has a natural aptitude for languages and is a good cook. She tries to get me to recall some Hakka words and insists that if I stay long enough, I will be speaking Hakka.

She takes me to visit her brother-in-law, who will make us a steamed rice cake. Ping Kuang Chen (also known as P. K.), now seventy-five, was born in Meixian, China. In 1948, when he was fifteen, he moved to India. He eventually owned a tannery in Calcutta, where he lived for fifty years. Four generations of his family lived in India, starting with his grandfather. His father had two wives, one in India and one in China. P. K. tells me, "A hundred years ago, the Hakka came to Tangra. They built eight hundred tanneries, but when the pollution got bad, the government pushed them out with no repayment." Most of the Chinese in India own beauty salons, shoe stores, hotels, tailor shops, and businesses making paper art for funerals. The Indians were envious of the Chinese businesspeople making money. After the Sino-Indian War in 1962, the younger generation started to leave. In 1990, P. K. and his wife came to Toronto because their children had moved here. "If the Hakka have a route, they will go," he says.

## STEAMED RICE CAKE WITH TOASTED GARLIC OIL

This steamed white rice cake serves as a neutral platform for the tasty condiments you spoon on top—sweet soy sauce, hot red chile sauce, and toasted garlic oil. Serve it as a snack or appetizer. Its texture is more like a firm pudding: smooth, dense, and a bit bouncy—a texture Asians appreciate.

This is a simplified version of P. K. Chen's recipe. The batter is quite thin. P. K. cooks part of it to make a thick paste and blends it with the remaining batter to hold it together. He also preheats the pan in the steamer to allow the cake to start cooking immediately, so that the thin batter doesn't have time to settle. The texture is best when served freshly steamed. Leftover pieces can be pan-fried or coated in batter and deep-fried. Extra garlic oil can be stored in a covered jar in the refrigerator.

*Makes 12 to 18 pieces, 6 to 8 servings as an appetizer*

### GARLIC OIL

½ cup vegetable oil

⅓ cup evenly minced garlic (see notes)

**1 FOR THE GARLIC OIL:** In a 6- to 8-inch frying pan over medium heat cook the oil and garlic, stirring occasionally, just until most of the garlic begins to turn gold,

## RICE CAKE

1 tablespoon vegetable oil

2 cups water

1½ cups rice flour (7 ounces)

1 teaspoon baking powder

¼ teaspoon salt

Sweet soy sauce, homemade (page 269) or purchased *kecap manis*

Chile sauce, homemade (page 268) or purchased

3 to 5 minutes (do not brown). Remove from the heat and pour into a bowl. The garlic will continue to brown once off the heat. Let cool. Makes about ½ cup.

2 **FOR THE RICE CAKE:** Coat a 9-inch shallow heatproof dish that will fit inside a steamer, such as a Pyrex pie pan, with the oil. Set the dish on a rack over 2 to 4 inches boiling water in a steamer or wok (if the bottom is round, place on a wok ring to stabilize). Preheat the dish, uncovered, over medium heat. If the water evaporates before you're ready to steam, replenish with more boiling water.

3 In a blender, combine 1½ cups of the water, flour, baking powder, and salt; whirl until smoothly blended, holding the blender lid down. Remove 3 tablespoons of the mixture and mix with the remaining ½ cup water in a 1-quart pan. Stir over high heat until it boils and thickens into a smooth paste, 1 to 2 minutes. Scrape the paste into the blender and whirl with the remaining mixture until smooth, holding the blender lid down.

4 Pour the thin batter into the hot oiled dish on the steaming rack. If the steamer lid is flat metal, wrap the lid with a towel to reduce condensation dripping on the food. Cover and steam over high heat for 10 minutes. Reduce the heat to low and steam until the center of the cake is firm to the touch (surface may be tacky) and the cake is an even white color throughout, about 5 minutes longer. Remove the cake from the steamer and let stand 3 to 5 minutes.

5 Cut the cake (which will be slightly sticky) into strips about 1½ inch wide. Repeat, cutting diagonally across the first cuts to make 1½-inch diamonds. Or cut into wedges. Lift out pieces with a wide spatula. Serve hot or warm with sweet soy sauce, chile sauce, and toasted garlic oil to spoon over pieces to eat.

**Notes:** Finely chop the garlic so the pieces are close to the same size. When fried in oil, the pieces will cook more evenly. If there's a great variation in size, some garlic pieces will burn while others remain raw. The goal is golden toasted garlic.

If you have leftover rice cake, cool, cover, and chill the pieces up to 2 days. Chen coats the pieces in flour and then a thin batter made from a mix and deep fries them. Or you can pan-fry the slices in a little oil in a nonstick frying pan over medium heat until golden on both sides. Serve the fried slices with the same toppings. ■

# CHICKEN AND GOJI BERRY SOUP

Jenny Liao's grandson often requests this chicken soup. He likes the dried orange-red goji berries, also known as wolfberries or red medlar, which add a faint sweet fruitiness to the broth. The berries are also said to improve eyesight. Any part of the chicken, with or without bone, can be used to make this soup. In my somewhat modern interpretation, velvety chunks of boneless chicken breast poach in the ginger-scented broth punctuated with goji berries. The dried red yeast rice tempers the sweetness and contributes a ruddy hue to the soup. I find the results elegant and sophisticated without requiring much work or time. For a more rustic version, use bone-in chunks of chicken, but allow additional time for the chicken to cook to tenderness.

*Makes 4 servings as part of a multicourse meal*

1 teaspoon red yeast rice (optional)

4 cups chicken broth, homemade (page 267) or purchased

6 thin slices fresh ginger, lightly crushed

1 teaspoon cornstarch

1 teaspoon Chinese rice wine (shaoxing) or dry sherry

1 teaspoon vegetable oil

¼ teaspoon sugar

¼ teaspoon salt, or to taste

6 to 8 ounces boneless, skinless chicken breasts

¼ cup dried goji berries

2 tablespoons cilantro leaves, for garnish

**1** In a fine strainer, rinse and drain the red yeast rice. Place the red yeast rice in a 3- to 4-quart pan. Add the broth and ginger. Bring to a boil over high heat. Reduce heat, cover, and simmer until the red yeast rice is soft and the broth has turned pink and has a mild ginger flavor, about 5 minutes.

**2** Meanwhile, in a small bowl, mix the cornstarch, wine, oil, sugar, and salt. Cut the chicken into ½-inch cubes and stir into the cornstarch mixture.

**3** Add the chicken mixture to the simmering broth; stir to separate the pieces. Place the goji berries in a wire strainer and rinse. Add the goji berries to the broth, and bring to a boil over high heat. Reduce the heat, cover, and simmer until the chicken is no longer pink in the center of the thickest part (cut to test), 3 to 4 minutes. Add additional salt to taste. Ladle the soup into a serving bowl, and garnish with cilantro. ∎

# From Kanpur to Toronto

Liu Ying Hsien's father moved to India from Meixian, China, over eighty years ago. His family lived in Kanpur, also known as the "Manchester of India," an industrial city with leather tanneries and textile mills in the state of Uttar Pradesh. They ran a shoe shop, a Chinese restaurant, and several ladies' hair salons. Ying Hsien compares his life in Kanpur, a city in northern India, to those of the Hakka who lived in Calcutta, 665 miles southeast: "Calcutta had twenty to thirty thousand Hakkas. The disadvantage is that very few worked and mixed outside of the Chinese community. The advantages were that they could speak Hakka more fluently and were immersed in Hakka culture and customs. There weren't many Hakkas where I lived. But I had a greater opportunity to mix and learn about things in India—its people, its customs, and the Hindi and English languages."

It was difficult to find work in India after the 1962 Sino-Indian War. "We needed a police permit to travel to any place in India other than where we lived, even for a job interview," says Ying Hsien. In 1967, he came to Canada. Five years later, his wife, Maggie, followed, and now all their relatives live nearby. They still enjoy cooking the foods of their childhood, from Indian curries to Hakka favorites.

Onions

# SWEET SOY CHOW MEIN

Most Hakkas in India stash a bottle of a special sauce in the refrigerator for this Hakka stir-fried noodle dish called *hung mee chow mein,* says Liu Ying Hsien. It's a family favorite for many. Once you taste these salty-sweet noodles, you'll see why. Stir-fry meat and vegetables; then add cooked noodles and the magic ingredient, sweet soy sauce (also known as *hung mee* or red sauce). It's an easy sauce to make (see page 269), or you can buy the Indonesian *kecap manis* for a quick substitute. The aromatic syrupy sauce imparts a blackish-brown glossy finish and intense flavor to the noodles.

Another reason to make this chow mein often is its flexibility. You can vary the meat and vegetables based on what's in your fridge. This version is threaded with pork, red bell pepper, onion, and carrots. Other popular alternatives include Chinese barbecued pork, chicken, cabbage, green beans, and cauliflower.

*Makes 3 servings as a main dish or 6 servings as part of a multicourse meal*

8 ounces boneless pork butt or shoulder, trimmed of fat

1 medium onion (about 8 ounces)

1 medium red bell pepper (about 6 ounces)

1 medium carrot (about 3 ounces), peeled

12 ounces Chinese dried wheat or egg noodles

2 tablespoons vegetable oil

1 tablespoon minced garlic

½ teaspoon coarsely ground black pepper, or to taste

¼ teaspoon salt, or to taste

¼ cup sweet soy sauce, homemade (page 269), or purchased *kecap manis,* or to taste

⅓ cup thinly sliced green onions, including green tops, for garnish

1 Cut the pork into thin matchsticks, about ¼ inch wide and 3 inches long. Cut the onion into thin slivers 2 to 3 inches long. Stem and seed the bell pepper and cut into thin slivers, 2 to 3 inches long. Cut the carrot into thin slivers, 2 to 3 inches long.

2 In a 6- to 8-quart pan over high heat, bring 3 to 4 quarts water to a boil. Add the noodles, stir to separate, and cook until barely tender to the bite, 4 to 6 minutes. Drain the noodles, rinse well with hot water, and drain again.

3 Set a 14-inch wok over high heat. When the pan is hot, after about 1 minute, add the oil and rotate the pan to spread. Add the pork and stir-fry until it begins to brown, 2 to 3 minutes. Add the onion, red pepper, carrot, garlic, black pepper, and salt. Stir-fry until the onion is lightly browned, 3 to 4 minutes. Add the noodles and sweet soy sauce. Stir-fry until the noodles are hot, about 2 minutes. Transfer to a serving dish and sprinkle with green onions. ■

# SOY-GLAZED BLACK PEPPER CHICKEN

Liu Ying Hsien learned this four-ingredient recipe from his mother in India. I love it because each ingredient packs a powerful punch. Coat bone-in, skin-on chicken thighs in dark soy sauce and freshly ground black pepper and pack snugly into the bottom of a pan. As the chicken thighs cook on low heat, their juices ooze out and mingle with the soy sauce and pepper to create a sauce with a lively bite.

*Makes 3 servings as a main dish or 6 servings as part of a multicourse meal*

6 bone-in, skin-on chicken thighs (about 2 pounds total)

1 tablespoon freshly ground or cracked black pepper (see note)

2 tablespoons dark soy sauce

Cilantro leaves, for garnish

1 Trim off and discard the large pads of fat from the chicken. Rinse the chicken and pat dry. In a heavy-bottomed 5- to 6-quart pan or deep 10- or 11-inch frying pan (bottom should measure 8 to 10 inches), mix the soy sauce and pepper. Add the chicken and turn until the pieces are completely coated. Arrange the chicken, skin side down, in a single layer so that it covers the pan bottom completely.

2 Cover the pan tightly and cook over low heat until the skin is dark brown, 15 to 20 minutes. Turn the chicken and continue cooking until it is no longer pink at the bone (cut to test), 20 to 25 minutes longer. If the juices completely evaporate before the chicken is done, add about ¼ cup water.

3 Transfer the chicken to a serving platter. Skim off and discard the fat from the pan juices. Pour the pan juices over the chicken, and garnish with cilantro.

Note: To crack pepper, place 1 tablespoon black peppercorns on a board and with the bottom of a heavy pan, firmly press down to coarsely crush. Or use a mortar and pestle. ∎

## Spanakopita Meets Egg Rolls in Toronto's Greektown

Dolmas and baklava dominate the stretch of Danforth Avenue known as "Greektown" in Toronto. Yet Anthony Lin and Sandra Chung, the owners of Danforth Dragon, offer a different dining adventure that fuses their Hakka and Indian roots. In this casual restaurant, they blend Indian spices such as *jeera* (cumin) and chile with Chinese soy sauce and rice wine for a distinctive cuisine that explodes with flavor.

Anthony Lin's parents made shoes in India. Even though his mother was born in India, she enforced Chinese traditions at home: "We ate with chopsticks. No Hindi was spoken. 'You're Chinese, speak Chinese at home,' Mom would say." Anthony left school early and has worked in restaurants from the age of twelve. "There was no future in India," he says. In 1989, at the age of fifteen, he followed his mother to Canada.

In 1999, Anthony opened Danforth Dragon, originally a fast-food joint. He brought the Indian-Chinese food popular in Calcutta to his Canadian customers in Toronto. Hakka chefs created this cross-cultural mix, which is wildly popular with customers from India. Most restaurants that offer this fusion cuisine are in Toronto's northern suburbs and attract primarily Indian customers who are familiar with this hybrid food.

More Canadians than Indians live near Danforth Dragon, so Anthony adapts his dishes to the North American palate. His Canadian customers don't eat much rice, so he reduces the amount of salt, soy sauce, and gravy in popular dishes like chile chicken. Pork is taboo for Muslims, but his Canadian customers request it. For Hakka customers, he'll cook more traditional dishes off the menu when requested.

"At home, Mom cooks the food, so it's pretty simple," says Anthony. They eat curry once a week, dal (Indian spiced lentils), and pan-fried whole fish with sweet and sour sauce. "*Hung mee* is also very popular among Indian Hakka families. And we often eat mixed wonton noodles at home and at the restaurant since they are convenient to make."

## CHILE CHICKEN

Customers love the explosion of hot, salty, and sweet flavors in this popular dish at Danforth Dragon. Soy-seasoned caramelized onions and fiery chiles tumble over chunks of crisp fried chicken. It's one of the most requested Hakka-Indian dishes at the restaurant.

*Makes 3 to 4 servings as a main dish or 6 to 8 servings as part of a multicourse meal*

### CHICKEN

1 pound boneless, skinless chicken thighs, trimmed of fat

1 tablespoon soy sauce

**1 FOR THE CHICKEN:** Cut the chicken into 1-inch chunks and place in a medium bowl. Mix in the soy sauce, ginger, garlic, and pepper. Marinate for 15 to 30 minutes.

1 tablespoon minced fresh ginger

1 tablespoon minced garlic

½ teaspoon ground black pepper

Vegetable oil, for deep-frying

1 large egg, lightly beaten

¼ cup all-purpose flour

## STIR-FRY

3 tablespoons water

2 tablespoons dark soy sauce

1 teaspoon soy sauce

1 teaspoon cornstarch

2 cups thinly slivered onions (about 8 ounces)

2 to 5 tablespoons thinly sliced jalapeño chile

Cilantro leaves, for garnish

**2** Set a 14-inch wok (if the bottom is round, place on a wok ring to stabilize) or 5- to 6-quart pan over medium-high heat and add oil to a depth of about 1½ inches. Heat the oil until it reaches 350°F on a thermometer; adjust the heat to maintain the temperature.

**3** Meanwhile, add the egg to the chicken and mix well to coat. Sprinkle with flour and gently toss to lightly coat chicken. When the oil is hot, add one-quarter to one-third of the chicken (don't crowd the pan) and stir to separate the pieces. Cook, turning occasionally, until browned and crisp and no longer pink in the center of the thickest part (cut to test), 2 to 3 minutes. Lift out with a slotted spoon and drain on paper towels. Repeat to fry remaining chicken.

**4 FOR THE STIR-FRY:** In a small bowl, mix the water, dark soy sauce, soy sauce, and cornstarch. Set a 14-inch wok or 12-inch frying pan over high heat. When the pan is hot, after about 1 minute, add 2 tablespoons of the frying oil and rotate the pan to spread. Add the onions and chile to taste, and stir-fry until the onions are browned, 2 to 3 minutes. Stir the soy sauce mixture and add to the pan; stir-fry until the sauce boils, and then stir in the fried chicken. Stir until the chicken is hot and coated with sauce, about 1 minute. Transfer to a serving bowl and sprinkle with cilantro. ■

Jalapeño chile

# CHILE BEEF

This beef version of the popular chile chicken skips the messy deep-frying for an easier dish to make at home. Spiked with hot green chiles and soy-stained sweet onions, it needs plenty of steamed rice to temper the heat. I like to eat this dish with a cool salad of sliced cucumbers, red onions, and red bell peppers marinated in seasoned rice vinegar.

*Makes 2 to 3 servings as a main dish or 4 to 5 servings as part of a multicourse meal*

## BEEF

12 ounces beef flank steak

1 tablespoon soy sauce

1 tablespoon minced fresh ginger

1 tablespoon minced garlic

½ teaspoon ground black pepper

## STIR-FRY

¼ cup water

2 tablespoons dark soy sauce

1 teaspoon soy sauce

1 teaspoon cornstarch

3 tablespoons vegetable oil

2 cups thinly slivered onions (about 8 ounces)

3 to 5 tablespoons thinly sliced jalapeño chile

3 tablespoons cilantro leaves, for garnish

1 **FOR THE BEEF:** Cut the beef crosswise into strips ⅛ inch thick, 2 to 3 inches long, and 1 inch wide. In a medium bowl, mix the beef, soy sauce, ginger, garlic, and pepper. Marinate for 10 to 15 minutes.

2 **FOR THE STIR-FRY:** In a small bowl, mix the water, dark soy sauce, soy sauce, and cornstarch. Set a 14-inch wok or 12-inch frying pan over high heat. When the pan is hot, after about 1 minute, add 1 tablespoon of the oil and rotate the pan to spread. Add half the beef mixture and stir-fry until lightly browned, 1 to 2 minutes. Transfer the meat to a serving dish. Repeat with 1 tablespoon oil and remaining meat mixture.

3 Return the pan to high heat. Add the remaining 1 tablespoon oil, onions, and chile; stir-fry until the onions are browned, 2 to 3 minutes. Stir the soy mixture and add to the pan; stir until the sauce boils. Add the beef and stir-fry until the meat is hot, about 30 seconds. Transfer to a serving dish and garnish with cilantro. ∎

# STIR-FRIED CUMIN BEEF

At Danforth Dragon, Anthony Lin stir-fries fragrant *jeera* (cumin) seeds, three kinds of chiles, and soy sauce with thin slices of beef or chicken to create a dish that will make your taste buds dance. Although the spices generously coat the meat, it's a dry stir-fry, meaning that there's no sauce. At the restaurant he blanches the beef in a pan of hot oil to quickly seal in the juices and separate the meat slices. At home, eliminate this messy step and simply stir-fry the meat. Serve with plenty of rice to buffer the heat.

*Makes 2 to 3 servings as a main dish or 4 to 6 servings as part of a multicourse meal*

12 ounces beef flank steak

3 tablespoons vegetable oil

½ cup chopped onion

1 tablespoon minced garlic

1 tablespoon minced fresh ginger

2 teaspoons cumin seeds

2 teaspoons sesame seeds

2 teaspoons coarsely chopped jalapeño chile, or to taste

½ teaspoon ground black pepper

¼ teaspoon dried hot chile flakes, or to taste

⅓ cup sliced green onions, including green tops

1 tablespoon dark soy sauce

2 teaspoons soy sauce

½ teaspoon chile sauce, homemade (page 268) or purchased, or to taste

**1** Cut the beef across the grain into strips ⅛ inch thick, 2 to 3 inches long, and about 1 inch wide.

**2** Set a 14-inch wok or 12-inch frying pan over high heat. When the pan is hot, after about 1 minute, add 1 tablespoon of the oil and rotate the pan to spread. Add half of the beef and stir-fry until lightly browned, about 2 minutes. Transfer the meat to a serving dish. Return the unwashed pan to high heat and repeat using another 1 tablespoon oil and the remaining meat.

**3** Return the unwashed pan to high heat. Add the remaining 1 tablespoon oil, onion, garlic, and ginger. Stir-fry until the onion is lightly browned, about 1 minute. Add the cumin seeds, sesame seeds, chile, black pepper, and chile flakes; stir-fry until the cumin is fragrant, 15 to 30 seconds. Add the beef, green onions, dark soy sauce, and soy sauce. Stir-fry until the meat is hot and coated with seasonings, about 1 minute. Stir in the chile sauce. Transfer to a serving bowl.

**Stir-Fried Cumin Chicken:** Substitute 12 ounces boneless, skinless chicken thighs, trimmed of fat, for the beef. ▪

# SPICY EGG ROLLS

The package looks Chinese; the filling tastes Indian. Chef Lin fills Chinese egg roll wrappers with a ground meat and pea mixture spiced with Indian curry and fries the rolls until crisp. He serves them with a mildly sweet Chinese plum sauce. Anyone can make this appetizer with his simplified filling and rolling technique. The rolls make a perfect hors d'oeuvre to pass around at a party. The meat mixture can be cooked a day ahead. Fill the rolls the morning of the party, but fry them shortly before serving. They will stay crisp in a warm oven for at least thirty minutes. To make a smaller batch, cut the recipe in half.

*Makes 20 to 24 rolls*

## FILLING

¾ cup water

2 tablespoons soy sauce

1 tablespoon cornstarch

2 tablespoons vegetable oil

1½ cups chopped onion

2 to 4 tablespoons minced jalapeño chile

2 tablespoons minced fresh ginger

1½ tablespoons minced garlic

¾ teaspoon salt, or to taste

2½ tablespoons curry powder

1½ pounds ground chicken or ground pork

1½ cups frozen petite peas, rinsed with hot water and well drained

⅓ cup chopped cilantro

## WRAPPING

¼ cup all-purpose flour

¼ cup water

**1  FOR THE FILLING:** In a small bowl, mix the water, soy sauce, and cornstarch. Set a 14-inch wok or 12-inch frying pan over medium-high heat. When the pan is hot, after about 1 minute, add the oil, onion, chile, ginger, garlic, and salt. Stir-fry until the onion is lightly browned, about 2 minutes. Add the curry powder and stir until fragrant, about 30 seconds. Add the chicken or pork and stir-fry until crumbly and lightly browned, 3 to 4 minutes. Stir in the peas and cilantro. Stir the soy sauce mixture, add to the pan, and stir until the sauce boils, about 30 seconds. Add more salt to taste. Remove from the heat and cool to room temperature, stirring occasionally, 15 to 20 minutes. Or cool, cover, and chill until the next day. Makes about 6 cups.

**2  FOR THE WRAPPING:** In a small bowl, mix the flour and water until smooth. Place a wrapper on a board. Cover the remaining wrappers with plastic wrap. Spread a narrow strip of flour paste along the 4 edges of the wrapper. Place ¼ cup filling in a 1½-inch-wide band across the bottom edge of the wrapper to within ¾ inch of the sides and bottom. Starting at the bottom, roll the wrapper up tightly to enclose the filling, pressing and sealing the edges as you roll. Place the filled rolls slightly apart on flour-dusted baking pans while you fill the remaining wrappers. Keep the finished rolls covered

20 to 24 egg roll or spring roll
wrappers, each 6½ to 8 inches
square, thawed if frozen (see notes)

Vegetable oil, for frying

Plum sauce, for dipping

with plastic wrap. If making ahead, cover and chill up to 8 hours.

3  Set a 14-inch wok (if the bottom is round, place on a wok ring to stabilize) or 5- to 6-quart pan over medium-high heat, and add oil to a depth of about 1½ inches. Heat the oil until it reaches 350°F on a thermometer; adjust the heat to maintain the temperature. Fry 3 or 4 rolls at a time, turning as needed, until golden brown on both sides, about 2 minutes total. Remove with a slotted spoon or tongs and drain on a baking pan lined with paper towels. Keep warm in a 200°F oven. Repeat to fry all. Offer the rolls whole or cut crosswise in halves or thirds. Serve with plum sauce for dipping.

Notes: Chef Lin uses pasta-like egg roll wrappers, which resemble a large version of wonton wrappers. You may also use spring roll wrappers, refrigerated or frozen, which resemble pale, thin, stretchy crêpes. Both types work.

The rolls are best when freshly fried, but if you have leftovers, cover and chill. To reheat, place slightly apart on a baking sheet and bake in preheated 350°F oven until crisp, 16 to 18 minutes. Rolls may not be as crisp when reheated. ∎

# CRISPY GINGER BEEF

Anthony Lin saw this dish served in many Chinese restaurants in India. Although most chefs coat the meat in a thick batter, he prefers a light veil of flour. When fried, the beef turns extra crispy. Anthony coats the thin slices with a glaze spiked with lots of ginger and a kick of chile. His customers love the crispy, sweet, and spicy character of the dish. I serve it with hot rice and a green salad dotted with cherry tomatoes and dressed with rice vinegar, sesame oil, and sugar.

*Makes 3 to 4 servings as a main dish or 6 to 8 servings as part of a multicourse meal*

## BEEF

1 pound beef flank steak

Vegetable oil, for frying

1 cup all-purpose flour, or as needed

## STIR-FRY

¼ cup sugar

¼ cup rice vinegar

2 tablespoons Chinese rice wine (shaoxing) or dry sherry

1 tablespoon soy sauce

1 tablespoon oyster sauce

1 teaspoon chile sauce, homemade (page 268) or purchased

2 tablespoons thinly slivered fresh ginger

1 tablespoon minced fresh ginger

1 tablespoon minced garlic

Cilantro leaves, for garnish

1 **FOR THE BEEF:** Thinly slice the beef across the grain ⅛ inch thick, 2 to 3 inches long, and ½ inch wide.

2 Set a 14-inch wok (if the bottom is round, place on a wok ring to stabilize) or 5- to 6-quart pan over medium-high heat, and add oil to a depth of about 1½ inches. Heat the oil until it reaches 350°F on a thermometer; adjust heat to maintain temperature.

3 Place the flour in a large bowl. Add one-quarter to one-third of the meat, tossing slices to coat with the flour. Lift out the beef and shake off the excess flour; spread out on a plate. Repeat to coat the remaining slices.

4 When the oil is hot, add about one-quarter of the floured beef strips, stir to separate, and fry until the beef is crisp and lightly browned, 2 to 3 minutes. Lift out with a slotted spoon and drain on a plate lined with paper towels. Repeat to cook the remainder.

5 **FOR THE STIR-FRY:** In a small bowl, mix the sugar, vinegar, wine, soy sauce, oyster sauce, and chile sauce. Set a 14-inch wok or 12-inch frying pan over high heat. When the pan is hot, after about 1 minute, add 1 tablespoon of the frying oil and rotate the pan to spread.

Add the slivered ginger, minced ginger, and garlic, and stir-fry until the garlic softens, about 30 seconds. Add the vinegar mixture and stir often until the sauce is bubbly all over, 45 seconds to 1 minute. Add the beef and stir-fry over high heat until the slices are coated and hot, about 1 minute. Transfer to a serving bowl and sprinkle with cilantro. ▪

# MIXED WONTON NOODLES

Anthony says that this is a popular dish in small family restaurants in India. Basically, it's a dry, soupless version of noodles and wontons. Anthony tosses boiled wontons and noodles with soy sauce, garlic, and a flavorful oil. It's a wonderfully versatile concept for a quick and easy one-bowl meal, especially if you have wontons stashed in the freezer. If you don't have any wontons, leave them out and add more noodles instead. You can use almost any kind of noodles—thin, round, or flat—just don't overcook them. If you like, top with sliced cooked meat and raw or blanched vegetables.

*Makes 2 servings as a main dish or 4 to 6 servings as part of a multicourse meal*

1 tablespoon Asian sesame oil or vegetable oil (see note)

1 tablespoon minced garlic, or to taste (see note)

¼ teaspoon ground white pepper

12 to 16 fresh or frozen wontons, homemade (recipe follows) or purchased

10 ounces fresh Chinese egg or wheat noodles, or 8 ounces dried

½ cup chopped cilantro

¼ cup thinly sliced green onions, including green tops

2 tablespoons soy sauce, or to taste

**1** In each of two large (2½- to 3-cup) bowls, place half of the sesame oil, garlic, and pepper.

**2** Fill a 5- to 6-quart pan with about 3 quarts water and bring to a boil over high heat. Add the wontons to the boiling water, stir to separate, and cook until the filling is no longer pink in the center (cut to test), 3 to 4 minutes. With a slotted spoon or shallow wire strainer, lift out the wontons, drain off excess water, and place half the wontons in each bowl. Mix the wontons lightly with the oil mixture; cover and keep warm.

**3** Pull the fresh noodles apart. Add the fresh or dried noodles to the boiling water. Stir to separate, and boil gently, uncovered, until the noodles are barely tender to the bite, 2 to 3 minutes for fresh noodles, 5 to 6 minutes for dried. Drain, rinse well with very hot water, and drain again. Add half of the following to each bowl: noodles, cilantro, green onions, and soy sauce. With chopsticks, mix lightly.

**Note:** Instead of using sesame oil and raw garlic, cook the garlic in 2 tablespoons vegetable oil over medium heat, stirring occasionally, just until golden, 1 to 2 minutes.

**Boiled Wontons** Make Steamed Pork Hash (page 148), except do not steam. Place 1 teaspoon of the pork mixture in the center of a wonton skin, bring the wonton skin up around the filling, and at the top of the filling, gather the skin and squeeze gently to seal. The wontons will look like pouches with gathered tops. Place ▶

slightly apart in a single layer on flour-dusted baking sheets. Cover with plastic wrap while filling the remaining skins. Boil as directed in step 2, or cover and chill up to 8 hours. Or freeze until solid, and then transfer to airtight containers. Boiled wontons can also be added to broth for soup or served as an appetizer with a flavorful sauce, such as the one used for Ginger-Garlic Chicken (page 205). Boiled wontons will stick together if allowed to sit in a big clump. Place slightly apart or put in sauce. Makes 5 to 6 dozen. ∎

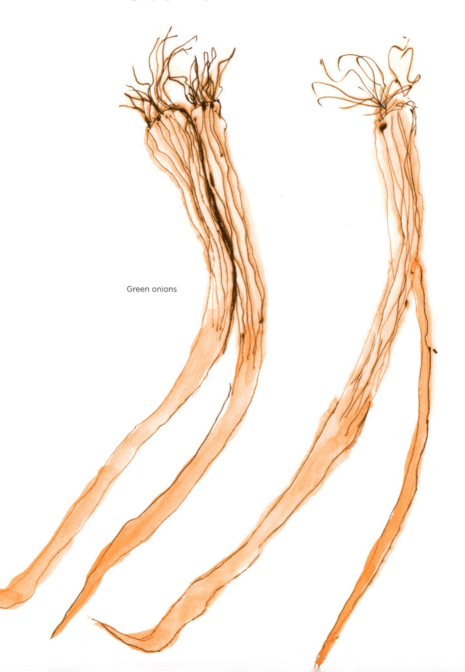

Green onions

# FRIED WONTONS WITH VEGETABLE EGG FLOWER SAUCE

Anthony pours a sauce streaked with stir-fried vegetables and threads of egg over fried pork-filled wontons. The chunky vegetable sauce slightly softens the fried wontons so that each mouthful is both chewy and crisp. To easily manage this dish, fry the wontons ahead, then reheat them in the oven while you quickly cook the vegetable sauce.

*Makes 2 to 3 servings as a main dish or 4 to 6 servings as part of a multicourse meal*

2 dozen fried wontons (page 149)

1⅓ cups chicken broth, homemade (page 267) or purchased

2 teaspoons cornstarch

¼ teaspoon salt, or to taste

¼ teaspoon ground white pepper

1 tablespoon vegetable oil

2 large cloves garlic, minced

1 tablespoon minced fresh ginger

½ cup thinly slivered onion

1 medium carrot (about 3 ounces), peeled and thinly slivered

6 ounces green cabbage, cut into ¼-inch-wide strips (about 3 cups)

1 large egg, lightly beaten

3 tablespoons chopped cilantro, for garnish

**1** If the wontons are freshly fried, keep them warm in a 200°F oven for up to 30 minutes. If the fried wontons are frozen or cold, spread them slightly apart on a shallow baking pan and bake in a preheated 350°F oven until hot and crisp, 10 to 12 minutes.

**2** In a small bowl, mix the broth, cornstarch, ¼ teaspoon salt, and white pepper. Set a 14-inch wok or 12-inch frying pan over high heat. When the pan is hot, after about 1 minute, add the oil and rotate the pan to spread. Add the garlic, ginger, onion, and carrot; stir-fry until the onion is lightly browned, 1 to 2 minutes. Add the cabbage; stir-fry until the cabbage wilts, 1 to 2 minutes. Push the vegetables to the sides of the pan. Stir the broth mixture and add to the center of the pan. Stir until the sauce boils.

**3** Remove the pan from the heat and, with chopsticks, slowly stir the beaten egg into the sauce until it forms long strands. Add salt to taste. Stir the vegetables into the sauce.

**4** Place the hot wontons on a platter or individual plates. Just before serving, spoon the vegetable sauce over the wontons and sprinkle with cilantro. ▪

# Hakka-Indian Flavors in New York

In the winter of 2005, Jacqueline Newman, editor of *Flavor and Fortune,* the magazine of the Institute of the Science and Art of Chinese Cuisine, introduced me to the Lo family, owners of Tangra Masala, a small restaurant in Elmhurst, Queens. The dishes at Tangra Masala defied traditional descriptions. They were neither pure Chinese nor pure Indian, but a delicious blend of Indian spices, soy sauce, and Chinese techniques merged together to create an enticing mix of flavors. When I find out the owners are Hakkas from Calcutta, I know I'll be back.

On my next trip to the East Coast, I meet the family at their second and newest restaurant, Tangra Asian Fusion Cuisine in Sunnyside, Queens. Peter Lo and his brother Lo Sim Fook greet me. I'm lucky to find them, because there are few Hakkas in the area—the Los believe there are only ten to fifteen Hakka families in the state. In 1916, their grandparents came from Meixian, China, to Calcutta, and then moved to Darjeeling, in the mountains. They had three sons and three daughters. "China had problems; the rule was bad and there were economic hurdles," says Sim Fook. In those days, the British ruled half the world, and the East India Company paved the path. Because India was the closest country to China, many Chinese emigrated there during that time.

Tangra is the name of the Chinese neighborhood in Calcutta. Most of the Chinese residents there worked in the tannery business or as dentists, carpenters, or shoemakers. The Lo family was in the shoe business. "At one time, the Chinese presence was very strong in Calcutta. We had beautiful Chinese schools. The Taiwanese government gave us books and we had a Canadian school run by priests," says Sim Fook. Then India closed the tanneries and tried to move the Hakka to undesirable areas. "The Chinese are invisible there now. The government feels Hakkas don't exist. We have no identity." In the 1962 Sino-Indian War, many Chinese residents were put under house arrest. After the war, many left India.

In 1983, the Los' sister came to the United States. Soon, most of the family followed to pursue a better future. All the siblings worked different jobs before eventually opening Tangra Masala together. Peter Tseng, a Hakka chef from Calcutta, joined them as a partner.

Peter Lo, who also cooks, talks about the restaurant's food: "Originally our food was like what we ate in China, but over time it changed. Spices were available and we experimented. Eventually we moved from the mainstream. In India, there is very little pork, because Muslims don't eat it. Chicken is universal. We add spices and chiles for chile chicken, our most popular dish. Pakora is an Indian dish. We use different spices and the batter is different. We sharpen the flavors of the food for the customers' tastes. Indian customers like a crispy texture and spicy taste."

Soon an Indian couple enters the restaurant, and Sim Fook greets them in Hindi. Others follow. As we dig into our tangra beef, we taste that crispy, spicy flavor that their customers like. We love it, too.

## TANGRA MASALA BEEF

This intensely spiced dish combines Indian spices with Chinese stir-frying technique. It starts with a masala, or spice paste, that explodes with hot chiles, warm cumin, fragrant coriander, and zesty ginger. Chef Peter Tseng makes a big batch of red masala to use in various dishes. He adds spoonfuls to stir-fries to infuse them with vivid red color and a spicy background. He boosts the flavor with extra chiles, garlic, and fresh ginger as he stir-fries the ingredients. I've simplified the basic masala recipe and omitted the food coloring for a more natural brick-red color. Double or triple the masala to use another time; it will keep in the refrigerator for a few weeks. Use the versatile spice paste with beef, lamb, chicken, or shrimp.

*Makes 3 to 4 servings as a main dish or 5 to 6 servings as part of a multicourse meal*

### MASALA

2 tablespoons sweet paprika

1 teaspoon ground coriander

½ teaspoon cayenne

½ teaspoon ground ginger

½ teaspoon salt

¼ teaspoon garlic powder, or
   1 teaspoon minced garlic

1 tablespoon vegetable oil

2 teaspoons cumin seeds

2 tablespoons chopped onion or shallot

1 teaspoon sugar

1½ to 2 tablespoons water, or as
   needed

**1 FOR THE MASALA:** In a small bowl, mix the paprika, coriander, cayenne, ginger, salt, and garlic powder. Set a 6- to 10-inch frying pan over medium heat. When the pan is hot, after about 1 minute, add the oil and cumin seeds. Shake the pan until the seeds are lightly browned, about 30 seconds. Add the onion and stir occasionally until it begins to brown, 30 seconds to 1 minute. Add the paprika mixture and stir until blended and fragrant, 30 seconds to 1 minute. Remove the pan from the heat. Stir in the sugar and enough water to make a moist paste.

**2 FOR THE MEAT:** Thinly cut the beef across the grain into slices ⅛ inch thick, 2 to 3 inches long, and 1 inch wide. In a medium bowl, mix the egg white, cornstarch, oil, salt, and pepper. Add the meat and stir until coated. ▶

## MEAT

1 pound beef flank steak

1 large egg white

1 teaspoon cornstarch

1 teaspoon vegetable oil

½ teaspoon salt

¼ teaspoon ground black pepper

## STIR-FRY

3 tablespoons vegetable oil

2 tablespoons chopped onion
or shallot

2 tablespoons minced garlic

1 tablespoon minced fresh ginger

2 to 3 teaspoons minced jalapeño
chile

½ cup water

¼ cup thinly sliced green onions,
including green tops

**3  FOR THE STIR-FRY:** Set a 14-inch wok or 12-inch frying pan over high heat. When the pan is hot, after about 1 minute, add 1 tablespoon of the oil and rotate the pan to spread. Add half of the meat mixture and stir-fry until the meat is lightly browned, 2 to 3 minutes. Transfer the meat to a serving dish. Return the pan to high heat and repeat with an additional 1 tablespoon oil and the remaining meat.

**4**  Return the pan to medium-high heat. Add the remaining 1 tablespoon oil to the pan. Add the onion, garlic, ginger, and chile; stir-fry until the onion softens, about 30 seconds. Add the masala and water and stir to blend. Add the meat and green onions. Stir-fry until the meat is hot and well coated with the masala, about 1 minute. Transfer to a serving dish.

**Notes:**  If you plan to make this dish often, you can triple the masala and store, airtight, in the refrigerator up to about 3 weeks. Use about 3 tablespoons masala for each recipe. Stored masala may be drier than fresh-made; if needed, add more water to blend into a sauce in step 4. Shop at ethnic markets, such as Indian, Asian, or Middle Eastern, for fresh spices sold in bulk at reasonable prices.

| | |
|---|---|
| **Tangra Masala Chicken** | Substitute 1 pound boneless, skinless chicken thighs, trimmed of fat, for the beef. |
| **Tangra Masala Lamb** | Substitute 1 pound boneless leg of lamb or lamb top round, trimmed of fat, for the beef. |
| **Tangra Masala Shrimp** | Substitute 1 pound peeled, deveined shrimp (31 to 35 per pound) for the beef. In step 2, slice the shrimp in half lengthwise. In step 3, stir-fry the shrimp just until pink, about 1 minute. ■ |

# GARLIC NOODLES AND SHRIMP

Many Indians know this dish as Hakka chow mein or lo mein, or Hakka noodles. At Tangra Asian Fusion Cuisine, this popular dish is called garlic noodles. The restaurant offers many versions of this noodle dish, using different vegetables or meats, or making it vegetarian. Extra chiles, garlic, and pepper give these stir-fried noodles a spicy Indian flavor. In India, a dish of soy sauce with minced chiles is often served alongside, to add to taste.

*Makes 2 to 3 servings as a main dish or 6 to 8 servings as part of a multicourse meal*

14 to 16 ounces fresh Chinese wheat or egg noodles, or 12 ounces dried

8 ounces broccoli florets, cut into ¾-inch chunks (about 2 cups)

12 ounces peeled, deveined shrimp (31 to 35 per pound)

2 teaspoons Chinese rice wine (shaoxing) or dry sherry

½ teaspoon salt, or to taste

½ teaspoon ground black pepper

2 tablespoons vegetable oil

2 tablespoons minced garlic

2 to 5 teaspoons minced jalapeño chile

1 cup thinly slivered red bell pepper

1 cup thinly slivered onion

½ cup thinly slivered carrots

2 tablespoons soy sauce

1  In an 8- to 10-quart pan over high heat, bring 3 to 4 quarts water to a boil. Pull the noodles apart and drop into the water; stir to separate. Boil gently just until noodles are barely tender to the bite, 2 to 3 minutes for fresh, 5 to 6 minutes for dried. Add the broccoli to the noodles. Cook just until the broccoli is bright green, about 30 seconds. Drain the noodles and broccoli, rinse well with hot water, and drain again.

2  In a medium bowl, mix the shrimp, wine, salt, and pepper.

3  Set a 14-inch wok over high heat. When the pan is hot, after about 1 minute, add the oil and rotate the pan to spread. Add the garlic, chile, bell pepper, onion, and carrots. Stir-fry until the onion begins to brown, 1 to 2 minutes. Add the shrimp mixture and stir-fry until the shrimp are pink, about 2 minutes.

4  Reduce the heat to medium. Add the noodles with broccoli and the soy sauce. Stir-fry until the noodles are hot and the ingredients are well blended, 2 to 3 minutes. Add salt to taste, if needed. Transfer to a serving dish or individual plates.

**Note:** Use a well-seasoned or nonstick wok so the noodles won't stick. ■

# SOFT TOFU IN SWEET RICE WINE SAUCE

Whenever I cook this dish, we can't stop eating it. By meal's end, our plates are scraped clean. Morsels of soft tofu mingle with bits of minced shrimp and pork or chicken in a mellow rice wine sauce. This is a favorite dish of Peter Tseng, the chef at Tangra Asian Fusion Cuisine. He adds fermented sweet wine rice, the wet sediment from making sweet rice wine, and dried red yeast rice to counter the sweetness with a slight astringency and earthiness. The yeast also speckles the sauce with red. These fermented rice products add a boozy complexity to the sauce, but you can a make a simple, and still delicious, rendition without them. Peter's technique of blanching the soft tofu in boiling water firms and plumps the silky bean curd so that it retains its seductive texture without falling apart.

*Makes 3 to 4 servings as a main dish or 6 to 8 servings as part of a multicourse meal*

## SAUCE

2 teaspoons red yeast rice (optional; see notes)

3 tablespoons boiling water

⅓ cup chicken broth, homemade (page 267) or purchased

⅓ cup fermented sweet wine rice, including liquid (see notes)

2 tablespoons Chinese rice wine (shaoxing) or dry sherry

1 tablespoon soy sauce

1 teaspoon cornstarch

½ teaspoon salt

¼ teaspoon ground black pepper

## STIR-FRY

14 to 16 ounces soft tofu

4 ounces boneless, skinless chicken thighs, trimmed of fat, or pork butt (see notes)

**1 FOR THE SAUCE:** Place the red yeast rice in a fine strainer and rinse well. Pour into a small bowl and cover with the boiling water. Let stand until the red yeast rice is soft, about 5 minutes. Stir in the broth, wine rice, wine, soy sauce, cornstarch, salt, and pepper.

**2 FOR THE STIR-FRY:** In a 3- to 4-quart pan over high heat, bring 1½ to 2 quarts water to a boil. Drain the tofu and invert onto a rimless dinner plate or wooden board. Cut the tofu into ½-inch cubes and gently slide the tofu into the boiling water. When the water begins to barely simmer, remove the pan from the heat. Let the tofu stand in the hot water until ready to stir-fry.

**3** Finely chop the chicken and shrimp. Gently drain the tofu in a colander.

**4** Set a 14-inch wok or 12-inch frying pan over high heat. When the pan is hot, after about 1 minute, add the oil and rotate the pan to spread. Add the garlic, chicken, and shrimp. Stir-fry until the meat mixture is slightly browned and crumbly, 1 to 2 minutes. Stir the sauce mixture and add to the pan. Stir until the sauce boils, about 30 seconds. Add the drained tofu to the pan and cook, stirring gently, until the tofu absorbs some of the

4 ounces peeled, deveined shrimp (about 8 shrimp, 31 to 35 per pound; see notes)

2 tablespoons vegetable oil

1 tablespoon minced garlic

3 tablespoons thinly sliced green onions, including green tops, for garnish

sauce, 1 to 2 minutes. Transfer to a serving dish and sprinkle with the green onions.

Notes: If you can't find red yeast rice and fermented sweet wine rice, make this less complex sauce: Mix ⅓ cup chicken broth, ⅓ cup cream sherry, 3 tablespoons water, 2 tablespoons dry sherry, 1 tablespoon soy sauce, 2 teaspoons cornstarch, ½ teaspoon salt, and ¼ teaspoon ground black pepper.

For a shortcut, use 8 ounces ground pork instead of chopping the chicken and shrimp. ∎

## STIR-FRIED GROUND BEEF AND SALTED MUSTARD GREENS

Peter Lo learned to cook from his mother. For a quick, flavorful meal for the restaurant staff or his family, he stir-fries ground beef and salted mustard greens with a little chile to give it Indian heat. Sim Fook, his brother, likes to eat this loose hash with hot rice for breakfast.

*Makes 2 to 3 servings as a main dish or 4 to 6 servings as part of a multicourse meal*

1 cup chopped salted mustard greens, homemade (page 146) or purchased

1 tablespoon vegetable oil

1 tablespoon minced garlic

1 to 2 tablespoons minced jalapeño chile

8 ounces ground beef

2 teaspoons soy sauce, or to taste

1 teaspoon sugar, or to taste

1 teaspoon rice vinegar, or to taste

Chopped cilantro, for garnish

1 Rinse the mustard greens and place in a medium bowl. Cover with water and soak 5 to 10 minutes. Drain well and squeeze out excess water.

2 Set a 14-inch wok or 12-inch frying pan over high heat. When the pan is hot, after about 1 minute, add the oil and rotate the pan to spread. Add the garlic, chile, and beef. Stir-fry until the beef is crumbly and lightly browned, 2 to 3 minutes. Add the mustard greens, soy sauce, sugar, and vinegar. Stir-fry until the greens are hot, about 1 minute. Transfer to a serving bowl and sprinkle with cilantro. ∎

Clams, chile, and cilantro

# SIX

# Return to Gold Mountain

Even though I found my Hakka roots in China, Gold Mountain is my home. Popo entered this county with uncertainty and fear, but she prevailed so that I could prosper and succeed. As my journey tracing the Hakka diaspora returns to where it started, I wish that Popo were here to teach me how to cook and to answer my many questions. More than fifty years have passed since she lectured me about my Hakka identity. In the last seven years, I've interviewed over fifty Hakkas around the world. I saw common traits among a great majority of them, especially the women. Many reminded me of Popo. A steely streak of determination ran through their core. A practical, no-nonsense attitude pervaded any task they managed. They adapted and survived in any situation.

One such woman becomes my Hakka mentor in California. With Popo and my parents gone, I need someone nearby to show me the basics of how a Hakka cooks at home. As a youngster, I wasn't ready to pay much attention to cooking. Now the time is right. I find my Hakka cooking coach in an old friend, Fah Liong. Like Popo, Fah arrived in Gold Mountain as a young wife—not from China, but from Indonesia. Her ingredients from a Southeast Asian kitchen vary a bit from Popo's, but that's the richness of the Hakka traveling kitchen. Like Popo, she once ran a restaurant briefly and learned to adapt to California ingredients and tastes. I marvel at the simple ease with which she uses her small paring knife to fastidiously trim fat from meat and cut vegetables into thin slivers. "It's all in your hands," she says. "Different people can work with the same ingredients, but the results are up to the hands of the cook." Her hands teach my hands. Fah learned to cook in order to recapture the flavors of her home, and now she is teaching me to do the same. Finally, I have fulfilled Popo's wishes. Yes, Popo, I'm proud to be Hakka.

After eating a diverse array of Hakka food around the globe, I'm also pleased to find two interesting Hakka restaurants right in my own backyard. One is more than three decades old; the other is a fledgling. Although traditional, both feature dishes appealing to my California-bred tastes. Flavors taste brighter. More fresh seafood and vegetables appear, and many dishes feel leaner and lighter.

## My Hakka Mentor

I met Fah Liong in 1971 when I joined the staff of *Sunset* magazine, where she also worked. She was one of the first Hakkas I met to whom I wasn't related. Throughout my journey, this self-taught cook, who took great inspiration from her Indonesian parents, agrees to share her repertoire of Hakka dishes and answer my many questions. We shop and cook.

Fah, husband Henry, and daughter Irene sailed from Indonesia to California when Henry came to study at Stanford in 1962. "I had to learn to cook; otherwise, we would have starved," says Fah. For this young wife and mother, cooking was a matter of survival. Fah arrived with no practical cooking skills, but she hungered for the aromas and flavors of her mother's kitchen. There were very few Hakkas in the San Francisco Bay Area. "When I shopped in Chinatown, the Cantonese shopkeepers just turned away from me. I had to learn to speak Cantonese," she explains.

Fah grew up as the youngest of eight siblings in Sumatra. Her mother, who was from Perak, Malaysia, married her father, from Sumatra, in 1918. "Meme [Mother] cooked all the meals. I used to watch her. My dad loved to eat and was also a good cook. He mostly went to the market to get groceries. But I never learned." In California, missing the foods of home, Fah taught herself to cook many of the dishes of her youth. Phone calls to her mother in Indonesia guided her. Like her mother, she is a natural, intuitive cook, creating recipes with what she has on hand. "What I cook at home is what I grew up with," she says. "My family ate Chinese and Indonesian food, but rarely mixed them. Their flavors are different."

Her mother gave her this cooking advice: "Always use the highest-quality ingredients. Keep practicing until you're good; you need to be patient when cooking. Prepare your ingredients first, and then cook, so you don't waste your time." Her mother's words and spirit guided Fah when she and her husband, Henry, opened Fah's Restaurant, an Indonesian restaurant in Redwood City, California. They ran the restaurant for four years, until Henry's health issues forced them to close. Now, more than forty years later, she helps me make sense of my jumble of recipes and remember the Hakka foods of my youth. Most of all, she shows me how to cook Hakka comfort food for the soul.

## SOY-GLAZED CHICKEN MORSELS

A sweet soy sauce glaze, embedded with bits of garlic and ginger, cloaks chunks of chicken. Fah uses the aromatic Indonesian sweet soy sauce known as *kecap manis,* but you can also make your own. Serve these delicious chicken nuggets as an appetizer or main dish. Leftovers can be eaten over a bowl of noodles, tossed with a little soy and shreds of lettuce.

*Makes 4 to 5 servings as a main dish or 8 to 10 servings as an appetizer or as part of a multicourse meal*

1½ pounds boneless, skinless chicken thighs, trimmed of fat

2 tablespoons vegetable oil

2 tablespoons minced garlic

2 tablespoons thinly slivered fresh ginger

¼ cup Chinese rice wine (shaoxing) or dry sherry

2 tablespoons sweet soy sauce, homemade (page 269), or purchased *kecap manis* (see note)

⅛ teaspoon ground white pepper

Thinly sliced iceberg or romaine lettuce, for serving

Cilantro sprigs, for garnish

Cherry tomatoes, for garnish

**1** Cut the chicken into 1-inch chunks.

**2** Set a 12-inch nonstick frying pan over high heat. When the pan is hot, after about 1 minute, add the oil and rotate the pan to spread. Add the chicken in a single layer, and cook until lightly browned, about 3 minutes. Turn over and continue cooking until the chicken is lightly browned on the other side and no longer pink in the center (cut to test), 3 to 4 minutes longer. Reduce the heat to medium-high.

**3** Push the chicken to the sides of the pan and add the garlic and ginger. Stir until the garlic begins to brown, about 15 seconds. Add the wine, sweet soy sauce, and white pepper. Stir often until the sauce glazes the chicken, 1 to 2 minutes. Transfer to a serving plate lined with lettuce. Garnish with the cilantro and tomatoes.

**Note:** For a quick alternative to sweet soy sauce, mix 1½ tablespoons dark soy sauce and 1½ tablespoons packed brown sugar. ∎

# PORK AND SEAFOOD LETTUCE WRAPS

Fah stir-fries a mixture of pork, shrimp, cabbage, and squid to create a delicious filling for cool, crisp lettuce cups. Although she uses dried squid in this recipe, I prefer the taste and texture of fresh calamari. Small calamari are widely available fresh or frozen, and are sometimes sold already cleaned. Eat as an appetizer or as a main course for two with rice. Spoon a little rice into the bottom of the lettuce cups to soak up the savory juices.

*Makes 2 servings as a main dish or 4 to 6 servings as an appetizer or part of a multi-course meal*

3 or 4 fresh small squid or calamari (about 4 ounces total)

2 tablespoons Chinese rice wine (shaoxing) or dry sherry

4 ounces peeled, deveined shrimp (about 10 shrimp, 36 to 40 per pound)

6 ounces boneless pork shoulder or loin, trimmed of fat

1 teaspoon soy sauce

2 tablespoons vegetable oil

1 tablespoon minced garlic

6 ounces cabbage, thinly sliced (about 2 cups)

1 tablespoon oyster sauce

½ teaspoon salt, or to taste

¼ teaspoon ground black pepper

10 to 12 iceberg lettuce leaves, each about 5 inches wide (see note)

1 To clean fresh squid: Pull the tube and head apart. Pull out and discard the long, clear quill in the tube. Press out the insides of the tube. Pull off and discard the thin speckled membrane covering the tube. Cut in front of the eyes to sever the tentacles; discard the eyes and attached material. Squeeze the tentacles near the cut end to pop out the hard beak; discard the beak. Rinse the tubes and tentacles well and drain. Cut the tubes crosswise into ¼-inch-wide rings; leave the tentacles whole.

2 In a small bowl, mix the squid with 1 tablespoon of the wine. Cut the shrimp in half lengthwise through the back. In another small bowl, mix the shrimp with the remaining 1 tablespoon wine.

3 Cut the pork into matchsticks ¼ inch thick and 2 to 3 inches long. In a small bowl, mix the pork with the soy sauce.

4 Set a 14-inch wok or 12-inch frying pan over high heat. When the pan is hot, after about 1 minute, add the oil and rotate the pan to spread. Add the garlic and stir-fry just until lightly browned, about 15 seconds. Add the pork; stir-fry just until the pork loses its pinkness, about 1 minute. Add the shrimp with wine. Stir-fry until the shrimp begin to turn pink, about 30 seconds. Add the cabbage and squid with wine; stir-fry just until the cabbage begins to wilt, about 1 minute. Stir in the oyster sauce, salt, and pepper.

**5** Transfer to a serving dish. Serve with the lettuce leaves. Scoop the hot pork and seafood mixture into a leaf and roll up to eat.

**Note:** To make lettuce cups: Set 1 head iceberg lettuce, stem side down, on a cutting board. About 3 inches above the base, cut the lettuce at a 45-degree angle through the core. Repeat around all 4 sides of the head. Lift off and discard any wilted outer leaves and cut away any remaining core. Turn the head cut side up and rinse well. Turn the head over and drain well, shaking out excess water. Wrap the lettuce in a towel. Slip into a plastic bag and chill until crisp, at least 30 minutes or up to 1 day. Lift off lettuce cups to use. Cut cups in half, if desired. ■

Iceberg lettuce

# STIR-FRIED CHICKEN AND CUCUMBERS

When cucumbers are briefly cooked, as in this stir-fry, they retain much of their fresh coolness and crunch. Fresh red chile streaks the dish with color and heat, while a mild sweet-sour sauce ties it all together. It's a bit like eating a hot salad.

*Makes 2 servings as a main dish or 4 servings as part of a multicourse meal*

## CHICKEN

8 ounces boneless, skinless chicken thighs, trimmed of fat

1 teaspoon vegetable oil

1 teaspoon cornstarch

1 teaspoon soy sauce

⅛ teaspoon ground white pepper

## SAUCE

⅓ cup water

1 tablespoon rice vinegar

2 teaspoons sugar

1½ teaspoons cornstarch

1 teaspoon soy sauce

¼ teaspoon salt

⅛ teaspoon ground white pepper

## STIR-FRY

1 large cucumber (about 12 ounces)

1 small fresh chile (preferably red), such as jalapeño or Fresno, or to taste

2 tablespoons vegetable oil

3 tablespoons thinly slivered fresh ginger

2 tablespoons minced garlic

⅓ cup water

**1 FOR THE CHICKEN:** Cut the chicken into strips ¼ inch thick, 2 inches long, and ½ inch wide. In a small bowl, mix the chicken with the oil, cornstarch, soy sauce, and white pepper.

**2 FOR THE SAUCE:** In a small bowl, mix the water, vinegar, sugar, cornstarch, soy sauce, salt, and white pepper.

**3 FOR THE STIR-FRY:** Peel down the length of the cucumber, alternating a ½-inch strip of green skin alongside each peeled strip for a striped effect. Cut the cucumber in half lengthwise. With a spoon, scoop out and discard the seeds. Cut each half in half lengthwise. Cut each quarter diagonally into ½-inch-thick slices; discard the ends. Cut the chile in half lengthwise. For less heat, scrape out all or some of the seeds and veins. Thinly slice the chile crosswise.

**4** Set a 14-inch wok or 12-inch frying pan over high heat. When the pan is hot, after about 1 minute, add the oil and rotate the pan to spread. Add the ginger and garlic; stir-fry until the garlic begins to brown, about 15 seconds. Add the chicken mixture. Stir-fry until the chicken begins to brown, 2 to 3 minutes. Stir in the cucumber. Add the water and stir-fry until the cucumber is barely tender to the bite but still retains some crunch, 2 to 3 minutes. Stir the sauce mixture and add to the pan. Stir-fry until the sauce boils, about 30 seconds. Stir in the chile to taste. Transfer to a serving dish. ∎

# BRAISED CHICKEN WINGS IN BEAN SAUCE

I love the way the smooth-textured flesh slips off the bones in this simple stew made with chicken wings. The salty fermented ground bean sauce and a generous measure of black pepper give the pan juices robust body and a spicy kick.

*Makes 3 to 4 servings as a main dish or 6 to 8 servings as part of a multicourse meal*

2 tablespoons vegetable oil

2 pounds chicken wing sections, meaty sections preferred

2 tablespoons minced garlic

2 cups water, or as needed

2 tablespoons ground bean sauce or hoisin sauce

1 tablespoon soy sauce, or to taste

1 tablespoon sugar (omit if using hoisin sauce)

½ teaspoon coarsely ground black pepper

Cilantro leaves, for garnish

1  Set a 14-inch wok or 5- to 6-quart pan over high heat. When the pan is hot, after about 1 minute, add the oil and rotate the pan to spread. When the oil is hot, add the chicken wing sections and stir occasionally until lightly browned, 5 to 8 minutes. Stir in the garlic; cook until soft, about 15 seconds. Add the water, bean sauce, soy sauce, sugar, and pepper. Return to a boil.

2  Reduce heat, cover, and simmer, stirring occasionally, until the meat is tender when pierced, 35 to 45 minutes. With a slotted spoon, lift out the wings and place on a serving dish; cover to keep warm. Skim off and discard the fat from the pan juices. Measure the juices. If more than ¾ to 1 cup, boil, uncovered, over high heat until reduced to that amount. If less than ¾ to 1 cup, add water to make that amount and bring to a boil. Pour the pan juices over the wings, and garnish with the cilantro.

### Braised Pork Spareribs in Bean Sauce

Substitute 2 pounds pork spareribs for the chicken wings. Ask the butcher to saw across the ribs to make 1-inch-wide strips. Rinse the ribs and pat dry. Trim off the excess fat and cut between the bones to separate into bite-sized pieces. In step 2, the ribs may take 50 to 70 minutes to become tender. ■

# SOY-BRAISED CHICKEN AND MUSHROOMS

This is a popular stew with several variations in the Hakka repertoire. Dark, meaty mushrooms, chicken, and pungent ginger braise in sweet soy sauce for a mahogany-hued stew. My mother used dark soy sauce and sugar to achieve the traditional glossy sauce on pieces of bone-in chicken. Fah uses *kecap manis* (sweet soy sauce), popular in her home in Indonesia, on boneless chunks of chicken thighs.

*Makes 4 to 6 servings as a main dish or 8 servings as part of a multicourse meal*

12 dried shiitake mushrooms, each about 2 inches wide

3½ cups hot water, or as needed

1½ pounds boneless, skinless chicken thighs

2 tablespoons vegetable oil

3 tablespoons thinly slivered fresh ginger

2 tablespoons minced garlic

3 tablespoons sweet soy sauce, homemade (page 269), or purchased *kecap manis* (see note)

½ teaspoon salt, or to taste

¼ teaspoon ground white pepper, or to taste

3 green onions, including green tops, cut into 2-inch lengths

1 Rinse the mushrooms and place in a medium bowl. Cover with the hot water. Soak until the mushrooms are soft, 20 minutes for thin caps to 2 hours for thick caps. Squeeze excess water out of the mushrooms and reserve the soaking water. Remove and discard the mushroom stems, and cut the caps in half.

2 Meanwhile, trim off and discard the excess fat from the chicken. Cut the chicken into 1-inch chunks.

3 Set a 14-inch wok or 5- to 6-quart pan over high heat. When the pan is hot, after about 1 minute, add the oil and rotate the pan to spread. Add the ginger and garlic and stir-fry until the garlic begins to brown, 15 to 30 seconds. Add the chicken and stir often until it begins to brown, 4 to 5 minutes. Add the mushrooms and 1½ cups of the mushroom-soaking water, pouring carefully so the sediment stays behind. Add the sweet soy sauce, and bring to a boil.

4 Reduce the heat, cover, and simmer, stirring occasionally, until the mushrooms are soft and the chicken is tender when pierced, 15 to 20 minutes. Transfer the meat with a slotted spoon to a serving bowl. Skim off and discard the fat from the pan juices. Measure the juices. If more than 1¼ cups, boil, uncovered, over high heat, until reduced to that amount. If less than 1¼ cups, add hot water to make that amount and bring to a boil. Add the salt and white pepper. Stir in the green onions. Pour into the serving bowl.

Note: For a quick substitute for the sweet soy sauce, mix 2 tablespoons dark soy sauce and 2 tablespoons packed brown sugar. ∎

# GINGER-GARLIC CHICKEN

This robust sauce combines ginger-and-garlic-infused oil with soy sauce. Fah serves this sauce over chunks of boiled dark-meat chicken. I have adapted the concept to this somewhat modern presentation and serve the sauce over moist chicken breasts that have been gently cooked using a Chinese technique. The versatile sauce is also delicious over blanched Chinese broccoli, bok choy, steamed fish, or boiled wontons. To stretch this recipe into a one-bowl meal with noodles, see the variation that follows.

*Makes 3 to 4 servings as a main dish or 5 to 6 servings as an appetizer or part of a multicourse meal*

## SAUCE

3 tablespoons vegetable oil

3 tablespoons evenly minced garlic (see note)

2 tablespoons minced fresh ginger

3 tablespoons soy sauce

½ teaspoon sugar

## CHICKEN

2 cups shredded iceberg or romaine lettuce

About 1 pound Steeped Chicken Breasts (page 22), warm or cool

2 to 3 tablespoons thinly sliced green onions, including green tops, or cilantro leaves, for garnish

**1 FOR THE SAUCE:** In a 6- to 8-inch frying pan over medium heat, stir the oil, garlic, and ginger until the garlic is light gold, 2 to 3 minutes. Do not overcook. Pour into a small bowl and stir in the soy sauce and sugar.

**2 FOR THE CHICKEN:** Place a bed of lettuce on a platter. Slice the chicken across the grain ½ inch thick. Attractively arrange the chicken on the platter. Stir the sauce to blend and spoon a few tablespoons over the chicken. Sprinkle with green onions. Offer the remaining sauce to add to taste.

Note: Finely chop the garlic so the pieces are close to the same size. When fried in oil, the pieces will cook more evenly. If there's a great variation in size, some garlic pieces will burn while others remain raw. The goal is golden toasted garlic.

## Ginger-Garlic Chicken over Noodles

In a 6- to 8-quart pan over high heat, bring about 3 quarts water to a boil. Add 8 to 10 ounces dried Chinese wheat or egg noodles to the boiling water, stir, and cook until barely tender to the bite, 5 to 6 minutes. Drain, rinse the noodles with very hot water, and drain again. Place the noodles in three large (3-cup) bowls. Top each bowl with equal portions of the shredded lettuce and chicken. Drizzle the ginger-garlic sauce over the noodles to taste. Sprinkle with the green onions. Makes 3 servings. ∎

# STIR-FRIED CARROTS, RADISHES, AND SHRIMP

Fah's mother cut dense carrots and Asian white radish into thin slivers and then stir-fried them with shrimp for a light, colorful dish with fresh crunch.

*Makes 2 servings as a main dish or 4 servings as part of a multicourse meal*

8 ounces peeled, deveined shrimp (31 to 35 per pound)

2 tablespoons Chinese rice wine (shaoxing) or dry sherry

¼ teaspoon salt

2 medium carrots (about 6 ounces total)

4 ounces Asian white radish, such as daikon

2 green onions

2 tablespoons vegetable oil

1½ tablespoons minced garlic

½ cup water or chicken broth, homemade (page 267) or purchased

1 tablespoon fish sauce, or to taste

⅛ teaspoon ground white pepper, or to taste

**1** In a small bowl, mix the shrimp, 1 tablespoon of the wine, and the salt.

**2** Peel the carrots and radish. Thinly slice the carrots and radish on the diagonal ¼ inch thick. Stack a few slices and cut lengthwise into ¼-inch-wide slivers; you should have about 1 cup of each. Trim the ends off the green onions. Cut the green onions into 1-inch lengths, including the green tops. Cut the thick end pieces in half lengthwise.

**3** Set a 14-inch wok or 12-inch frying pan over high heat. When the pan is hot, after about 1 minute, add 1 tablespoon of the oil and rotate the pan to spread. Add the garlic; stir-fry until lightly browned, about 15 seconds. Add the marinated shrimp. Stir-fry until the shrimp turn pink, 1 to 2 minutes. Transfer the shrimp to a serving dish.

**4** Return the pan to high heat. Add the remaining 1 tablespoon oil along with the carrots and radish; stir-fry to coat the vegetables with oil. Add the water and stir-fry until the vegetables are crisp-tender, 2 to 3 minutes. (If the liquid evaporates before the vegetables are done, add 2 to 3 tablespoons water and continue cooking.) Add the green onions, shrimp, remaining 1 tablespoon wine, fish sauce, and white pepper; stir-fry until the shrimp are hot, about 30 seconds. Transfer to a serving dish. ∎

# STIR-FRIED BEAN SPROUTS, BEEF, AND PICKLED MUSTARD GREENS

A mildly piquant sauce lightly coats crunchy bean sprouts and tender beef strips. Red pepper slivers streak it with vivid color. The addition of pickled or salted mustard greens sharpens the flavor profile and provides a Hakka accent.

## BEEF

8 ounces beef flank steak, trimmed of fat

1 tablespoon soy sauce

1 teaspoon cornstarch

½ teaspoon vegetable oil

⅛ teaspoon ground white pepper

## SAUCE

3 tablespoons water

1 tablespoon rice vinegar

2 teaspoons soy sauce

2 teaspoons sugar

1 teaspoon cornstarch

¼ teaspoon salt

⅛ teaspoon ground white pepper

## STIR-FRY

⅔ cup thinly slivered pickled or salted mustard greens, homemade (page 147) or purchased

2 tablespoons vegetable oil

3 tablespoons thinly slivered fresh ginger

1 tablespoon minced garlic

1 cup thinly slivered red bell pepper

6 cups bean sprouts (about 12 ounces)

⅓ cup coarsely chopped cilantro (optional)

**1** **FOR THE BEEF:** Cut the beef across the grain into slices ⅛ inch thick, ½ inch wide, and 2 to 3 inches long. In a small bowl, mix the beef with the soy sauce, cornstarch, oil, and white pepper.

**2** **FOR THE SAUCE:** In a small bowl, mix the water, vinegar, soy sauce, sugar, cornstarch, salt, and white pepper.

**3** **FOR THE STIR-FRY:** Rinse the mustard greens and place in a small bowl. Cover with water and soak about 5 minutes. Drain the greens and squeeze out excess water.

**4** Set a 14-inch wok or 12-inch frying pan over high heat. When the pan is hot, after about 1 minute, add the oil and rotate the pan to spread. Add the ginger and garlic; stir-fry until lightly browned, about 15 seconds. Add the beef mixture; stir-fry until lightly browned, 2 to 3 minutes. Stir in the red pepper. Add the bean sprouts and mustard greens; stir-fry until the sprouts have barely wilted but still retain their crunch, 1 to 1½ minutes.

**5** Stir the sauce mixture and add to the pan. Stir-fry until the sauce boils, about 30 seconds. Stir in the cilantro, and pour into a serving dish. ■

# SOY-GLAZED PORK AND MUSHROOM NOODLES

At a small noodle shop near her home in Indonesia, Fah Liong always ordered the same thing: a bowl of noodles topped with dark soy-glazed pork and mushrooms. She eventually asked the Hakka vendor for the recipe. Luckily for us, he shared it. Pork strips and earthy mushrooms braise in dark soy sauce and sugar until infused with a salty sweetness. Serve the glazed pork over noodles with bok choy and crisp bean sprouts; top it off with a clear broth. This savory combination provides the centerpiece for a casual kitchen party. Set out the components and let guests build their own noodle bowl. Or assemble the bowls completely in the kitchen. The robust braised pork topping can be made ahead.

*Makes 6 to 8 servings as a main dish or 12 servings as part of a multicourse meal*

## PORK TOPPING

10 dried shiitake mushrooms, each about 2 inches wide, or 4 ounces fresh shiitake mushrooms

2 pounds boneless pork butt, trimmed of fat

3 tablespoons vegetable oil

1½ cups thinly sliced shallots or red onion (about 6 ounces)

3 tablespoons dark soy sauce

2 tablespoons sugar

1 teaspoon salt

½ teaspoon ground white pepper

## VEGETABLES

8 small heads baby bok choy or *choy sum* (about 1 pound total)

8 cups bean sprouts (about 1 pound)

⅓ cup thinly sliced green onions, including green tops

1  **FOR THE PORK TOPPING:** Rinse the mushrooms. Place the dried mushrooms in a small bowl. Cover with hot water and soak until soft, 20 minutes for thin caps to 2 hours for thick caps. Squeeze out the excess liquid from the soaked mushrooms. Remove and discard the mushroom stems and cut caps into ¼-inch strips.

2  Cut the pork into strips ¼ inch thick, 2 inches long, and ½ inch wide. Place a 14-inch wok or 5- to 6-quart pan over high heat. When the pan is hot, after about 1 minute, add the oil and rotate the pan to spread. Add the shallots and stir often until lightly browned, 3 to 4 minutes. Add the pork and stir often until the meat loses its pinkness, 3 to 4 minutes. Add the sliced mushrooms, dark soy sauce, sugar, salt, and white pepper. Reduce the heat, cover, and simmer, stirring occasionally, until the meat is tender to the bite, 20 to 25 minutes. (If the meat begins to sticks before it is tender, add a few tablespoons of water.) Remove from the heat and cover to keep warm.

3  Shortly before serving, if the pan is dry, add a few tablespoons water and reheat, covered, over medium heat until pork is hot. Uncover and stir often over high heat until most of the juices evaporate and the meat is glazed with sauce. Transfer to a serving dish.

## NOODLES

2 pounds fresh Chinese egg or wheat noodles, or 1¾ pounds dried

3 tablespoons Asian sesame oil

2 tablespoons vegetable oil

2 tablespoons dark soy sauce

¼ teaspoon ground white pepper

## BROTH

2½ quarts chicken broth, homemade (page 267) or purchased

½ cup thinly sliced green onions

⅓ cup Tianjin (Tientsin) preserved vegetable, rinsed, or salt or soy sauce to taste

**4 FOR THE VEGETABLES:** Cut the bok choy lengthwise into ½-inch-wide sections at the base, then crosswise into 2-inch lengths. Up to 30 minutes before serving, fill an 8- to 10-quart pan with about 1 quart water and bring to a boil over high heat. Add the bok choy and cook, uncovered, stirring occasionally, until crisp-tender, 3 to 4 minutes. Stir in the bean sprouts and drain at once. Transfer to a large bowl. Sprinkle with the green onions.

**5 FOR THE NOODLES:** Shortly before serving, in the same 8- to 10-quart pan (no need to wash), bring about 4 quarts water to a boil over high heat. Pull the fresh noodles apart and add to the pan; stir to separate. Cook the noodles until barely tender to the bite, 2 to 3 minutes for fresh, 5 to 6 minutes for dried. Drain, rinse well with very hot water, and drain again. In a large bowl, mix the sesame oil, vegetable oil, dark soy sauce, and white pepper. Add the noodles and mix to coat; cover to keep warm.

**6 FOR THE BROTH:** Pour the broth into a 5- to 6-quart pan or the rinsed pan used for the noodles and bring to a boil over high heat. Add the green onions and preserved vegetable. Leave in the pan or pour into a large bowl. Cover to keep hot.

**7** To serve: Equally distribute the noodles into six to eight large (2- to 3-cup) bowls. For buffet style, offer the pork, vegetables, and hot broth to spoon over the noodles. Or, in the kitchen, distribute the toppings and broth equally over noodles. Or serve the broth in a small bowl alongside the noodles.

**Notes:** The pork topping can be made up to 2 days ahead. After simmering until tender, cool, cover, and chill. Reheat, covered, over medium-low heat, adding a little water if the meat sticks. Then stir over high heat to evaporate the juices until the meat is glazed with sauce.

To bolster the flavor of the broth, after taking the pork out of the pan, add a few cups of the broth to the unwashed pork pan and stir over high heat to loosen the brown film and deglaze the pan. Add the deglazing liquid to the remaining broth. ∎

# STIR-FRIED CHINESE BROCCOLI AND CHICKEN

Every Chinese cook has a basic stir-fry recipe that can be varied with the seasons. Fah uses this one, which keeps the vegetables crisp, the seasonings uncomplicated, and the sauce minimal. The secret to any good stir-fry is to cut the vegetables and meat into similar sizes and shapes and to prepare all the ingredients before turning on the heat. If you can't find Chinese broccoli, broccolini, broccoli raab (rapini), and common broccoli will also work, as long as you cut them into thin, even pieces.

*Makes 2 servings as a main dish or 4 servings as part of a multicourse meal*

12 ounces Chinese broccoli

8 to 10 ounces boneless, skinless chicken thighs, trimmed of fat

2 tablespoons vegetable oil

1½ tablespoons minced garlic

1 tablespoon thinly slivered fresh ginger

½ cup water or chicken broth, homemade (page 267) or purchased, or as needed

2 tablespoons Chinese rice wine (shaoxing) or dry sherry

½ teaspoon salt, or to taste

¼ teaspoon ground white pepper, or to taste

¼ teaspoon sugar

1 Trim off the tough stem ends from the broccoli. Peel the skin off the stalks, if tough. Cut the broccoli into 2-inch pieces, about ½ inch thick; split the stalks lengthwise if thicker than ½ inch. Rinse and drain. Cut the chicken into thin slices, about 2 inches by ½ inches.

2 Place a 14-inch wok or 12-inch frying pan over high heat. When the pan is hot, after about 1 minute, add the oil and rotate the pan to spread. Stir in the garlic and ginger. Add the chicken and stir-fry until lightly browned, 2 to 3 minutes.

3 Add the broccoli and stir-fry to coat with oil. Add the water, wine, salt, white pepper, and sugar. Stir-fry until the broccoli is crisp-tender, 2 to 3 minutes. If the liquid evaporates before the broccoli is done, add about ¼ cup water and continue stir-frying. Add more salt and white pepper to taste, if needed. Transfer to a serving dish. ∎

Chinese broccoli

# PORK AND WHITE RADISH SOUP

Asian white radish (also known as turnip or daikon) softens and sweetens as it simmers with pork in this homespun soup. Fah makes the soup with a base of water and dried squid when she is out of broth. As the pork and radish simmer together, their earthy juices infuse the water to make a light-tasting broth. For a richer flavor, start with chicken broth.

*Makes 6 to 8 servings as part of a multicourse meal*

3 cups chicken broth, homemade (page 267) or purchased, or water (see note)

3 cups water

1 piece dried squid, about 4 inches square (optional)

8 to 10 ounces boneless pork butt or shoulder, trimmed of fat, cut into ½-inch chunks (see note)

12 ounces Asian white radish, such as daikon (an 8- to 10-inch section)

½ to 1 teaspoon salt

¼ teaspoon ground black pepper

⅓ cup coarsely chopped cilantro, for garnish

1 In a 3½- to 4-quart pan, bring the broth and water to a boil over high heat.

2 With tongs, hold the squid 1 to 2 inches over a high flame, turning as needed, until lightly toasted on both sides, about 30 seconds total. Add the squid and pork to the broth and return to a boil. Reduce the heat, cover, and simmer for about 10 minutes.

3 Meanwhile, peel the radish and cut crosswise into 1½-inch lengths. Then cut each piece lengthwise into ½-inch-thick wedges. Add the radish to the broth and return to a simmer over high heat. Reduce the heat, cover, and simmer until the pork and radish are very tender when pierced, about 45 minutes longer.

4 Remove and discard the squid. Skim off the fat from the soup and discard. Add the salt and pepper. Ladle into individual bowls or a large serving bowl and sprinkle with cilantro.

Note: For a more flavorful soup, use all broth. Instead of boneless pork, replace with about 1 pound bone-in pork neck, cut into bite-size chunks. In step 2, simmer the pork neck and squid for about 30 minutes. ∎

# SHRIMP AND CHIVE FRITTERS

Guests will love these lacy shrimp and chive fritters. The secret is a simple thick batter that loosely binds the shrimp and garlic chives together as they fry in hot oil. Fah learned this recipe from her Indonesian mother, Min Kiauw, who invented it with the ingredients she had on hand. You'll find these crisp, craggy morsels positively addictive. Serve them with your favorite red chile sauce; my preference is the Thai sweet chile sauce made by Mae Ploy.

*Makes 8 to 10 servings as an appetizer or as part of a multicourse meal*

6 ounces garlic chives, or 6 ounces green onions plus 2 tablespoons minced garlic

1 cup all-purpose flour (4½ ounces)

¾ teaspoon salt

¼ teaspoon ground white pepper

⅔ cup water, or as needed

1 pound peeled, deveined shrimp (31 to 35 per pound), rinsed and well drained

Vegetable oil, for frying

Chile sauce, homemade (page 268) or purchased

1  Trim off and discard the ends of the chives. Discard any wilted chives. Cut the chives into 2-inch lengths to make about 3 cups. If using green onions, cut into 2-inch lengths, including green tops, then lengthwise into ¼-inch-wide slivers.

2  In a medium bowl, mix the flour, salt, and white pepper. Whisk in ½ cup of the water until blended. Gradually whisk in more water, a tablespoon at a time, until the batter is smooth and the consistency of thick pancake batter. (It should be just thick enough to hold the pieces together. Stir in a little water, if too thick, or more flour, if too thin.) Stir in the chives and shrimp until the batter coats all of the pieces.

3  Set a 14-inch wok (if the bottom is round, place on a wok ring to stabilize) or 5- to 6-quart pan over medium-high heat. Fill the pan with oil to a depth of about 1½ inches. Heat the oil until the temperature reaches 375°F on a thermometer. Adjust the heat to maintain the temperature.

4  With a large flat spoon, scoop up 1 shrimp with about a tablespoon-sized clump of chives; hold near the surface of the oil. With a spatula or another spoon, carefully push the mixture off the spoon into the hot oil. Fry 3 or 4 fritters at a time, placing the fritters slightly apart. Fry until crisp and golden, turning once, 1½ to 2 minutes total. With a slotted spoon or wire strainer, lift out the fritters and drain in a single layer on pans lined with paper towels. Repeat to fry the remainder. Serve at once or place, uncovered, in a 200°F oven up to 30 minutes to keep warm. Serve hot with the chile sauce. ∎

# PORK AND SHRIMP BALL SOUP

Dried ingredients play a big part in the Hakka diet. In this recipe, black fungus, bean thread noodles, and woodsy-tasting lily buds contribute a varied palette of textures and flavors to a clear, healthful broth studded with carrots, potatoes, and pork and shrimp meatballs. You'll need to shop at an Asian market for the dried fungus and lily buds; the dried noodles can be found in the ethnic section of many supermarkets.

*Makes 4 servings as a main dish or 8 servings as part of a multicourse meal*

⅓ cup lightly packed dried lily buds

⅓ cup dried black fungus, such as cloud ears

1 package (1.7 to 2 ounces) dried bean thread noodles

7 cups chicken broth, homemade (page 267) or purchased

1 large carrot (about 5 ounces), peeled and cut into ½-inch cubes

8 ounces peeled, deveined shrimp (31 to 35 per pound)

8 ounces ground pork

2 teaspoons Chinese rice wine (shaoxing) or dry sherry

1½ teaspoons cornstarch

½ teaspoon salt, or to taste

⅛ teaspoon ground white pepper, or to taste

1 large boiling potato such as Yukon Gold (about 8 ounces)

⅓ cup thinly sliced green onions, including green tops

1 Rinse the lily buds and black fungus. Place in a medium bowl and cover with hot water; let stand until soft, 15 to 20 minutes. In another bowl, soak the bean thread noodles in hot water until soft, 5 to 10 minutes. Drain the lily buds and fungus, rinse well, and squeeze out excess water. Tie a knot in the center of each lily bud to keep the buds intact as they cook; if the ends are hard, trim off and discard. Pinch out and discard the hard knobby centers from the fungus; cut the fungus into 1-inch pieces. Drain the noodles. With scissors, cut the noodles into 6-inch lengths.

2 In a covered 5- to 6-quart pan over high heat, bring the broth to a boil. Add the carrot and return to a boil. Reduce the heat, cover, and simmer until the carrot is almost tender when pierced, about 10 minutes.

3 Meanwhile, chop the shrimp until it forms a chunky paste. In a bowl, mix the shrimp, pork, wine, cornstarch, salt, and white pepper until well blended.

4 Add the potato, lily buds, and fungus to the carrot, and return to a boil. Cover and simmer until the potato is almost tender when pierced, about 10 minutes.

5 With a wet hand, pick up a handful of the pork mixture and squeeze to force the mixture through the opening between your thumb and index finger. Scrape off 1-inch meatballs as formed and drop into the simmering ▸

broth. Or, with wet hands, form mixture into 1-inch balls and place on an oiled plate. Slide the meatballs into the simmering broth. Cover and simmer until the meatballs are no longer raw in the center (cut to test), about 5 minutes. Add the drained noodles and bring to a simmer. Add the salt and white pepper to taste. Ladle into bowls and sprinkle with green onions.

Note: The soup (without noodles) can be made up to 1 day ahead, cooled, covered, and chilled. Reheat to simmering, then add soaked drained noodles shortly before serving. ▪

Shrimp and chives

# FAH'S STUFFED TOFU TRIANGLES

Fah Liong uses fish sauce, popular in her native Indonesia, to impart a mild sea flavor to the pork and shrimp filling in these tofu triangles. Bits of shiitake mushrooms add meaty flavor and texture. Steam or poach the triangles in broth; then serve with chile sauce and soy to embellish their fresh, light flavors.

*Makes 2 to 3 servings as a main dish or 4 to 6 servings as part of a multicourse meal*

2 dried shiitake mushrooms, each about 1½ inches wide

4 ounces peeled, deveined shrimp (about 8 shrimp, 31 to 35 per pound)

4 ounces ground pork

2 tablespoons thinly sliced green onions, including green tops

1 tablespoon fish sauce

2 teaspoons cornstarch

¼ teaspoon salt

⅛ teaspoon ground white pepper

1 pound firm tofu

Thinly sliced green onions, including green tops, for garnish

Soy sauce, for serving

Chile sauce, homemade (page 268) or purchased, for serving

**1** Rinse the dried mushrooms and place in a small bowl. Cover with hot water and soak until soft, 20 minutes for thin caps to 2 hours for thick caps. Squeeze out excess liquid. Remove and discard the mushroom stems and finely chop the caps. Finely chop the shrimp. In a small bowl, mix the mushrooms, shrimp, pork, green onions, fish sauce, cornstarch, salt, and white pepper.

**2** Rinse the tofu, and then drain for about 5 minutes. Cut the tofu into 4 squares or rectangles, each about 1 inch thick and 2½ to 3 inches wide. Cut the pieces in half diagonally to make triangles. Lay the tofu triangles in a single layer on a double thickness of towels. Set another double layer of towels on top and press gently to remove excess moisture. Cut a slit down the center of the widest side of each tofu triangle so that it comes within ½ inch of the ends. Cut around the slit to form a generous ¼-inch-wide opening and carefully dig out the tofu to form a pocket. Gently fill the pocket with about 1 tablespoon filling, using a chopstick or small spoon to push the filling into the pocket; the filling can mound slightly on top. Repeat to fill all. Reserve the tofu scraps for another use.

**3** Stand the tofu triangles, filling side up, slightly apart in a 9-inch shallow heat-proof dish that will fit inside a steamer, such as a Pyrex pie pan. Set the dish on a rack over 2 to 4 inches boiling water in a steamer or wok (if the bottom is round, place on a wok ring to stabilize). If the steamer lid is flat metal, wrap lid with a towel to reduce condensation dripping on the food. Cover and steam over high heat until the filling is no longer pink in the center (cut to test), 10 to 15 minutes. Watch the water level, adding more boiling water as needed. Carefully remove the dish from the steamer. ▸

**4** Garnish with green onions. Serve hot with soy sauce and chile sauce to add to taste.

**Stuffed Tofu Soup** Make the recipe through step 2. In a 3- to 4-quart pan over high heat, bring 6 cups chicken broth to a boil. Add the filled tofu triangles and bring to a simmer. Reduce the heat, cover, and simmer until the filling is firm, about 5 minutes. Add ¼ cup thinly sliced green onions and salt and pepper to taste. Ladle into bowls. Makes 6 to 8 servings as part of a multicourse meal. ■

# LOOFAH SQUASH IN EGG FLOWER SAUCE

The delicate, refreshing flavor and soft, silky texture of loofah squash is enriched in this dish with a gentle swirl of beaten egg in its poaching liquid. Angled loofah (also known as Chinese okra or silk squash) resembles a long, slightly curved English cucumber with green, rough, ridged skin and a soft, white, slightly spongy interior.

*Makes 3 to 4 servings as part of a multicourse meal*

1 pound angled loofah squash
  (2 medium, each about 12 inches)
  or zucchini (about 3 medium)

1 tablespoon vegetable oil

2 tablespoons minced garlic

¾ cup water

½ teaspoon salt, or to taste

⅛ teaspoon ground white pepper

1 large egg

**1** Peel the loofah to remove all green skin (zucchini does not need peeling). Cut the squash into 1-inch pieces.

**2** Set a 14-inch wok or 10- to 12-inch frying pan over high heat. When the pan is hot, after about 1 minute, add the oil and rotate the pan to spread. Add the garlic and stir-fry until it begins to turn golden, about 15 seconds. Add the squash, water, salt, and white pepper. Cook, covered, over medium heat, stirring occasionally, until the squash is tender when pierced, 5 to 6 minutes.

**3** Break the egg into the pan and, with a chopstick, break the egg up and stir gently into the liquid to form shreds. Remove from the heat; the egg will slightly thicken the liquid. Add more salt to taste, if needed. Transfer to a serving dish. ■

Loofah squash

# PAN-STEAMED FISH IN BEAN SAUCE

Fah departs from the traditional Chinese steamed fish in this Hakka variation that requires no special steaming equipment. The fish steams in a flavorful liquid spiked with wine, ginger, garlic, green onions, and savory bean sauce in a frying pan. Slivered carrots contribute sweetness and color to the pan juices.

*Makes 2 servings as a main dish or 4 to 6 servings as part of a multicourse meal*

1 small whole fish (about 1½ to 2 pounds), such as black bass, rockfish, tilapia, or striped bass, cleaned and scaled (see note)

¼ teaspoon salt

2 tablespoons vegetable oil

⅓ cup thinly slivered carrots

2 tablespoons thinly slivered fresh ginger

1 tablespoon minced garlic

3 green onions, cut into 2-inch lengths, including green tops

½ cup water

3 tablespoons Chinese rice wine (shaoxing) or dry sherry

1 tablespoon ground bean sauce or black bean sauce

¼ teaspoon sugar

**1** Rinse the fish; pat dry. Make 3 or 4 slashes, about ¼ inch deep, 2 inches long, and 1 inch apart, down each side of the fish. Lightly sprinkle the inside and outside of the fish with the salt.

**2** Set a 12-inch frying pan over high heat. When the pan is hot, after about 1 minute, add the oil and rotate the pan to spread. Add the carrots, ginger, and garlic. Stir-fry until the garlic softens, about 15 seconds. Add the green onions; stir until bright green, about 30 seconds.

**3** Add the water, wine, bean sauce, and sugar. Bring to a boil. Add the fish to the pan and reduce the heat to low. Cover and simmer for 5 minutes. With a wide spatula, carefully turn the fish over. Cover and simmer just until the fish is barely opaque in the center of the thickest part (cut to test), 5 to 8 minutes longer. Transfer the fish to a serving platter. Pour the pan juices and vegetables over the top.

**Note:** The Chinese prefer to eat whole fish with heads and tails attached. Most Asian markets carry a selection of small whole fish. Choose one that will fit into a 12-inch frying pan, or trim off the head and tail. Look for fish with shiny eyes and red gills, signs of freshness. If you can't find a whole fish, you can substitute ¾ to 1 pound skinless fish fillets, 1 to 1¼ inch thick. Use a 10-inch frying pan for fillets. Check the Monterey Bay Aquarium's website (www.montereybayaquarium.org/cr/seafoodwatch.aspx) for sustainable choices. ■

# PORK SPARERIB AND BEAN CURD STICK SOUP

When soybean milk is heated, a skin forms on the surface. The skin is gathered and dried into golden sticks, known as bean curd sticks. When they cook in this simple, wholesome soup, the sticks unfurl into golden ribbons that absorb the flavor of the pork ribs. Chunks of carrot brighten the soup and lend a natural sweetness.

The thick parts of the bean curd sticks can take a long time to soak, so plan ahead and start soaking a few hours before cooking. Or, better yet, start soaking them the night before. The soup can be made ahead and reheated.

*Makes 6 servings as a main dish or 10 to 12 servings as part of a multicourse meal*

1 package (6 ounces) dried bean curd sticks

4 cups chicken broth, homemade (page 267) or purchased

4 cups water

1½ to 2 pounds pork spareribs, sawed across the bones into 1-inch-wide strips (see note)

4 large carrots (about 1 pound total)

1 teaspoon sugar

½ teaspoon salt, or to taste

¼ teaspoon ground black pepper

1 cup thinly sliced green onions, including green tops

**1** Break the bean curd sticks in half, if needed, to fit into a large bowl. Cover with hot water and soak, turning occasionally and replacing with more hot water as needed, until soft, at least 2 hours at room temperature or overnight in the refrigerator. Drain well. Cut the bean curd sticks into 1-inch pieces.

**2** In a 6- to 8-quart pan over high heat, bring the broth and water to a boil. Meanwhile, trim the excess fat off the pork. Rinse the spareribs and pat dry. Cut between the bones of the spareribs. Add the pork to the broth and return to a boil. Reduce the heat, cover, and simmer for 45 minutes.

**3** Meanwhile, peel the carrots and cut into ½-inch chunks.

**4** After the pork has cooked for 45 minutes, add the bean curd sticks, carrots, sugar, salt, and pepper and return to a boil. Reduce the heat, cover, and simmer until the pork, bean curd, and carrots are tender when pierced, 30 to 45 minutes longer. (If the bean curd sticks are not thoroughly soaked, they will absorb lots of liquid; add more water, if needed, to maintain about 8 cups liquid during cooking). Skim off and discard any fat. Stir in the green onions. Ladle the soup into bowls or a large tureen.

**Note:** Remember to ask the butcher to saw across the spareribs in about 1-inch-wide strips. At Asian markets, you may find them precut in strips. ▪

# BRAISED TARO IN BEAN SAUCE

Ground bean sauce, made from fermented soybeans, robustly seasons a sauce that coats chunks of smooth, sweet taro, a starchy tuber. This hearty vegetable dish tastes almost like a Chinese version of potatoes in gravy. In fact, if you can't find the small, shaggy, dark-skinned taro, use potatoes instead. You can also serve this dish in Western meals, as a companion to meat.

*Makes 4 to 6 servings as part of a multicourse meal*

1 pound small taro or boiling potatoes, such as Yukon gold

1 tablespoon vegetable oil

2 tablespoons minced garlic

1 cup water, or as needed

1 tablespoon ground bean sauce or hoisin sauce

1 teaspoon soy sauce

½ teaspoon sugar (omit if using hoisin sauce)

¼ teaspoon ground black pepper

3 tablespoons thinly sliced green onions, including green tops, for garnish

**1** Peel the taro. If you have sensitive hands, wear rubber gloves or peel under water. Cut the taro into ¾-inch chunks.

**2** Set a 14-inch wok or 10-inch nonstick frying pan over medium-high heat. When the pan is hot, after about 1 minute, add the oil and rotate the pan to spread. Add the garlic and stir-fry just until golden, about 15 seconds. Add the taro and stir-fry until lightly browned, about 2 minutes.

**3** Add the water, bean sauce, soy sauce, sugar, and pepper. Reduce the heat, cover, and simmer, stirring occasionally, until the taro is tender when pierced, about 15 minutes. If the liquid evaporates and the taro begins to stick, add a little more water. With a slotted spoon, lift out the taro and place in a serving dish. Measure the pan juices. If more than ½ cup, boil, uncovered, over high heat until reduced to that amount. If less than ½ cup, add water to make that amount and bring to a boil. Pour the pan juices over the taro. Sprinkle with the green onions. ■

# STIR-FRIED BEEF AND WATER SPINACH

Stir-fried meat and vegetables are a basic component of the Hakka diet. The flavors are direct and natural, with no sauce added. This version combines water spinach—a hollow-stemmed green with long, pointed leaves—and beef. The thinly sliced marinated meat and spinach are stir-fried separately, and then mixed together.

*Makes 2 servings as a main dish or 4 servings as part of a multicourse meal*

## BEEF

8 ounces beef flank steak

2 teaspoons soy sauce

1 teaspoon cornstarch

1 teaspoon vegetable oil

⅛ teaspoon ground white pepper

## STIR-FRY

10 to 12 ounces water spinach or spinach

3 tablespoons vegetable oil

2 tablespoons water

¼ teaspoon salt, or to taste

1 tablespoon thinly slivered fresh ginger

1 tablespoon minced garlic

1 **FOR THE BEEF:** Cut the beef across the grain into slices ⅛ inch thick, 2 to 3 inches long, and ½ inch wide. In a small bowl, mix the beef with the soy sauce, cornstarch, oil, and white pepper.

2 **FOR THE STIR-FRY:** Remove and discard any yellow or wilted leaves from the greens. Trim off and discard the woody stem ends from the water spinach, usually the bottom 3 to 4 inches. Cut the tender stems with leaves into 3- to 4-inch lengths. If the stems are woody and tough, discard them and use only the leaves. (For spinach, trim off the root ends and tough stems and cut into 4-inch lengths.) Wash well and drain. You should have 8 to 10 cups of greens.

3 Set a 14-inch wok or 12-inch frying pan over high heat. When the pan is hot, after about 1 minute, add 1 tablespoon of the oil and rotate the pan to spread. Add the water spinach, water, and salt. Stir-fry until the greens are wilted, about 1 minute. (If all the greens don't fit into the frying pan, add about half the greens and turn until they begin to wilt and shrink, then add the remainder.) Transfer to a serving dish.

**4** Return the pan to high heat. When the pan is dry, add the remaining 2 table-spoons oil and rotate the pan to spread. Add the ginger and garlic; stir-fry just until garlic is lightly browned, about 15 seconds. Add the beef mixture and stir-fry until the beef is lightly browned, 2 to 3 minutes. Return the water spinach and accumulated liquid to the pan and stir-fry, scraping free any browned bits, until the ingredients are lightly mixed and spinach is hot, about 1 minute. Add salt to taste. Transfer to a serving dish. ▪

Water spinach

# SOY-SIMMERED PORK AND SALTED MUSTARD GREENS

Salted mustard greens, a Hakka staple, cut the richness of pork in this simple, dark, savory-sweet stew. The greens and pork simmer together in a generous measure of rice wine seasoned with garlic and both dark and sweet soy sauce. Serve with mounds of hot rice.

*Makes 6 to 8 servings as a main dish or 10 to 12 servings as part of a multicourse meal*

3 cups homemade salted mustard greens (page 145), or 2 packages (10 ounces each) purchased salted mustard greens

2 pounds boneless pork butt, trimmed of fat

¼ cup vegetable oil

⅓ cup minced garlic

2 cups Chinese rice wine (shaoxing) or dry sherry

3 tablespoons sweet soy sauce, homemade (page 269), or purchased *kecap manis* (see notes)

2 tablespoons sugar, or to taste

2 tablespoons dark soy sauce

Salt

1 Rinse the mustard greens well and cut into 1½-inch squares. If the pieces are thicker than 1 inch, split in half so the pieces are about ½ inch thick. You should have about 3 cups. In a large bowl, soak the mustard greens in water to cover for at least 1 hour or up to 4 hours, changing the water occasionally.

2 Cut the pork into 1½-inch chunks. Drain the mustard greens and squeeze out excess water.

3 Set a 14-inch wok or 5- to 6-quart pan over high heat. When the pan is hot, after about 1 minute, add the oil and rotate the pan to spread. Add the garlic and stir-fry until lightly browned, about 15 seconds. Add the pork and cook, stirring occasionally, until lightly browned, 5 to 8 minutes. Add the wine, mustard greens, sweet soy sauce, sugar, and dark soy sauce.

4 Bring the pork mixture to a boil. Reduce the heat, cover, and simmer, stirring occasionally, until the meat is tender when pierced, 1½ to 2 hours. If liquid evaporates before the pork is tender, add up to 1 cup of water and continue simmering. Skim off the fat from the pan juices and discard. With a slotted spoon, lift out the pork and greens and transfer to a serving bowl. If the pan juices taste watery, boil over high heat, uncovered, until reduced to about 1 cup. Taste the sauce and add salt and more sugar, if desired. Pour over pork.

**Notes:** For a quick substitute for the sweet soy sauce, mix 2 tablespoons dark soy sauce and 2 tablespoons packed brown sugar.

If the stew is made a day ahead, cool, cover, and chill. Reheat, covered, over medium heat, stirring occasionally. Add a little water if the meat begins to stick. ▪

# STIR-FRIED TRIPE AND BEAN SPROUTS

Although the Hakka and many Chinese eat all parts of the animal, I've never been a big fan of most innards. One exception is beef tripe—not any kind, but the kind called book tripe, also known as leaf tripe or bible tripe. This type of tripe, with thin tissues attached to a thicker base, resembles pages in a book. When cooked, it has a pleasant crunchy texture and mild flavor. In this light stir-fry, Fah Liong deftly combines the tripe with crisp bean sprouts and a tangy-sweet sauce spiked with red chile and ginger.

Look for book tripe in Asian markets. Most tripe is sold cleaned and par-boiled. Fah cleans and boils it further, until crisp-tender.

*Makes 2 servings as a main dish or 4 servings as part of a multicourse meal*

## TRIPE

3 tablespoons salt, or as needed

8 ounces beef book tripe

## SAUCE

3 tablespoons water

2 tablespoons rice vinegar

1 tablespoon sugar

2 teaspoons soy sauce

2 teaspoons cornstarch

½ teaspoon salt, or to taste

⅛ teaspoon ground white pepper

## STIR-FRY

2 tablespoons vegetable oil

3 tablespoons thinly slivered fresh ginger

1 tablespoon minced garlic

6 to 8 thin rings fresh chile (preferably red), such as Fresno or jalapeño

4 cups bean sprouts (about 8 ounces)

½ cup coarsely chopped cilantro

**1 FOR THE TRIPE:** Sprinkle 1½ tablespoons of the salt over the tripe and rub well. Rinse off the salt and then repeat with the remaining salt. In a 4- to 5-quart pan over high heat, bring about 2 quarts of water to a boil. Add the tripe and boil for 5 minutes. Pour off the water. Add 2 to 3 quarts of fresh water to the tripe and return to a boil. Reduce the heat, cover, and simmer until the thickest part of the tripe is tender when pierced, about 1 hour. Drain and rinse well with warm water. Squeeze out excess water. Cut the tripe into slices ½ inch wide and 2 to 3 inches long.

**2 FOR THE SAUCE:** In a small bowl, mix the water, vinegar, sugar, soy sauce, cornstarch, salt, and white pepper.

**3 FOR THE STIR-FRY:** Set a 14-inch wok or 12-inch frying pan over high heat. When the pan is hot, after about 1 minute, add the oil and rotate the pan to spread. Add the ginger, garlic, and chile; stir-fry just until the garlic softens slightly, about 15 seconds. Add the tripe and stir-fry until hot, about 1 minute. Add the bean sprouts and stir-fry until they barely wilt, 1 to 2 minutes.

**4** Stir the sauce mixture and add to the pan. Stir-fry until the sauce boils, about 30 seconds. Stir in the cilantro, and transfer to a serving dish. ∎

# A Humble Hakka

San Francisco's Ton Kiang Restaurant proudly announces "Hakka Cuisine" right under the name on its sign. The restaurant has long been popular for its dim sum, wide variety of Chinese dishes, and Hakka specialties. It is named after the Ton Kiang (East River) in Guangdong Province, where many Hakkas settled.

William Wong always introduces himself as the manager, but I feel sure that he is the owner. I ask him again and he says, "I call myself the manager. I'm a very humble man." He is also a successful entrepreneur who has managed to keep this restaurant in business for more than three decades.

William's father started the restaurant in 1977. He originally came from Meixian, China, and then went to Burma, where William was born. When the Burmese began to resent the success of Chinese residents of their country, the family came to the United States and opened Ton Kiang, which at one point grew into a chain of three branches. Now William and two of his siblings run the one remaining location on Geary Boulevard in San Francisco's Richmond District.

Fah and I sit down to a Hakka lunch at Ton Kiang. Many Hakka dishes are listed in the clay pot section of the menu; others, not explicitly labeled Hakka, are scattered in other sections. We order several classic Hakka dishes to share. We're especially curious about the seafood with house-made rice wine sauce and pickled greens. The sauce is made from the by-products of making rice wine and is not served in many restaurants.

Before the food arrives, the waiter brings an unexpected carafe of rice wine. The fragrant golden wine tastes mildly sweet, smooth, and mellow, with a fruity plum finish. It's my first taste of this wine in the United States since I returned from China. We're privileged to sample this special treat. The waiter tells us that the owner makes it at home and, unfortunately, it's not for sale.

After lunch, we interview Ton Kiang's chef, who has worked at the restaurant for more than twenty years. Originally from the Hakka heartland in China, he came here via Hong Kong, where he learned to cook Hakka dishes in restaurants. We ask about the Hakka dishes we sampled, and he tells us how they're made. "At Ton Kiang," he says, "we adjust the food to the tastes of Americans and overseas Chinese." This Hakka adaptability may be the key to Ton Kiang's long-term success.

# SPINACH AND FISH BALL SOUP

Many Hakkas remember their grandmothers or mothers patiently using a spoon to scrape every fiber of flesh from fish bones to make fish paste, which was used in many ways. Certain fish—such as Spanish mackerel, wolf herring, or bonefish—were used to create the preferred springy texture. The flesh was chopped and beaten, and salt water was gradually added until the mixture held together. Then the fish was thrown against a chopping block or the sides of a bowl to develop the characteristic bouncy texture, the criteria for a good fish ball.

Today, few people have the patience to scrape fish flesh from bones, so many buy a ready-to-use fish paste in Asian supermarkets. However, fish paste is relatively easy to make with a food processor or electric mixer and a variety of readily available fish fillets.

At Ton Kiang in San Francisco, cooks form the fish paste into balls and poach them in a clear broth with ginger, spinach, and mushrooms for a refreshing soup.

*Makes 2 to 3 servings as a main dish or 4 to 6 servings as part of a multicourse meal*

## FISH PASTE

8 ounces skinless fillet from a white-fleshed fish, such as snapper, lingcod, or tilapia

1 large egg white

3 tablespoons cornstarch

2 tablespoons ice water

¾ teaspoon salt

¼ teaspoon ground white pepper

3 tablespoons thinly sliced green onions, including green tops

## SOUP

6 cups chicken broth, homemade (page 267) or purchased

**1 FOR THE FISH PASTE:** Rinse the fish, pat dry, and cut into ½-inch chunks. With a food processor or knife, whirl or chop the fish until minced and pasty. If using a knife, transfer the minced fish to a bowl. Add the egg white, cornstarch, water, salt, and white pepper. Whirl in a food processor or beat with an electric mixer on medium-high speed until smooth and fluffy. Add the green onions and whirl or beat until well distributed. If not using right away, cover the paste and chill for up to one day.

**2 FOR THE SOUP:** In a 4- to 5-quart pan over high heat, bring the broth, mushrooms, and ginger to a boil. Reduce the heat, cover, and simmer for 5 minutes.

**3** With wet hands, roll the fish paste into 1-inch balls and place slightly apart on an oiled plate. When all the paste has been shaped, gently scrape the fish balls into the simmering broth. Reduce the heat and simmer until ▸

6 ounces fresh button or cremini mushrooms, each about 1½ inches wide, rinsed and quartered lengthwise, or 1 can (15 ounces) straw mushrooms, rinsed and drained

8 thin slices fresh ginger, lightly crushed

6 ounces spinach leaves (about 6 cups), rinsed and drained

2 teaspoons Asian sesame oil (optional)

Salt

Ground white pepper

the fish balls are opaque in the center (cut to test), 2 to 3 minutes. Stir in the spinach and cook just until it wilts, 1 to 2 minutes. Add the sesame oil, salt, and white pepper to taste. Ladle the soup into individual bowls or a serving bowl.

**Notes:** Most Asians prefer fish balls to have a bouncy texture. If you prefer slightly softer fish balls, reduce the cornstarch to 2 tablespoons.

For a shortcut, instead of making the fish paste, buy 8 ounces ready-to-use fish paste from the fish counter at an Asian market. ∎

## SALT-POACHED CHICKEN

Ton Kiang's steamed salt-baked chicken is actually a shortcut version, in which the bird is poached in brine. It is easy to duplicate at home. This technique disguises even slightly overcooked chicken. The secret is to keep the water at a bare simmer. When the chicken is done, a brief dip in an ice-water bath cools it rapidly so it doesn't overcook and contracts the skin so it is smooth and firm. With chicken so moist and smooth, who cares if it isn't wholly traditional. Eat the white chicken with a lively fresh ginger paste, slightly tamed by hot oil.

*Makes 5 to 6 servings as a main dish or 10 to 12 servings as part of a multicourse meal*

One 4- to 4½-pound chicken, preferably free-range or organic

6 quarts water, or as needed

1 cup plus 3 tablespoons kosher salt, or as needed

2 to 3 ounces peeled fresh ginger

½ teaspoon table salt or ¾ teaspoon kosher salt, or to taste

3 tablespoons vegetable oil

1 If the head, neck, and feet are present on the chicken, remove for another use or leave attached. If the neck and giblets are in the body cavity, remove for another use. Remove and reserve the lumps of fat near the entrance of the body cavity. Rinse the bird inside and out. In a deep (at least 6 inches tall) 10- to 12-quart pan over high heat, bring 6 quarts water, the kosher salt, and the reserved chicken fat to a boil. Immerse the chicken in the water, breast side up. If the water doesn't completely cover the chicken, add enough boiling

3 tablespoons slivered green onions, including green tops, for garnish

Soy sauce, for serving

water to cover plus 3 tablespoons kosher salt for each additional quart of boiling water. Return the water to a simmer, cover, and adjust the heat so that only a few small bubbles barely break the surface. If it is difficult to maintain heat this low, leave the pan lid slightly ajar.

2 Cook the chicken for 40 minutes. Insert a large spoon into the chicken cavity, tilt slightly to drain the water out of the cavity, and lift out the bird, placing it in a shallow dish. Insert an instant-read thermometer through the center of the thickest part of the breast until it touches the bone; it should read about 170°F. Or cut a slit into the meat where the thigh joins the body to check that the meat is no longer pink. If the chicken is not done, return to the water and cook, covered, about 5 minutes longer.

3 Once done cooking, immerse the chicken in a large bowl of ice water until the surface of the chicken is cool, 2 to 3 minutes. Lift out the chicken, draining the water from the cavity, and let rest about 10 minutes.

4 Meanwhile, with a microplane or the rough holes of a box grater, grate the ginger onto a plate to make ¼ cup. Place the ginger pulp, including any juices, in a 1-cup heatproof bowl. Mix in the table salt. In a 6- to 8-inch frying pan over high heat, warm the oil until it ripples when the pan is tilted, about 1 minute. Pour the hot oil over the ginger and salt and mix to blend; it will bubble vigorously.

5 Cut the chicken into pieces for serving (page 243). Arrange the pieces attractively, preferably in the shape of a chicken, on a platter. Sprinkle with the green onions. Serve with the ginger paste and soy sauce, to add to taste. ∎

# SHRIMP AND PICKLED MUSTARD GREENS IN RICE WINE SAUCE

A Hakka shrimp stir-fry at Ton Kiang is seasoned with the boozy sediment from sweet rice wine and dried red yeast rice to produce a russet sauce with an earthy sweetness. Slivers of pickled or salted mustard greens add a tangy, pungent accent. You'll need to visit an Asian market to get the key ingredients.

*Makes 2 to 3 servings as a main dish or 4 to 6 servings as part of a multicourse meal*

## SAUCE

1½ teaspoons red yeast rice (optional)

6 tablespoons boiling water

¼ cup fermented sweet wine rice, including liquid, or cream sherry

2 tablespoons Chinese rice wine (shaoxing) or dry sherry

4 teaspoons soy sauce

1½ teaspoons cornstarch

## STIR-FRY

½ cup thinly slivered pickled or salted mustard greens, homemade (page 147) or purchased

2 tablespoons vegetable oil

1 tablespoon minced fresh ginger

12 ounces peeled, deveined shrimp (31 to 35 per pound)

½ cup thinly sliced green onions, including green tops

Salt

**1 FOR THE SAUCE:** In a fine-mesh wire strainer, rinse and drain the red yeast rice. Pour the red rice into a small bowl and cover with the boiling water. Let stand until the rice is soft, about 5 minutes. (If red yeast rice is not used, omit soaking and boiling water. Mix 6 tablespoons cold water with the other sauce ingredients.) Add the fermented sweet wine rice, wine, soy sauce, and cornstarch to the soaked red rice, and stir to blend.

**2 FOR THE STIR-FRY:** Rinse the mustard greens well and soak in water for about 5 minutes. Drain and squeeze out excess water.

**3** Set a 14-inch wok or 12-inch frying pan over high heat. When the pan is hot, after about 1 minute, add the oil and rotate the pan to spread. Add the ginger and shrimp. Stir-fry until the shrimp are pink, about 2 minutes. Stir in the mustard greens and green onions. Stir the sauce mixture and add to the pan. Stir-fry until the sauce boils, about 30 seconds. Add salt to taste. Transfer to a serving dish.

**Chicken in Rice Wine Sauce:** Substitute 12 ounces boneless, skinless chicken thighs for the shrimp. Cut the chicken into strips ¼ inch thick, 3 inches long, and ½ inch wide. In step 3, stir-fry the chicken until lightly browned, 2 to 3 minutes. ∎

# Cooking from the Heart

Just as my recipe research is almost complete, I discover a new restaurant on Cabrillo Street in San Francisco. This small, family-run business is simply called Hakka Restaurant. Chinese families pack into the noisy dining room on a Friday night—a good sign. It is obvious that customers come not for the ambience, but simply to eat good food. We concentrate on the Hakka specialties; most are listed on the menu as chef's specials. I'm pleased that we have preordered the chicken with preserved mustard greens. A whole chicken, stuffed with a mixture of greens, mushrooms, and pork, is braised and served with a sauce made from the reduced pan juices. The salty-savory flavor is pure Hakka. My husband insists that we order another Hakka favorite, Chinese bacon with preserved mustard greens. The restaurant's rendition is delicious. Soft, succulent, greaseless slices of pork belly lie on a bed of savory preserved mustard greens. Finally, a dish of vivid green Chinese broccoli with sweet rice wine crunches with freshness. The food possesses a clarity and pureness of flavor.

"I cook from my heart," says the chef, Jin Hua Li. "I have to be happy in what I do; then I get the best product. I use high-quality ingredients to prepare healthy food that is not very greasy and enhances the natural flavor of the ingredients." Li learned to cook Hakka food at home in Guangdong Province in China. In 1985, he began cooking at a restaurant in China, and in 1987 he came to the United States, where he opened Golden Mountain Restaurant in Hayward and cooked at the highly rated Koi Palace in Daly City. I ask him how to cook some of the dishes and am surprised to discover that they are far easier to make than I expected. Try them. Just start with good ingredients and a happy heart.

# CHINESE BROCCOLI IN SWEET RICE WINE

Chef Li stir-fries vegetables quickly and simply with this easy technique. The broccoli emerges bright green with a gentle crunch. Be picky when choosing the broccoli. Select only young, tender, thin-skinned, slender stalks. Your finished dish will only be as good as the quality of your produce. Shop at the farmers' market for the freshest produce. The pieces should be about the same thickness to cook evenly; if needed, cut thick stalks in half lengthwise. This technique can also be adapted to other vegetables, such as bok choy or asparagus.

*Makes 4 servings as part of a multicourse meal*

12 ounces Chinese broccoli or broccoli raab (rapini)

1 tablespoon vegetable oil

3 tablespoons water

2 to 3 teaspoons crushed Chinese brown slab sugar or packed brown sugar

½ teaspoon salt, or to taste

2 tablespoons Chinese rice spirits or vodka (see note)

1  Trim off the stem ends of the broccoli and peel the skin off the stalks, if tough. Cut the broccoli into 3-inch pieces. Split the bottom ends and stalks lengthwise if thicker than ½ inch.

2  Set a 14-inch wok or 12-inch frying pan over high heat. When the pan is hot, after about 1 minute, add the oil and rotate the pan to spread. Add the broccoli and stir-fry to coat with the oil. Add the water and continue stir-frying until the broccoli is bright green and crisp-tender, 2 to 3 minutes. Add the sugar and salt; stir-fry until the sugar melts. Stir in the rice spirits and bring to a boil. Transfer to a serving dish.

**Note:** Chef Li uses a clear spirit distilled from rice called Kiu Kuang Shuang Jin Chiew made by Pearl River Bridge, for its clean, neutral taste. It is about 29 percent alcohol. Chinese rice wine (shaoxing) will also work, but will have a more pronounced flavor. ∎

Chinese broccoli

# CHILE-SPICED CLAMS WITH BASIL AND CILANTRO

The Hakka in Thailand inspired Chef Li when he created this new dish, which he calls house special clams. It's spicy, with two forms of chile, but mild compared to true fiery Thai-style dishes. Lots of fresh basil and cilantro add a fresh herbal scent. Serve with hot rice to soak up the delicious juices.

*Makes 2 servings as a main dish or 4 to 6 servings as part of a multicourse meal*

2 tablespoons vegetable oil

8 thin slices fresh ginger

8 to 10 thin slices jalapeño chile

1 green onion, including green top, thinly sliced

2 pounds small hard-shelled clams in their shells, scrubbed

¾ cup water

1 tablespoon fresh lime juice

1 tablespoon fish sauce, or to taste

1 teaspoon Asian sesame oil

1½ teaspoons cornstarch

½ teaspoon sugar

¾ teaspoon chile sauce, homemade (page 268) or purchased, or to taste

1 cup fresh Thai or Italian basil leaves

½ cup cilantro leaves

1 Set a 14-inch wok or 5- to 6-quart pan over high heat. When the pan is hot, after about 1 minute, add the oil and rotate the pan to spread. Add the ginger, chile, and green onion. Stir-fry until the chile softens slightly, about 30 seconds. Stir in the clams and ½ cup of the water. Cover and cook until the clams pop open, 2 to 5 minutes.

2 Meanwhile, in a small bowl, mix the remaining ¼ cup water, lime juice, fish sauce, sesame oil, cornstarch, and sugar. Add to the clams and stir until the sauce boils, about 1 minute. With a slotted spoon, transfer the clams to a serving dish. Discard any unopened clams. Stir the chile sauce into the sauce. Stir in half of the basil and half of the cilantro and pour the sauce over clams. Garnish with the remaining basil and cilantro. ∎

# EMERGING HAKKA CLASSIC
# Braised Chicken Stuffed
# with Preserved Mustard Greens

梅菜雞 Hakka: *moi choi gai;* Mandarin: *mei cai ji*

To my taste, Chef Jin Hua Li's signature dish, chicken with preserved mustard greens, has the potential to become a Hakka classic. The San Francisco chef created this festive stuffed chicken packed with Hakka flavors for Chinese New Year. It reminds me of a Chinese version of Thanksgiving turkey and gravy. Chef Li stuffs a whole chicken with a mixture of preserved mustard greens, dark mushrooms, and pork. He then braises the bird in broth and finishes it with a sauce created from the umami-rich pan juices.

The dish shares the savory, robust character of another popular Hakka classic, pork belly with preserved mustard greens. Both dishes use chewy dried mustard greens, which infuses them with a distinctive sweet-salty pungency. With chicken, the final package seems lighter, but just as satisfying. In the twenty-first century, perhaps the chicken version will gain fans among the health-conscious new generation and their cholesterol-counting grandparents.

Mustard greens

# BRAISED CHICKEN STUFFED WITH PRESERVED MUSTARD GREENS

You'll have to order this festive stuffed chicken a day ahead if you want to eat it at Chef Li's Hakka Restaurant in San Francisco. If you're too far away, make it at home. You can prepare the mustard green stuffing a day ahead. About one hour before serving, reheat the mixture, and stuff the bird shortly before cooking. Chef Li prefers to use a large clay pot for braising, but a wok also works well.

*Makes 5 to 6 servings as a main dish or 8 to 10 servings as part of a multicourse meal*

4 ounces preserved mustard greens

8 dried shiitake mushrooms, each about 2 inches wide

4 ounces boneless pork butt or shoulder, trimmed of fat

3 tablespoons vegetable oil

6 tablespoons Chinese rice wine (shaoxing) or dry sherry

4 tablespoons oyster sauce

1 chicken (about 4 pounds), preferably organic or free-range

1 tablespoon dark soy sauce

6 cups chicken broth, homemade (page 267) or purchased

8 thin slices fresh ginger

3 green onions, including green tops, cut into 2-inch lengths

3 pieces dried tangerine peel, each about 1 inch wide, rinsed

1 teaspoon whole white peppercorns

2 tablespoons water

2 tablespoons cornstarch

Cilantro sprigs, for garnish

**1** Chop the mustard greens into ¼- to ½-inch pieces to make about 1 cup, and place in a large bowl. Fill the bowl with hot water and rub the greens to remove the salt and sand; rinse and drain several times. Cover with more hot water and let stand, changing the water occasionally, until the thick stem pieces are soft, 30 minutes to 1 hour. Drain, rinse, and drain again. Press and squeeze the excess water out of the greens.

**2** Rinse the mushrooms. Place the dried mushrooms in a small bowl. Cover with about 1½ cups hot water and soak until soft, 20 minutes for thin caps to 2 hours for thick caps. Lift out the mushrooms and squeeze out the excess liquid. Reserve the soaking water. Remove and discard the stems of the mushrooms; cut the mushroom caps into ¼-inch strips.

**3** Cut the pork into matchsticks, about ¼ inch thick and 2 inches long.

**4** Set a 14-inch wok over high heat. When the pan is hot, after about 1 minute, add 1 tablespoon of the oil and rotate the pan to spread. Add the pork and stir-fry until lightly browned, about 1 minute. Add the mustard greens and mushrooms. Stir-fry until the mixture is well blended, about 1 minute. Add 1 cup of the reserved mushroom-soaking water (slowly pour the water off and leave the sediment behind), 2 tablespoons of the wine, and 2 tablespoons of the oyster sauce. Reduce the heat to low, cover, and simmer until the liquid is absorbed ▸

and the pork is tender when pierced, 10 to 15 minutes. Remove from the pan. Wash and dry the pan.

5 If the head, neck, and feet are present on the chicken, remove for another use or leave attached. If the neck and giblets are in the body cavity, remove for another use. Remove and discard the lumps of fat near the entrance of the body cavity. Rinse the bird inside and out; pat dry. Firmly pack the body cavity and, if accessible, the neck cavity with all of the hot mustard green mixture. Overlap the skin at the openings and weave thin skewers through the skin and body to close the openings of the chicken. Pat the chicken skin dry. Rub the outside of the chicken with dark soy sauce.

6 Set the wok (if the bottom is round, place on a wok ring to stabilize) over medium-high heat. When the pan is hot, after about 1 minute, add the remaining 2 tablespoons oil and rotate the pan to spread. Set the chicken in the pan and cook, turning as needed with 2 large spoons or spatulas, until browned on all sides, 6 to 8 minutes total. (If using a 4½-quart clay pot, transfer the chicken now.) Add the broth, ginger, green onions, remaining ¼ cup wine, remaining 2 tablespoons oyster sauce, tangerine peel, and peppercorns to the pan. Bring to a boil over high heat. Reduce the heat, cover, and simmer for 25 minutes. Gently turn the chicken over and continue cooking until it is no longer pink at the thigh bone when pierced, 20 to 25 minutes longer.

7 Lift out the chicken and set on a platter. Remove the skewers and scoop out the stuffing into a serving bowl. Cover the stuffing and keep warm. Lightly cover the chicken and let rest about 10 minutes. Pour the pan juices through a strainer set over a bowl. Discard the solids. Or sweep a small wire strainer through the juices to remove the solids. Skim off and discard the fat from the pan juices. Return the juices to the pan and boil, uncovered, over high heat for about 15 minutes, or until reduced to about 3 cups.

8 Meanwhile, cut the chicken into pieces for serving (page 243) and attractively arrange on a platter. In a small bowl, mix the water with the cornstarch. Add to the reduced pan juices and stir until the juices thicken and boil. Pour some sauce over the chicken and stuffing and pour the remaining sauce into a bowl to serve alongside. Garnish the chicken with cilantro.

Note: You can make the stuffing a day ahead, and then cover and chill. Reheat the mixture in a nonstick pan, covered, over low heat, stirring occasionally and adding a little water if it sticks. When the mixture is hot, stuff the bird and braise. Do not stuff the chicken until just before cooking. ∎

# The Hakka Kitchen

## Tools

Given the Hakkas' frugal nature and transitory lifestyle, it's most likely that their kitchens were portable and spare. Perhaps the basic kitchen centered on a large lidded wok, a spatula, and several ladles, steaming racks, and cleavers. To-day, we have dedicated gadgets and Western appliances to make cooking easier. But for Chinese cooking, basic equipment and techniques still prevail.

## Woks

If I could choose only one pan for my kitchen, it would be a wok. In the Chinese kitchen, the wok is an all-purpose pan, used for stir-frying, steaming, braising, and deep-frying. Add a curved wok spatula, lid, steamer basket, and wok ring for support, and you have the basic tools for most Chinese cooking. With these tools, you'll be able to cook an endless variety of dishes for life.

The best choice for Western home kitchens is a 14-inch, flat-bottomed, enamel-clad wok made of cast iron or rolled carbon steel. The flat bottom sits stably on electric or gas burners and effectively captures heat. Round-bottomed woks can also sit comfortably on many gas burners, but may need a ring for support on electric burners. Cast-iron and carbon-steel woks, sold in Asian cookware stores and markets, are value priced. A good source for these woks is the Wok Shop in San Francisco (www.wokshop.com/store). Used often, these traditional woks will darken and develop a patina that acts like a natural nonstick finish. Before you use these pans for the first time, season them as you would a cast-iron pan.

There are many ways to season a wok. Since woks last a lifetime, I've seasoned only a few. The last time, I used this technique suggested by expert Tane Chan, owner of the Wok Shop: Scrub the pan, inside and out, with soapy water to remove the oily film, rinse, and dry thoroughly by setting over high heat. Coat the interior and exterior (no need to coat the exterior of an enamel-clad wok) with a light film of vegetable oil. If the wok has wood handles, remove or wrap with a wet towel and heavy-duty foil. Bake the wok, upside-down, in a preheated 425°F oven for 20 minutes to develop an even patina. Place the wok on the stove over medium heat. To remove the metallic taste, add a big handful of cut-up pungent vegetables such as garlic chives, green onions, onion, ginger, or garlic and a couple tablespoons of oil. Stir-fry, pressing the vegetables into the pan sides, until the bottom and two-thirds up the pan sides turn black, 10 to 15 minutes. Toss out the charred vegetables. Let cool. Gently wash the pan; do not scrub with soap. Dry by heating the wok over high heat until all the water evaporates. Then you're ready to stir-fry.

I clean carbon-steel or cast-iron woks with lightly soapy water and a gentle scrub, if needed. Don't get aggressive with scrubbing or you may remove the patina. If food is stuck, fill the pan with water and soak until the food is loose, and then scrub gently. Rinse well, and then place over high heat until all the water evaporates. The pan may rust if stored damp. If the wok is new and you don't use it often, coat the interior lightly with oil.

The best way to keep the pan seasoned is to use it frequently for stir-frying or deep-frying. Avoid steaming in a newly seasoned pan. After steaming, or if you haven't used the pan in a while, reseason by popping corn in it: Heat the wok over medium-high heat. When the pan is hot, add about 3 tablespoons vegetable oil and ⅓ cup popcorn kernels. Cover the wok and shake the pan often until the popping subsides, 2 to 3 minutes. Pour the popcorn into a bowl and wipe out the pan with a towel; the wok should be nicely coated with oil and ready for stir-frying.

Today, many manufacturers produce high-priced woks that don't require seasoning. However, many of these pans have nonstick finishes that don't stand up to high heat. Without high heat, it is difficult to sear food and attain the browning that stir-frying requires. Nonstick and stainless steel woks are suitable for steaming or deep-frying.

Consider adding a wok spatula, wok ring, and domed lid to make a wok perform even better. A curved, shovel-like wok spatula slides down the sloping sides of a wok smoothly so that stir-frying becomes an easy, rhythmical motion. If you have a round-bottomed wok, a wok ring helps stabilize the wok over the burner when deep-frying, steaming, or braising, preventing it from accidentally tipping over and spilling its contents all over the floor. A domed lid is designed to make steaming in a wok easier.

## Chinese Steamers

You can steam food without a Chinese steamer, but it's so much easier with equipment designed to hold wide dishes. Most Chinese steamers consist of round shallow baskets with slotted or perforated bottoms that act as racks and let in the steam. A lid covers the basket to keep in the steam. The steamer baskets can be stacked to steam several foods at one time. They may be made with bamboo or metal. The most versatile size is 11 to 12 inches in diameter, wide enough to accommodate large plates with enough space for the steam to circulate.

Bamboo steamers are designed to fit into a wok. The sloping sides of the wok naturally elevate the steamer baskets over water. The bamboo lid breathes, reducing condensation. However, the base of the bamboo rack can scorch, especially if the water level gets too low. Make sure that the bottom rim is just covered with water while steaming to prevent the rack from burning. Watch the water level closely. Frequent steaming can strip the patina from a well-seasoned wok. Alternate with stir-frying, make popcorn in the wok, or reseason as needed. Or use a noncorrosive stainless steel or nonstick wok for steaming.

Metal steamers are often sold as a self-contained unit with a base to hold water, plus two racks and a domed metal lid. They are a good choice if you steam often. Look for metal steamers at Asian markets and cookware stores and online at www.wokshop.com/store or http://importfood.com.

Round flat steamer racks, metal or bamboo, are designed to fit into woks and may also be found at Asian markets. With these, you'll need a round, domed lid to cover the pan. With a domed lid, most of the condensation rolls down the sides rather than drips over the food. If you use a flat metal lid, wrap it with a towel to reduce condensation.

## Clay Pots

Many Chinese cooks prefer using rustic clay pots (also called sand pots) to slowly cook stews, rice, braised dishes, soups, and herbal tonics. The handsome pots, which can double as serving dishes, have an unglazed sand- to beige-colored exterior with a shiny, dark-brown glaze inside. Many believe that slow-cooked foods taste purer, sweeter, and more natural when cooked in a clay pot. Pots vary in size, from small ones made for individual portions to large ones used for soups and tonics. Sometimes a thin wire cage wraps around the pot to add extra strength and improve heat conductivity. The clay may be rough and coarse or smooth and more refined. The pots are generally squat, with sides that flare out slightly, and are topped with a lid. Taller spouted pots are used for herbal tonics or soups. Shop for clay pots at Asian markets and cookware stores, or online at www.wokshop.com/store or Amazon.com.

Clay pots can last a long time if treated gently. Before using for the first time, soak the clay pot in water overnight to seal the pores, and then dry. Coat the bottom exterior lightly with vegetable oil. Avoid extreme temperature changes.

Don't set a cold pot from the refrigerator over high heat; it may crack. Never place an empty pot on the heat; it should contain some liquid. Clay pots can sit directly on gas burners. With electric burners, a heat diffuser is recommended. If using in the oven, don't preheat. Set the pot in the cold oven and let it gradually heat. To clean, soak the pot until stuck-on food is soft, and then wash with lightly soapy water and rinse.

## Cleavers

I find a Chinese cleaver to be the perfect all-purpose chef's knife. It can handle all the basic cutting chores and its wide rectangular blade adds advantages. Slam the flat side of the blade across garlic cloves to crush. Use the broad blade to scoop up ingredients. It's sturdy enough to cut through chicken bones.

Traditional Chinese cleavers have carbon blades that rust if left wet. They come in different weights: light, for slicing and boning; midweight, for chopping, slicing, and cutting through poultry bones; and heavy, for whacking through thick bones. Select a midweight cleaver to use as an all-purpose knife. The model I've used for years is one designed by Martin Yan; it has a nonstaining blade, but the same traditional shape.

# Techniques

In this book's recipes, you'll find certain techniques used over and over. Learn these basics, and you'll find that cooking Chinese food will become second nature.

## Stir-Frying

Fuel was a precious commodity in Chinese kitchens. The stove was a hole over a fire chamber. Underneath, there was an opening to feed the fire. A wok, with its round bottom and bowl-shaped pan, fit over the lipped hole and efficiently captured the heat. With a small fire, the wok got very hot. The cook would add a little oil and small pieces of food to the wok, which were then stirred and tossed in the pan. Within minutes, the food was cooked. Meats browned, and vegetables retained their bright colors and textures. This technique of cooking over high heat with constant motion became known as stir-frying.

**SET-UP**   The wide bowl-shaped wok, with its high sloping sides, works perfectly for stir-frying. The heat is concentrated on the bottom, while the sides stay a bit cooler. The curved sides of the pan make it easy to toss the food over and over. The high sides help contain splattering oil and leafy greens. A 14-inch wok is a good size for home kitchens. See the description of the wok under Tools (page 235) for more details.

Wide frying pans with sloping sides can sometimes work as a suitable substitute if you don't have a wok. Because of their wide, flat cooking surfaces, you may need more oil or a splash of water to keep food from sticking and burning. Liquid will evaporate more quickly, so you may need to add a little more liquid if sauces thicken too much. If you use a frying pan, choose one that conducts heat well and can take high heat.

**TIPS**   *Prep all ingredients in advance.* Since this fast-paced cooking method takes only minutes, prep and measure all your ingredients in advance. In these recipes, it is assumed that all produce is rinsed and that garlic, ginger, and onions are peeled. Cut all ingredients into small, even-sized pieces and place ingredients in separate piles. To cut down on dishes, mound several ingredients on the serving dish or a cutting board. Bulky vegetables can sit in the colander. Meats go in a small bowl. Assemble the sauce mixtures. Set everything near the range and you're ready to go.

*Use high heat.* Fast-paced stir-frying requires high heat. Turn up the heat and allow the pan to warm for at least 1 minute before adding your ingredients. If water is sprinkled onto the hot surface, it should immediately vaporize. Once the pan is hot, drizzle a neutral vegetable oil with a high smoking point, such as canola or an oil blend, around the edges of the pan and rotate the pan to spread. The hot oil should ripple when the pan is tilted.

*Less is more.* Most home ranges can't compete with high-powered restaurant ranges, so limit your quantities. If you add too much food at one time, the pan temperature will cool and the food will stew, rather than sear. It's better to cook several small batches than to fill a pan too full.

For thinly sliced meats, you will get the best results if you limit each batch to 8 to 12 ounces in a 14-inch wok. Drier foods, cornstarch-coated pieces, or thicker pieces can sometimes be stir-fried up to 1 pound at a time.

Limit most vegetables to 4 to 6 cups at a time (or 8 to 10 cups for leafy greens). Add vegetables at different times based on their density: thick or dense vegetables should be added first and cooked longer; thinner or leafy pieces should be added later and cooked only briefly. If vegetables start to burn or if you are cooking dense vegetables, such as broccoli or carrots, add a splash of water to create a little steam or cover the pan briefly to finish cooking.

## Deep-Frying

When food is immersed in hot oil, it quickly turns golden and crisp. The effects of deep-frying can be seen in the crunchy skin of fried wontons or egg rolls, pebbled with tiny bubbles. Sometimes this technique is also used as a preliminary step, such as when making stuffed tofu or steamed pork belly with preserved mustard greens. This deep-frying step enriches the color and flavor of a steamed dish.

Restaurants often use this process because it is the fastest way to brown food quickly and evenly. Home cooks use the technique less often because it can be messy. Yet there are times when no other cooking method can produce the right result. And when done properly, deep-fried food can taste light and greaseless.

**SET-UP**    The bowl shape of the wok, with its narrow base and wide opening, works especially well for deep-frying. Since the pan base is narrow, you end up using far less oil than with other wide, deep pans. If you are using a round-bottomed wok, stabilize it by setting it on a wok ring so it doesn't tip over.

A 5- to 6-quart pan can also be used. With these pans with wider bases, you'll need more oil. If you use this technique often, consider buying an electric deep fryer.

**TIPS**    *Use the right type of oil.* Use a neutral-tasting oil that has a high smoking point, such as canola oil or a vegetable oil blend. Pour the oil into the wok to a depth of about 1½ to 2 inches in the center.

*Maintain the right temperature.* Heat the oil over medium-high heat until it reaches the desired temperature, usually between 350°F and 375°F. A thermometer is the most accurate way to gauge the temperature. Regulate the heat to maintain the temperature while frying. It's normal for the temperature to drop when food is added. If you have not overloaded the pan with too much food, the temperature will return to the desired temperature rather rapidly. Between each batch, make sure the oil is back to the desired temperature before adding more food. Regulate the heat to maintain a fairly constant temperature; medium-high works well on my range.

*Do not crowd the pan.* Allow enough room for oil to circulate around the food. Adding too much food at one time can lower the temperature for too long, resulting in soggy food.

*Remove fried food carefully.* Use a Chinese wire strainer (sometimes called a spider) or slotted spoon to lift out fried foods. Have a pan or plate lined with paper towels ready to drain fried foods on. Most fried foods can be kept warm in a 200°F oven for up to 30 minutes.

## Steaming

Steaming is one of the major Chinese cooking techniques. Composed dishes cook gently in a moist environment, preserving succulence and nutrients. It's an easy and healthful way to cook: just set food on a rack above boiling water, cover, and steam until done. All you need is the right steamer set-up.

**SET-UP**  You will need a base to hold water, a rack to suspend food over water, and a lid to keep the steam in. Possible combinations include:

- A 14-inch wok with a domed lid and round cake or steamer rack. If the wok wobbles, set it on a wok ring, a perforated metal ring that stabilizes it on the burner. Place the rack in the wok; the sloping sides of the wok will naturally elevate the rack over the water. The wide opening of the wok makes it easier to remove dishes.

- A Chinese bamboo steamer with a lid. Place 11- to 12-inch steamer baskets in a 14- to 16-inch wok. If a round-bottomed wok wobbles on the burner, set it on a wok ring. Layer baskets to cook more than one dish at a time.

- A Chinese metal steamer. This self-contained unit includes a pan for water, topped with stackable metal steamer baskets, and a domed lid. Choose an 11- to 12-inch metal steamer for the greatest versatility. Stack the racks to cook several dishes at a time.

- A wide, deep pan, such as a kettle or frying pan, with a lid and a round rack. Set the removable rim of a cheesecake pan or three empty 2- to 3-inch-tall cans with both ends removed in the pan, and place the rack on top.

The dish that holds the food must be at least 1 inch smaller than the width of the pan or steamer basket. Chinese cooks often use 9-inch Pyrex pie pans or shallow, heatproof 8- to 9-inch-wide bowls.

**TIPS**  *Watch the water level.* The water should be at least 1 inch below the food so it doesn't bubble into the food. Watch the water level, especially when steaming for a long time, to make sure that the pan does not boil dry. If using a bamboo steamer, keep the bottom rim submerged in water to prevent scorching. Replenish with more boiling water as needed.

*Avoid waterlogged food.* Wrap flat metal lids with a thin, clean dish towel to reduce condensation dripping onto food, tying the towel ends on top so they don't burn. If you are steaming more than one layer at a time in a metal steamer, wrap the bottom of the top rack so it doesn't drown the center layer with condensation. Condensation is generally less of a problem with porous bamboo lids or domed lids.

*Remove hot food carefully.* First, turn off the heat to reduce the chance of burning your hands. If using Chinese steamer baskets, remove the basket with lid from the hot water and set down on a plate or towel. Open the lid away from you, and then lift out the dish. If not using steamer baskets, carefully lift out the steamed dish using pot holders. If it is difficult to get hold of the dish, slip a wide spatula underneath the dish and lift up slightly until you can grab the dish with pot holders, and then lift out.

Or use a plate lifter or fashion a string harness. In Asian markets, you can sometimes buy a three-pronged plate lifter or giant tongs with wide grips that look similar to canning tongs. They grip the edges of the hot plate and help you lift it out. Have pot holders ready to grab the dish, in case it slips. You can also fashion a string harness. Align two lengths (three to four times the width of the dish) of cotton string and tie a knot in the center. Open up to form an *X*. Place the dish of food in the center of the *X*. Bring the string ends together, knot them, and place the strings on top of the food. After steaming, carefully lift up the string harness, and then grab the bowl with pot holders to stabilize.

## Braising

The two-step technique known as braising produces food with rich color and moist, tender texture. First cook the food to create a brown or golden exterior. Do this by stir-frying, pan-browning, deep-frying, or even broiling. Then add liquid, cover the pan, and simmer the food over low heat. In this moist environment tough meats become tender and vegetables soften. The process can take hours or minutes, depending on the food. Meats such as pork butt or oxtails may take hours. A stew like Soy-Braised Chicken and Mushrooms (page 204) cooks in less than half an hour. Vegetables such as eggplant soften in a few minutes.

**SET-UP**   Use a wok, a frying pan, or a large, deep pan to stir-fry or pan-brown the food. Add liquid, and then cover the pan with a lid. If using a Chinese clay pot, brown the food in a metal pan first, then transfer food to the clay pot, add liquid, cover, and cook slowly.

**TIPS**   *Cut ingredients equally.* Cut ingredients into pieces of equal size so that they become tender in the same amount of time.

*Use high heat.* In most cases, use medium-high to high heat for browning to give rich color to meats or vegetables. If the heat is too low, the food will simply stew in its own juices; it won't brown until all the liquid evaporates. When browning large amounts, don't crowd the pan. Divide into smaller batches and brown each separately. Then return all the browned meat to the pan, add liquid, cover, and simmer.

*Cover tightly.* After adding liquid, bring the liquid to a simmer or boil, then reduce the heat to low. Cover the pan tightly to keep moisture in. If the lid is loose, check often and add more liquid as needed.

*Reduce pan juices.* Once the food is done, transfer it to a dish with a slotted spoon. Taste the pan juices. If they are watery, boil uncovered over high heat to concentrate the flavor. Or if there isn't much liquid left, add water as directed by the recipe or dilute to your taste and bring the sauce to a boil. Pour the juices over the food.

## Cutting

Chinese cooking requires good knife skills, especially for stir-frying, where thin, even-sized pieces are critical. You can use a sharp all-purpose chef's knife or, my preference, a Chinese cleaver. Keep the blade sharp to minimize the effort.

In these recipes, some cutting terms are frequently used. Here's how I define them and how to achieve the results.

*Thinly slivered.* Also known as "julienned," "finely shredded," or "cut into matchstick-sized sticks or thin strips." In these recipes, "thinly slivered" refers to skinny strips about 1 to 3 inches long and $\frac{1}{16}$ to $\frac{1}{4}$ inch thick. One way to produce such pieces is to cut the food, such as fresh ginger or carrots, into thin slices the length of the desired strip. Then, stack 2 or 3 slices and slice lengthwise into thin slivers. For onions, cut in half lengthwise, trim the ends, peel, and then cut each half lengthwise into thin slivers. For green onions, trim the ends, and then cut into 2- to 3-inch lengths. Stack 2 or 3 of the green tops and cut lengthwise into thin slivers. Cut the thick white ends lengthwise into thin slivers.

*Minced.* Also known as "finely chopped." In these recipes, I use "minced" to mean cut into tiny, irregularly shaped pieces, each about $\frac{1}{8}$ inch wide. The pieces should be roughly the same size so they cook evenly.

*Chopped.* The same as minced, except pieces are larger, $\frac{1}{4}$ to $\frac{1}{2}$ inch.

### CUTTING WHOLE POULTRY

Chinese chefs, with practiced strokes, chop cooked or raw birds through the bones to make bite-sized pieces that are easy to pick up with chopsticks. With the help of a mallet or small hammer to force the blade of a midweight or heavier cleaver or a large, heavy chef's knife through the bones, you can achieve similar results with more control.

1 Chickens and ducks sold in Asian markets often have heads, necks, and feet attached. Cut these parts off and reserve for another use, or discard. Or, if

desired, leave attached. If the bird is raw, remove the giblets and neck from the cavity and reserve for another use. Remove and discard the large pads of fat near the entrance of the body cavity. Rinse the bird inside and out; pat dry with towels.

2 To split the bird in half: Lay the bird, breast side up, on a board. With a cleaver or large chef's knife, work the blade down the center length of the breast. With a flat mallet or the heel of your hand, tap the blade through the breastbone. Pull the halves apart and position the blade down one side of the backbone. With a mallet or the heel of your hand, tap the blade through the bone to split the bird in half.

3 To remove the legs: Lay the halves, cut side down, on a board. Pull one of the legs, with thigh attached, out from the body, and cut through the joint that attaches the thigh to the body. Separate the thigh and drumstick at the joint. Place the blade across the thigh or drumstick and use a mallet or the heel of your hand to tap the blade through the bone to cut 1- to 1½-inch slices down the length of each piece. Or, if you prefer not to cut across the bone, cut lengthwise alongside the thighbone to cut in half and leave the drumstick whole.

4 To remove the wings: Pull the wings away from the body, and cut through the joint that attaches the wing to the breast. Cut the wings apart at the joints.

5 To cut the body: Lay the body pieces, cut side up, on the board. Cut down the length of the body through the rib bones to separate the breast from the back. If desired, reserve the bony back pieces to make broth. Cut the breast and back pieces crosswise into 1- to 1½-inch-wide pieces.

   For boneless breast pieces on cooked birds: Do not cut the breast crosswise through the bone into small pieces. With a boning knife or a knife with a slender blade, cut down each side, from the top of the breastbone along the rib bones, to remove an entire half breast. Cut each boneless breast section crosswise into 1-inch slices.

6 To present cooked birds, arrange the pieces to resemble a whole bird. Using a wide spatula or the blade of a cleaver, transfer the back pieces, if using, down the center of the platter. Set the breast pieces on top. Place the head above the breast. Arrange the wings, legs, and feet along the sides as in a whole bird.

# Around the Hakka Table

Chinese meals are usually eaten family style. Several different dishes are served together or cooked in quick succession. Each person gets a bowl of rice, a pair of chopsticks, and sometimes a small plate.

In the recipes in this book, you'll often see a number of servings listed as a main dish or as part of a multicourse meal. For the simplest and most basic of meals, serve one dish per person and rice. Many of these recipes serve two as a main course with rice and a vegetable. For each additional diner, add another dish, or figure on a total of about 4 ounces of total protein per serving for the meal. Vary the dishes based on texture, taste, ingredients, and cooking technique.

Multicourse meals for small groups are a matter of organization and good advance preparation. Include some dishes that don't require much active last-minute cooking. Cut and measure all ingredients ahead of time and place with the serving dish. Many meals we ate in China started with a few small plates, such as fried peanuts, pickled vegetables, cool seasoned meats, or cool spiced cooked vegetables. For four to six guests, consider a soup, a steamed dish, a stew or braised dish, one or two stir-fries, and rice. Many soups, steamed dishes, and stews can be made partially or completely ahead and held briefly while you quickly stir-fry the last dish. Serve the courses one or two at a time. At informal family meals, it's common to put all the dishes on the table at the same time. For the novice cook, it takes practice to produce a multidish Chinese meal. Enlist help. Get a cooking partner or ask willing guests to lend a hand.

Producing a multicourse banquet for a large group can be intimidating. For a special occasion, prepare one Hakka classic, such as Salt-Baked Chicken (page 64), Taro Abacus Beads (page 125), or one of the stuffed tofu dishes (page 31). Supplement the meal with potluck contributions. Plan a menu and send guests a recipe. Choose from the many simpler recipes throughout the book. Ask each guest to bring a dish, completed or ready to cook on-site. With a little planning, it's easy to share Hakka fare with your family and friends.

For casual parties, I like to concentrate on one great dish that can be made at least partially in advance. Choose a classic, such as Savory Pounded Tea Rice (page 119) or Hakka Soup Noodles with Egg Roll (page 169), and serve buffet style, letting guests tailor the dish to their taste. Another option is Basin Feast (page 82), a multicourse banquet layered in one pan. A day or two before your party, prepare the different parts and assemble. When guests arrive, turn on the heat and add the finishing touches. For a soup and sandwich party, assemble either of the pork belly with preserved mustard greens dishes (page 42) a day ahead. Do the steaming the day of the party and present the guests with small buns so they can make mini sandwiches. Serve with Pickled Carrots and Radishes (page 60) and a simple soup, such as Chicken and Goji Berry Soup (page 176).

In the West, beer, wine, and tea are served with Chinese meals. In China, diners might choose Chinese wines, such as the sherry-like shaoxing or stronger distilled rice spirits. Hakkas make an aged wine from glutinous rice that tastes much like a cream sherry. However, it is not readily available, and I like it better as an aperitif or after-dinner drink. Western wines also work. With so much variety in a Chinese meal, it is sometimes difficult to choose just one wine or beer that works with every dish. I find the most accommodating wines are dry rosé, pinot gris, pinot noir, or sparkling wines such as brut or rosé. Or offer two or three different wines and let your guests choose. Consider serving a sauvignon blanc if you're having many seafood or vegetable dishes. With heavier pork dishes, offer a more full-bodied red wine, such as zinfandel or merlot. Avoid high-alcohol, highly tannic, or heavily oaked wines. For beer, choose a pale lager to go with the widest range of foods. Or invite friends to bring a selection.

If you prefer a nonalcoholic beverage, I like the cleansing attributes of tea. For an all-purpose choice, serve a semifermented tea such as oolong. With rich, heavy dishes, consider *pu erh,* a dark tea that aids digestion. Most Chinese restaurants offer sparkling cider with their banquets, as the bubbles help clear the palate.

Dessert doesn't play a big part in Chinese meals. The easiest and most appreciated is fruit: oranges, tangerines, Asian pears, watermelon, or pineapple, cut into sections or wedges for easy eating. End with a soothing cup of fragrant jasmine tea.

# The Hakka Pantry

You can make many dishes from this book with a few basic ingredients: all-purpose soy sauce, dark soy sauce, Chinese rice wine, fresh ginger, garlic, various cuts of pork, tofu, bean sauce, fresh vegetables, and long-grain rice. You'll find most of these ingredients, or suitable alternatives, at a well-supplied supermarket. Look for the vegetables at a farmers' market. To add more Hakka flavor to your cooking, seek out an Asian market to find some of the preserved ingredients, such as Chinese sausage, Chinese bacon, salted mustard greens, Tianjin (Tientsin) preserved vegetable, fermented black beans, preserved mustard greens, preserved radish, and red fermented bean curd. Large Asian supermarkets found in areas with major Chinese populations offer most of the ingredients called for in these recipes.

The following list is a shopping guide for many of the ingredients used in this book. Read the recipe carefully, and if you find unfamiliar ingredients, refer to this list. Consider shopping for Chinese ingredients an adventure. Since there are many different Chinese dialects, the same word may be pronounced and spelled in different ways. Labels may be vague, generic, or downright confusing, especially when written in English.

To help you out, I have included traditional Chinese characters for these ingredients. Look for these characters on the package and see if you can match them, or show them to a Chinese clerk. In this list, the Chinese characters are followed by transliterated Chinese names and other names used for the ingredient. The first transliteration is the standard Mandarin transliteration of the characters, followed by other names and spellings used for the ingredient. The description of the product will help guide you to the right choice. Check the label ingredients lists; they sometimes more clearly indicate what you are getting.

amaranth 莧菜 (*xian cai, yeen choy;* Chinese spinach): This leafy green tastes similar to spinach, with an earthy edge. Chinese cooks prefer the variety with fuchsia splotches on thin, flat green leaves. Use in soups and stir-fries. Spinach works as an alternative. Store loosely covered in the refrigerator.

anchovies, dried 江魚仔 *(jiang yu zi, ikan bilis):* Tiny dried silvery-white anchovies are commonly used in Southeast Asia. They can be deep-fried and eaten as a crisp snack or appetizer or used to make fish broth. Store airtight in the refrigerator or a cool, dry place.

arrowhead 慈菇 *(ci gu, chi gu):* This tuber looks like a large ivory-colored water chestnut. It tastes like a cross between a potato and a sunchoke, with a mild flavor that sometimes has a bitter edge. Peel and trim off the spongy base and shoots before cooking. Boil until crisp-tender, or longer for a softer, more potato-like texture. Choose large, firm corms. Store immersed in a bowl of water in the refrigerator. Substitute small red boiling potatoes.

Asian eggplant 茄子 *(qie zi, ke zeem;* found as Chinese eggplant, Japanese eggplant): The Chinese variety may be up to 12 inches long, with a smooth lavender skin and firm, silky flesh. Japanese eggplants are shorter, up to 6 inches long, with dark purplish-black skin. Both are long and slender and have few seeds. They hold their shape better than globe eggplant, which can be used as an alternative. Store loosely covered in the refrigerator.

Asian sesame oil 麻油 *(ma you, ma yul, ma yo):* This aromatic, golden-brown oil is made from toasted sesame seeds and has a strong nutty fragrance and flavor. It is better as a seasoning oil than a cooking oil, as the aroma dissipates with high heat and long cooking. Drizzle over vegetables, float on soups, or use in sauces. Do not confuse it with Western cold-pressed sesame oils that are made with raw seeds and have a neutral flavor. Store airtight at cool room temperature or in the refrigerator, if used rarely. The best brands, such as Kadoya, are pure sesame oils, not blends.

Asian white radish 白蘿蔔 *(bai luo bo, bak lo bok, bai luo boh;* found as daikon, Chinese turnip): The Japanese variety is called daikon and is basically interchangeable with the Chinese white variety also known as turnip. Both are slender ivory roots that generally range from 8 to 12 inches long and 2 to 4 inches wide. The Chinese variety is stubbier, with a scruffier skin than the smooth white daikon. Both have crisp white flesh and are mild and slightly sweet compared to small European radishes. Look for heavy, firm roots with green tops. Use raw in pickles and salad and cooked in soups, stir-fries, stews, and radish cakes. Asian white radishes turn sweet and mellow with long, slow cooking. Store loosely covered in the refrigerator.

baby bok choy 小白菜 *(xiao bai cai;* Shanghai bok choy): This leafy cabbage has small (4- to 10-inch) jade-green heads with pale green stems. The heads may be steamed or blanched whole, or cut in halves or quarters lengthwise. They can also be sliced and stir-fried. Store loosely covered in the refrigerator. *See also* bok choy bamboo shoots 竹筍 (*zhu sun, jook soon*): These large tan or brown cone- or tusk-shaped winter shoots can sometimes be found fresh in Asian markets. Peel or cut off the fibrous exterior and woody bottom to reach the sweet crunchy heart. *Do not eat fresh bamboo shoots raw.* They need to be cooked to remove toxic hydrocyanic acid. Slice the shoots and boil in salted water until crisp-tender and no longer bitter, 5 to 10 minutes; drain. Show off the fresh shoots unadorned, as a simple stir-fried or braised vegetable dish. Store the shoots loosely covered in the refrigerator. If fresh bamboo shoots are unavailable, use good-quality canned shoots, such as Ma Ling or Companion Winter Bamboo Shoots, or vacuum-packed shoots. Rinse canned shoots, and if desired, blanch in boiling water briefly to freshen.

bean curd. *See* bean curd sticks, dried; five-spice pressed tofu; fried tofu; pressed tofu; red fermented bean curd; tofu

bean curd sticks, dried 腐竹 (*fu zhu, foo jook, ful jook;* dried tofu sticks): When soybean milk is heated, a skin forms on the surface. The skin is removed and gathered into sticks and dried over rails. To use, soak the golden sticks in hot or warm water until soft, which can take a few hours. Start soaking the night before to ensure that the sticks are completely rehydrated. Cut and use the sticks in soups or stews, where their neutral taste readily absorbs flavors. Store tightly covered at cool room temperature.

bean sauce, ground 磨豉醬 (*mo chi jiang, meen see, mo see chiang;* bean sauce, brown bean sauce, yellow bean sauce, bean paste): This thick, pasty sauce is made with ground fermented soybeans. It has a salty, pronounced fermented bean flavor, akin to soy sauce. Some varieties are spiced with chiles. Use to season stir-fries, stews, and meats. Store airtight in the refrigerator. I used ground bean sauce from Koon Chun Sauce Factory in my testing.

bean thread noodles, dried 粉絲 (*fen si, xi fen, sai fun;* cellophane noodles, glass noodles): Dried, thin, wiry noodles made from mung bean starch turn clear and translucent when cooked. They are usually soaked before cooking. Use bean thread noodles in soups, stir-fries, and salads. Unsoaked noodles can also be deep-fried. They instantly turn crisp and slightly puffy, and are often used to add texture to chicken salad. Store airtight at room temperature.

beech mushrooms 鴻禧菇 (*hong xi gu, hon shi goo; hon-shimeji;* clamshell mushrooms): These white or light-brown cultivated fresh mushrooms with small, smooth caps and thick, tender stems have a mild flavor and juicy flesh. They are often attached at the base and sold in clumps. Stir-fry, braise, simmer, or deep-fry. Store in a paper bag in the refrigerator; use promptly.

bitter melon or gourd 苦 瓜 (ku gua, foo gwa): Bitter accurately describes the taste of this green vegetable. The preferred Chinese variety ranges from 6 to 10 inches long and 1½ to 2 inches wide. Its smooth green skin is furrowed with deep wrinkles, and a white pith and seeds fill the interior. Cut the melon in rings and scrape out the spongy center. Stuff the cavity with a savory mixture and steam, braise, or poach. Bitter melon can also be sliced and stir-fried. Store loosely covered in the refrigerator.

black fungus, dried 黑 雲 耳 (hei yun er, wun yee; cloud ears) or 黑 木 耳 (hei mu er, mook yee; wood ears): Use the dark fungus for its crunchy texture, rather than its neutral flavor. Packages are often simply labeled "dried black fungus." There are two kinds. The small, thin ones known as cloud ears are best for quick-cooked dishes such as stir-fries or soups. They look like tiny brittle leaves and are dark-colored on both sides. Wood ears are larger, thicker, and tougher. They are two-toned: black on one side and beige on the other. Use them in long, slow cooking. Both types of black fungus are also often sold in thin strips. Rinse and soak the cloud ears or wood ears in water; they will double or triple in size. Pinch out the hard knob in the center, if present, and discard. Rinse well to remove any dirt. The Chinese believe that the fungus helps to keep the blood fluid, a good defense against atherosclerosis. Store airtight at room temperature.

black vinegar 鎮 江 醋 (zhen jiang cu, hock naw mai cho, Chinkiang chu; Chinkiang vinegar, black rice vinegar): This dark vinegar made from glutinous rice is often aged, which lends it complex, smoky overtones. Gold Plum's Chinkiang vinegar is a favorite. Use it in dipping sauces, dressings, and stir-fries. Store airtight at room temperature. Use balsamic vinegar as an alternative.

bok choy 白 菜 (bai cai, pak choi, pai tsai; Chinese white cabbage): White, smooth, juicy stalks with broad dark-green leaves and a mild cabbage-like flavor. Heads vary in length from 6 to 20 inches. Slice and stir-fry, blanch, steam, or add to soups. Store loosely covered in the refrigerator. See also baby bok choy

broad-stemmed Chinese mustard greens 包 心 芥 菜 (bao xin jie cai, dai gai choy, bao shin jay tsai; broad-leaf mustard cabbage, wrapped heart mustard, Swatow mustard): These mustard greens have big, jade-green heads and thick, broad, juicy stems with ruffled leaves. Since they are prized for their stems, which are often pickled, salted, or preserved, heads may be sold with the leaves trimmed off. The heads and stems may be straight, but are often curved into a semiclosed heart. The leaves can be sliced and added to soups.

brown slab sugar 片 糖 (pian tang, peen tong, wong tong; brown candy): Flat bars of layered brown sugar are used to make sweet soups, savory sauces, and desserts. Store airtight at cool room temperature. Use ¼ cup packed brown sugar for one slab (5 inches by 1 inch, about 4 ounces) as an alternative.

celtuce 芹萵 (*qin wo, ching woh, woh sun;* Chinese lettuce, A-choy, stem lettuce, celery lettuce, asparagus lettuce): This popular Chinese vegetable looks like a little tree, with a thick stem and green romaine-like lettuce leaves sprouting from the top. The long, firm green stem has a texture similar to a broccoli stem; peel deeply to reach the tender part, which can be sliced and pickled, stir-fried, or added to soups. The leaves are usually stir-fried or added to soups. In Asian markets in North America, the leaves and stems are usually sold separately. Store loosely covered in the refrigerator. Use romaine lettuce as a substitute for the leaves, broccoli stems for the stem.

chiles, fresh 鮮辣椒 (*xian la jiao, seen laat ziu, hsien la chiao*): In this book, I have used mostly readily available chiles, such as the plump, round-shouldered, thick-walled jalapeño or the thinner, more triangular-shaped Fresno. These 3- to 4-inch chiles are usually medium-hot, although heat varies with each one. Jalapeños are usually sold green. Fresno chiles are sold yellow and often red. Red chiles are generally preferred in Chinese cooking for their bright color and sweeter flavor. Most of the heat is contained in the veins that run down the inner walls of the chile, which rub against the seeds. For less heat, remove the seeds and veins. For more heat, include all the seeds and veins or use a hotter variety, such as serrano. Store chiles loosely covered in the refrigerator.

chile sauce or paste 辣椒醬 (*la jiao jiang, la chiao chiang;* chile garlic sauce): This spicy condiment is made from chiles, usually red. Chinese versions are generally made from fermented or dried red chiles, salt, and oil. Some add garlic, fermented black beans, soybeans, or preserved radish. Southeast Asian producers often add vinegar or sugar. Use as a seasoning, table condiment, or dipping sauce. Store airtight in the refrigerator after opening.

Chinese bacon 臘肉 (*la rou, lop yok;* winter-cured pork, soy sauce pork, Chinese-style cooked pork strips, dried smoked pork belly): These strips of pork belly marinated in soy sauce and five-spice powder and dry-cured over a fire might have been the world's first bacon. Look for the dark, dry strips hanging from strings in Chinese meat markets or vacuum packed in the refrigerator section of Asian supermarkets. To soften the hard, dry strips, steam or simmer in water or another liquid. Trim off the tough rind if you don't plan on cooking the bacon for very long. The fat-striped pork adds a smoky, earthy flavor to stewed, steamed, and braised dishes. Small bits are also used to season fillings. Choose bacon with a high proportion of lean meat. Store airtight in the refrigerator.

Chinese barbecue sauce. *See sa cha* sauce

Chinese broccoli 芥 蘭 (*jie lan, gai lan, chieh lan;* Chinese kale): Chinese broccoli has a texture similar
to the American version, with a mildly bitter, earthy flavor somewhat akin to
kale. Instead of large crowns, the structure is mostly narrow crunchy stems with
stiff leathery leaves and small white buds or flowers. A whitish bloom dulls its
dark-green color. Check the ends of cut stalks; those with a slight translucence
will be the youngest and most tender. Peel the stems if the skin is tough. Stir-
fry, steam, or blanch. Drizzle with oyster sauce and sesame oil for a simple and
delicious presentation. Store loosely covered in the refrigerator. Use broccoli
raab (rapini), broccolini, or regular broccoli as a substitute.

Chinese celery 芹 菜 (*qin cai, qin choy*): This vegetable, with its skinny, stringy stalks and flat parsley-
like leaves, has an assertive herbal flavor. Add it to stir-fries and soups. Store
loosely covered in the refrigerator. Use the common North American thick-
stalked variety as a mild-mannered substitute; add some flat-leaf parsley to
mimic the flavor, if desired.

Chinese chives. *See* garlic chives

Chinese lettuce. *See* celtuce

Chinese mustard greens 芥 菜 (*jie cai, gai choy, jay tsai*): Chinese mustard greens come in different forms
with confusing names. All have a brilliant jade-green color and sharp mustard
flavor. Use the greens in stir-fries, soups, braises, and pickles. Substitute
American or Southern curly mustard when used in soups or stir-fries. Store
loosely covered in the refrigerator. *See also* broad-stemmed Chinese mustard
greens; leaf mustard; pickled mustard greens; preserved mustard greens or
cabbage; salted mustard greens

Chinese noodles, fresh or dried 麵 條 (*mian tiao, mein*): Chinese wheat noodles are sometimes labeled as
egg noodles, even though the ingredients may not include eggs. These noodles
are usually white, but some have a golden hue, due to egg or coloring. They may
be round or flat, thick to thin. Store fresh noodles airtight in the refrigerator
and dried noodles airtight at room temperature.

Chinese rice spirits 雙 蒸 酒 or 米 酒 精 or 米 威 士 忌 酒 (*shuang zheng jiu, mi jiu jing, mi wei shi ji jiu,*
*mi chiew, mi jeow;* white rice wine): This clear spirit distilled from rice has a clean,
neutral taste. Its alcohol content starts around 30 percent. Use in soups, sauces,
stir-fries, and marinades. Choose a brand that is good for drinking, such as Pearl
River Bridge's Kiu Kuang Shuang Jin Chiew. Those labeled cooking wine contain
salt and should be avoided. Use vodka as an alternative. Store airtight at room
temperature.

Chinese rice wine 紹興酒 (*shao xing jiu, siu hing zul, Shao hsing hua tiao chiew*): Shaoxing wine is named after the city in the eastern province of Zhejiang in which it is produced. It's distilled from fermented glutinous rice, rice millet, yeast, and spring water. This aged amber wine has a flavor and alcohol content (about 18 percent) similar to that of dry sherry, which makes a good substitute. Japanese sake, also made from rice, has a lighter color and different flavor profile, but could be used in small amounts as an alternative. Mirin, sweetened sake, is too sweet. A respected shaoxing wine for drinking and cooking is the blue-labeled Pagoda brand's Hua Tiao Chiew. Drink Chinese rice wine warm as a beverage or use in stir-fries, stews, braised dishes, and drunken dishes. Avoid the salted version labeled cooking wine. Store airtight at room temperature.

Chinese sausage 臘腸 (*la chang, lop chong*): This dried sausage is most commonly made with pork, pork fat, and sugar. Lower-fat versions and a variation with liver are also available. The slightly sweet sausage resemble a small, slender salami, with a similar texture and color, but only about ½ inch thick and 6 inches long. Chinese sausages are sold vacuum-packed in the refrigerator section of Asian markets or hanging in pairs from a cord in Chinese meat markets. Steam or slice and stir-fry the firm links. Store covered in the refrigerator.

Chinese sesame paste 芝麻醬 (*zhi ma jiang*): Toasted sesame seeds are ground into a dark aromatic paste with a deep nutty flavor. Use sesame paste in sauces for noodles and salads and in sweet fillings. Stir oil into the paste before using. Store airtight in the refrigerator.

*choy sum* 菜心 (*cai xin, bok choy sum*): *Choy sum* translates to "vegetable heart" and is applied to a variety of greens. However, when the name is used by itself, *choy sum* usually refers to a less-mature bok choy or the small heart of the larger bok choy. The small hearts with white juicy stems and green leaves have a delicate flavor. If small, halve lengthwise or leave whole and blanch or steam. If large, slice and stir-fry, blanch, steam, or add to soups. The term *choy sum* is sometimes used for another green called *yao choy* (page 266). Store loosely covered in the refrigerator.

cilantro 香菜 or 芫荽 (*xiang cai, yan sui, yeem sai, yuan chien;* fresh coriander, Chinese parsley): This herb looks similar to flat-leaf parsley, with a softer texture and a refreshing, assertive flavor that people either love or hate. Use it as a garnish and seasoning. Store loosely covered in the refrigerator, stem ends immersed in water.

cloud ears. *See* black fungus, dried

coriander, fresh. *See* cilantro

daikon. *See* Asian white radish

dark soy sauce 老抽 (*lao chou, low zul;* black soy sauce, double black soy sauce, mushroom soy sauce): Dark soy sauce is aged longer than all-purpose soy sauce and blended with a little molasses to give it a darker color and slight caramelized sweetness. Mushroom soy is a dark soy sauce flavored with straw mushrooms to impart a deep, rich taste. Use in stir-fries, stews, and marinades to give a deep, dark color and rich, robust flavor. For a simple substitute, mix two parts soy sauce with one part molasses. Store at room temperature.

eggplant. *See* Asian eggplant

egg roll wrappers 蛋卷皮 or 春捲皮 (*dan juan pi, chun juan pi, chun guen pay;* spring roll skins, pastry wrappers): Thin wrappers or skins (6½ to 8 inches square) are used to make egg or spring rolls. Pasta-based wrappers, similar to large wonton skins, blister when fried and have a sturdy texture. Spring roll wrappers or skins also refer to dry crêpe-like squares or rounds. Both types are interchangeable for frying, but the drier crêpe-like wrappers hold up better if made ahead before frying and have a thinner, crisper texture. Store airtight in the refrigerator or freeze for longer storage.

enoki mushrooms 金針菇 (*jin zhen gu, gin jun chun goo;* enokitake): These creamy white, slender mushrooms with long, skinny stems and small caps have a delicate, mild, fruity flavor and a crisp texture. Trim off the ends of joined stems, separate the mushrooms, and add near the end of cooking. Store in the refrigerator, lightly covered, and use before the mushrooms lose their crisp texture.

fermented black beans 豆豉 (*dou chi, dul see;* salted black beans, preserved black beans): Small, black soybeans are fermented with salt and spices until pungent and aromatic. Rinse or soak in water, and use whole or crushed to season meats, steamed fish, or vegetables. To make black bean sauce, fermented black beans are crushed with garlic and sometimes ginger, and mixed with soy sauce. Purchased black bean sauce can be used as a substitute. Store airtight in the refrigerator.

fermented sweet wine rice 甜酒釀 (*tian jiu niang, tien jeow niang, lao zao;* sweet rice, rice pudding, rice sauce): Wet fermented sediment or lees are the result of making sweet rice wine. The soft, fermented glutinous rice lees are packaged with some of the clear to cloudy sweet wine. Ingredients are water, glutinous rice, and yeast. Both the soft rice lees and sweet wine are used in savory sauces and desserts. Fermented sweet wine rice is sold refrigerated or on the shelf in Asian markets. Store airtight in the refrigerator for several months.

fish paste 魚漿 (*yu jiang*): Fresh white-fleshed fish, salt, seasonings, and sometimes additives such as starch or egg white are ground into a dense paste, which is used to make fish balls, fish cakes, or stuffed tofu. When cooked, it typically has a springy, bouncy texture. Fish paste is sold at the seafood counter of Asian markets. You can also make your own (page 225). Store covered in the refrigerator for one or two days.

fish sauce 魚露 (*yu lu, nam pla, nuoc mam*): Amber-colored fish sauce is made from fermented salted anchovies and water. Potent and salty, it is used much like salt or soy sauce in Southeast Asian countries. Use salt as an alternative. Store airtight at room temperature.

five-spice powder 五香粉 (*wu xiang fen, ngh heung fun, wu shiang fen;* Chinese five-spice): This aromatic Chinese spice blend usually combines five spices, although the number and combination may vary. The most common components are cinnamon, fennel or anise, cloves, star anise, Sichuan peppercorns, and sometimes ground ginger. Use with meats as a rub, in a marinade, and in braising liquids. Store airtight at room temperature. If you can't find premade five-spice powder, try making your own supermarket alternative using equal parts ground ginger, finely crushed anise or fennel seeds, ground cinnamon, and ground cloves, plus a pinch of ground white pepper.

five-spice pressed tofu (or bean curd) 五香豆腐乾 (*wu xiang dou fu gan, nge hiong dul foo gawn;* marinated bean curd, seasoned *dou fu*): Pressed tofu is flavored with soy sauce and five-spice powder, giving it a brown surface. Use for stir-fries. Store covered in the refrigerator. Discard if it becomes slimy or smells sour.

fried tofu (or bean curd) 油豆腐 (*you dou fu, yo dul foo;* oil tofu, yellow bean curd): Squares of firm tofu that have been lightly fried have a golden surface and firm, white interior. Use fried tofu for stir-fries. Store covered in the refrigerator. Discard if it becomes slimy or smells sour. For a substitute, pan-fry firm tofu: Rinse and drain firm tofu. Cut into slabs about ½ inch thick. Pat dry and drain on towels. Gently press the top surface with additional paper towels to remove excess moisture. Set a 12-inch nonstick frying pan over medium-high heat. When the pan is hot, after about 1 minute, add 2 tablespoons vegetable oil and rotate the pan to spread. Lay the tofu in a single layer in the pan and cook, turning halfway through, until golden brown on both sides, 7 to 8 minutes total.

galangal, ground 沙姜 (*sha jiang, kencur, cekur;* sand ginger, lesser galangale): *Kaempferia galanga,* a rhizome related to ginger, has a peppery, camphor flavor. Use the dried ground spice to make a sauce for chicken. Store airtight at room temperature.

garlic chives 韭菜 (*jiu cai, gau choy;* Chinese chives): These grass-like dark-green blades have a strong garlic flavor. Add to stir-fries, soups, eggs, and seafood. Store loosely covered in the refrigerator. Use thinly slivered green onions with a little extra minced garlic as a substitute.

ginger 薑 (*jiang, kiong, geung*): Fresh ginger, in its mature stage, looks like a knobby irregular hand with rough tan skin and fibrous yellow flesh. This rhizome has a strong, pungent, spicy flavor. Peel, slice, sliver, mince, or grate to use as a seasoning in stir-fries, soups, stews, sauces, and steamed dishes. In Asia, "old ginger" is distinguished from "young ginger," which has a thin, smooth ivory skin with pink shoots and a milder flavor and less fibrous texture. Young ginger is also available in North America, usually in the summer and fall. Slice and pickle the young ginger. Store mature ginger uncovered in the refrigerator for up to a few weeks. Young ginger should be used fairly promptly.

glutinous rice 糯米 (*nuo mi, naw mai;* sweet rice, sticky rice): Glutinous long- or short-grain rice contains more amylopectin, a starch that makes the rice naturally sticky, than other rice. It is used to make rice wine, fermented sweet wine rice, savory fillings, and desserts. Store covered at room temperature. *See also* fermented sweet wine rice

glutinous rice flour 糯米粉 (*nuo mi fen, naw mai fun;* sweet rice flour): Milled from glutinous rice, this flour contributes a sticky, chewy texture to sweet snacks and desserts. Store airtight in a cool, dry place. *See also* rice flour

glutinous rice wine 糯米酒 (*nuo mi jiu, hock mai zul;* Tung Kiang glutinous rice wine): This golden or brown Hakka wine, made by fermenting cooked glutinous rice with wine yeast, tastes sweet and mellow with nutty, fruity overtones, like a cream sherry or tawny port. Drink as a beverage or cook with chicken to make a restorative tonic for new mothers after childbirth. Store airtight at room temperature. Use cream sherry or tawny port as an alternative.

goji berries 枸杞 (*ju qi, gay zee, gou qi zi;* red medlar, wolfberries): The reddish-orange oval berries of the matrimony vine, *Lycium barbarum,* look similar to small, slender red raisins. They're sweet, with slight anise overtones, and have tiny pits that don't need to be removed. The Chinese believe that the red berries improve eyesight. Use in soups, stews, and desserts. Goji berries are sold in Chinese herb shops, Asian markets, and health food stores. Store airtight in a cool, dry place.

hoisin sauce 海鮮醬 (*hai xian jiang, hoisin zheung*): This thick brown sauce is a sweetened, spiced version of bean sauce. It's often served as a condiment with Peking duck. It can be used as a more available alternative to basic bean sauce when small amounts are needed. Store airtight in the refrigerator once opened.

jujubes. *See* red dates, dried

kabocha 南瓜 (*nan gua, nam gwa;* Japanese pumpkin, Japanese squash): *Kabocha* is a generic term for Japanese winter squash. Sizes and shapes vary. One of the most common varieties is round with a flattened top and bottom and thin dark-green skin, sometimes mottled with slate-colored stripes; orange-skinned varieties also exist. Asians like the squash's vivid orange color and smooth, sweet flesh. Steam, simmer, or bake. Store at cool room temperature; after cutting, store covered in the refrigerator.

king oyster mushrooms 杏鮑菇 (*xing bao gu, shing bao goo;* king trumpet mushrooms, royal trumpet mushrooms, Trumpet Royale mushrooms): These big, fleshy, meaty mushrooms have thick, white, bulbous stems and rather small brown caps. Their firm, solid texture holds its shape when cooked. These flavorful mushrooms are often sold in Asian markets. Trim the stem ends. Braise, stir-fry, sauté, or deep-fry. Store in a paper bag in the refrigerator, and use within a few days. *See also* oyster mushrooms

leaf mustard 小芥菜 or 芥菜心 (*xiao jie cai, jie cai xin, gai choy sum, jay tsai shin, juk gai choy;* small *gai choy,* bamboo mustard, mustard green heart): Small bunches with narrow or celery-shaped stems and thin leaves.

light soy sauce. *See* soy sauce

lily buds, dried 金針 (*jin zhen, gum tzum, gin jun;* golden needles, tiger lily buds): Lily buds are the dried unopened flowers of yellow and orange daylilies. The thin, flexible strands range in color from golden to brown; the light-colored ones are fresher. Soak in water until soft, trim off the bump at the end, and tie in a knot so it stays together. Lily buds contribute a light floral fragrance and woodsy, earthy flavor to soups and stir-fries. Store airtight in a cool, dry place.

lily bulbs, fresh 百合 (*bai he, pak hup):* The edible bulbs of the *Lilium* flowering plant have smooth, fleshy ivory-colored layers, like petals. Each bulb is about the size of a large head of garlic. Separate the layers, rinse well, and stir-fry. Fresh bulbs add a subtle bittersweetness, crisp bite, and a trace of potato-like starch. Check the produce section for the fresh bulbs. Use shallots as an alternative for the fresh bulbs. Store in the refrigerator.

long beans 豆角 (*dou jiao, dul gock, tou chiao;* yard-long beans, asparagus beans): These skinny green beans usually range from 18 to 24 inches long. Their color is light or medium green. They have an intense bean flavor and a drier, chewier, heartier texture than common green beans. They're more akin to cow peas or black-eyed peas. Trim the stem ends; no need to string. Stir-fry, blanch, or steam. Store loosely covered in the refrigerator. Use green beans as a substitute.

long-grain rice 長粒米 (*chang li mi):* Long-grain white rice is the everyday grain of the Hakka diet. Boil or steam. Store at room temperature in a cool, dry place.

loofah, angled 絲瓜 (*si gua, see gwa;* angled luffa, silk squash, Chinese okra): Long and slender with a graceful curve, this summer squash has a dull, rough green skin that conceals soft, mild-flavored white flesh. Protruding ridges run down the sides. If the squash is young and tender, peel off the ridges and leave strips of green skin. When cooked with some skin, the center will be soft and the edges slightly crunchy. If the squash is more mature with leathery skin, or for a soft texture throughout, peel off all the skin before cooking. Steam or add to stir-fries, soups, or braises. Store loosely covered in the refrigerator. Use zucchini as an alternative.

lotus root 蓮藕 (*lian ou, leen gnul):* This rhizome of the lotus plant looks like a string of sausage links with holes tunneling through the sections. When the flesh is peeled and sliced crosswise, the holes form a pretty, lacy pattern. The ivory-colored flesh is crisp and slightly sweet and starchy, somewhat like jicama or water chestnut, but a bit woodier and not as juicy. Peel, thinly slice crosswise, and blanch to use in salads or pickles. Add to stir-fries, soups, and stews. Store loosely covered in the refrigerator.

mushrooms. *See* beech mushrooms; black fungus, dried; enoki mushrooms; king oyster mushrooms; oyster mushrooms; shiitake mushrooms; straw mushrooms

mustard greens. *See* broad-stemmed Chinese mustard greens; Chinese mustard greens; leaf mustard; pickled mustard greens; preserved mustard greens or cabbage; salted mustard greens

napa cabbage 黃白菜 (*huang bai cai, wong gna bock;* Chinese cabbage, celery cabbage): These elongated barrel-shaped or cylindrical heads with white, satiny stems and light-green, ruffled leaves have a sweet, delicate, mild cabbage flavor. Thinly slice for salads, add to soups, or braise or stir-fry. Store loosely covered in the refrigerator.

noodles. *See* Chinese noodles, fresh or dried

*ong choy. See* water spinach

orange peel, dried. *See* tangerine peel, dried

oyster mushrooms 蠔菇 (*hao gu, hou goo, how goo;* abalone mushrooms, tree oyster mushrooms): These mild, tender, soft cultivated mushrooms have a cream or taupe color with spoon-shaped or round caps. They usually grow in clusters. Trim off the stem ends and separate the mushrooms. Braise, stir-fry briefly, sauté, or deep-fry; avoid serving raw. Store in a paper bag in the refrigerator, and use within a few days. *See also* king oyster mushrooms

oyster sauce 蠔油 (*hao you, hoe yul, oe yul):* This thick, dark-brown sauce is made from oyster extract, sugar, and salt. Use it to infuse stir-fries, sauces, and vegetables with intense savory flavors. I prefer the Lee Kum Kee brand, which has a picture of a woman and boy in a boat on the label. Store airtight in the refrigerator once opened.

palm sugar 棕櫚糖 (*zong lu tang, nam tan peep;* jaggery, java sugar, coconut sugar): Golden and grainy, this sugar is made by boiling down the sap of various palm trees. The sugar adds a maple syrup–like sweetness to stews and desserts. It is often formed into firm cakes. Store airtight at room temperature. Use brown sugar as a substitute.

peas, edible-pod 豌豆 (*wan dou, hoh laan dau, wan dul;* found as snow peas, sugar peas, sugar-snap peas): These peas can be eaten whole, including the unlined pod. In Chinese dishes, the flat-pod snow pea with immature peas has long been popular for its crisp crunch and bright grass-green color. Plump sugar-snap peas, with their thick juicy pods and fully developed peas, offer a sweeter, more succulent alternative. Remove the strings and briefly blanch or stir-fry. Store loosely covered in the refrigerator.

pickled mustard greens 酸菜 (*suan cai, soen choi, suan tsai;* pickled mustard cabbage): Similar to salted mustard greens. Sugar and vinegar give these greens a sweet-tart finish; most are from Southeast Asia. Some brands add yellow coloring to give the greens a golden tinge. Buy pickled mustard greens in Asian markets in plastic bags or in cans. They can often be used interchangeably with salted mustard greens in stir-fries, soups, and stews. To make your own, see page 147. *See also* salted mustard greens

pickled plums 酸梅子 (*suan mei zi, soen moi, shoon moy):* These golden plums are packed in water and salt. I like the Koon Chun brand. Use the salty-sour fruit to make plum sauce or cook with poultry or meat. Store airtight in the refrigerator once opened.

plum sauce 酸梅醬 (*suan mei jiang, shoon moy zheung, suan mei chiang):* This golden sweet-tart sauce is made from cooked plums, sugar, salt, ginger, and chiles. It can be found in Asian markets and the international section of supermarkets. Use as a dipping sauce. Store airtight in the refrigerator once opened.

pork belly 五花肉 (*wu hwa rou;* five-flower pork, three-layer pork, side pork, fresh bacon): Hakkas love this succulent cut of pork, streaked with layers of fat and meat and topped with chewy skin. It is steamed or braised for hours until it attains a melt-in-the-mouth texture. Look for evenly thick pieces with a high proportion of lean meat. Store covered in the refrigerator.

preserved lime or lemon 鹹檸檬 or 酸石灰 (*xian ning meng, suan shi hui;* pickled lemon or *limón,* salted lemon or lime): The green-skinned citrus fruit that North Americans call lime is called *limón* or lemon in many other countries. Look for the preserved lime packed in brine in jars. The ingredients should include lime or lemon, water, and salt. Use it in sauces to add refreshing tartness, citrus aroma, and slight bitterness. Store-bought preserved lime or lemon can be used as a substitute for homemade salted lime or lemon. I used a pickled lemon produced in Thailand for testing. Refrigerate after opening.

preserved mustard greens or cabbage 梅菜 or 梅干菜 (*mei cai, moi choy, mei tsai, mei gan cai, mei gan tsai;* preserved vegetables, dried vegetables, plum-dried vegetables): Dry, pliable, yellowish-brown stalks of mustard cabbage, preserved in salt and sugar, are often steamed with pork belly in the Hakka specialty *kiu ngiuk moi choi.* Labels are very vague, so check ingredients lists to get more specific descriptions. Sometimes the leaves are trimmed off and just the hearts are sold. Salt content varies. Generally, the softer, lighter-colored greens are sweeter and less salty. Chop, rinse, and soak the greens in water, changing water occasionally to remove excess salt. Squeeze dry, then cook. Store airtight at room temperature, and refrigerate after opening. The brands Stone Crane and Shun Fat Yuen do not use preservatives (the greens are labeled dried vegetable).

pressed tofu (or bean curd) 豆腐乾 (*dou fu gan, dul foo gawn, nigari;* pressed *dou fu,* super-firm tofu): Water is pressed out of bean curd so the cakes have a very firm texture. The pressed cakes are then vacuum packed without water. This tofu holds its shape when stir-fried or grilled. Store, covered, in the refrigerator. Discard if it becomes slimy or smells sour. *See also* five-spice pressed tofu

red dates, dried 紅棗 (*hong zao, hong zoe;* jujubes): These dry, leathery red dates have an apple-raisin flavor. Add to soups, stews, steamed dishes, and desserts. Soak and pit before cooking. Store airtight in a cool, dry place.

red fermented bean curd 南乳 (*nan ru, nom yu;* red bean cheese, red wet bean curd, red preserved bean curd): Small cubes of bean curd are inoculated with a special mold and then soaked in a brine with Chinese rice wine, salt, and dried red yeast rice until they ripen to soft, pungent, red nuggets, much like a smelly aged cheese. Hakkas often use the fermented curd to add intense flavor to pork. Stored airtight in the refrigerator, it will keep almost indefinitely.

red yeast rice 紅米麴 (*hong mi qu, kuk):* Tiny dried dark-red particles are a fermentation by-product of the red yeast *Monascus pupureus* growing on cooked nonglutinous rice. The dried red yeast rice is used as a natural dye and preservative, adding a deep red color and faint mineral flavor to fermented bean curd, wine, soups, and sauces. The dried red yeast rice is used medicinally to improve blood circulation and digestion. It is believed to help combat cholesterol. Store airtight at room temperature or freeze or refrigerate for longer storage. May be difficult to find.

rice. *See* glutinous rice; long-grain rice

rice flour 粘米粉 (*nian mi fen, zeem mai fun, mi fun;* rice powder): Rice flour is a white flour made from ground long-grain rice and used to make noodles and savory steamed cakes. It is not interchangeable with glutinous rice flour. Store airtight in a cool, dry place. *See also* glutinous rice flour

rice noodles, dried 米粉 (*mi fen, mai fun;* rice vermicelli, rice sticks): These thin noodles are made from long-grain rice and water. When boiled, the brittle dried noodles soften into tender white noodles. When fried in hot oil, they puff into crisp strands almost instantly. Store covered at room temperature.

rice vinegar 米醋 (*mi cu, mi chu*): This mild, amber-colored vinegar made from rice wine lees is less acetic (usually around 4 percent) and less harsh than most other vinegars. Use for pickles, stir-fries, and sauces. Store airtight at room temperature.

rice wine. *See* Chinese rice spirits; Chinese rice wine; fermented sweet wine rice; glutinous rice wine

*sa cha* sauce 沙茶醬 (*sha cha chiang;* Chinese barbecue sauce): This potent oily paste is made from ground dried brill fish, chile, garlic, dried shrimp, peanuts, coconut, and spices. Use the paste to season stir-fries, brush on meat before grilling, or use as a dipping sauce for hotpot or as a soup base. It contributes an aromatic seafood flavor. The one made in Taiwan is simply labeled barbecue sauce in English. Do not confuse it with another Chinese barbecue sauce from Hong Kong with hoisin sauce as a base. Check the ingredients list to see if it has the dried brill fish. Refrigerate after opening.

salted mustard greens 鹹菜 (*xian cai, hahm choi, hom choy, shen tsai;* salted mustard cabbage): Stems and heads of mustard cabbage are soaked in brine. The wet-brined, olive-green vegetables are generally sold in plastic bags in the refrigerator section or on the shelf at Asian grocery stores. Chop, if needed, rinse well, and soak, changing water occasionally, to remove excess salt, and then squeeze dry. Use in stir-fries, soups, and stews. Salted mustard greens are interchangeable with pickled mustard greens. To make your own, see page 146. Store airtight in the refrigerator. *See also* pickled mustard greens

salted radish 鹹菜脯 (*xian cai fu, hom choy poo, shen tsai poo;* preserved radish, salted turnip, preserved turnip): The Asian white radish is preserved in salt, sugar, and sometimes soy sauce to transform it into a chewy, golden- to tan-colored cured vegetable. It is similar to sweet radish, but may be saltier and drier. Soak in water to remove excess salt. Use it to add a chewy texture and salty-sweet flavor to eggs, meats, rice soups, and dumpling fillings. Refrigerate or store airtight in a cool, dry place. *See also* sweet radish

sesame oil. *See* Asian sesame oil

shiitake mushrooms 冬菇 or 椎茸 (*dong gu, chui rong, doong goo, schway long goo*; Chinese mushrooms, black mushrooms, black forest mushrooms): Available fresh or dried, these dark, meaty, aromatic mushrooms have a deep flavor with hints of pine and garlic. Braise whole or add to stir-fries, fillings, soups, and stews.

> *Dried shiitakes.* The best have thick, lighter-colored caps with tiny white cracks; they may be called flower mushrooms (*fa goo*). Mushrooms with darker, thinner caps tend to be cheaper and less meaty. Chinese cooks often prefer dried shiitakes for their concentrated flavor and high quality. The dried brown or black mushrooms range from 1 to 3 inches wide. Rinse and soak them in hot water until soft; this can take as little as 20 minutes for thin caps and as long as 2 hours for thick caps. Remove and discard the tough stems. Reserve the flavorful soaking water to add to sauces or soups by carefully pouring off the clear soaking liquid and leaving the gritty sediment behind. Store dried shiitakes airtight in the freezer or refrigerator, or at room temperature.

> *Fresh shiitakes.* Look for thick, solid curled-under caps with a slight whitish bloom. Avoid big, flabby mushrooms. Shiitakes are dense, firm, and drier than most fresh mushrooms. Store fresh shiitakes in a paper bag in the refrigerator, and use within a few days.

shrimp, dried 乾蝦米 (*qian xia mi, ha mai, gawn kan hsia mi*): Small dried shrimp add a briny flavor to fillings, stir-fries, and sauces. They may be labeled small (½ inch) to extra-large (about 1 inch). Choose ones with bright orange color, and rinse and soak before use. Store airtight in the refrigerator.

Sichuan peppercorns 花椒 (*hua jiao, fa ziu, hua chiao*; Chinese pepper, *fagara*, Szechuan pepper, *sansho*) These small, dry, reddish-brown berries (*Xanthoxylum piperitum*) are not related to peppercorns (*Piper nigrum L.*). They have a spicy, woodsy, citrusy aroma and produce a numbing sensation when eaten. Toast in a dry pan until they begin to smoke, then finely grind in a mortar and pestle. Use in seasoned salts, rubs for meats, and flavored oils. Store airtight at room temperature.

snow peas. *See* peas, edible-pod

soy sauce 醬油 (*jiang you, see yul, chiang yo*; white soy sauce, thin soy sauce, light soy sauce): This all-purpose dark, aged seasoning liquid made from naturally fermented soybeans and wheat is indispensable in a Hakka kitchen. Chinese soy sauces, such as Pearl River Bridge Superior Light Soy Sauce, contain more soybeans and have a stronger, more pronounced soy essence than Japanese sauces, such as Kikkoman, which contain more wheat and are lighter, mellower, smoother, and less intense. Some Chinese cooks call this all-purpose soy sauce light (not referring to low-sodium) or white to distinguish it from dark or black soy sauce.

Use to season stir-fries, marinades, and dipping sauces, and with lighter foods. Choose only naturally brewed sauces. Store airtight at room temperature or in the refrigerator. *See also* dark soy sauce; sweet soy sauce

squid, dried 乾魷魚 *(qian you yu, gawn yo yue):* Dried squid has a distinct smell of the sea and a chewy texture. The large, flattened tan pieces are toasted and added to soups to deepen the flavor. For stir-fries, soak in water with baking soda (about 1 teaspoon baking soda to 1 cup water) until soft and pliable; then clean, removing the ink sac, cellophane-like quill, and eyes, if present. Rinse and soak in plain water to remove the baking soda. Baking soda tenderizes and plumps dried squid. Thinly slice and cook. Store airtight in the refrigerator.

star anise 八角 *(ba jiao, buot guok, pa chiao):* This aromatic spice is shaped like an eight-pointed star, about the size of a quarter. The reddish-brown star infuses stews and braises with a distinctive licorice flavor. If a recipe calls for one star anise and it is missing some tips, add some broken tips to make a total of eight. The spice is ground and used in five-spice powder. It is also sometimes sold ground in Asian markets. If you can't find it ground, pound it in a mortar and pestle, then finely grind in a blender. Use about 1 teaspoon fennel or anise seeds as a substitute for each star anise. Store airtight at room temperature.

straw mushrooms 草菇 *(cao gu, tsao ku goo):* These delicate, meaty mushrooms with dome-shaped brown caps and thick straw-colored stems are commonly available peeled and canned in North America. Sometimes they are also packed unpeeled; with their edible shroud-like caps, they resemble quail-sized brown eggs. Rinse the mushrooms well and use in soups, stir-fries, and stews.

sugar. *See* brown slab sugar; palm sugar

sugar snap peas. *See* peas, edible-pod

sweetened black vinegar 甜醋 *(tian cu, teem cho, tien chu;* sweetened black rice vinegar): This dark, syrupy sweetened vinegar is used primarily to cook pickled pig's feet. Store airtight at room temperature.

sweet radish 甜菜脯 *(tian cai fu, thiam choy poo, tian tsai poo;* sweet turnip): Sweet radish or turnip is similar to salted radish, but slightly sweeter, lighter in color, and more pliable. Most brands come from Southeast Asia. *See also* salted radish (for description and use)

sweet rice. *See* fermented sweet wine rice; glutinous rice

sweet soy sauce 甜醬油 *(tian jiang you, thiam see yul, tien chiang yo, kecap manis;* Indonesian sweet soy sauce): Chinese cooks from Southeast Asia often use *kecap manis,* a sweet soy sauce from Indonesia. Soy sauce is sweetened with palm syrup for a dark, syrupy, salty-sweet condiment. Add to stews, meats, noodles, and stir-fries, or use as a dipping sauce. To make your own, see page 269. For a simple substitute to use in cooking, mix equal parts of dark or all-purpose soy sauce and packed brown sugar.

tangerine peel, dried 橘皮 or 陳皮 (*ju pi, chen pi, guo pay, gee pi, jian pi;* dried orange peel): Brownish pieces of dried tangerine peel (often labeled orange peel) add a subtle citrus fragrance to soups, stews, and meat mixtures. Older peel is valued for its more effective medicinal properties. To make your own, peel a tangerine and tear the skin into 1- to 2-inch pieces. Scrape off and discard the thick white pith with a knife. Air dry or sun dry until hard. A small amount of grated fresh tangerine or orange peel can be used as an alternative. Store airtight in a cool, dry place.

tapioca pearls 木薯珍珠 (*mu shu zhen zhu, muh shuu jen ju*): Dry balls of tapioca starch are used in drinks, such as *boba* tea or pearl tea, and desserts. Boil until soft and chewy. Store airtight in a cool, dry place.

tapioca starch 菱粉 (*ling fen, ling fun;* tapioca flour): This fine, silky white flour or starch comes from cassava root and is used to make tapioca. It resembles cornstarch with its smooth powdery texture. Add to dough for dumplings and taro abacus beads to give a chewy texture and slight translucence. Store airtight in a dry place.

taro 芋頭 (*yu tou, woo tau;* dasheen, Chinese taro, eddoes): At most Asian markets in North America, you'll find two basic types of taro: small or large. Chinese taro are usually small, shaggy, ridged, brown-skinned corms that range in shape from crescents to barrels to tops; some have pink tips. Their firm white flesh turns moist, tender, mild, and slippery when cooked. The larger type, sometimes called dasheen, are barrel-shaped, tan- or brown-skinned corms encircled by ridged rings and hairy skin. The dense flesh varies from white to a grayish-lavender, sometimes flecked with purple fibers. When cooked, large taro may be drier, with chestnut and coconut overtones. The flesh may turn gray or beige, often shadowed with purple. They may take longer to cook and absorb more liquid than small taro. Raw taro contains crystals of calcium oxalate and can irritate skin. If you have sensitive skin, wear rubber gloves or peel the tubers under water. Immerse in water until ready to cook, to prevent discoloration. *Do not eat raw taro.* The Chinese prepare taro much like a potato—peeled, boiled, steamed, mashed, stewed, or thinly sliced or shredded and deep-fried. Sometimes, when cooked in a sauce, potatoes may be used as a substitute. Store, uncovered, in a single layer at cool room temperature.

Tianjin (Tientsin) preserved vegetable 天津冬菜 (*tian jin dong cai, doong choy, choong choy):* Tan-colored, semi-dry, chopped napa cabbage leaves with garlic and salt are often sold in small, squat, dark-brown crocks or plastic bags. Add small amounts to lend a distinctive fermented, salty flavor to steamed meats, rice soups, and vegetables. Store airtight in the refrigerator.

tofu 豆腐 (*dou fu, dul foo;* bean curd): Fresh bean curd is commonly called tofu. Soybean milk is mixed with a coagulant to make curds, which are then pressed to form rectangular or small square cakes. Tofu is sold refrigerated in sealed water-packed plastic tubs or in bulk in tubs at Asian markets. Tofu comes in different degrees of firmness: soft or silken, regular or firm, and sometimes extra-firm. Soft or silken tofu has a delicate, custard-like texture; it should be handled gently and used in soups or desserts. Regular or firm tofu, often pressed into squares, can be stuffed, diced, or sliced. Use it in stir-fries, braises, soups, and steamed dishes. Store all types of tofu in the refrigerator, covered with water. Use promptly; tofu will smell sour when too old. *See also* bean curd sticks, dried; five-spice pressed tofu; fried tofu; pressed tofu; red fermented bean curd

vinegar. *See* black vinegar; rice vinegar; sweetened black vinegar

water chestnuts, fresh 馬蹄 (*ma ti, ma tai):* These small dark brown–skinned corms look like flower bulbs. Their white flesh has a sweet, juicy crunchiness, much like a jicama or apple. The sweet flavor seems to disappear when canned. Look for large firm corms. Peel to use raw or cooked. Water chestnuts add a crunchy texture to meat mixtures, stir-fries, salads, soups, stews, puddings, and sweet drinks. Refrigerate in a bowl of water, changing water every few days. Do not confuse them with water caltrops, which look like ebony water buffalo horns but are also commonly called water chestnuts.

water spinach 蕹菜 or 空心菜 or 通心菜 (*weng cai, kong xin cai, tong xin cai, ong choy, kong sin tsai, toong sin tsai, rau muong;* swamp spinach, morning glory, water convolvulus): Long pointed leaves branch off skinny hollow stems. The greens have a mild spinach-like flavor. Inspect the base of the stems and avoid those with a white cottony center that indicates woodiness. Trim off and discard the tough stem ends. Cut the tender stems with leaves into about 3-inch lengths. Rinse well, and add to stir-fries and soups. Store loosely covered in the refrigerator. Use spinach as a substitute.

white radish. *See* Asian white radish

wolfberries, dried. *See* goji berries

wonton skins 餛飩皮 (*hun tun pi, hun dun pi;* wonton wrappers): These small squares of fresh pasta are used to enclose a filling to make wontons. In Asian markets, they are often available in different thicknesses. Thin or medium are best for soup, medium for frying. Store airtight in the refrigerator, or freeze for longer storage.

wood ears. *See* black fungus, dried

*yao choy* 油菜 (*you cai, yu choy, yo tsai, choy sum, ching choy sum;* flowering green, flowering cabbage, oil vegetable): These slim, bright-green, leafy stalks may have tiny yellow buds or flowers. *Yao choy* has an earthy, slightly mustardy flavor. Young small stalks may be called *choy sum.* Stir-fry, blanch, or steam. Store loosely covered in the refrigerator.

# Basic Recipes

## CHICKEN BROTH

In my mother's kitchen, there was always a pot of homemade broth brewing on the stove. It was a haphazard affair. She would throw bones and vegetable trimmings into the pot as they accumulated. She never refrigerated the broth; she just boiled it furiously once a day. She said that the boiling killed all the bacteria. We're still alive, but I suggest a safer routine: As you collect bones and scraps, freeze them. When you collect enough, make broth. Or you can readily buy chicken carcasses and pork bones (see note) at Asian supermarkets.

Broth can be stored in small portions in the freezer, ready to use. Most Chinese broths are light and clear. For a richer, more concentrated flavor, use a whole chicken.

*Makes 2½ to 3½ quarts*

4 to 5 pounds meaty chicken bones, such as a carcass, backs, wings, or necks, or 1 whole chicken (3½ to 4 pounds), rinsed (see note)

6 quarts water

3 green onions, including green tops, ends trimmed

8 thin slices fresh ginger

3 large cloves garlic

1 teaspoon black peppercorns

1 tablespoon kosher salt, or to taste

1  Fill a 12-quart pan with the bones. Cover with the water. Bring to a simmer over high heat. Reduce the heat and simmer, uncovered, for 30 minutes, skimming off foam every few minutes.

2  Meanwhile, cut the green onions in half. With the flat blade of a knife, lightly crush the green onions, ginger, and garlic. After the water has simmered for 30 minutes, add the green onions, ginger, garlic, and peppercorns. Continue cooking, uncovered, so that the water barely simmers, until the broth is reduced by about half, 3 to 3½ hours. Skim off the foam and fat occasionally.

3  With a slotted spoon, lift out the large bones and discard. Set a colander or large fine wire strainer over a large bowl or pan (for a clearer broth, line the colander ▸

with a double thickness of damp cheesecloth). Pour the broth into the colander. Discard the solids. If there is a lot of sediment, let the broth stand until the sediment settles, 20 to 30 minutes. Carefully ladle or pour off the clear broth into a large bowl, leaving the sediment behind.

**4** Add salt to taste; it's best to salt lightly and do the final salting when the soup is complete. Use the broth or cover and chill up to 3 days. Or freeze in small portions in airtight containers, allowing at least 1 inch of headspace.

**Note:** For a meatier flavor, replace half of the chicken pieces with about 2 pounds of meaty pork pieces, such as spareribs or pork neck. ■

## CHILE SAUCE

It is easy to make fresh chile sauce to suit your taste. I styled these red and green sauces after those I tasted at Ton Kiang in San Francisco. The heat of the chile is concentrated in the yellow veins of capsaicin that run down the walls of the chile and in the seeds, which rub against the veins. Control the heat by the amount of the seeds and veins you use. These medium to medium-hot sauces keep in the refrigerator for a few months.

*Makes about ¾ cup*

6 ounces chiles (about 6 large), such as red Fresno or green jalapeño (see note)

2 large cloves garlic, crushed

2 tablespoons rice vinegar or distilled white vinegar

1 teaspoon sugar

½ teaspoon salt

**1** Cut off the sides of the chiles, leaving the seed core and stems behind. If you prefer a very hot sauce, include all the seeds and the yellow veins that line the walls of the chile. Or reserve some of the seeds and veins and add later to taste. Coarsely chop the chiles to make about 1 cup.

**2** Place the chiles, garlic, vinegar, sugar, and salt in a blender. Blend just until the chiles are coarsely ground, scraping the container occasionally. Taste. For a hotter sauce, add some of the chile seeds and blend briefly. Use or chill in an airtight container for up to 3 months.

**Note:** Other chile varieties can be used. Generally, smaller chiles, such as serrano, are hotter, and larger chiles are milder. Sauces made with green chiles will have a yellowish-green color. ■

# SWEET SOY SAUCE

In India, Hakkas call sweet soy sauce *hung mee,* which translates to "red sauce." The name doesn't seem to fit, since in reality the sauce isn't red, but brownish-black. No one I met could explain the origin of its name. Name issue aside, it is one of those magic ingredients that instantly transforms the ordinary into the extraordinary. It's easy to make: just boil soy sauce, sugar, and fragrant seasonings until thick and syrupy. Don't worry about the large quantity of sugar. The salty soy sauce balances the sugar so that the result tastes savory rather than dessert-like. Aromatic, sweet and salty, and thick and syrupy, sweet soy sauce imparts a deep, dark color and glossy sheen to noodles, stir-fries, stews, and sauces. It closely resembles the Indonesian *kecap manis,* which can be used as a quick alternative. The sauce keeps for months in the refrigerator.

*Makes 1⅓ cups*

1 piece dried tangerine peel, about 2 inches wide

1 stalk fresh lemongrass, about 10 to 14 inches long

3 thin slices fresh ginger

1½ cups water

¾ cup dark soy sauce

¾ cup packed brown sugar

1 cinnamon stick, about 3 inches long

1 star anise

1 Soak the dried tangerine peel in hot water until soft, about 15 minutes, and then drain. Trim off and discard the leafy tops and base of the lemongrass. Rinse the stalk and cut into 3-inch lengths. Lightly crush the lemongrass and ginger with the flat side of a knife blade.

2 In a 2½- to 3-quart pan over high heat, bring the water, soy sauce, brown sugar, tangerine peel, lemongrass, ginger, cinnamon, and star anise to a boil. Reduce the heat to medium-high, and boil gently until the liquid is greatly reduced and slightly syrupy, about 20 minutes. Pour the sauce through a wire strainer set over a 1-quart glass measuring cup or bowl and measure the sauce. If more than 1⅓ cups, boil, uncovered, over medium-high until reduced to that amount. If less than 1⅓ cups, add water to make that amount and bring to a boil. Discard the solids. Leftover sauce can be refrigerated in an airtight container for up to 6 months. ∎

# STEAMED RICE BOWLS

In Meizhou, we were served rice from small clay bowls. We were told that the Hakka often steamed rice in small lidded clay bowls with brown glazed interiors and unglazed exteriors. Back home, I tried Chinese porcelain rice bowls and found that they worked, too.

If you own a large stacked steamer, this method is a neat way to steam individual bowls of rice. Simply rinse the rice, place equal portions of rice and water in each bowl, and steam until tender. It's also an energy-saving technique if you are already steaming another dish. Just add another steamer basket and fill with bowls of rice.

*Makes 6 servings*

2 cups long-grain white or jasmine rice

2 cups water

1  Place ⅓ cup of the rice in a wire strainer and rinse under running water, swishing around a few times, until the water runs clear. Drain and place the rice in a small bowl. Repeat to fill a total of 6 bowls. Level the rice and cover each bowl with ⅓ cup water.

2  Set the bowls on a rack over 2 to 4 inches boiling water in a steamer or wok (if the bottom is round, place on a wok ring to stabilize). If the steamer lid is flat metal, wrap the lid with a towel to reduce condensation dripping on the food. Cover and steam over high heat until the rice is tender, 25 to 30 minutes. Watch the water level, adding more boiling water as needed. Carefully remove the dish from the steamer and serve.

**Note:** You can easily adjust the size of this recipe. Just use equal parts of rice to water for each bowl. Allow room for the rice to expand; it will triple in volume. After cooking, leave the rice in the covered steamer to keep warm. ■

# Table of Equivalents

## LIQUID AND DRY MEASURES

| U.S. Standard | Fluid Ounces | Metric |
| --- | --- | --- |
| ¼ teaspoon | — | 1.25 milliliters |
| ½ teaspoon | — | 2.5 milliliters |
| 1 teaspoon | — | 5 milliliters |
| 1 tablespoon (3 teaspoons) | ½ fluid ounce | 15 milliliters |
| 2 tablespoons | 1 fluid ounce | 30 milliliters |
| ¼ cup (4 tablespoons) | 2 fluid ounces | 60 milliliters |
| ⅓ cup (5⅓ tablespoons) | 3 fluid ounces | 90 milliliters |
| ½ cup (8 tablespoons) | 4 fluid ounces | 120 milliliters |
| ⅔ cup (10⅔ tablespoons) | 5 fluid ounces | 150 milliliters |
| ¾ cup (12 tablespoons) | 6 fluid ounces | 180 milliliters |
| 1 cup (16 tablespoons) | 8 fluid ounces | 240 milliliters |
| 1 pint (2 cups) | 16 fluid ounces | 480 milliliters |
| 1 quart (4 cups) | 32 fluid ounces | 960 milliliters |

## WEIGHT MEASURES

| | |
| --- | --- |
| ½ ounce | 14 grams |
| 1 ounce | 28 grams |
| 8 ounces (½ pound) | 227 grams |
| 1 pound (16 ounces) | 454 grams |
| 2.2 pounds | 1 kilogram |

## LENGTH MEASURES

| U.S. Standard | Metric |
| --- | --- |
| ⅛ inch | 3 millimeters |
| ¼ inch | 6 millimeters |
| ½ inch | 12 millimeters |
| 1 inch | 2.5 centimeters |

## OVEN TEMPERATURE

| Fahrenheit | Celsius | Gas |
| --- | --- | --- |
| 250 | 120 | ½ |
| 300 | 150 | 2 |
| 350 | 180 | 4 |
| 400 | 200 | 6 |
| 450 | 230 | 8 |

# Bibliography

*Resources that provide background information on the Chinese and Hakka diaspora are listed under "General," below. My comments appear in brackets. Following, in alphabetical order, chapter by chapter, are the sources that are most directly relevant to each section.*

## General

Chen, Patrick D. Laminated map. "The Hakka Chinese Migration: The Five Major Migrations of the Hakka Chinese within China and the World Distribution of Overseas Chinese." Ottawa, Canada: Patrick Chen, 2008.

Constable, Nicole. *Guest People: Hakka Identity in China and Abroad.* Seattle: University of Washington Press, 1996.

———. "Hakka." In *Encyclopedia of World Cultures.* Encyclopedia.com, 1996. www.encyclopedia.com/topic/Hakka.aspx. Accessed December 26, 2011.

Kwan, Cheuk, producer and director. *Chinese Restaurants.* DVD series. Toronto, Canada: Tissa Films, 2005.

Lee, Siu-Leung. "Hakka: An Important Element of Chinese Culture." Asiawind: Bridging East and West in Business Technology and Culture. www.asiawind.com/hakka.

Lozada, Eriberito P. "Hakka Diaspora." In *Encyclopedia of Diasporas,* edited by Melvin Ember, Carol Ember, and Ian Skoggard, 92–102. Boston: Kluwer/Plenum, 2003.

Pan, Lynn. *The Encyclopedia of the Chinese Overseas.* Cambridge, Mass.: Harvard University Press, 1999.

———. *Sons of the Yellow Emperor: A History of the Chinese Diaspora.* New York: Kodansha America, 1994.

Wu, David Y. H., and Sidney C. H. Cheung. *The Globalization of Chinese Food.* Honolulu: University of Hawaii Press, 2002.

# Introduction

Bohr, P. Richard. "Transforming China: Hakka Identity and the Taiping Revolution, 1851–1864." Speech given at the Roundhouse Reunion, Toronto Hakka Conference, June 2008. [On the "world's bloodiest civil war."]

Carstens, Sharon A. "Hakka Malaysian Culture." In Constable, *Guest People,* 124–48. [On gender work roles, see pp. 132–33.]

Cohen, Myron L. "The Hakka or 'Guest People.'" In Constable, *Guest People,* 36–79. [On Hakka migrations, see pp. 41–48.]

Constable, Nicole. "Introduction: What Does It Mean to Be Hakka?" In Constable, *Guest People.* [On identity and the Hakka label, see pp. 9–13.]

———. "Hakka." In *Encyclopedia of World Cultures.* Encyclopedia.com, 1996. www.encyclopedia.com/topic/Hakka.aspx. Accessed December 26, 2011. [Source of worldwide Hakka population figures.]

Fong, Adam. "Ending an Era: The Huang Chao Rebellion of the Late Tang, 874–884." East-West Center Working Papers, International Graduate Student Conference, no. 26, 2006. www.eastwestcenter.org/fileadmin/stored/pdfs/IGSCwp026.pdf. [On the second Hakka migration, see pp. 2–10.]

Han, Suyin. *The Crippled Tree.* London: Panther Books, 1972. First published 1965 by Jonathan Cape Limited. [On Hakka origin theories and the Hakkas' pioneer reputation, see pp. 22–23.]

Hu-DeHart, Evelyn. "Spanish America." In Pan, *The Encyclopedia of the Chinese Overseas,* 254–60. [On the Hakka in Spanish America, see p. 260.]

Kwok Kian Woon. "Singapore." In Pan, *The Encyclopedia of the Chinese Overseas,* 200–217. [On the Hakka in Singapore, see p. 204.]

Lai, Walton Look. "The Caribbean." In Pan, *The Encyclopedia of the Chinese Overseas,* 248–53. [On the Hakka in the Caribbean, see p. 249.]

Lee, Siu-Leung. "Hakka: An Important Element of Chinese Culture." Asiawind: Bridging East and West in Business Technology and Culture. www.asiawind.com/hakka. [On the metaphor of Hakkas as dandelions.]

Lozada, "Hakka Diaspora," 92–102. [On Hakka origin theories and arguments, see pp. 92–94.]

Oxfeld, Ellen. "India." In Pan, *The Encyclopedia of the Chinese Overseas,* 344–46. [On the Hakka in India, see p. 345.]

Pan, *The Encyclopedia of the Chinese Overseas,* 25–27. [For the source of the quote by G. William Skinner and statements about the hill people, fighting in the 1850s, and misconceptions in Luo's theory, see pp. 25–27.]

Spence, Jonathan D. *God's Chinese Son.* New York: W. W. Norton, 1996. [On Hong Xiuquan and the Taiping Rebellion, see pp. xxi–xxvii, 86.]

Tong, Niew Shong. "Malaysia." In Pan, *The Encyclopedia of the Chinese Overseas,* 172–86. [On the Hakka in Malaysia, see pp. 173, 183–85.]

Willmott, W. E. "The South Pacific, Tahiti." In Pan, *The Encyclopedia of the Chinese Overseas*, 299–302. [On the Hakka in Tahiti, see p. 301.]

## 1 Popo's Kitchen on Gold Mountain

Arrival Investigation Case Files, 1884–1944. National Archives at San Francisco, San Bruno, CA. RG 85, box 1513. No. 19981/5–8, February 28, 1921. [Angel Island interview.]

Chang, Iris. *The Chinese in America*. New York: Penguin Books, 2004. [On the number of Chinese women legally permitted to enter the United States from 1906 to 1924, see pp. 173–74; on the date Asians could buy property, see p. 161; on the Magnuson Act, see p. 227; on the 1877 event in Chico, see p. 127.]

Lau, Alan Chong. "Tonight, we eat our fill and remember dad." *The International Examiner*, October 29, 1982. [On Harry Chong Lau's story.]

## 2 Hakka Cooking in the Homeland

Cheung, Sidney C. H. "Consuming 'Low' Cuisine after Hong Kong's Handover: Village Banquets and Private Kitchens." *Asian Studies Review* 29 (September 2005). [On the origin and history of basin feast, see pp. 263–65.]

———. "Food and Cuisine in a Changing Society." In *The Globalization of Chinese Food*, edited by David Y. H. Wu and Sidney C. H. Cheung, 100–112. Honolulu: University of Hawaii Press, 2002. [On Hakka food in Hong Kong, see pp. 104–106.]

"Luodai Ancient Town in Chengdu." Cultural China: Understanding China's 5000-Year Culture. http://scenery.cultural-china.com/en/130Scenery6434.html. [Source of Luodai statistics.]

*Xinhua*. "Sichuan to Host World Hakka Convention." May 30, 2005. http://english.peopledaily.com .cn/200505/30/eng20050530_187428.html. [Source of statistics on the number of Hakka in Sichuan.]

## 3 Leaving the Mainland

Barmé, Geremie R. "Strangers at Home." *Wall Street Journal,* July 17–18, 2010. [On the Chinese population in Southeast Asian countries.]

Chang, May Y. H., ed. *Xinzhuxian Kejia yinshi wenhua diaocha jihua* [Hsinchu County Hakka dietary culture report]. Taipei: Xinzhu xianzhengfu wenhuaju [Cultural Affairs Bureau of the Hsinchu County Government], 2005. [On the story of fried pork drumsticks, see p. 59; on Hakka little stir-fry, see p. 28; on the Beipu tea ceremony, see pp. 100–101.]

"Hakka in Mauritius." Asiawind: Bridging East and West in Business Technology and Culture. www .asiawind.com/pub/forum/fhakka/mhonarc/msg00122.html. [Source of statistics on the percentage of Hakkas in Mauritius.]

"Mauritius: Population." Cap Soleil. www.capsoleil-maurice.com/en/island-infos/mauritius-population.html. [Source of statistics on the Chinese population in Mauritius.]

Moey, S. C. *Chinese Feasts and Festivals*. Hong Kong: Periplus Editions, 2006. [On the Winter Festival, see p. 112.]

Pan, *Sons of the Yellow Emperor*. [On the Chinese entry into Southeast Asia, see p. 172; on the Hakka-dominant Chinese population in Mauritius, see p. 61.]

Wang, Lijung. "Diaspora, Identity and Cultural Citizenship: The Hakkas in Multicultural Taiwan." Paper presented at the Chinese Culture Research Conference, Taiwan Hsinchu Jiaotong University, January 2005. [Source of information on the Hakka population in Taiwan and its history and activism.]

Wong, Amy. *Famous Cuisine Home Recipes*. Kuala Lumpur: Famous Cuisine Publishing, n.d. [Source of savory pounded tea rice recipe, pp. 18–19.]

———. *Malaysian Gourmet*. Kuala Lumpur: Famous Cuisine Publishing, 2003. [Source of taro abacus recipe, p. 19.]

## 4 Across the Pacific

Balbi, Mariella. *Los Chifas en el Peru* [Chinese restaurants in Peru]. Lima: Universidad de San Martín de Porres, 1999. [Source of salted mustard green recipe, p. 223.]

Chou, Jin-Hong, ed. *Lianlian Kejia wei: yanzi shipin pian* [Love Hakka taste, salt-preserved food book]. Taipei: Miaoli xian wenhuaju [Miaoli County Cultural Bureau], 1992. [On the history of pickles, see pp. 6–11.]

Hu-Dehart, Evelyn. "Spanish America." In Pan, *The Encyclopedia of the Chinese Overseas*, 254, 260. [On the Hakka in Peru.]

Lai, Him Mark. "The United States." In Pan, *The Encyclopedia of the Chinese Overseas*, 262. [On the Hakka in Hawaii.]

Lum, Dee, ed. *Everyone, Eat Slowly: The Chong Family Food Book*. Ka'a'awa, Hawaii: Chong Hee Books, 1999. [Source of steamed savory egg custard recipe, p. 30; on En Fah Kong Yap, see p. 26.]

Michener, James. *Hawaii*. New York: Random House, 1959. [Source of Wu Chow's Auntie character.]

Phillips, Carolyn. "Salted Limes." *Out to Lunch* (blog). http://carolynjphillips.blogspot.com/2011/01/hakka-salted-limes.html. [Source of salted lime recipe.]

Salazar, Jorge. "Chinese Flavors of Peru." *Flavor and Fortune* 9, no. 2 (Summer 2002): 15–16. [Source of history on the Chinese in Peru.]

Wilmont, W. E. "The South Pacific." In Pan, *The Encyclopedia of the Chinese Overseas*, 299–301. [On the Hakka in Tahiti.]

## 5 Multiple Migrations

Chang, Winston H., Jr. *Foods of the Hakka Shops*. Toronto, Ont.: Electra Syndicate, 2003. [Source of stuffed bitter melon recipe, p. 77.]

"The Chinese Community in Canada." Statistics Canada, vol. 2006, no. 1, www.statcan.gc.ca/pub/89–621-x/89–621-x2006001-eng.htm. Accessed December 27, 2011.

Chung, Yoon-Nan. "Chinese in Canada." Asiawind: Bridging East and West in Business Technology and Culture. www.asiawind.com/pub/forum/fhakka/mhonarc/msg01861.html. [Source of statistics on the percentage of the Canadian Chinese population that is Hakka.]

Duncan, Dorothy. "Chinese Food and the Canadian Experience." *Flavor and Fortune* 5, no. 2 (June 1998). [On Canada's restrictive immigration practices, see pp. 11–12, 16.]

Ng, Wing Chung. "Canada." In Pan, *The Encyclopedia of the Chinese Overseas*, 234–47. Cambridge: Harvard University Press, 1999. [On discrimination against and the economic future of the Chinese in Canada, see p. 234.]

## The Hakka Kitchen and Pantry

Cost, Bruce. *Asian Ingredients*. New York: HarperCollins, 2000.

Dunlop, Fuchsia. *Land of Plenty*. New York: W. W. Norton, 2003

Hom, Ken. *Chinese Technique*. New York: Simon & Schuster, 1981.

Lo, Eileen Yin-Fei. *Mastering the Art of Chinese Cooking*. San Francisco: Chronicle Books, 2009.

———. *New Cantonese Cooking*. New York: Viking Penguin, 1988.

Miller, Gloria Bley. *The Thousand Recipe Chinese Cookbook*. New York: Grosset & Dunlap, 1976.

Schneider, Elizabeth. *Vegetables from Amaranth to Zucchini: The Essential Reference*. New York: William Morrow, 2001.

Trang, Corinne. *Essentials of Asian Cuisine*. New York: Simon & Schuster, 2003.

Yan, Martin. *Martin Yan's Asia*. San Francisco: KQED Books & Tapes, 1997.

———. *A Simple Guide to Chinese Ingredients and Other Asian Specialties*. Foster City, Calif.: Yan Can Cook, 1994.

Young, Grace. *Stir-Frying to the Sky's Edge*. New York: Simon & Schuster, 2010.

———. *The Wisdom of the Chinese Kitchen*. New York: Simon & Schuster, 1999.

Young, Grace, and Alan Richardson. *The Breath of a Wok*. New York: Simon & Schuster, 2004.

# Index